BAR BRITISH SE1
ARCHAEOLC
VOLUME 4

AIN

BELONGING AND BELONGINGS

*Portable artefacts and identity
in the civitas of the Iceni*

Natasha Harlow

BAR
PUBLISHING

Published in 2021 by
BAR Publishing, Oxford

BAR British Series 664

Archaeology of Roman Britain, volume 4
Belonging and Belongings

ISBN 978 1 4073 5701 0 paperback
ISBN 978 1 4073 5702 7 e-format

DOI https://doi.org/10.30861/9781407357010

A catalogue record for this book is available from the British Library

COVER IMAGE *Colchester Derivative triple Rearhook brooch,*
Necton (PAS: NMS-AE1FF0)

BAR
PUBLISHING

BAR titles are available from:

BAR Publishing
122 Banbury Rd, Oxford, OX2 7BP, UK
EMAIL   info@barpublishing.com
PHONE   +44 (0)1865 310431
FAX   +44 (0)1865 316916
www.barpublishing.com

ARCHAEOLOGY OF ROMAN BRITAIN

Series Editors: Edward Biddulph (Oxford Archaeology) and
Martin Pitts (Exeter University)

Roman Britain presents a dynamic and exciting field of study, with an abundance of data amenable to multi-disciplinary approaches, 'big data' studies, the application of theoretical approaches, and a variety of visually stimulating artefacts and reconstructions that speak to our own age in a remarkably direct way. This series promotes research relating to the Roman province of Britannia, spanning a broad period from the late Iron Age to post-Roman Britain (roughly from the 1st century BC to the 5th century AD), as well as encompassing studies that examine the interaction between the British Isles, the nearby Continent, and other parts of the connected Roman empire.

If you are interested in publishing in the *Archaeology of Roman Britain* series, please contact editor@barpublishing.com.

Also in the Subseries

The Clayton Collection
An archaeological appraisal of a 19th century collection of Roman artefacts from Hadrian's Wall
Frances McIntosh

Oxford, BAR Publishing, 2019   BAR British Series **646**

Archaeology of Roman Britain, 1

Worcester Magistrates Court
Excavation of Romano-British homes and industry at Castle Street
Andy Boucher

Oxford, BAR Publishing, 2020   BAR International Series **658**

Archaeology of Roman Britain, 2

London's Roman Tools
Craft, agriculture and experience in an ancient city
Owen Humphreys

Oxford, BAR Publishing, 2021   BAR British Series **663**

Archaeology of Roman Britain, 3

Other titles of Related Interest

Pattern and Process in the Material Culture of Anglo-Saxon Non-elite Rural Settlements
Hana Lewis

Oxford, BAR Publishing, 2019   BAR British Series **649**

Later Iron Age Norfolk
Metalwork, landscape and society
Natasha C.G. Hutcheson

Oxford, BAR Publishing, 2004   BAR British Series **361**

For more information, or to purchase these titles, please visit **www.barpublishing.com**

Acknowledgements

I would like to extend my thanks to the following people who made this research project possible: my PhD supervisors, Will Bowden (University of Nottingham) and Colin Haselgrove (University of Leicester) and the AHRC/Midlands3Cities Doctoral Training Partnership. Historic Environment Record and Portable Antiquities Scheme staff facilitated my data collection, in particular Gaby Day, Ben Donnelly-Symes, Heather Hamilton, Rik Hoggett, Faye Minter, Jude Plouviez, Anna Booth, Garry Crace, Adrian Marsden, Julie Shoemark and Alastair Willis. Wendy Scott (Leicestershire County Council) and Julia Farley (British Museum) were welcoming placement hosts. Norfolk Museums Service staff, past and present, have encouraged me over many years: Steven Ashley, John Davies, Natasha Hutcheson, Tim Pestell, Jan Pitman, Andrew Rogerson and Alan West.

My gratitude is also due to the metal-detectorists who took the time to answer my interview questions and to colleagues who generously shared aspects of their research: Colin Andrews (seal-boxes), Robin Bendrey (horses), Alex Bliss, Dot Boughton and Jack Davy (miniatures), Tom Brindle (RRS), Nina Crummy and Ellen Swift (bracelets), Matt Fittock (figurines), Adam Parker (anatomical votives), Martin Pitts (objectscapes), Stuart McKie (curse tablets), Michael Marshall (torcs, bracelets), Gwladys Monteil (samian), Michelle Statton (personal ornament), Naomi Sykes (zooarchaeology) and John Talbot (coins). Brian Read (Historical Metallurgy Society) assisted me with archive materials. Katherine Robbins (University of Leicester) provided Roman road and coastline map layers. Caistor Roman Project members Jenny Press and Ian Jackson supplied small finds images and Caroline Lowton kindly proofread the manuscript. Lastly, thanks to my friends and family for their support and encouragement.

This project was supported by funding from the Norfolk and Norwich Archaeological Society.

Dedicated to my grandparents,
Pia and Richard

Contents

Digital dataset is available at https://doi.org/10.30861/9781407357010.dataset1

List of Figures

List of Tables

List of Abbreviations

ADS   Archaeology Data Service

BAR   British Archaeological Report

BM   British Museum

CAMARC   Cambridgeshire Archaeology

CBA   Council for British Archaeology

CCC   Cambridgeshire County Council

CHER   Cambridgeshire Historic Environment Record

CRP   Caistor Roman Project

EAA   East Anglian Archaeology

FLO   Finds Liaison Officer

HER   Historic Environment Record

LIA   Late Iron Age

LPRIA   Late Pre-Roman Iron Age

NA   Norfolk Archaeology

NAHRG   Norfolk Archaeological and Historical Research Group

NAU   Norfolk Archaeological Unit

NCC   Norfolk County Council

NHER   Norfolk Historic Environment Record

NMS   Norfolk Museums Service

NRC   Norfolk Research Committee

NWHCM   Norwich Castle Museum

OAE   Oxford Archaeology East

PAS   Portable Antiquities Scheme

PCAS   Proceedings of the Cambridge Antiquarian Society

PPS   Proceedings of the Prehistoric Society

PSIA(H)   Proceedings of the Suffolk Institute of Archaeology (and History)

RRS   Roman Rural Settlement Project

SAU   Suffolk Archaeological Unit

SCC   Suffolk County Council

SHER   Suffolk Historic Environment Record

Naming Conventions and Source Material

Throughout the text, sites and objects are referred to using a code which combines a prefix (NHER, SHER, CHER or PAS) followed by the individual reference number. Objects labelled CRP, NWHCM or BM followed by an alpha-numeric sequence are registered finds of the Caistor Roman Project, Norwich Castle Museum and the British Museum respectively.

All maps were created by the author and contain OS data © Crown copyright and database right (2014-17), provided through EDINA Digimap and OS Opendata services. Roman Road and Coastline layers provided by K. Robbins, based on data from Ancient World Mapping Centre (2012), Norfolk Archaeological Trust (2012-16), Fenland Survey (1994), McCormick *et al.* (2013 DARMC Scholarly Data Series) and English Heritage.

All PAS images are used courtesy of the Portable Antiquities Scheme under a CC BY-SA 4.0 licence.

Digital data were supplied by:

Norfolk Historic Environment Record (licence 232, 25/11/2014)

Suffolk Historic Environment Record (licence 06/11/2014)

Cambridgeshire Historic Environment Record (licence 15-2029, 01/05/2015).

Abstract

This book is a revised and updated version of my doctoral thesis, carried out at the University of Nottingham between 2013 and 2018.

The Late Iron Age in northern East Anglia ended with the Boudican revolt in 60/61 CE, after which the people known as the Iceni were subsumed by the Roman empire. This study tests the archaeological evidence for the Iceni as a defined group, demonstrated by the distinctive character of material culture in the region. It investigates the theory that they were slow to adopt Roman imports and luxury goods, either as a form of deliberate resistance or due to cultural retardation following the Boudican revolt. It also questions the interpretive narrative of the Iceni as 'Other', in both classical and modern sources.

My research expands upon previous studies, which have often been restricted to a single county, time period or artefact class. It includes a broad study of the three counties most closely associated with the Iceni: Norfolk, Suffolk and Cambridgeshire. The chronological range (*circa* 100 BCE-200 CE) incorporates the pre-Roman Iron Age, the invasions of Caesar and Claudius, the Boudican rebellion and its aftermath, and the early part of the Roman occupation of Britain.

A large dataset of over 14,000 object records has been examined, drawn from county Historic Environment Records (HERs) and the Portable Antiquities Scheme (PAS). Object categories studied include brooches and other forms of personal ornament, grooming and cosmetic implements, objects associated with religious practices, such as votive miniatures and figurines, aspects of literacy and sealing, and the many artefacts related to horse harness and vehicles found in the region.

This project reassesses many of the long-held stereotypes about the Iceni in the light of the dramatic increases in metal-detector finds over the past 20 years. It demonstrates that:

- A single unified social entity ('the Iceni') is not archaeologically visible across the study area, although there is complex and nuanced intra-regional patterning.

- Iron Age modes of expressing status and identity persisted under Roman rule, through the manufacture, use and display of objects.

- Evidence is lacking for regional impoverishment and depopulation in the aftermath of the Boudican revolt.

- Metal-detected surface finds have a significant impact on the archaeological interpretation of the region, particularly when viewed across a wide area and in conjunction with stratified sites.

The Land of the Iceni

1.1. Introduction

To the aristocratic male writers of classical histories, Britain signified a savage land in need of Roman civilisation. However, many Britons were familiar with Roman architecture, language and artefacts. Southern parts of the British Isles had experienced nearly a century of engagement with the empire, between Julius Caesar's abortive expeditions of 55/54 BCE and Claudius's successful conquest in 43 CE (Creighton 2006: 14-34; Woolf 2011b: 89-91). Imports arrived in large numbers from the Mediterranean and Gaul, with wheel-turned pottery, coinage and cremation burials becoming increasingly visible in the archaeological record (Mattingly 2007: 68-84).

The land of the Iceni falls within the modern counties of Norfolk, Suffolk and Cambridgeshire (Figure 1.1). Settlements cluster on the higher ground at the Fen-edge, in a line running up the northwestern side of Norfolk.

Along this ridge run two major routes, the Icknield and Peddars Ways. The Icknield Way (NHER: 1398) enters the region from the southwest, running past important Iron Age sites at Thetford and Snettisham, arriving at the Wash near Holme-next-the-Sea. This routeway marks the chalk escarpment above the Fen-edge and is considered to have prehistoric origins. The Peddars Way (NHER: 1289) marks the western watershed and is thought by some to be a military road, along with the Pye Road and the Fen Causeway, driven through the territory in the wake of the invasion (Andrews 2012: 63; Fairclough 2010: 64; Gurney 1993: 34; Hutcheson 2004: 7). The precise routes and dating remain uncertain.

The territory was located between two great wetlands, the Fen Basin to the west and the so-called 'Great Estuary' on the east coast. Increased flooding in the Late Iron Age (LIA) made parts of the Fenlands less habitable until a fall in sea levels and large-scale drainage in the first century CE made reoccupation possible. An Imperial

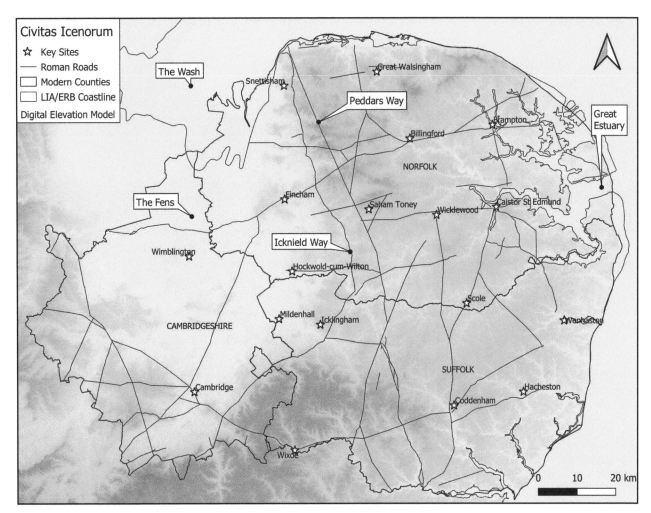

Figure 1.1. Key modern and historic features of the *Civitas Icenorum* showing elevation.

estate has been mooted in the Fens in the later Roman period. The Great Estuary had formed by the Iron Age, with submersion of a spit of land allowing tidal ingress of the North Sea near modern Great Yarmouth. In the Roman period, a vast landscape of saltmarsh and mudflats existed, with estuarine conditions reaching far inland. The tributaries of the Great Estuary are the modern Rivers Yare, Bure and Waveney, forming the main river valleys of today's Norfolk Broads. The Great Estuary would have been a major gateway to the area, with the *civitas* capital at *Venta Icenorum* sited on a navigable but shallow branch (Bescoby *et al.* forthcoming). The Estuary silted up again in the Anglo-Saxon period, attributed to rising sea levels and the re-emergence of the sandbar upon which Yarmouth now sits (Albone *et al.* 2007a: 3-6; Catling 2014; Frere 1991: 267; Gurney 1993: 34).

The landscape was intensively farmed where suitable, with relatively sparse settlement dotted across the fertile areas. Different patterns of agriculture and stock-rearing may explain the lack of surrounding earthworks, which are found in other regions. Similarly, the tradition of fortified hilltops seen in southern and western Britain seems to have been less common here, partly due to the low-lying geography of the area. However, several putative hillfort-type sites have been identified. Enclosures are known at various locations in west Norfolk: Warham, Narborough, Holkham, Thetford and South Creake. Barnham in northwest Suffolk may also fit into this category. There are also exceptional sites at Snettisham, Stonea Camp and Thetford (Fison Way), interpreted as foci of ritual behaviour (Clarke 1939; Davies 1996, 1999; Hill 1999; Hutcheson 2004; Malim 2005; Martin 1999). Most homesteads were unenclosed (construed as undefended) and there were few of the extensive LIA nucleations usually described as *oppida* (Fernández-Götz 2014b; Moore 2012; Pitts 2010). Davies considers the settlements at Thetford, Saham Toney and *Venta Icenorum* as potential candidates for *oppida* in Norfolk (1999: 33-37), while Pitts includes only Cambridge and Burgh (2010: 36 table 1). Some of these designations will be challenged below.

1.2. The Iceni in the Late Iron Age and Early Roman Periods

The Iceni is the name given to the people living in what is now northern East Anglia, immediately before contact with the Roman world and during the period of Roman rule in Britain.[1] The LIA in the polity is normally dated to *circa* 100 BCE to 60/61 CE, the change from self-governance to full Roman rule marked by the Boudican revolt (Davies 1996: 65).[2] The Iceni people seem to have subscribed to a different way of life, following less hierarchical

settlement patterns, social structures and burial practices than their neighbours, the Trinovantes in south Suffolk and Essex and the Catuvellauni in Cambridgeshire. They set themselves apart by 'the absence of imported wine-vessels and certain types of pottery' (Green 1993: 32). Instead, they expressed wealth and rank through their numerous harness and chariot fittings and personal ornaments, at the pinnacle of which were their golden torcs.

The Icenian territory was atypical compared to other parts of southern Britain. Few imported goods seem to have reached the region. Dressel 1 wine *amphorae* and imported finewares are rare, unlike other parts of southern and eastern England in the LIA (Champion 2016: 159; Ralph 2007: 108; Rippon 2018: 62-65).[3] Highly ornamented fine metalwork, including torcs and horse gear, was crafted and deposited, often in hoards, across the region. Production of this distinctive indigenous material culture continued into the early Romano-British period, frequently developing hybrid forms. Gold coins were being struck from *circa* 65 BCE, with silver issues appearing in the record from about 35 BCE (Davies 1996, 1999; Hutcheson 2004). There is minimal archaeological indication of developed social hierarchies or warfare, and an almost complete absence of the 'warrior chieftain' funerary rites typified by Aylesford-Swarling or Welwyn in the southeast, or the extravagant 'Arras-style' chariot burials of Yorkshire (Clarke 1939; Davies 2011b; Hill 1995, 2007; Martin 1999; Rippon 2018: fig. 2.9). This finds parallels with the Eburones polity on the Lower Rhine, an area which also showed a fondness for hoards of gold coins and torcs in the second-first centuries BCE. This region was similarly decentralised, with a lack of *oppida* and burials, apparent resistance to Mediterranean imports and a late advent of coinage. Other societies without *oppida*, such as the Menapii, are 'characterised by a lower degree of social and territorial hierarchisation [and] more inclined towards egalitarianism and a more heterarchical social landscape' (Fernández-Götz 2014a: 214-19).

Funerary rites left little trace in the LIA across much of Britain. Human remains may have been deposited in water, which has parallels with the prehistoric tradition of metalwork deposition in wet places (Johnson 2002; Sykes 2014: 65). Urned cremation burial was a local tradition in southeastern Britain, from the early first century BCE into the post-conquest period. Burial of partial remains in pits, often alongside animal bones, was another common method of disposing of the dead. Human remains were perhaps also scattered, excarnated or deposited in middens or wells. It is estimated that 90-95 per cent of the population did not receive a formal interment, although

---

[1] Discussing 'the Iceni' as an entity is problematic. The name is retained throughout as a familiar epithet, but should be understood as a convenience, not a statement of ethnicity. Likewise, I use the names of adjacent peoples, such as the Trinovantes and Catuvellauni, as shorthand.
[2] Talbot (2015: 241) presents reasonably convincing numismatic evidence for 61 CE, although the unrest may have continued over a period of several months.

[3] Dressel 1 *amphorae* have been found along the Stour Valley and at Snailwell (Moore et al. 1988: 14). The concentration of Dressel 1 in Essex highlights this gap in Suffolk, Norfolk and Cambridgeshire. This distribution has been suggested to mark a boundary between the Iceni, and their southern neighbours, the Trinovantes (Sealey 2015). Small numbers of Dressel 20 oil *amphorae* (which peak in the Antonine period in Britain) have been found at Denver, Feltwell, Hockwold, Weeting, Brancaster, Scole and Caister-on-Sea (Tyers 2014).

inhumation became popular from *circa* 200 CE across the western empire (Carr and Knüsel 1997; Cool 2011; Gurney 1998; Hill 1995a; Merrifield 1987; Sealey 2016). This major shift corresponds to several other changes in material culture and practice beginning in the third century CE, which will be explored further below.

The Iceni way of death was distinct from neighbouring regions and other provinces and, at the same time, similar to other parts of Britain. Iron Age and Roman burials are infrequent, especially in Norfolk and north Suffolk (Figure 1.2).[4] Mapping from the Roman Rural Settlement (RRS) Project confirms this trend (Figure 1.3). Despite strong evidence for production of horse and vehicle trappings (chapter eight), there are no confirmed chariot burials.[5] The discussion of pipeclay figurines in children's burials (section 6.8) presents evidence for some intra-regional differences.

According to Tacitus (*Ann*. 12.31, 14.31), after the invasion instigated by the emperor Claudius in 43 CE, some groups, including the Iceni, were affiliated with the Roman empire as client-kingdoms. This allowed local rulers to control their own internal affairs providing they followed Roman policy. Client-kingdom status meant they could draw on the security and might of the Roman army when necessary, without the need for a permanent military presence. Gift-giving, diplomacy and trade advantages may have also sweetened the deal for such semi-independent states (Hanson 1997; Mattingly 2011: 85-93; Richardson 1984: 13-14; Wacher 1976: 226-27). The client-kingdom may account for the restricted numbers of forts and military material culture in the Iceni heartland (Eckardt 2005: 150-51; Mattingly 2007: 138-39), which is discussed further below.

Tacitus (*Ann*. 12.31) states an uprising among the Iceni in 47 CE was prompted by their forcible disarming by the incoming governor Ostorius Scapula. This might suggest that they were not one of the kingdoms to submit to Claudius at the original invasion (Salway 1981: 90, fn. 1, 101). Mattingly interprets this event as a skirmish more than a full-blown revolt, as the client-kingdom status was maintained (2007: 101-2). Some numismatists suggest it may have been at this point that Prasutagus became king of a unified Iceni (Allen 1970: 16; Davies 1996: 85, 1999: 41), although Hutcheson discerns an earlier change in social organisation in the late first century BCE/early first century CE (2007: 369).

1.3. The Boudican 'War of Independence'

The breakdown of the client-kingdom relationship and the ensuing 'War of Independence' (Crummy *et al*. 2015) has been much discussed (Collingridge 2005; Gambash 2012; Hingley and Unwin 2005; Trow 2003, to name but a few). Classical sources describe how the oppressed indigenes (the Iceni and some of their near neighbours) rose up in an ill-fated revolt against the occupation under their leader Boudica, Prasutagus's widow, during the reign of Nero (Dio *Hist. Rom*. 62.1-12; Tac. *Ann*. 14.29-39). This was eventually put down under the serving provincial governor Suetonius Paulinus (for concise summaries see Hingley and Unwin 2005: 41-61; Mattingly 2007: 106-13; also Braund 1996; Webster 1993). This rebellion marks the demise of the client-kingdom and is generally accepted as the end of the Iron Age in Iceni territory.

Direct archaeological evidence for the revolt is limited. Destruction levels at *Camulodunum* (Colchester) and *Londinium* (London) tally with the written accounts. A less comprehensive destruction horizon is seen at *Verulamium* (St Albans), while *Caesaromagus* (Chelmsford), although not mentioned in the classical texts, may also have suffered the same fate (Gambash 2012: 2; Hingley and Unwin 2005: 63-107). Settlement shifts are sometimes also attributed to the revolt (Perring and Pitts 2013: 246). Mid-first century CE burnt levels and hoards of coins and metalwork are usually interpreted as 'Boudican'. These hoards, dating to the 60s CE, occur in Norfolk, north Suffolk and north Cambridgeshire. However, the 'Trinovantian' territory of Essex and south Suffolk has not produced similar hoards, suggesting regional variation in deposition (Chadburn 2006: 174; Todd 1999: 72-73). There may be an element of circularity here, in which Icenian mid-century hoards are expected to be Boudican, whereas elsewhere the narrative is different. There has been a tendency to interpret archaeological remains in the study area through the lens of the Boudican story and this is explored as a key theme throughout this book.

The end of the client-kingdom and ensuing full Roman control of the Iceni territory is one of the most interesting periods in this part of Britain. Davis and Gwilt (2008: 146) suggest that, prior to the revolt and for several generations beyond, the Iceni people used items of portable wealth to both passively and actively resist incorporation into the Roman world. These ideas will be revisited below in the discussion of identities, resistance and material culture.

1.4. The *Civitas Icenorum*

I use the term *civitas Icenorum* to describe the territory populated by the people known as the Iceni in the post-client-kingdom phase from 61 CE onwards.[6] This was

---

[4] An HER search (with wide parameters for Iron Age and Roman cemeteries, cremations or inhumations) returned Cambridgeshire (53), Norfolk (39) and Suffolk (38). Many of these were antiquarian finds, or early records without strong dating or contextual information, so should not be regarded as definitive. The broad date range also means that many Late Roman cemeteries were included.

[5] At Mildenhall in 1812, workmen 'discovered a human skeleton of large dimensions, stretched at its full length between the skeletons of two horses, arranged in a parallel order. On one side of the warrior lay a long iron sword, on the other his celt: he had a torques of gold; but the temptation of this precious metal induced the labourers to conceal for a time their discovery. The torques was conveyed secretly to Bury, sold to a petty silversmith and immediately melted down' (Clarke 1939: 43). The unknown fate of this skeleton and his/her grave goods means we cannot draw any firm conclusions on the nature of the burial.

[6] 'Civitas' is defined as: an organised community; a state; the persons living within such a community; a city and its surrounding district (Glare 2012) and the condition or privileges of a (Roman) citizen; the citizens united in a community; the body-politic (Lewis and Short 1969).

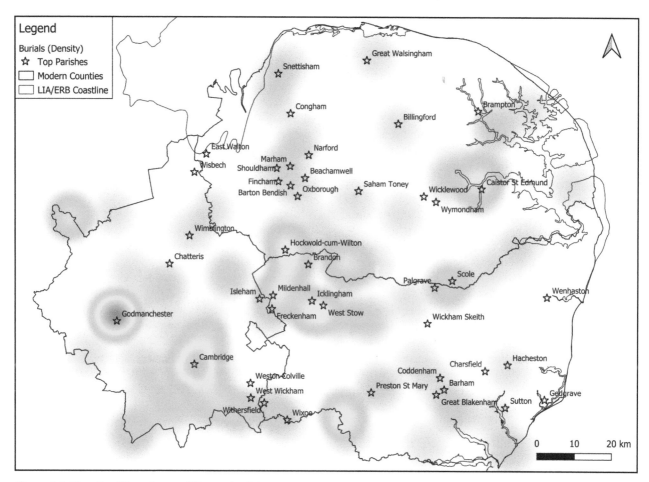

Figure 1.2. Density of Iron Age and Roman burials.

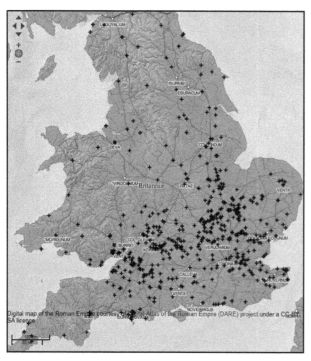

Figure 1.3. Funerary sites (Rural Settlement of Roman Britain, CC by-SA).

effectively a Roman administrative district with its capital at *Venta Icenorum*, which is one of this study's key sites, located approximately 6 km (4 miles) south of Norwich. The Latin usage of the word *civitas* encompasses a sense of citizenship of the people, as well as their state or community. *Civitas* is generally accepted as defining a political, rather than ethnic, identity. However, Tacitus (*Ann.* 12.31) also refers to the Iceni as *gens* which could be translated as 'clan' or 'people' (Moore 2011: 339-40).

Frere suggested a strong military redeployment and refortification of the province after the rebellion, with new forts at Great Chesterford, Coddenham, Ixworth and possibly Saham Toney (1991: 73-74). This assumed militarisation is not currently supported by archaeological evidence, although this may be due to a lack of recovery and poor dating (Millett 1990: 55). Evidence for overt military control of the territory is lacking; instead, there may have been more subtle impacts on the landscape of the region. Some see a deliberate reordering of the indigenous landscape, through the development of the road network and schemes of centuriation, by which land was mapped, measured out and allocated (Dilke 1971; Frere 2000; Williamson 1986). British centuriation schemes may have respected pre-Roman field systems and land-use, but evidence is scarce and highly contested (Mattingly 2007: 359-62).

4

The narrative of widespread depopulation and abandonment in the aftermath of the rebellion, based on Tacitus (*Ann.* 14.38), has gone relatively unquestioned. Studies of coins and horse harness do not support the assertion that the territory was a 'cultural backwater', disengaged from wider socio-political changes (Davies and Gregory 1991: 77; Hutcheson 2004: 95). The Iceni are perceived to have rejected the civic trappings and imposing architecture found elsewhere in Roman Britain, in the form of large towns, villas, mosaics and inscriptions, preferring traditional modes of displaying status through portable wealth (Andrews 2012: 66; Fincham 2002: 83; Mattingly 2007: 111-13; Trow 2002: 104). We will return to this 'reluctance' again throughout this study.

1.5. The *Civitas* Capital: *Venta Icenorum*

The *civitas* capital has been described as 'an afterthought' and 'poorly developed'. It is considered to have failed as an urban centre, due to the impoverishment of the Icenian people and their 'local nobility' subsequent to the Boudican rebellion (de la Bédoyère 2006: 137; Frere 2000: 354; Millett 1990: 100-1). These typify standard, but outmoded, views of the town and demonstrate the persistence of the 'barbarians vs. civilisation' narrative. Excavations were carried out between 1929 and 1935 by Donald Atkinson (Frere 1971, 2005). Influenced by Haverfield (1901), Atkinson dated the formal layout to *circa* 70 CE, as part of a punitive Roman response to the revolt, describing the 'conservative character of the Iceni' and their 'imperfect degree of Romanisation' (1931: 133, 1932: 42).

Despite its tenacity in most subsequent literature, the narrative of stunted urban development at *Venta Icenorum* has been challenged by the Caistor Roman Project (2009-present). Bowden states it is no longer possible to think of the *civitas* capital as part of the post-revolt 'pacification' of the Iceni, as excavations have found little evidence for significant settlement before *circa* 120 CE (2012, 2013a, 2013b, 2017) nor for a high degree of militarisation (Harlow in Bowden forthcoming).

1.6. '*Igni atque ferro vastatum*': Harried with Fire and Sword

'The tribes which had shown themselves dubious or disaffected were harried with fire and sword. Nothing, however, pressed so hard as famine on an enemy who, careless about the sowing of his crops, had diverted all ages of the population to military purposes' (Tac. *Ann.* 14.38).

Another intransigent hypothesis, based on Tacitus, states that after the rebellion the population was annihilated, and the region laid waste (Hutcheson 2004: 95). 'Tribes' (plural) reminds us that, in the classical telling, the Iceni were joined in revolt by their neighbours, the Trinovantes, and perhaps other groups (Tac. *Ann.* 14.31). According to Caesar, a similar fate was meted out to the Eburones of

the Lower Rhine, whose *civitas* was razed and pillaged in retribution for the revolt of Ambiorix (Fernández-Götz 2014a: 235).

Often, the same evidence is used to make contrasting statements based on the perception of the Icenian character. For example, the absence of villas and an 'aristocratic class of landowners' in the Fenland is considered evidence for a possible Imperial estate. The lack of military posts in the same area 'implies a compliant population' (Catling 2014). By contrast, in the Iceni heartland these are considered evidence for cultural conservatism and the depopulation of the area after the revolt. The proposed Imperial estate depends on the Boudican narrative to provide the conditions for colonisation of a ravaged and empty land with few survivors (Malim 2005: 42).

Increasing evidence for LIA and early Roman settlement, particularly from developer-led projects, does not support a post-revolt vacuum in the Fens. Numerous sites are also suggested by field survey and aerial photography. Roads and canals (like the Fen Causeway and Car Dyke) were not planned strategic expansions, but local improvements on existing networks (Catling 2014; Smith *et al.* 2016; Taylor 2007). The narrative of depopulation and retribution features less strongly in archaeological or historical presentations of the LIA in Suffolk or Essex. Moore *et al.* (1988: 21, 82) observed there was little evidence of either a 'dramatic disruption' or new settlers in Suffolk, while the small towns at Hacheston and Coddenham developed uninterrupted.[7] Shifts in settlement (e.g. Chelmsford and Great Chesterford) and artefactual patterns in Essex are attributed by some to post-Boudican repression and military intervention (Perring and Pitts 2013: 246). These constructions are part of the discourse of the Iceni as 'Other'.

Tacitus claims that 70,000 Roman citizens and their allies were killed in the destruction of *Camulodunum* and *Verulamium*, and that 80,000 Britons fell at a cost of 400 Romans in Suetonius Paulinus's victory (*Ann.* 14.33, 14.37). It is practically impossible to estimate the numbers of inhabitants of the territory either directly before or after the revolt, but it is commonly assumed that a great many people died or were displaced as a consequence of the fighting, or the subsequent famine (Clarke 1939: 60-61; Millett 1990: 100-1; Webster 1993: 101, 129). 'Almost a complete generation of men of marriageable and procreative age would have been wiped out in battle while poverty, starvation and slavery will have reduced the number of survivors. It seems doubtful whether the population could have been restored to its original level

---

[7] The study of Roman urbanism and the classification of 'small towns' is beyond the scope of this book (see Burnham and Wacher 1990; Clarke 1995; Gurney 1995; Rodwell and Rowley 1975; Rust 2013; Taylor 2013; Todd 1970). The term is adopted here for convenience to describe nucleated settlements that are larger than villages, but not on the scale of *civitas* centres or *coloniae*. Small towns may have played a role in the introduction and distribution of new material culture and practices in the *civitas* (Plouviez 2005: 162).

within a generation, if indeed it ever was' (Wacher 1976: 229).

The post-Boudican impoverishment of the Iceni is often referred to, and yet is little supported by material evidence. Hutcheson notes the continued production of horse equipment on Roman period sites in Norfolk: 'The assumption that this region was devastated in the aftermath of the rebellion is not sustained by a close reading of the archaeological record. "Iron Age" cultural attributes do not disappear' (2004: 97-98). She advocates further research on this topic, which this study attempts to address. The Iceni disappear from the sparse written records, the name preserved only in the *civitas* capital and on lead ingots from a fourth century CE shipwreck off the Armorican coastline (L'Hour 1987). This is the fate of many other named communities which may have been creations of the colonial administration. It is necessary to evaluate the material remains carefully with this in mind.

The slow adoption of new material culture and practices has been ascribed to a social inwardness or an unwillingness to adopt a 'Roman' way of life (e.g. Atkinson 1932: 42; Millett 1990: 100-1), although critiques of 'Romanisation' have rightly questioned these concepts (e.g. Barrett 1997; Grahame 1998; Hingley 2008; James 2010). Cultural conservatism can instead be regarded as part of a dynamic of resistance in response to imperial oppression (Hill 2001; Hingley 1997; Scott 1990). This may reflect an alternative engagement with a vastly unequal power, or the extension of significant pre-conquest differences. It is possible that the Iceni were simply following a broader trend in LIA Britain, creating a strong regional identity in opposition to outside pressures (Davis and Gwilt 2008: 176).

1.7. How has the Icenian 'Other' been defined?

1.7.1. Creating the Iceni

The people known to the Romans as Iceni or Eceni may be synonymous with the *Cenimagni*, one of the groups who surrendered to Julius Caesar during his brief British expeditions in the 50s BCE (*BG* 5.21). Chadburn (2006: 322-23) tentatively suggests that the word *Eceni* could be related to the Latin *equus* (equine), making them 'Horse' people. A graffito on a greyware sherd from *Venta Icenorum* appears to read IQVINI (Figure 1.4). Nash Briggs disagrees on linguistic grounds, relating ECEN to a Germanic root meaning 'oak' (2011: 86, 2017: 154-55).

The ethnicity of Iron Age Britons has been contested on many fronts. Classical writers used a variety of terms to refer to the social structures of those with whom they came into contact, including 'peoples', 'nations' and 'states'. Earlier narratives in archaeology saw 'Celtic' or 'Belgic' invasions and ethnic links with the Gauls (e.g. Bulst 1961; Childe 1980; Clarke 1939; Hawkes and Dunning 1930). Ancient Britain was defined through classical texts and

coinage as 'a mosaic of bounded monolithic ethnic or tribal units' (Jones 1997: 31). These structures have since been replaced by ideas of independent 'insular evolution', combined with generations of cultural contact across the North Sea (Mattingly 2007: 83).

As Davies observes, the 'peoples of this island were neither unified nor uniform' (1999: 14). Some pre-conquest British societies may have been loose allegiances which coalesced around particular leaders or clans in response to the invasion. Named groups like 'the Iceni' are unlikely to reflect genuine indigenous identities or political structures. They may have emerged as a response to engagement with external forces in the administrative context of Roman occupation. Moore cautions against mapping named groupings onto modern boundaries, as this 'tribalization' denies the 'potentially multifaceted and fluid nature' of Iron Age societies (2011: 354). It is also essential to question our vocabulary and reflect upon the potential for multiple identities and groupings.[8]

Ethnicity is a focus within and between groups, usually based on common descent or cultural identification. Emberling (1997: 305) notes that societies structured around kinship are less hierarchical than those based on status or class. Jones (1997) warns that ethnicity is not simply a reflection of the *habitus*; material culture contributes to, and is reciprocally structured by, the creation of identity. Ethnic groups are dynamic and can be strategically manipulated to accommodate social and political tensions. Under Roman occupation, changing interactions and social relationships created new 'manifestations of ethnicity' (*ibid.*: 133). Holding multiple levels of ethnicity was not antithetical to Roman identity. In addition, 'acculturation' was not forced upon Roman subjects (Kurchin 1995: 128). Roman administrators were more interested in the political allegiances of those they had conquered or were trading with, than their ethnic or 'tribal' origins. Revell (2016) found it impossible to delineate a single 'Roman ethnicity' to which provincials were supposed to aspire. Derks and Roymans's volume on ethnic constructs (2009) demonstrates the variety of potential readings of ethnicity from an archaeological standpoint, stressing the difficulties, perhaps impossibilities, of reconciling cultural and ethnic identities through material artefacts, or even language. If 'being Roman' was a mark of citizenship, not ethnicity, which identity are we looking for?

---

[8] 'The use of the term "state" is justified for the LIA polities in Gaul and Britain as this is the term, *civitas*, used by the Latin writers who refer to them and had direct experience of them; the common translation into English, 'tribe', has unfortunate connotations in the anthropological literature, as it implies a lower level of social organisation' (Collis 2007: 524). The use of 'tribe' is thus only relevant when referring to classical texts (Moore 2011). Ross suggests replacing 'tribe' with 'community', thereby highlighting differences and networks (2011: 3), although uncritically substituting 'community' for 'tribe' is not especially useful. I will refrain from repeating this flawed terminology except in direct quotation, preferring to describe the Iceni *civitas*, territory, people or polity. Similarly, I replace 'native' with 'indigenous' or 'local', as it is loaded with contemporary post-imperial connotations.

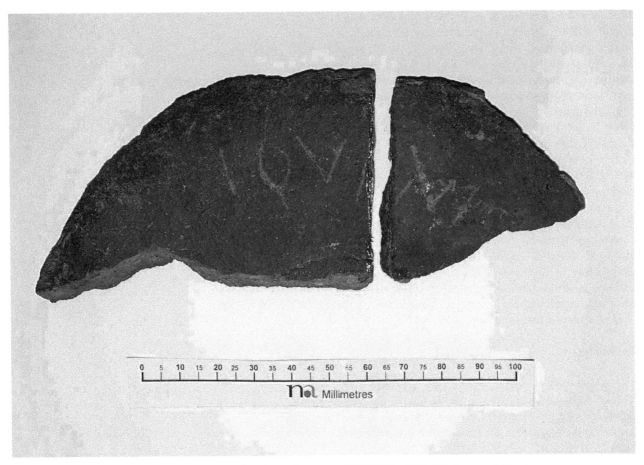

Figure 1.4. Greyware vessel with IQVINI graffito, *Venta Icenorum* (NWHCM: 1929.152; Image: Author).

1.7.2. Mapping 'Tribal Territories'

The Icenian territory resists definition; it has been characterised using coin distributions, despite issues with this rather narrow interpretation of the data (Allen 1970; Chadburn 2006: 333; Clarke 1939: 42, 81; Kimes *et al.* 1982).[9] Evidence from settlements and material culture shows well-developed and distinctive regional and intra-regional identities, with subtle variations in materials and distribution (Davies and Williamson 1999: 8). The 'social, political and territorial structure of Late Iron Age Britain was much more complex than the accepted "tribal map" implies' (Haselgrove 1992: 128). In recent years, regional distinctiveness has become a cause célèbre; modern preoccupations with devolution, migration and multiculturalism inevitably entering the archaeological debate.

Geographical features have also been used to establish boundaries. Davies (2011c: 1) identifies the River Waveney (the modern Norfolk-Suffolk county division) as a possible southern limit, whereas Martin fixes the line much further south, between the River Lark and the Alde (1999: 85). Rippon views the Lark-Gipping valleys in Suffolk as one

of the 'stable boundaries' in the East Anglian cultural landscape, potentially remaining a focal point for centuries (2018: 10). The Fen-edge is clearly an important boundary in the west, although this seems to have attracted activity rather than formed a barrier. Waterways can be considered connective rather than divisive. These boundaries, if they were conceptualised as such, were changeable, permeable and intangible.

Liminal zones or areas of intersection are where identities are most cherished and contested. The social study of boundaries, both symbolic and physical, has been approached scientifically, anthropologically and experientially (Barth ed. 1969; Bradley 2000; Kimes *et al.* 1982). Parker discusses different types of frontier and the potential for religious, cultural, economic and democratic borders (2006). Borderlands are therefore essential to understanding the territory. One of the aspects of this research is to look for patterns in the archaeological evidence which could be interpreted as zones of overlap between distinctive regional material culture assemblages.

1.7.3. Neophiles and Neophobes

The concepts of Icenian cultural retardation and backwardness are a foil to the idea of other southern British peoples as early adopters or 'neophiles'. The Iceni have been defined in opposition as 'neophobes',

---

[9] Chadburn reports that hoards containing only Icenian coins are found within a line running approximately from Great Yarmouth-Diss-Bury St Edmunds-Cambridge-March-The Wash (2006: 333, 470 map 17).

resisting the onward march of progress. In some ways, this rhetoric still exists in the common perception of Norfolk today as a sleepy backwater. Imported goods and appropriated traditions may signify a new way of belonging, perhaps desirable to those who would benefit from increased access to the Roman system of towns, roads and currency. The southern lands of LIA Britain had closer contact with Roman expansion for longer, whereas the east perhaps maintained earlier networks with northern Britain or northern Europe (Davis 2014: 217; Hunter 1997: 109; MacGregor, M. 1976: 103, 134; Mackreth 2011: 188). However, not all imports represent adoptions of identity; they can be imposed as part of wider power relationships (Haselgrove and Moore 2007: 8). Cultural capital and technical 'know-how' can be inclusive or exclusive. Different cultural practices and new objects can alienate or disempower those without this cultural knowledge. Conversely, acquisition or appropriation of these behaviours and belongings can be empowering or used to express difference (Swift 2017: 13).

1.8. Summary

The land of the Iceni seems to have been defined by what it is not. As the old adage relates, 'in Norfolk we do things different'. This 'Do Different' rhetoric has been applied to the Iceni (Clarke 1939: 85, attributed to R.H. Mottram; Davies 2011b: 104; Fairclough 2010: 105; Marsden 2012: 52, 64). There is a strong sense that in the past, as today, the region was defiantly independent. The Iceni are thought to have stood apart from other peoples of pre-Roman Britain. Their distinctive use of material culture reflects changing expressions of status and identity. The making of the Icenian 'Other', which began in the classical texts, has continued to structure our understanding of the period. In this book, I consider this discourse and illuminate some responses to major changes, both internal and external, through the everyday personal belongings of the period.

This brief summary of the historical and archaeological background sets the scene for the following research questions: Is there a distinctive material culture in the region which can be identified with the Iceni? What is the historical discourse of 'the Iceni' and does it stand up to archaeological scrutiny? Were displays of portable artefacts favoured over other symbols considered to demonstrate status, and were personal belongings used to show resistance to Roman influence? Is there evidence for the claimed post-rebellion famine, depopulation and reallocation of land? How significant are unstratified surface finds recovered by metal-detector in creating new interpretations?

To address these questions, I created a database of over 14,000 object records, drawn from the county HERs and PAS records for Norfolk, Suffolk and Cambridgeshire. The date range spanned 300 years, from 100 BCE to 200 CE. Excavation reports, 'grey literature' and other published sources, such as county archaeological journals, were consulted. Further detail on the research methodology is discussed in the next chapter and the Appendices.

Understanding Change and Looking for Difference

2.1. Introduction

The complex subject of the Roman interlude in Britain raises questions about identity and ethnicity, resistance and agency.[1] This chapter reviews our current state of knowledge on the key issues of belonging (identity) and belongings (material culture). It situates my research within contemporary theoretical thought and considers the interpretive models suitable for large-scale data analysis. These will be discussed under two overarching themes: How do we understand cultural contact and change? How are private and public, individual and group identities expressed through material culture?

This study considers the role of portable artefacts in identity formation. It focusses on practice, display and difference as expressed through personal belongings (Eckardt 2014; Gardner 2007; Revell 2016). My approach combines Crummy's functional categories (1983), which are allied to *praxis*, with an object-centred view of agency in which 'things' engage in social and material networks (Gell 1998; Gosden 2005; Hodder 2012). An introduction to the research methodology used is outlined in section 2.4, with more detailed discussion in Appendices A and B.

2.2. How do we understand cultural contact and change?

The prevailing Romanisation paradigm of the late 19th and 20th centuries coloured archaeological understandings of interactions between Iron Age Britain and the Roman empire. Its application to the Iceni and the *civitas* capital (Atkinson 1931, 1932; Haverfield 1901) resulted in the persistent 'cultural backwardness' stereotype. Romanisation has been heavily critiqued over the past 30 years (e.g. Hingley 2008; James 2010; Mattingly 1997, 2007; Millett 1990; Webster and Cooper 1996; Woolf 1997). In the ensuing theoretical vacuum, questions remain over the evidence for continuity and change during Britain's term as a Roman province (Gardner 2007, 2013; Versluys 2014; Woolf 2014).

Romanisation explained the incorporation of diverse groups of indigenous people into the monolithic imperial body as part of a progressive framework (Barrett 1997: 51). Classical descriptions and numismatic evidence were used to conceptualise 'tribal' groups and territories (section 1.7.2). One narrative saw emergent 'native elites' in the LIA maintaining power through the control of rare and imported products. The deliberate acculturation of 'native aristocracies' paved the way for assimilation into the empire. Certain groups were permitted to retain local dominance in exchange for their loyalty (Frere 1991). Literary claims that indigenous princelings were taken 'hostage' to Rome, returning home to impart a cultured touch to their countryfolk, may have had a comforting resonance for antiquaries familiar with the Grand Tour, but there is minimal evidence in the archaeology (see Creighton 2000: 89-92). An alternative approach considered the importance of social reciprocity and the desire to acquire prestige. Cultural change trickled down the social hierarchy by a process of emulation (Haselgrove 1996; Millett 1990, 2002). Gifts, honours and privileges may have overcome the potential culture clash between conquerors and colonised (Grahame 1998; Kurchin 1995). Both these viewpoints rely on an economic model for social change. The idea of 'native elites' is rarely questioned, but the social structure of the Iceni would have played a large part in whether these strategies found favour.

James develops this approach by emphasising 'elite negotiation' to explain the profound material changes in the artefactual record, with new coinage, burial rites and personal adornment apparent in the century before the Claudian invasion. Long-standing contact and trade links with Gaul influenced lowland Britain's relationship with Rome (James 2010). Despite the region's geographical proximity to the mainland, this suite of novel ideas and objects was not adopted in the Iceni territory with the same enthusiasm as other parts of southeastern England.

Regional differences were homogenised by the 'Romans vs. Natives' opposition of Romanisation (Hill 2001: 12). The tendency to see imperialism as a unilateral process failed to explore the role of the colonised in creating and subverting the *status quo*. Reassessment of 'Britain in the Roman Empire' (Mattingly 2007) highlights resistance, regional diversity and the active construction of identities, rather than the straightforward adoption of *romanitas* (Creighton 2006; Gardner 2013; Grahame 1998; James 2010; Keay and Terrenato 2010).[2] Within this 'nativist' critique, the diversity of material culture and social practice across the provinces has been given greater attention (Crummy and Eckardt 2003: 44). These approaches still make certain assumptions about social structure, leadership and value systems.

---

[1] Mattingly also refers to the 'Roman interlude', praising the recent convergence of Iron Age and Roman specialists 'working across this divide' (2008: 214).

[2] *Romanitas* denotes Roman self-image and identity, expressed through cultural attributes such as villas and townhouses (Kurchin 1995: 127), although neither the term nor concept appears in the documentary record until *circa* 200 CE (James 2010: 200).

If Romanisation has been discredited as, at best, a historical discourse and, at worst, an irrelevant fiction, how does this affect any attempt to seek Icenian identities? What traces might the two-way process of adaptation and appropriation between groups leave in the artefact record? Much has been written on potential replacements for Romanisation as a narrative to explain cultural process and change, and their application to material culture. These include globalisation and glocalisation, discrepant experience and institutional archaeology (e.g. Gardner 2013; Hodos ed. 2017; Laurence 2001; Mattingly 2011; Pitts and Versluys eds. 2014; Woolf 2014). I have attempted to integrate the nuances of discrepancy and hybridity within a wider post-colonial analysis of power and discourse. Gardner (2013) recommends that small finds are interpreted as manifestations of *praxis* – ritual or habitual action. His 'institutional archaeology' considers interactions of practice, structure and agency over time and space. These institutions may be anything from customs and ethnicity to more structured organisations. By looking at a large geographical area and a 300-year timespan, I will attempt to demonstrate some of these relationships in areas such as religion, literacy and transport.

2.2.1. Persistent Identities: Resistance and Discrepancy

In the late 20th century, archaeological debates moved away from Romanisation to address overlooked areas such as class, age, gender and regionality. This socially-aware archaeology reflected political fights for equality and consideration of individual power for change. The revisionist approach (Haselgrove 1996, 2002; Millett 1990) was criticised for its focus on elites and the 'trickle down' effect on the wider population. Cultural contact was redrawn as a multifaceted experience which allowed a range of 'discrepant' identities and greater agency among occupied peoples. Instead of simple submission or slavish emulation, people responded to Roman influence with a dynamic re-creation of identities (Hill 2001; Mattingly 2007).

Ideas of resistance and 'cultural conservatism' are key concepts in the discourse of the Iceni. I define 'resistance' in Hingley's sense, in which material culture is used in indirect forms of opposition (1997: 88), or the 'hidden transcripts' of Scott (1990), which may be expressed as an alternative, or a counterpart, to outright insurgence. While the average peasant-farmer may have had limited potential to effect large-scale change, the will to resist may have been expressed through simple personal belongings, such as brooches.

Davies argues for a series of 'cultural indicators' and 'deliberate exclusions' which set the Iceni apart from other Iron Age Britons (2011b: 104). Indicators like language, dress and cuisine can mark out cultural interactions and may tell us about attitudes to citizenship in the past. The persistence of older forms, styles and perhaps also meanings, into the post-revolt period may reveal this process. The re-forging of identities, creating a creolised

Romano-British character, may have reinforced or challenged the new administration (Davis and Gwilt 2008: 146-47; Hingley 1997: 96; Mattingly 2008: 218).

2.2.2. Globalisation and Connectivity

While the study of a small territory within a marginal province of the Roman empire does not provide enough data to consider global-scale shifts, the topic of globalisation and its close companion, fragmentation, deserve mention. Pitts and Versluys characterise globalisation as 'processes by which localities and people become increasingly interconnected and interdependent' (2014: 11), while Hodos defines it as 'a wide-scale flow of ideas and knowledge alongside the sharing of cultural customs, civil society, practices and the environment' (2017: 4). Hodos champions globalisation as an 'alternative paradigm' which allows for difference and a variety of responses at different scales (*ibid.* 8-9).

One of the challenges is how to interpret interconnectivity in the past through the lens of material culture. Can we see evidence of shared practices and identities, without homogeneity and uniformity, in 'an incomplete and ambiguous synchronisation' (Hodos 2017: 6)? The process of 'glocalisation' involves local adaptations of shared global practices and ideas, resulting in hybrid identities and transformations (Gardner 2013: 7). This balancing act between the global and local emerged in LPRIA Britain, when widespread forms of material culture and practice were appropriated, transformed and incorporated by 'dynamic and interconnected' societies, while still maintaining strong local identities and traditions (Gosden and Hill 2008: 2). Under circumstances such as imperial expansion, we encounter this odd paradox whereby cultural convergence is paralleled by cultural differentialism (Hodos 2017: 4).

2.2.3. What is the power of the dispossessed?

To understand interactions between indigenous groups and colonial powers, we must query the mechanisms for social change and the role of state and individual. In the early to mid-20th century, Marxist archaeologists posited that past societies were aligned along class lines, emphasising domination by the powerful and resistance among minority or oppressed groups. Internal struggles for power instigated social transformations. Processual archaeologies drew heavily on anthropological theory, science and linguistics to interpret the spread of Roman culture, taking a long view of social change (Tilley 1990; Trigger 2006: 386-483). Structuralist analyses compared Roman unity with Iron Age diversity; Roman order with Iron Age chaos (Woolf 1992: 351-52).

Social theorists like Giddens (1984) criticised the Marxist/structuralist approach for lacing too tight a social straitjacket around the individual agent. Sociologists (e.g. Bourdieu 1977) viewed individuals at the nexus of a constantly renewed web of relationships, practices and interactions with both institutions and other social actors. Structural relationships of domination and exploitation are still valid in this model, but are tempered by individual actions. However, these analyses tend to neglect the agency of the less powerful and the masses (Grahame 1998: 5). James sees local elites reinforcing their roles through the control of cultural capital. They sought to maintain and express a social hierarchy which validated their privileged position, defining themselves through 'distinction from their subordinates through new symbols of exclusion' (2010: 199).

In Roymans's discussion of Belgic Gaul and the Rhineland, Roman 'cultural uniformisation' occurs, while continuing cultural differences were 'reformulated in interaction' (1996: 10). Some peoples held ambiguous identities which bridged the perceived gap between 'civilised' Gallic and 'barbarian' Germanic societies. A 'failure to Romanise' left those on the margins 'doomed to chaos and barbarism'. Those areas which felt the impact of Rome less heavily were differently integrated into the empire, often based on what they could provide, like military conscripts or agricultural surpluses (*ibid.*: 101-3). There were multiple unequal power structures and relationships of exploitation within the Roman provinces. Where on this spectrum of engagement did the *civitas Icenorum* fall?

Under the client-kingdom, the 'Icenian aristocracy' (Gurney 1998: 27) included Prasutagus and Boudica, or their equivalents. After the revolution was subdued, were the remnants of this 'elite' enslaved or permitted to take up positions of power under the new administration? During the *civitas* period, we can only imagine the dynamics at work between local power-brokers, resettled veterans, active military personnel and the administrative class, as well as the average subsistence farmer. Yet, this viewpoint still assumes that hierarchy was the norm. There are possibilities for a re-reading of the Boudican uprising, using concepts of consensus and collective action (DeMarrais 2016).

Scott's 'hidden transcripts' (1990) allow for marginalised and subordinate groups to express dissent through cultural forms. People may tolerate periods of domination if they believe they will be eventually liberated. This can be related to the Iceni both during the client-kingdom and the occupation. Perhaps this explains the lack of militarisation in the territory before Ostorius Scapula's programme of disarmament reportedly triggered the first uprising (Hingley and Unwin 2005: 26; Mattingly 2007: 101; Tacitus *Ann.* 12.31). The idea of cultural resistance has been critiqued by Sauer, who accuses resistance theorists of an 'anti-colonialist mission' to find archaeological proof of 'otherwise unrecorded widespread resistance' (2004: 119). If material culture was a means of expressing resistance to Roman rule, how do we recognise the 'ironic potential' for satire, mimicry and subversion (Webster 2003: 35)?

Britons who were friendly to the Romans must have been aware of these hidden meanings. Many members of the client-state would have been pro-Roman and may even have contested the revolt. Scott acknowledges the difficulties of finding subordinate discourses, both past and present. Overt resistance may be expressed in domains of domination: against taxation and appropriation of goods and lands, public rituals and ideological displays. Hidden transcripts are transmitted most keenly where control is weakest, for example through popular culture and personal religious expression (1990: 108-35). Counter-cultural dissonance can be expressed through dress and language, and it is these things which may leave traces in the archaeological record.

Taking up the Roman way of dress may have paid cynical lip-service to the incoming hegemony, but maintained contradictory or subversive attitudes (Grahame 1998: 2). Carroll discusses the blending of 'ethnic' clothing in Germany and Gaul (2012) and notes a 'pronounced diffidence' towards Roman female attire on the second century CE tombstone of the Catuvellaunian woman, Regina, at South Shields. Depending on the strictures of the occupiers, resistance may have been subtle or overt; if wearing one's British heritage on one's sleeve was considered dangerous or rebellious, this may have been restricted to times when surrounded only by close kin or sympathetic community members. If, however, it was seen as a parochial but harmless fashion, indigenous dress may have been retained as a means of sustaining pre-Roman beliefs and traditions throughout the occupation, and to pass these on to future generations, along with rituals, oral histories and dialects.

2.3. How does identity relate to material culture?

Born out of heavily artefact-based prehistoric studies, material culture theory can be applied to historical archaeology to balance the classical sources. An object-centred approach views artefacts as active. Human socialisation derives from and impacts upon the material world: 'things create people'. This standpoint gives us the opportunity to consider how objects can actively create membership of groups. Becoming Romano-British may have entailed 'a series of subtle, but fundamental shifts' in personal presentation and behaviour (Gosden 2005: 193-98). Small personal belongings can be examined for their role as 'cultural or regional identifiers' (Swift 2011: 209). Objects do not straightforwardly reflect the social context of their production. Instead, artefacts recovered by excavation or surface collection have reached the most recent milestone in their life histories, a biography of materiality stretching back to their inception in the maker's imagination (Appadurai ed. 1986; Beaudry *et al.* 1991; Gosden and Marshall 1999; Hodder ed. 1991; Hodder and Hutson 2003; Joy 2009, 2010).

In this section, I outline several theoretical approaches to relationships between identity and the material world. These encompass ideas of display, aesthetics and hybridity, and the role of elites. I highlight some of the key issues in the construction of identities through material culture with relevance to the study of the Icenian polity, including coinage, hoarding and craft production.

2.3.1. Personhood and Adornment

The complex process of interaction between people and things can create gender, ethnic and group identities. Revell (2016) explores the plural, varied and personal nature of identity formation. Identity is both product and performance, mutually constituted through practice and often mediated by material culture. Practice is thus the connective tissue between belongings and belonging. Identities are 'socially constructed, situational and mutable' (Crummy and Eckardt 2003: 44). Fowler proposes the more reflexive notion of 'personhood' (2004), which may be analysed in social, political and spatial terms. This is a dynamic process whereby identities are created both internally and externally through practice or 'strategies' (Pudney 2010: 116). How people chose, or were expected, to decorate themselves and their clothing gives us clues to past personhood. Through their association with the body, adornment, costume and grooming are common points of focus when discussing gendered identities. It is important to remember that, like all socially constructed identities, gender norms vary over time. Archaeology has developed as a discipline using rather fixed binary gender categorisations which have only recently been challenged.

A multifaceted set of personal and social meanings can be communicated through items such as jewellery, clothing, hairstyles and other personal accessories (Swift 2011: 206). These symbols would have been consumed in varied ways by different individuals depending on their social background. As agents in the social life of the community, individuals manifested multiple forms of identity throughout their lives and in varying social contexts. Material culture played an active part in the creation of 'a complex interlocking series of connections and identities' which can potentially be recognised in artefactual distributions and contexts (Hunter 2007: 286-87).

Crummy and Eckardt recommend exploring the inter-woven strands of social practice and identity embodied within objects (2003: 45). Changes in *praxis* can occur which utilise the same material culture and *vice versa*. Artefactual conservatism, innovation and hybridity can demonstrate changing patterns of display and behaviour. Although material agency without context, and intentionality in resistance, have been questioned (Ribeiro 2016; Russell 2004), objects can express and create feelings of (in)equality. This goes beyond the simple idea of 'haves' and 'have nots': not every symbol of rank or status is desirable to all. In this way, we can challenge the doctrine of 'tribal elites' which is a key part of the narrative of cultural contact. How did the people of the area express identity and status through material culture? Did it differ from their neighbours and the Roman occupiers? Is there evidence for discrepancy and dissonance?

2.3.2. Social Boundaries and Identity

The critique of Romanisation revealed its inherent unidirectional model of conquest and acculturation. Narratives are peppered with 'quick learning natives' in the towns and 'tribal nobles' in the country eagerly emulating Roman standards of living. Enthusiastically cooperating 'native elites' were grateful to be offered material trinkets or key positions in provincial life, from where they could exercise hegemony on behalf of their distant imperial masters (Fincham 2002; Hattatt 1982: 21; Millett 1990). In this model, the agency and potential of the masses is often 'neutralized', 'disempowered' and 'unprivileged' (James 2010: 199).

The evidence for Icenian elites derives largely from literature, rather than archaeology, and thus presents a problem. The assumed social structure has been based upon ideas of kingship and Iron Age 'warrior' societies with little supporting evidence. Ideas of social stratification are entangled with the interpretation of coinage as evidence of elites. Fernández-Götz has described the heterogenous nature of *civitates* with 'multiple conflicts of interests and power dynamics at all levels' including gender, age and status (2014a: 59). The possibilities of alternative power dynamics may be a genuine difference in the Iceni polity and reflect the way the empire interacted with its people (Lamb 2018). Perhaps the mechanism of occupation worked more smoothly through engagement with or creation of an active stratum of privilege. Imperial expansion and centralisation required the construction of defined 'tribal' territories with stratified leaderships, creating the conditions for 'effective interaction' (Wells 2001: 113-14). If the Iceni had an 'aristocracy' would that make them easier to govern? Could they have revolted without a unifying leadership? Material culture is also implicated in the construction of these narratives.

What constituted a 'British elite'? How involved were they in processes of capitulation and negotiation? Elite status and identity have been presumed to be 'self-evident, inevitable and unproblematic' (Revell 2016: 61). Within such meta-structures, numerous select groups may have coexisted, including military, mercantile, political, religious, ancestral and intellectual 'elites'. Dominant groups can only operate via the acquiescence or oppression of the non-elite (*ibid.*: 62). A change of landholder or overseer may have impacted little on ordinary people's lives. Structures of power may have continued, leaving the *status quo* virtually intact. Slave labour is undoubtedly a possibility in certain industries in Roman Britain (Watts 2005: 2). Iron shackles have been discovered at Saham Toney (Bates *et al.* 2000: 230; NHER: 29429) and dredged from the River Wensum at Worthing (NHER: 2984).

We must deconstruct this terminology and its application to archaeological groups and artefacts. The assumed membership of these elites, aristocracies and status groups needs to be questioned. I do not dispute the existence of social differentiation, but wish to raise the debate about how to recognise it archaeologically. An exclusive group based on access to specialised knowledge, such as a craft workshop or a religious cult, would leave a very different material signature to one based on communal ownership of livestock. What other models might have existed in later prehistoric and early Romano-British societies? How can they be recognised in the material culture?

2.3.3. The Material Elite Paradigm

The paradigm of the material elite is based on assumptions that past societies operated hierarchically through material wealth. Our conceptions of 'elite', 'big man' and 'slave' are part of an unsustainable progressivist view of history (Fernández-Götz 2014a: 33). The idea of inherited status is also seldom interrogated. Social status can nevertheless be predicated upon many other factors, including ownership of livestock, magico-ritual capital, prowess in battle or hunting, and links with ancestors or land. Individuals may have held membership of multiple, sometimes contradictory, social groups based on kinship, specialist knowledge, age, gender, inherited class or non-hereditary leadership (Tullett 2010: 65-67). Even in societies which are outwardly egalitarian, people continually monitor and evaluate each other (Wason 1994: 36-37). Many of these forms would leave little archaeological trace, but it is important to consider their existence (Hill 2011: 243). Naturally, not all archaeologists make such assumptions, but elites are rarely overtly problematised in the same way as gender, for example (on which, see Effros 2004; Gibbs 1987; Harlow 2004; Holmes 2012; Scott 1995; Sørensen 1987; Van Driel-Murray 1995).

Wells (2001) regarded pre-conquest male burials with weaponry, horse gear and luxury items as the hallmarks of an 'international warrior elite', dominant across much of Europe. Giles (2012) has questioned this in relation to the chariot burials in Yorkshire. Hill (2011) considered possible alternatives to stratified societies for the Iron Age, such as segmentary and non-hierarchical groupings, which lack elites and hold resources collectively. The idea of heterarchy has been explored in relation to complex societies and gender (Crumley 1987; Ehrenreich *et al.* eds. 1995; Levy 1999). Revell's (2016) search for non-elite provincial identities and Rathbone's 'anarchist archaeology' (2015) also provide interesting possibilities. Oosthuizen (2016) looks at the potential for collective land rights and 'horizontal' forms of governance. Given the frequency of hoards of torcs, coins and horse harness (Chadburn 2006: 174), it is conceivable that the Iceni held their wealth communally, rather than individually, in the form of precious metalwork or livestock. Production and hoarding of metalwork doubtless relate to social structures, which may have continued under Roman occupation. Such a social organisation would have an important impact on inheritance of land, power and wealth, and on our ability to recover these structures archaeologically.

The material elite paradigm has seeped into our understanding of artefacts and practices. There is also a tendency to refer to Roman 'industries', 'factories' and 'commodities' which is a relic of the progressive understanding of Roman imperialism (Webster and Cooper eds. 1996). Culturally-specific value systems can be hard to retrieve. During the early colonial period in North America, the Algonquians were keen to trade for refined copper at the expense of gold and silver. This seemed naïve to the European colonists, but 'within the indigenous world view it made complete sense': copper was a powerful, spiritual and political substance, particularly valued for its red colour (Farley 2012: 152-56). This should serve as a salutary warning to avoid retrofitting materialist and capitalist doctrines onto prehistory. Eckardt advises against applying ideologies of consumption to the Roman period, suggesting 'appropriation' more suitably represents the active process of constructing social meaning (2005: 140).

Classical texts emphasised the 'transgressive customs' of the 'barbarous' Britons (Stewart 1995: 3). In Boudica's rallying speech to her troops, Dio has her refer to British men, who hold all things in common, even their children and wives. She reminds her compatriots 'how much better is poverty with no master than wealth with slavery' (*Hist. Rom.* 62.3, 62.6). Of course, we have no archaeological evidence for Boudica herself, and Dio's dramatisation may be a reference to Caesar, who stated the Britons practised polygamy and had customs which determined the place of children within this marriage network (*BG* 5.14). Caesar's knowledge of Britain was extremely limited, and we have no information to confirm or disprove this social structure (see Hingley and Unwin 2005: 41-61 for a concise discussion of the classical sources). Tacitus also introduces other elements of social hierarchy, such as the role of priests or 'Druids' (*Ann.* 14.29).

Some client rulers were allowed to nominate heirs, but successions were moments of tension which could descend into chaos and violence (Mattingly 2011: 75-92). Power struggles after the uprising in 47 CE may have led to Prasutagus's accession to leadership (Frere 1991: 61). In turn, his disastrous attempt to share the kingdom between his own daughters and the emperor Nero precipitated the Boudican revolt (Tac. *Ann* 14.31). This may reflect hugely differing attitudes to the holding and transfer of power between these two, unequal entities. Clearly, the hints of alternative social organisation in the literary narratives cannot be taken at face value. The archaeology confounds any attempts to fit the classical texts, and it is necessary to derive new narratives which take material culture as the starting point.

2.3.4. Craft Specialisation

The division of labour which supports specialised craft practices is sometimes considered evidence for social differentiation. In this model, 'elites' exercise symbolic and economic power through controlling the skills of craftspeople and negotiating the exchange of prestige items. This commissioning of high-quality artefacts is seen as a political strategy which differentiates the (material) 'elite' from other levels of society (Wason 1994: 107-8). While there may be a relationship between specialist craft skills and social stratification, this model seems to me rather too analogous with the medieval system of patronage.

The image of the region as backward and culturally impoverished derives partly from the lack of familiar benchmarks for social stratification, and therefore the high degree of craft skill seems puzzling. In Joy's discussion of Middle Iron Age cauldrons, he observes little sign of the 'elite-sponsored' specialist workshops once thought to be the driving force behind the production of 'prestige' metalwork (in Baldwin and Joy 2017: 103-5). The frequency of metalworking debris in settlements confirms that small-scale, local production with idiosyncratic styles and methods continued into the LIA. Therefore, I would argue that highly-skilled craft production need not exist within a hierarchical, competitive social milieu.

2.3.5. Coins and Identity

Part of the construction of 'the Iceni' is the idea that coin distributions can be retrofitted to ethnic boundaries. While this has been roundly critiqued and found wanting, these 'tribe-sized' coinage groups refuse to dissolve, even as the concept of 'tribe' itself dematerialises (Moore 2011: 350), leaving us with some problematic archaeological evidence (Figure 2.1). It is likely that political allegiances were as important as ethnic factors of identity. Although not the focus of this study, coinage is vital for understanding the role of other material culture as portable wealth. Distributions of certain small finds also appear to match the estimated boundaries of *civitates*. Production centres may explain this zoning phenomenon (Eckardt and Crummy 2008: 68, 74). Are these 'tribal territories' actually evidence for the geographical range of specific workshops or exchange networks?

A reading of Icenian coinage refutes some of the conventions derived from the classical sources. Iron Age issues predominantly found in East Anglia are called 'Icenian', despite ECEN being a rare exception to the usual lack of ethnonyms on coins. While the distribution appears geographically contained (Figure 2.2), there are intra-regional variations and inter-regional similarities. Three main mints often produced issues in parallel (Talbot 2017: 60-62). Chadburn (2006; following Allen 1970), interpreted these as representing three *pagi* or subgroups, each with a leader named in coin legends, and in the case of Prasutagus, a king, '*Rex Icenorum*' (Tac. *Ann.* 14.31). The Prasutagus coins (e.g. PAS: CCI-780101) are now thought to relate to an otherwise unknown person called Esuprastus (Williams 2001: 9). This individual may also feature on neighbouring coinage, including AESV and IISVPRASV variants (Talbot 2017: 100). Coins with ANTED and ECEN legends were issued concurrently by the same mint with broadly similar

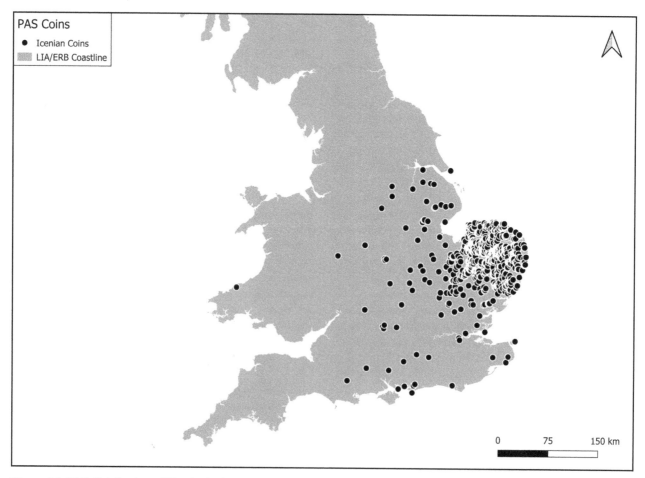

Figure 2.1. PAS distribution of 'Icenian' coins.

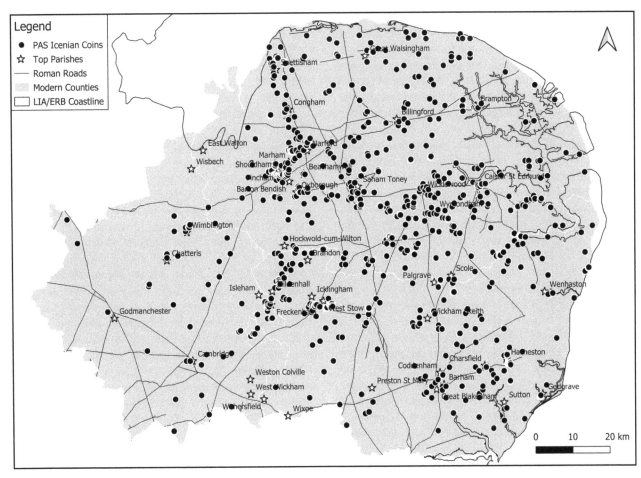

Figure 2.2. PAS distribution of 'Icenian' coins in the study area.

distributions, which does not support the idea of independent *pagi*. Talbot found these multiple, contemporaneous names inconsistent with the idea of dynastic sovereignty (2015: 310-11, 2017: 33). Alongside evidence for the flatter social organisation and greater political diversity of the region (Davies 1999; Hill 2011; Lamb 2018), the coins reveal 'no evidence of rigid centralised organisational structures' and kingship 'does not appear to be appropriate in Late Iron Age East Anglia' (Talbot 2017: 149). Leins argues for a similar lack of stratification in the northeastern coin-producing region (2012: 244-47).

Over 100 pellet mould fragments were found at Fison Way, Thetford (NHER: 5853; NWHCM: 1995: 60), identified as the location of an Iron Age mint (Talbot 2015: 155). Coin moulds have also been found at Saham Toney (NHER: 4697), Needham (NHER: 11071) and West Stow (SHER: WSW002). Chadburn also adds possible mints at Snettisham and Fincham (2006: 460-64). Minting of Icenian silver coinage during the client-kingdom has been debated (Creighton 1992, 1994; Gregory 1991a: 196). Talbot observed that production continued after the conquest into the client-kingdom in 'a steady orderly way', only ceasing after the 60/61 CE rebellion (2017: 125). He also noted that neither the invasion nor the revolt of 47 CE is 'directly detectable in the numismatic record' (*ibid.*: 150).

For the first few centuries of the occupation, monetisation in Roman Britain was patchy (Walton 2011: 290-91). Most transactions must have carried on as part of pre-existing barter or gift exchange systems. Coin hoards fit into the long tradition of Icenian metalwork deposition. Excess wealth may have been removed from the community by this process, acting to increase social equality (Wason 1994: 109-11). Hoards also reveal distributions which may reflect regional boundaries (Chadburn 2006: 333; Davies 1996: 85-87).

2.3.6. Hoarding and Deposition

Identity and material culture can often be entwined through the processes of deposition. Hoards are a particular form of intentional deposit which have attracted varied and changing archaeological interpretations. Although my dataset is primarily composed of surface finds, there are numerous significant hoards from the region, particularly of horse harness and jewellery. A few examples can show the potential of hoards to illuminate past *praxis* and personhood. Why did people deposit their belongings in hoards? Were hoards caches of individual or community wealth, valuables hidden in times of trouble, or displays of conspicuous consumption? Were they trophies, the spoils of war?

One of the practices which seems to set the Iceni apart archaeologically is the tendency to hoard decorated and precious metalwork. Norfolk tops the PAS tables for the most Iron Age and Roman hoards, of both coins and other artefacts. This hoarding tradition has been described as a 'culturally distinct phenomenon' which is not found to the same extent among neighbouring groups (Chadburn 2006: 174). Of course, hoarding as a practice is not specific to East Anglia or the LIA: people have been depositing selected artefacts for millennia, across the British Isles and beyond. The topic is a large one which cannot justly be explored here. For East Anglian case studies see Chadburn (2006), Creighton (1994), Hutcheson (2004, 2007), Johns (1997), Stead (1991) and Talbot (2015, 2017); for the wider picture see Davis and Gwilt (2008), Garrow and Gosden (2012), Haselgrove (2015) and Hunter (1997).

Archaeologists have sometimes been quick to ascribe mid-first century CE hoards to the 'War of Independence', although this can be a self-fulfilling argument. Hoards of Icenian coins are inevitably cited as evidence for the unrest of the Boudican revolt and its aftermath (Allen 1970: 16-18; Clarke 1939; Chadburn 2006: 161-63; Todd 1999: 72-73), although this assumption has been disputed (e.g. Leins 2008). Earlier hoards, like the Snettisham torcs (section 4.7), have been called 'tribal treasuries' (Stead 1991), whereas finds dating from the client-kingdom and rebellion are considered 'security' hoards. Creighton (1994) reassessed Icenian coin hoards from an archaeological perspective. He observed that Roman coins

were phased in gradually and increased over time, and both Roman and Icenian issues were hoarded together. A clear material distinction between invaders and indigenes is not supported. This blurring of boundaries is a common theme throughout my research. However, Talbot's work (2015, 2017) reveals that Icenian coin hoards were part of an episodic, not continuous, practice. This may give credence to the argument that hoards were a response to periods of danger or change, although the careful selection of coins by metal and denomination demonstrates a degree of forward planning rather than blind panic.

Occasionally, a link with the rebellion is a real possibility. The Fenwick Treasure (Figure 2.3) was found beneath the Boudican destruction levels in Colchester, one of three Roman towns destroyed during the uprising. The hoard includes both male and female personal effects: bracelets, rings and earrings, along with a coin-purse. Many of the items of jewellery were imported and followed contemporary Mediterranean fashions. A pair of silver bracelets and a medallion have been interpreted as '*armillae*' (section 4.4), military decorations possibly awarded during the Claudian conquest, belonging to a veteran living in the *colonia*. This is a rare example of a jewellery hoard from a domestic context. It was hidden in a small box under the floor of a house, which burned down on top, sealing the deposit. The hoard's owners never returned to retrieve their belongings (Crummy *et al.* 2015, 2016). It is highly likely that this was a flight hoard, deposited at the time of the Boudican crisis.

Figure 2.3. The Fenwick hoard, Colchester, Essex (PAS: ESS-058E5B).

Alternatively, hoarding can be read as a form of resistance, 'reinforcing community cohesion and solidarity', especially at times of change (Garrow and Gosden 2012: 312). The Iceni are thought to have deliberately excluded imports of wine in favour of locally-produced beer during the contact and client-kingdom periods (Davies 2011b: 103-4). This boycott has also been viewed as resistance among the Belgae, as described by Caesar (Pitts 2019: 36). Tankards, for communal consumption of beer, were regular components of LIA and early Roman hoards, including those from Santon (section 8.10.2) and West Stow, the latter which included votive figurines, staff terminals, headdress components and leaf/feather plaques (Horn 2015: 332-33; Worrell *et al.* 2011: 422-25). Wine-drinking may have introduced an intoxicating new suite of material culture and behaviour to be adopted or resisted.

Two significant hoards of vessels connected to wine-drinking expose the sheer variety of interpretations which may be placed on the same artefacts. At Crownthorpe (Wicklewood), copper alloy pans and dishes were packed inside a strainer, all of Italian origin, alongside two locally-manufactured drinking cups with 'Celtic' style ducks on the handles (Figure 2.4). Stylistically these have been dated to the 60s CE. Davies suggests they 'may have been owned by a prominent local person who had been hoping to enhance his status by adopting Roman modes of behaviour' and who 'may have been fleeing from Boudica's rebels' (2009: 139). Aldhouse-Green goes one step further, proposing the set belonged to 'a wealthy Icenian, almost certainly a Briton who had benefited from the Roman alliance and, maybe, even the king himself' (2006: 69). This deposit shows the connectedness of people, objects and practices at this time, whether indigenous or imported. It also reveals the way material culture has been structured within the narratives of acculturation and rebellion.

At Hockwold-cum-Wilton, on the Fen-edge, seven high-quality, silver drinking cups, some with Bacchic imagery, were deliberately broken up, flattened and buried. These late first century CE vessels have been variously described as loot, buried 'for temporary safe-keeping during the upheavals' (Davies 2009: 139), 'clearly a smith's bullion' (Davies and Robinson 2009: 32-33) or 'part of the wealth of a Romano-British shrine' (BM: 1962,0707). Aldhouse-Green proposes they were destroyed by 'nationalists' in a 'gesture of contempt' towards the imposition of a 'soft and decadent' Roman culture or, conversely, as a devotion to the 'old cult practices' of the Iron Age (2006: 69, 228). This hoard reveals some of the wide-ranging discourses applied to belongings which will be discussed in the following chapters.

Both these vessel hoards occurred at or near temples. The hoarding impulse at important religious sites and the suitability of objects for votive deposition carries through from the LIA into the occupation. Were people substituting one type of drinking paraphernalia for another within their votive practices? Were these objects considered appropriate deposits because of their (either positive or negative) associations with outsiders? If so, which outsiders? Elements of the Crownthorpe hoard were made locally; other parts came from Italy. Drinking sets were frequent components of high-status Gallic funerary assemblages. Grave goods in neighbouring parts of Britain were often hybridised, reflecting interconnectivity between multiple points of origin (Pitts 2019: 134). Did these mixed or hybrid hoards act as proxy burials in an area which did not have a strong custom of inhumation or cremation at this time? This idea is explored further below.

In the first century CE, hoarding shifted from gold to silver coins, then to deposits of decorated equestrian equipment. Roman-period deposits often combine jewellery, coinage,

Figure 2.4. A pair of pedestal cups with duck terminals, Crownthorpe (NWHCM: 1982.464; Image: © Norwich Castle Museum and Art Gallery).

harness, vessels and religious items. Although other practices died away with the conquest, hoarding continued well into the Roman occupation, contradicting the narrative that the Iceni were annihilated during or after the Boudican revolt (Hutcheson 2004: 90-93, 2007: 369) (section 1.6). Objects in harness hoards (section 8.10) were combined and fragmented in quite deliberate ways, possibly marking important events within a community. This separation and recombination process may have emphasised relationships between groups of people and sets of objects. Garrow and Gosden conclude that 'hoards were not the wealth of the elite or material for a smith to recycle, but elements of a dispersed community of people linked through artefacts' (2012: 191-92).

The enduring wealth of the region persisted into the later Roman period, with an unusually rich array of hoards of coins and precious metalwork, concentrated around the Lark Valley and along the Fen-edge. These later hoards, such as Mildenhall and Hoxne, tend towards pewter and silver plate vessels, sometimes with Christian or cult overtones (Davies and Gregory 1991: 86; Moore *et al*. 1988: 73, 82). Attitudes towards accumulation and disposal of metalwork may have altered, and the choice of appropriate artefacts, materials and locations varied. However, the practice of hoarding continued apace, structured within strong cultural conventions.

2.3.7. Similar but Different: Iron Age and Roman Aesthetics

'Celtic' art is characterised by its individuality, curvilinear decoration and rotational symmetry (Johns 1996b: 24; Swift 2011: 212). In the LIA, personal possessions became part of 'an expanding visual repertoire' related to identity, status and body-perception (Haselgrove and Moore 2007: 8). Decoration seems heavily stylised or abstracted to modern eyes. Many of these patterns may have been understood as apotropaic, that is, bringing good fortune to the owner or recipient (Gell 1998: 83-84). Representational depictions are rare in pre-Roman art, but animals are sometimes naturalistically modelled, especially on figurines and 3-dimensional objects. Davies notes the Iceni were especially fond of boars, bovids and waterbirds (2011a, 2014).

A significant shift in material culture occurs in the first century BCE/CE, as pre-Roman styles of jewellery disappear in favour of continental ornaments. This was 'highly significant in the renegotiation of social and personal identities' (Pudney 2010: 115). Hunter notes the enthusiasm with which Roman-style artefacts were acquired, and the development of 'new, distinctive and local' styles (2007: 288-89). Behaviour and usage are not always apparent from the form of artefacts, as functional features can change, and objects can have a range of functions (Swift 2017: 16, 102). Several such classes of objects will be discussed in this study. The curvilinear artwork of the LIA resurfaces around the time of the conquest, but is eventually replaced with a more symmetrical and geometric style.

Coins, brooches and ceramics are seen to become increasingly standardised and mass-produced, which Garrow and Gosden suggest had an impact on practice (2012: 152). Standardised products have no clear relationship to individual makers or end users, meaning they need guarantees like stamps for quality control. However, in the decades immediately post-conquest, many indigenous British groups 'retained the autonomy and wherewithal to make and wear their own distinctive styles of metalwork' (Davis and Gwilt 2008: 146, 178). I would argue that greater standardisation is superficial. Many artefacts produced in the first two centuries CE were distinctive, even unique, though produced in relatively large quantities (Jackson 2010: 26). Spratling describes this similar but different aesthetic as 'purposeful differentiation' (2008: 197). Some pre-conquest traits persist, such as multicoloured enamelwork and individual finishing. Imagery on LIA coinage undergoes a process of simplification over time, which gives the lie to evolutionary typologies which see progression from simple to complex (Garrow and Gosden 2012: 80).

A narrative of Roman standardisation leads us to expect decreasing individuality of ornament and form as artefacts become increasingly mass-produced. Our perceptions of these ideas are based on modern production techniques. In the past, objects made in small quantities could be made to strongly conventional prototypes, thus being very similar. Conversely, artefacts made in large numbers may have been individually hand-finished to the owner's specifications (Swift 2017: 14-16). However, the study period is one still strongly embedded in a small-scale workshop tradition. Most small finds produced during the early years of the Roman occupation were hand-finished and display great variety and difference, such as cosmetic grinders (Jackson 2010). Pitts proposes 'seriality' as an alternative to standardisation to describe the familial relationships of closely similar, but non-identical, forms of *fibulae* (2019: 40).

Garrow and Gosden perceive a reflexive process between objects and people, in which artefacts provide 'switch points' for new connections and identities to be created (2012: 152). Decoration is also a key facet - traditional objects may have been decorated with new styles creating a visual and conceptual fusion (Swift 2011: 212). This stylistic syncretism may have been recognised at the time. Hybrids developed amid the culture clash in regions which resisted Roman rule. New materials (e.g. brass) and technologies were selectively adapted to an older value system, perhaps retaining durable aesthetic codes.

Another major shift occurs in the later second century CE. Many artefact types disappear, and the archaeological record of the third/fourth centuries CE looks very different. Roman fashions were waning, possibly due to their political and cultural capital becoming less advantageous. A resurgence of earlier art styles and a re-creation of tradition perhaps ushered in another cycle of resistance and identity-building in the mid-late Roman period (Wells

1999: 197-98, 256). These changes and tensions over time will be addressed in relation to Icenian material culture.

2.3.8. Hybridity and Creolisation

The consumption and display of personal artefacts may have played an active role in indigenous interactions with the Roman world and in creating social distinction within the group. Objects can be active participants in social discourse, capable of unmaking, transforming and recreating relationships and identities. Hybridisation can result from innovative responses to the styles, materials and technologies of 'outside' sources (Davis and Gwilt 2008: 146). Woolf saw an entirely novel imperial culture in the Gallic provinces arising from this 'new cultural logic' (1997: 347). However, different groups may potentially have utilised the same items as badges of belonging or as statements of resistance. It is important not to become too polarised in our thinking about hybridity, as it can replicate the binary tropes of Romanisation. As Gosden proposes: 'We should not spend time trying to identify the original elements of a bipartite Romano-British culture, but rather look at the logics by which the pieces were combined' (2005: 209).

Change can take decades, even generations. This slow creep over time may be seen in the development of hybrid forms. Looking for locally-produced objects is one way to determine indigenous attitudes to regime change. Evidence for manufacturing processes includes unfinished, miscast and modified artefacts. Experimental objects may also show hybridity of technology and form. During data collection for this project, objects identified in this way were recorded and will be discussed below. 'Creolisation' provides a more nuanced alternative to hybridity which derives from post-colonial thought. It allows for the imbalance of power in colonial situations to be addressed. Deliberate ambiguity and the potential for subversion through art and artefacts are considered from the perspective of the subjugated (Carr 2003, 2006; Webster 2001, 2003).

Theories of resistance, creolisation and hybridisation, in turn, have their critics. Mattingly warns that creolisation risks simply inverting the tenets of Romanisation with all its attendant problems (2011: 203-4). The idea that Rome remained the instigator of cultural change fails to acknowledge the importance of pre-existing relationships with neighbouring provinces, such as Gaul (Revell 2016: 47). Resistance, adaptation and acceptance can also occur simultaneously (Carr 2006: 110). Continuity and transformation are not mutually exclusive. At Ditches, Gloucestershire, Trow *et al.* (2009: 64-71) identified a sense of ownership and the importance of place with an emphasis on the pre-Roman past, which was seemingly held simultaneously with a desire to engage with Gaulish culture, and through it, an interpretation of the Roman lifestyle.

Pitts and Versluys caution against substituting ideas such as globalisation or creolisation for Romanisation, as cultural processes of hybridity and resistance perpetuate the dichotomous discourse of 'Romans vs. Natives'. Instead they propose a focus on connectivity and communication (Pitts and Versluys 2014; Versluys 2014). Pitts's work on objectscapes in the northwest provinces explores shifts in funerary assemblages from standardisation, through local adaptation and innovation, to 're-universalisation' (2019: 14). He notes that 'connectivity created opportunities for local groups to participate and re-negotiate their places within the new imperial world through innovative selections of objects' (*ibid.*: 176).

This globalised and entangled approach to material culture has its benefits, but I am wary of deliberately discarding one doctrine in favour of another. It is important to consider the implications of cultural engagement and negotiation for all sides, with an open mind. While all artefacts are hybrids to some extent, I would argue that they can indicate fusion and experimentation. By flagging up objects which differ from the norm and considering their lineages and innovations, the role of hybrid or creolised objects has potential to draw attention to areas of interconnectedness. A brief summary of the research methods and their application to my database of portable artefacts is described in the next section. A more detailed discussion of the data collection process and project methodology can be found in Appendices A and B.

2.4. Research Methods

2.4.1. Function and Praxis

Crummy's work on Colchester (1983) has become one of the main reference publications for identifying Romano-British objects. I have adapted her small finds methodology, which is based around functional categories (1983, 2007b, 2012). In my database, copper alloy predominates, partly due to its durability in the soil and the high proportion of metal-detected finds. Other materials, such as bone, glass, iron and precious metals are to be found, albeit in small numbers. The inherent lack of stratigraphy of detector finds means contextual analyses are unfeasible and looking at social distribution is equally problematic. Therefore, the choice of function as a means of grouping the artefacts is more appropriate than selection by material or context. A hypothesis-testing model was impractical as a methodology; rather it was necessary to examine the data and the potential applications of theory as a holistic process, leading to observations and interpretations.

Function is an effective way to think about *praxis*, as the embodied application of skills or knowledge, in the past. Artefacts are embedded within dynamic and meaningful practices. Functional understandings of objects can help us appreciate the reproduction and transformation of differentiated identities (Gardner 2002: 332-34). For example, personal ornaments are involved with the social practices of 'appearing' and 'belonging'. The materialisation of agency through action or 'projects' emerges in relationships between people, and between people and things (Hodder 2012; Robb 2010).

Nevertheless, there are some drawbacks with this approach. The dataset from Colchester has a bias towards cemeteries and grave goods, which may skew the functional analysis in favour of personal effects and ornaments (Wardle 2013: 193). Functional categories are necessarily weighted towards modern interpretations of usage. Spradley (2001: 105) has questioned Crummy's justification for attempting to impose functions onto objects. Certain objects traverse such imposed boundaries, or embody intangible (and thereby potentially irretrievable) meanings. Artefacts may also have multiple, fluid functions over time; these cross-functional objects offer us numerous interpretive opportunities which we can choose to embrace.

2.4.2. Inclusions and Exclusions

Crummy proposed that her framework be adapted to fit other assemblages (1983: 4-5) and I have done so accordingly. As Crummy dealt primarily with Roman period artefacts, some Iron Age items do not fit neatly into her categories. Other groupings have been updated with more recent scholarship and revised to fit my own criteria.

As brooches form the bulk of my dataset, I have subdivided Crummy's Category 1 'Objects of personal adornment or dress' into two parts: brooches and other personal ornament. Chapter three looks exclusively at the brooches, from simple wire *fibulae* to elaborate enamelled plate brooches. Chapter four examines other items of adornment, including fasteners, toggles, bracelets, snake jewellery and torcs. Chapter five is based on Crummy's Category 2 'Toilet, surgical or pharmaceutical instruments', including nail cleaners and other implements. I have relocated cosmetic grinders (from Crummy's Category 14) into this chapter to reflect current scholarship (Jackson 2010). I have also added mirrors here as, although they do not feature amongst the Colchester assemblages, they find a natural home in a discussion of personal grooming. Although often poorly dated, I have included Roman mirrors, partly for comparison with the Iron Age examples, and because they provide an interesting example of recovery bias which will be discussed in section 5.6.

For chapter six, I have selected artefacts related to religious or votive practice (Crummy's Category 14): miniature objects, such as axes and wheels, and pipeclay figurines. Chapter seven looks at objects associated with written communications (Crummy's Category 7) as evidence of developing literacy in the *civitas*. These include seal-boxes, intaglio rings and wax *spatula* handles in the shape of the goddess Minerva. Chapter eight discusses artefacts associated with horses and wheeled transportation (Crummy's Category 8). This includes harness such as bridle-bits and strap fittings, as well as chariot furnishings, especially terret rings and linch-pins.

As portable artefacts and belongings are the prime focus of this research, articles such as furniture mounts and studs, and containers such as *paterae*, buckets and other vessels, were omitted. I excluded overtly military objects

(Crummy's Category 13), such as weaponry and armour, as my interest lies in the civilian population's interactions with the Roman world. Nevertheless, I retained personal items, such as some brooches and mounts, which have an uncertain military association. For instance, there is doubt over whether button-and-loop fasteners were military trappings; they certainly appear to predate the Roman conquest and are found on many settlements (section 4.2).

Unidentified (Crummy's Category 18) or undated material presents a problem. I referred to published catalogues to identify unknown items wherever possible, e.g. nail cleaners (Crummy 2016; Crummy and Eckardt 2003; Eckardt and Crummy 2008), seal-boxes (Andrews 2012) and brooches (Bayley and Butcher 2004; Fowler 1960; Haselgrove 1997; Hattatt 1982, 2007; Hull and Hawkes 1987; Mackreth 2011; Plouviez 2008, 2014; Snape 1993). Many objects were accorded only a broad 'Roman' date range, so only those which fitted into my parameters have been included here. Objects with this long dating, including needles, tweezers, earrings and *styli*, were reluctantly excluded. I did retain what I considered 'undated but interesting' records where appropriate, for comparative discussion, such as metal figurines and anatomical mounts.

Coinage is another significant category which I have deliberately omitted, as it is well discussed elsewhere. It is essential, however, to be aware of previous work on coins and their relationships with artefacts and identities (as summarised in section 2.3.5). Pertinent studies include Allen 1970; Chadburn 2006; Creighton 1992, 1994, 1995; Davies and Gregory 1991; Haselgrove 1992; Leins 2008, 2012; Nash Briggs 2011; Talbot 2011, 2015, 2017; Talbot and Leins 2010; Walton 2011, 2012.

2.4.3. Looking for Difference

In conjunction with the functional approach, I am interested in the processes of adoption and adaptation of artefact types and the hybridisation of Roman and indigenous forms and aesthetics. I find the methods of Eckardt (2014, 2018), Carr (2001, 2003) and Webster (2001) useful; rather than looking for patterns and objects which fit neatly into typologies and classifications, they aim to highlight difference, hybridity and change. Spradley looks for difference, focussing on the importance of recognising, and thinking through, unknown and ambiguous objects. Focussing on the oddities, the square pegs, not dismissing them because they fail to fit into neatly-defined categories, can be productive (2001: 104-11).

During the Roman occupation 'new traditions developed, adapting elements of both indigenous and introduced practices and style to create patterns different from any of the antecedents' (Wells 1999: 265). Many small finds specialists search for parallels and seek similarities for identification. I have tracked those objects recorded as 'unique', 'unusual' and 'unparalleled'. These are of course subjective classifications, but it is a useful way of flagging difference (Harlow 2017).

Sørenson (1987) looked at the dichotomy between standardisation and uniqueness. Objects with limited variability (less distance from the norm) can have 'automatically ascribed' meanings, whereas unusual, unique and varied objects require more thinking about, greater working through (*ibid.*: 97-98). This may be applicable to large datasets of small finds which lack context, assuming a norm can be established. This has influenced my decision to look for unusual variants in addition to grouping finds by functional category.

2.4.4. Working with Surface Finds

Projects taking unstratified finds as primary data have become commonplace over the past decade (Andrews 2012; Brindle 2010, 2014; Jackson 2010; Robbins 2012; Statton 2016; Walton 2012). Despite inherent biases, the quantity of information available is unparalleled by that from well-stratified sites (Figure 2.5). My research highlights the value of using surface finds in conjunction with excavated material (Haselgrove 1985; Marsden 2012; Worrell *et al.* 2010). The three counties provide a rich diversity of both stratified and metal-detected material to be investigated. Nevertheless, there are significant ethical and practical issues to be addressed with artefacts collected and reported by detectorists.

Questions have rightly been asked about the authenticity of records, particularly locational information. Marsden decries ongoing illegal detecting in Norfolk (2012: 51) and this is far from rare elsewhere. The debate remains hotly contested and, at times, divisive (Gill 2010; UKDFD 2007; van der Schriek 2014; Winkley 2016). However, as a source of research data, it is impossible to ignore the large quantities of artefacts reported annually, and new ways forward have been proposed to minimise the ethical implications (Chester-Kadwell 2009; Ulmschneider 2000; Worrell *et al.* 2010). This project deliberately explores some of these issues and contributes to this emerging branch of the discipline.

2.4.5. Potential Constraints and Bias

Although East Anglia's arable land is a hotspot for metal-detecting, there are many constraints. Urban and agricultural land-use, scheduled monuments, military zones, Forestry Commission, coastal and Crown properties restrict available search areas and influence recovery (for Norfolk see Chester-Kadwell 2009: 82-86, and 167 pl. 1). Both now, and in the past, extensive areas of wetland (the Great Estuary/Norfolk Broads and the Fens) limit access. The coastline has receded by as much as 2km since the Roman period (Albone *et al.* 2007b: 74). Recovery bias is always a potential issue (see Appendices A and B). Some key Iron Age sites in the HER files do not feature on the PAS, presumably because they are scheduled monuments with restrictions on casual use of metal-detectors. Interviews carried out with detectorists revealed other constraints on their practices. Peat build-up means the ancient land surface is buried metres below the surface in some places.

An increasingly efficient (or industrialised) agricultural cycle means that many fields are drilled immediately after harvest, and the pheasant shooting season is another factor which prevents detecting at certain times of year. Linear features may be explained by the tendency of detectorists to search along known prehistoric trackways and Roman roads.[3] A geographical bias is introduced by 'productive' sites attracting heavy detector use. These may show up in mapping as concentrations of finds.

As Chester-Kadwell's map (2009: 167 pl. 1) shows, a group of parishes in west Norfolk has seen extensive detector coverage. This shows up repeatedly in my own mapping, and reflects a high concentration of human activity and/or a high recovery rate. This area includes the possible ritual site and small town at Fincham, described as 'a prolific site actively detected over a long period, the detectorist having a good relationship with Norwich Castle Museum' (Talbot 2017: 94, 128). This patterning has twofold implications. Firstly, as several detectorists pointed out during interview, if there were nothing to be recovered, no amount of searching would create this pattern. Therefore, the finds must be there in the first place. High numbers of finds from a certain area, while perhaps disproportionate compared to other parishes, nevertheless show a concentration of settlement or other past activity. Secondly, Chester-Kadwell maps detector finds from all periods, not just Iron Age and Roman. A map of Roman brooches from Norfolk on the PAS database (Figure 2.6) shows there is county-wide detector coverage and the area around Fincham, while high, is not the highest, nor the only area producing many finds. Another area that warrants further archaeological investigation is represented by the noticeable gap, east of Brandon, produced by Thetford Forest. Metal-detecting is generally banned on Forestry Commission lands.

Cool and Baxter's work (2016a, 2016b) on morphological bias has an important bearing on this research project due to the high percentages of metal-detector finds in the database. Approximately 99 per cent of PAS and 64 per cent of non-PAS finds were metal-detected. The different county percentages (Table 2.1) may reflect the higher density of grey literature in my Cambridgeshire data and the selective incorporation of Norfolk HER material onto the PAS. The high proportion of brooches probably reflects the '*fibula* event horizon' phenomenon (Hill 1995a: 66) (section 3.2.1) and county variations in dating small finds. Vigilance for such biases in this study has flagged up some informative patterns which contribute to the ongoing debate.

Constraints are manifold, through the usual processes of deposition, survival, discovery and recording, as well

---

[3] Some may point to historic activity: I have identified a possible extension to the Icknield Way, perhaps a summer trackway along the Fen-edge, which manifests as a linear distribution of findspots stretching from near Hockwold-cum-Wilton to the Chippenham area (submitted to NAHRG Annual).

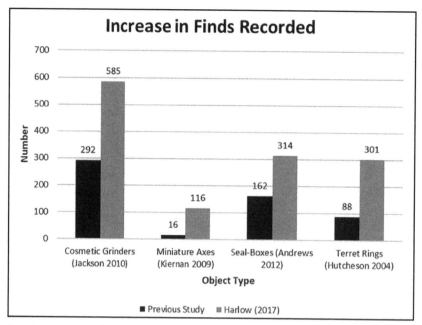

Figure 2.5. Increase in selected categories of finds recorded.

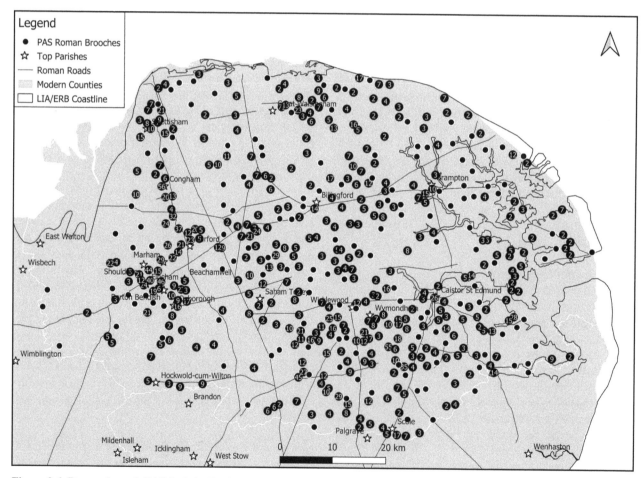

Figure 2.6. Roman brooch PAS finds in Norfolk.

Table 2.1. Percentages of brooches by county, collection type and source

Source	Cambs	Norfolk	Suffolk
Metal-Detected	241	1798	1622
Excavated	87	184	286
Other/Unknown	137	580	761
HER Brooch Total	465	2562	2669
HER All Finds	693	3997	3198
HER Percentage	67	64	83
Metal-Detected	413	2279	2563
Excavated	0	0	2
Other/Unknown	1	5	23
PAS Brooch Total	414	2284	2588
PAS All Finds	524	2759	2937
PAS Percentage	79	83	88

its people had different attitudes to portable wealth and were less easily swayed by imported goods and diplomatic gifts than other groups in Britannia. The role of 'elites' in the development of the *civitas* may have been minimal. Both my critique of the material elite and the idea of resistance may help illuminate the differences apparent in the *civitas*. If the Iceni were not a hierarchically structured and coherent group before the client-kingdom, or if they based their value systems, inheritance and prestige on non-material aspects, their interactions with the colonial power would be less visible, resulting in the 'culturally conservative' interpretation.

Due to an over-reliance on classical literature, Icenian identities have often been constructed around a Boudican narrative which bears little relevance to the archaeological record. Material culture, including hoards and coins, has been used to create a sense of coherence which can be explained in terms of 'tribal' interactions with the Roman incomers. This is clearly too simplistic. Evidence for continuity, dispossession and resistance needs to be examined afresh.

The following data-driven chapters fall naturally into two parts: Chapters three to five (ornament and grooming) being more directly related to the personal, the individual and the body; Chapters six to eight (votives, literacy and harness) having a greater interpersonal, social and external focus. In each of the following chapters, I take a different category of small finds and use its distributions and concentrations to investigate the key themes, beginning with brooches.

as physical restrictions on where people can search. My own collection biases will inevitably have further skewed the selection. Despite these issues, by compiling a large dataset, the sheer numbers may help to reduce the inherent slant and unpredictability. One of the benefits of working with large numbers of finds, mostly due to high metal-detector coverage, is that you derive a sense of overview, rather than the 'keyhole' approach of excavation. These are 'surface' finds in more than one way though, as the interpretation relies on quantity and concentrations in the absence of context and time-depth. The advantage of using a mixture of detected and excavated finds is that they complement each other and fill in gaps in the available information.

2.5. Summary

In this chapter, I have discussed the ways in which cultural contact and change have been approached through archaeology. Ideas of resistance and discrepancy can help us move away from elite-focussed studies and allow us insights into other potential sources of identity and power. However, it is important not to replace the doctrine of Romanisation with an uncritical view of identity (Pitts 2007). Change and continuity have respectively been seen as progressive and reactionary. There has been a tendency to fall back on the paradigm of the material elite and a teleological view in which neophilia is seen as positive and evolutionary, whereas neophobia stifles growth and creativity. The processes by which new ideas and things arrive, take hold, and become commonplace, are much more intricate.

Evidence for social hierarchy in the region is limited, although it appears to have been materially rich both before and after the conquest. Perhaps this signifies that

Badges of Belonging: Brooches

3.1. Introduction

An unprecedented amount of material relating to personal adornment was deposited or lost in the first and second centuries CE. These artefacts allow us to see change and continuity at work. The functional category of personal ornament is divided into two parts: this chapter is dedicated to brooches. Other forms of jewellery are dealt with in chapter four. The research questions will be tested using my dataset of over 10,000 brooches which form, at 78 per cent, by far the greatest proportion of the database (Table 3.1). This enables a detailed investigation of the role of belongings in the creation of personal and public identities across the three counties.

Although small and commonplace, the humble brooch can give us insights into a range of past practices and attitudes. A discussion of manufacturing evidence provides context for regional, ethnic, religious and gender identities. Changing technologies and aesthetics can be sought by looking for difference and hybridity. Analysis of brooches addresses some assumptions about the Icenian depopulation after the Boudican revolt and active resistance to Roman imports. It is also possible to test Cool and Baxter's hypothesis (2016a, 2016b) that some brooches were differentially recovered by metal-detecting based on their basic morphology (Appendix B).

My research adds to the growing picture of regional identity and adornment, building on recent work in adjacent regions and periods (Adams 2013; Farley 2012; Rosten 2007; Statton 2016). Mackreth (2011) and Hattatt's (1982, 1985, 1987) overviews of Iron Age and Roman brooches in Britain are invaluable typological and chronological sources. For *comparanda* from the European mainland, catalogues on Gaul (Feugère 1985) and the Low Countries (Heeren and van der Feijst 2017) have been consulted. Although metal production in the LIA and Roman period is not the focus of this book, I consider the evidence for metalworking and hybridity which result from a merging of technologies and designs (for various aspects of the subject see Bayley and Butcher 2004; Davis 2014; Dungworth 2016; Garrow and Gosden 2012; Heeren and van der Feijst 2017).

Table 3.1. Overall percentages of brooches by source

Source	All Brooches	All Finds	Percentage
HER	5696	7888	72
PAS	5286	6220	85
Total	10982	14108	78

3.2. Late Iron Age and Early Roman brooches

In early and middle Iron Age Britain, brooches were rare in burials and only found with adult remains, both male and female. Children may have worn different clothing or perhaps brooches were symbols of adulthood. Brooches were almost never worn in pairs. Toggles and pins, many in perishable materials, may have served the purpose of fasteners (Adams 2013: 217-32). Brooches were very rare in the Roman Mediterranean heartland, implying a pre-conquest and provincial tradition across central and northwest Europe (Heeren and van der Feijst 2017: 361). By the LIA, brooches were worn by all age groups and genders. This may suggest a change in clothing or the availability of metal. Their size and robustness depended on the fineness of the fabric being secured. Romano-British women used pairs of brooches to fasten their garments on each shoulder (Allason-Jones 1989: 61).

3.2.1. The Fibula *Event Horizon*

The massive increase in the deposition of brooches and other small personal belongings on settlements in southeastern Britain is known as the '*fibula* event horizon' (Hill 1995a: 66). Brooch usage did not happen overnight, as Hill's expression might imply, but a dramatic increase in finds does occur from the first century BCE (see Appendix C: Brooch Date Ranges). Hill questions whether this event resulted from greater abundance and loss, or changing cultural processes with higher archaeological visibility (*ibid.*: 66, 85; 1997: 96). This sudden growth in finds suggests either a shift away from the LIA focus on recycling or a materially rich and careless approach to objects (Cool 2006: 49). There seems to have been much less effort to reuse or retrieve lost and broken belongings, and a greater emphasis on deposition (Jundi and Hill 1997). Nonetheless, some items were worth conserving, as shown by repairs to certain brooches and tableware.

For centuries before the conquest, the people of Britain used distinctive brooches to fasten their clothing. Adams argues that major regional differences, and the techniques and components of brooch-making, already existed in the Middle Iron Age, rendering the 'horizon' somewhat less dramatic (2013). Gosden sees a shift in aesthetics, with a decline in the production of individual 'virtuoso objects' such as torcs, shields and swords and increased manufacture and deposition of small personal items (2005: 203). This bulge in production and the narrative of standardisation implies that more brooches were in use, and/or were recycled less frequently. As a result, they perhaps became less distinctive and precious as belongings. However, the explosion in brooches was not universal: regional and chronological variations suggest a sequence of 'multiple well-defined events or horizons' (Cool and Baxter 2016a: 86).

Unlike coins, which have restricted circulations, but are impersonal objects, wearing a brooch was an active, personal choice. Brooches were often large and elaborately decorated, clearly designed to be seen. Their archaeological ubiquity implies they were everyday items, although the more ornate examples may have been beyond the means of the average person. Brooches expressed more than their primary utilitarian function; visual appeal and symbolism became increasingly important and they were sometimes used as votive offerings (Eckardt 2005: 148; Marsden 2014: 66-67) (see chapter six).

Under Roman occupation, brooch forms and decoration changed, developing hybrid regional varieties which combined both imported and British elements. This may simply reflect changing fashions, or have been a political statement of continuing indigenous identity (Jundi and Hill 1998). Certain brooch types display regional patterning, from Dragonesques in Yorkshire to the Rearhook in Norfolk (Mackreth 2011: 60, 188). Regional preferences may have defined members of social groups (Gosden 2005: 204). Alternatively, distributions could reflect accessibility to local workshops.

3.2.2. The Fibula *Abandonment Horizon*

Cool and Baxter successfully show the '*fibula* event horizon' to be much more complex, regionally varied and sequential than previously thought (2016a, 2016b). I would suggest that like other forms of material culture, especially seal-boxes and cosmetic grinders, perhaps we are seeing multiple 'event horizons' through time and across different artefact types.

Brooches continued to multiply and diversify until the later second century CE when there is a sudden decline in the archaeological record, most likely due to a change in clothing style or the use of other types of fasteners. Some imported brooches remained in use, but manufacturing in Britain ceased. This change did not occur in the same way on the continent (Hattatt 1982: 35), although the continuity in distribution observed from the LIA to third century CE in the Low Countries became disrupted in the Late Roman period (Heeren and van der Feijst 2017: 413). Cool and Baxter coined the phrase '*fibula* abandonment horizon' (2016a: 94) to describe the abrupt decline in the everyday usage of brooches (as previously noted by e.g. Allason-Jones 1989: 126; Hattatt 1982: 35). I will return to this fascinating avenue of enquiry in more detail below (section 3.13, section 9.5).

3.3. Badges of Belonging?

Regional and chronological variations can be visualised through mapping the distributions of personal belongings. Brooches have been used, like coinage, to define regional groups and territories (Mackreth 2011; Martin 1999; Plouviez 2014). In this section, I address the problematic question of 'tribal boundaries' and the ascription of identity groups to material culture.

Based on distributions of finds, during the client-kingdom the Iceni are said to have made and worn a specific two-piece brooch as an ethnic identifier. The Rearhook 'was exclusively an Icenian brooch type […] pre-Boudicca in its homeland, and may well have been something by which members of the tribe could have been recognized' (Mackreth 2011: 60). Their neighbours, the Trinovantes and Catuvellauni, wore a related brooch, the Harlow type (*ibid.*: 50). It should be noted that Mackreth does not elaborate regarding the territorial limits, nor provide distribution maps.

3.3.1. Colchester Derivatives: Harlow and Rearhook

The Harlow brooch is a two-piece Colchester Derivative with a double pierced lug.[1] This method fixes the two parts securely together: one lug holds the spring, the other the chord (Figure 3.1). Harlow brooches were produced in great numbers and are very common in East Anglia, with a *floruit* 50-70 CE, although running on into the later first century CE. The Harlow was made in regular sizes and is less ornate than its cousin, the Rearhook. Mackreth asserts it was the natural successor to the pre-conquest Colchester brooch (section 3.8.5) in the 'home territory' of the Trinovantes and Catuvellauni (2011: 50).

As the Harlow replaced the Colchester brooch around the time of the Claudian invasion, so an idiosyncratic range of brooches using the Rearhook fixing method developed (Mackreth 2011: 234). Rearhook brooches are Colchester Derivatives with the spring secured by a rear-facing hook extending over the head of the bow (Figure 3.2). They are more decorative than Harlow types, which Mackreth interprets as a 'deeply rooted' regional preference (*ibid.*: 67). Rearhook brooches predominate in Norfolk, Suffolk and Cambridgeshire, inevitably prompting connections with named groups such as the Iceni (Plouviez 2014: 34-36, 40).

Plouviez used ratios of Harlow to Rearhook brooches to look for indigenous affiliations in Suffolk (in Martin 1999: 88-89). The small towns of Wenhaston and Pakenham had a ratio of 1:1, which she ascribed to an Icenian origin. Hacheston and Coddenham had a much lower ratio of Rearhooks to Harlows, which would place them in Trinovantian 'tribal' territory. Mackreth dates Rearhooks tightly to the invasion and assigns a marked endpoint for manufacture (43-60/65 CE) to the 'savage repression of the Iceni after the defeat of Boudicca' (2009: 144). Both this frequently repeated subjugation premise and the idea that brooches symbolised allegiance to a political or ethnic

---

[1] The name derives from Holbrooks site, Harlow, Essex and is applied both to the brooch and the spring system (Mackreth 2011: 50), which has recording implications, similar to Polden Hills.

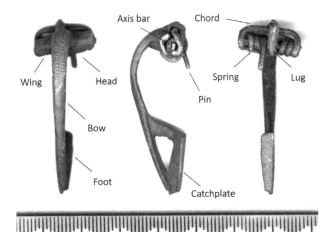

Figure 3.1. Colchester Derivative Harlow brooch showing terminology, South Elmham St Mary (PAS: SF5751).

Figure 3.2. Colchester Derivative Rearhook, Pulham Market (PAS: SF-C65E1A).

entity are problematic. It is necessary to rethink these brooches as badges of 'tribal' identity.

Mackreth's tight dating of Rearhook brooches suggests production ends *circa* 60/61 CE (in Gregory 1991a: 122-23; 2011: 60-69). This is derived from numerous examples from Colchester dated *circa* 49-61 CE, plus a few from other sites such as Fison Way (45-61 CE), Snettisham (mid-first century CE), Bagendon (43-50 CE, 50-60 CE), Hod Hill (49-61 CE) and Puckeridge (40-65 CE). However, he also records examples from Stonea (second/third century CE, 220-400 CE) and Snettisham (late first/early second century CE). Mackreth's dramatic cut-off point is only really recognisable at Fison Way and Colchester, both sites which clearly suffered destruction at this time, and which have 'Boudican' attributions based on readings of the literature. Many of the other dated examples are from late first century CE or later contexts. Rearhook brooches appear to have a long 'tail' in keeping with many other brooch types, especially at sites considered to be Icenian strongholds like Snettisham and Stonea.

Mackreth's sample of Rearhooks was small: Norfolk (276), Suffolk (23) and Cambridgeshire (42) (2011 Access database) in comparison to my own, which includes PAS finds. There are slightly more Rearhook than Harlow brooches in my dataset and together they comprise almost 24 per cent of the total. Suffolk has nearly three times as many Harlow brooches as Norfolk, but the two counties have roughly equal numbers of Rearhooks (Table 3.2).[2]

Neither Rearhook nor Harlow is common in northeast Norfolk or Cambridgeshire, perhaps reflecting geographical constraints, such as wetlands. The distributions look quite similar (Figure 3.3), but the densities tell a different story (Figure 3.4, Figure 3.5). Harlow brooches have a southerly bias, in line with Mackreth's observations. They particularly cluster in the southeast around Coddenham (45), Charsfield (37), Hacheston (35) and Wenhaston (57). The parishes around Withersfield (30) show concentrations of Harlows and a paucity of Rearhooks, again fitting the regional ascriptions. Conversely, Harlows are found in west Suffolk, with foci around Icklingham (17) and Freckenham (21) and west Norfolk around Fincham, areas usually considered Icenian territory.

Rearhooks abound in the central belt of settlement in Breckland and along the Icknield corridor. Concentrations occur at Palgrave (33), Saham Toney (61), Coddenham (35) and Wenhaston (44). There are also 25 at or near Crownthorpe temple, Wicklewood (NHER: 8897). While the hotspot in west Norfolk may derive in part from heavy detector use, the concentrations fluctuate over time and with different brooch types, and I believe these reflect real archaeological densities, perhaps slightly exaggerated by higher recovery levels.

So, what may account for these patterns? A shift in the importance of certain areas may have already occurred by the time of the client-kingdom. The focus of brooch findspots along the southern Fen-edge becomes less visible compared to the pre-conquest period (section 3.8). Both Rearhook and Harlow distributions avoid key sites of the supposed Icenian 'heartland', such as Thetford and Stonea. These are potentially ritual sites rather than permanent settlements (Hingley and Unwin 2005: 31, 36). Single brooches did not feature highly as votive offerings in the LIA, unlike at Romano-British temples.

When considered in tandem, these two brooch types share many centres of deposition. The hotspots appear very tightly focussed, almost restricted to certain areas, perhaps suggesting a lack of brooch loss or deposition in rural

---

[2] Recording bias potentially plays a part with Rearhooks. My figures include Colchester Derivatives identified as 'sprung Dolphins'. In Norfolk 'Dolphin' has been a valid category for some years, whereas in Suffolk it is rarely used (Ruth Beveridge, Suffolk Archaeology pers. comm. 21/04/2017). Nomenclature also affects the Harlow, with many PAS records giving 'Colchester Derivative double lug' or similar. I have followed Plouviez in considering the 'sprung Dolphin' and the Rearhook one and the same, distinct from Harlow and Hinged variants (2008: 171, 2014: 35-36).

Table 3.2. Harlow and Rearhook brooches by county

Brooch Type	Cambs	Norfolk	Suffolk	Total
CD Harlow	74	297	839	1210
CD Rearhook	38	684	671	1393

settlements (compare fasteners Figure 4.5, or cosmetic grinders Figure 5.5). The small towns of Coddenham and Wenhaston are hotspots for both, areas recognised as zones of interaction by Martin (1999: 86, 90). This 'Gipping Valley frontier' shows 'no clear tribal affiliation' and 'may reflect greater contact and cultural mixing' (Moore *et al.* 1988: 13). My updated figures roughly correlate with the distinctions Plouviez made in 1999, with approximately 1:1.3 in the parishes of Coddenham and Wenhaston, and 1:5 at Hacheston. Nevertheless, I disagree that these brooches represented 'tribal badges' and argue that many people could have owned and worn both types. These settlements certainly do not represent a boundary, rather a nexus in which different groups met and merged. This implies that both types of brooch were being made and worn across the area during the client-kingdom. A look at the evidence for production may confirm this.

3.4. Brooch Manufacture

Personal possessions form an important lens through which the significance of metalwork can be viewed. One of my key arguments is that the production and consumption of high-quality decorated metalwork played a central and long-standing role in the land of the Iceni. This preoccupation may also explain their reasonably early adoption of brooch-making and wearing. In this, they were certainly not lagging behind their neighbours (Mackreth 2011: 5, 60). This extends into the early Roman period and the manufacture of brooches in larger quantities.

Earlier Iron Age moulds or failed brooches are unknown in Britain. Metal (or the knowledge to produce it) may have been so precious that imperfectly-cast artefacts were always recycled or reworked, unlike in later periods. In the LIA, a range of production processes was used. Brooches were initially forged, and later, cast in two primary ways: piece mould and investment casting. Investment moulds were used for individual solid-cast objects, such as harness and chariot fittings. It is thought the lost-wax (*cire perdue*) process was utilised, although this is yet to be scientifically proven.[3] The wax 'former' melts away and the surrounding clay must be broken off once cool, meaning that lost-wax castings are unique artefacts even when made in multiples (Adams 2013: 143-44; Davis 2014: 25; Dungworth 2016: 539).

Piece moulds date from the Roman period and were made in matching pairs or 'valves' (Figure 3.6). A wooden, bone or lead pattern was impressed into both halves. For brooches, spacers for the spring, catchplate and attachment lugs were fitted into the mould before casting. Decoration was inscribed into the wet clay or worked into the finished object. Although piece moulds could only be used once, the pattern was reusable; multiple moulds could create groups of objects which looked very similar, but had subtle variations (Bayley 1995; Dungworth 2016: 539; Garrow and Gosden 2012: 93-96). These may have been accidents of manufacture, or part of a deliberate aesthetic of understated difference. This calls into question the idea that Romano-British small finds were highly standardised and mass-produced.

Bayley and Butcher (2004) analysed the metallurgical make-up of some 3,500 LIA and Roman brooches from Richborough, considered representative of the period. They found that there were preferences for different copper alloys over time. The colouration of brass is closer to gold than bronze, which may have been an important aesthetic choice. Manufacturers of Iron Age coins and torcs deliberately manipulated the colour of gold and silver by varying alloys and surface enrichment (Farley 2012: 47, 85, 193). This selectivity seems to persist into the Roman period with the choice of precise alloys for some brooches. Recent work by Heeren and van der Feijst confirms the specificity of certain alloys for different brooch types in the Netherlands (2017: 243-59).

3.5. Brooch Moulds and Patterns

Possible lead manufacturer's models have been found at Burgh Castle (NHER: 10471), Grimston (NHER: 43198) and Caistor St Edmund (NHER: 20452). A find which post-dated my data collection is a lead umbonate brooch pattern from Scole (PAS: NMS-091CB2).[4] A triskele die stamp from Hanworth (NHER: 30853) (Figure 3.7) has similarities with a double-sided mould from Whitby, Yorkshire (PAS: YORYM-466941) and a copper alloy mould from Leicestershire (PAS: LEIC-0B42E6) (Davis 2014: 92). These may have been formers for clay moulds or more likely, given their negative designs, used for making decorative repoussé plates, such as those applied to disc brooches.

Moulds and miscast objects can give us clues to the manufacturing of indigenous ornaments. Mackreth cautions that the survival of metal moulds is extremely rare as they were probably re-melted numerous times (2011: 5). According to Bayley *et al.*, Norfolk provides the only known metal bi-valve brooch moulds from the Roman empire (2001: 542). Their scarcity may simply be due to lack of preservation and recovery, or reflect genuinely restricted craft production. Mapping the findspots of artefactual evidence for brooch production shows that it was widespread, often related to centres of population (Figure 3.8). The distribution of manufacturing evidence for Rearhook and Harlow brooches (Figure 3.9)

---

[3] Julia Farley, Curator, BM (pers. comm. 09/05/2017).

[4] My thanks to Adrian Marsden, Numismatist (NCC) for bringing this to my attention.

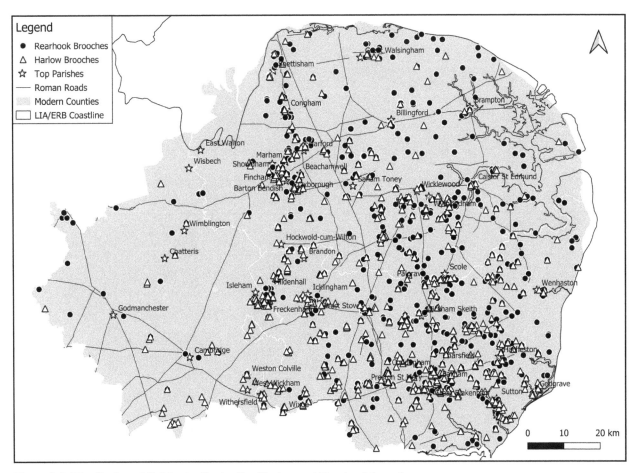

Figure 3.3. Distribution of Colchester Derivative Harlow and Rearhook brooches.

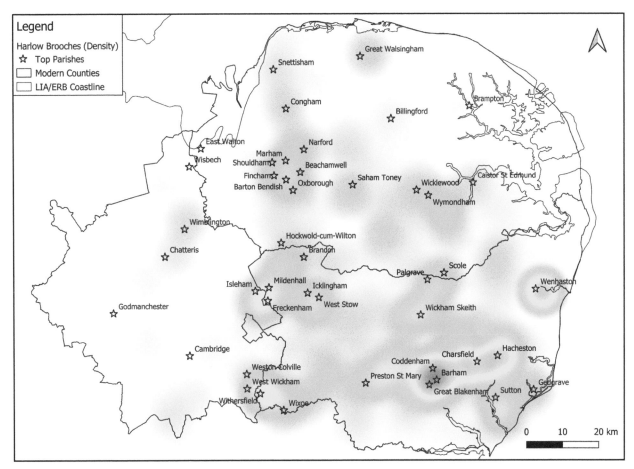

Figure 3.4. Density of Colchester Derivative Harlow brooches.

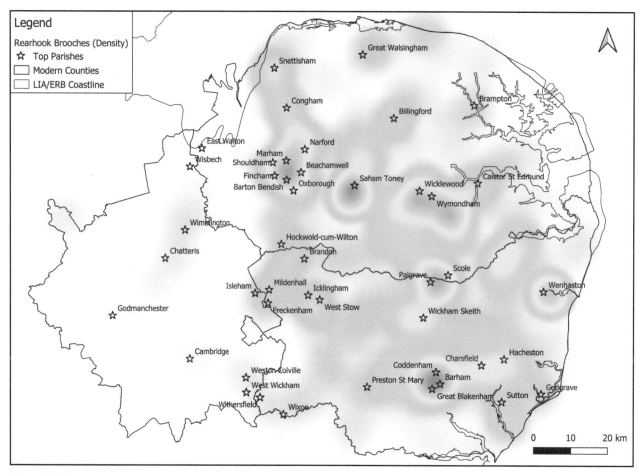

Figure 3.5. Density of Colchester Derivative Rearhook brooches.

Figure 3.6. Two valves of a piece mould, Old Buckenham (NHER 30864; Image: © Norwich Castle Museum and Art Gallery).

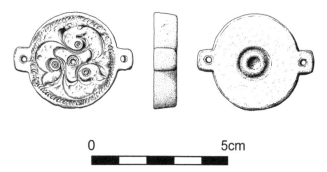

Figure 3.7. Triskele die stamp, Hanworth (NHER: 30853; Illustration by S. White © NCC Historic Environment Service).

shows that both types were largely found in the north of the region. This presents an intriguing puzzle. A more detailed analysis of these finds follows.

3.5.1. Felmingham

One valve of a copper alloy mould suggests that Rearhook brooches were being manufactured in Felmingham in the mid-first century CE. The mould has a deep recess for the spring housing, a central depression for the Rearhook and a channel for the formation of the catchplate (NWHCM: 2013.144) (Figure 3.10). The metal composition of this mould shows that it is a 'lightly leaded' bronze. The large mass ensures that it would not melt during casting. Bayley reports that it has an unusual sprue cup at the head end; moulds of this period are usually filled from the foot. This technology is better suited to early first century CE one-piece brooches, in which the sprue and runner were hammered out to form the pin/spring. Two suggestions are put forward to explain this: the awkward positioning of the Rearhook, with its derivation from the Colchester, or a personal preference of the maker (Bayley *et al.* 2004: 540-42). I would add that it may be an experimental form in which the manufacturer is trying new styles, while using the older method of filling the mould.

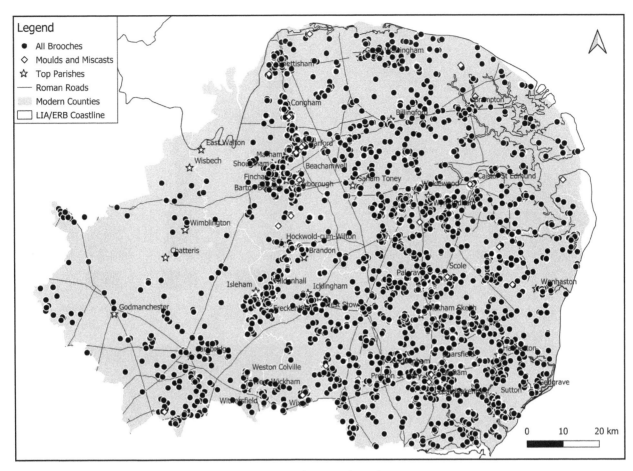

Figure 3.8. Distribution of all brooches showing evidence for manufacturing.

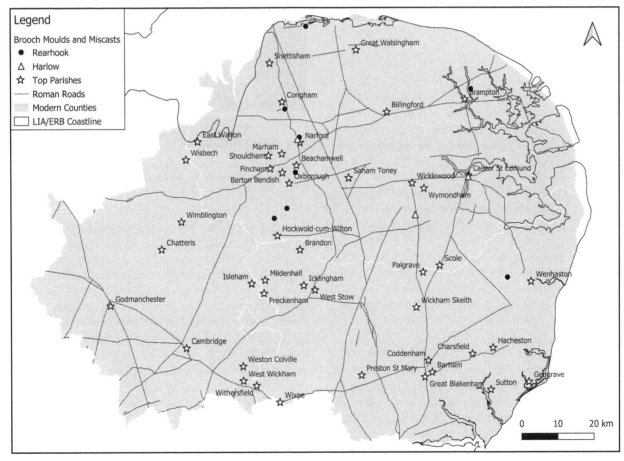

Figure 3.9. Distribution of Harlow and Rearhook moulds and miscasts.

Figure 3.10. Rearhook brooch mould, Felmingham (NWHCM: 2013.144; Image: © Norwich Castle Museum and Art Gallery).

Figure 3.11. Harlow brooch blank, Old Buckenham (PAS: NMS-2E1E91).

3.5.2. Brancaster

Another valve of a Rearhook brooch mould was found in the *vicus* of Brancaster shore fort (PAS: NMS-E99B33). Although the shore fort dates to 260 CE+ (Moore *et al.* 1988: 80), this type of brooch was in production in the mid-first century CE, so the *vicus* may stand upon an earlier settlement or metalworking area.

3.5.3. Old Buckenham

At Old Buckenham (NHER: 30864), metal-detecting in 1994 recovered an unprecedented collection of brooch blanks, moulds, failed castings and scrap metal. The bi-valve metal mould fragments, some still containing unfinished castings, were for production of a Colchester Derivative brooch (Figure 3.6). The brooch is an unparalleled subtype with the Harlow spring mechanism (section 3.3.1) (Bayley *et al.* 2001; Mackreth 2011: 5, 59). In 2012, the lower part of a Harlow brooch blank was found at the same site. This example has the casting sprue at the foot (Rogerson and Ashley 2013: 555-58 fig. 4.14; PAS: NMS-2E1E91) (Figure 3.11). Another 'highly distorted', possibly miscast, Colchester Derivative brooch comes from elsewhere in the parish (PAS: NMS-08AC82) (Figure 3.12).

The Old Buckenham moulds are unique survivals of experimental forms: 'The brooch type is truly a hybrid' (Bayley *et al.* 2001: 116). The brooch resembles the 'native Icenian habit' in form and decoration, but is sprung in the Harlow style with a double lug. This indicates that some innovative brooches had extremely limited production runs and/or distribution zones. Bayley *et al.* reflect that 'at the very moment that the Colchester was being replaced

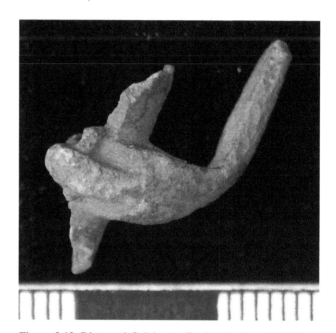

Figure 3.12. Distorted Colchester Derivative brooch, Old Buckenham (PAS: NMS-08AC82).

by its progeny, there were experiments with the new style of separately-made pins. They appear as hybrids, but in truth they should be seen as the failures they were' (2001: 111). Failures, perhaps, on an individual basis, but these tests and prototypes also represent lessons learnt and human adaptability in action. This demonstrates that the metalworkers were familiar with the Harlow fixing method and tried it out, but it ultimately was not adopted for use locally. The reasons for this are unclear, although I doubt it relates to a clash of 'tribal' identities.

3.5.4. Venta Icenorum

In 1938, investigations by Surgeon Commander Mann at Caistor Paddocks (NHER: 9816), between the *civitas* capital and its extra-mural temple, revealed a layer of ash containing metalworking debris, clay mould and crucible fragments. Hearths, a kiln and a furnace were also found. This site is interpreted as a bronze-casting workshop (Tylecote 1969: 46-47). Manufacture of razors, brooches, bracelets and pins is demonstrated by failed castings and mould fragments. Some burnt mould pieces preserved the shapes of the objects within, including the only known manufacturing evidence for Mackreth's Harlow Type 1.a1 brooch (2011: 50; Tylecote 1969).[5] Also found was an unfinished, forged Drahtfibel derivative brooch (Mackreth 2011: 22, Type 1.b1). The mixed production of brooch types is paralleled at Compton Dando, Somerset, where moulds were found for several brooches including 'Dolphin', T-shaped and Hod Hill (PAS: GLO-9090B6).

The moulds from *Venta* are the investment type for lost-wax casting. Both triangular Iron Age and hemispherical Roman crucibles were found. Among the fragments was a brooch spring and wound wires, an early sign of production of two-piece brooches (Tylecote 1969: 46-47). The presence of Iron Age and Roman crucibles, alongside investment moulding, indicates that Icenian bronzesmiths were using both indigenous and introduced technologies in parallel. These finds bear strong similarities to discoveries from Prestatyn, which included clay piece and investment moulds for a variety of objects. The two casting technologies were distributed in different buildings on that site. The crucibles were mainly triangular Iron Age forms, but contained traces of high zinc alloys from casting brass, which Bayley claims reflects a 'Romanised' industry (in Blockley *et al.* 1989: 179-81).

Harlow brooches date from *circa* 40-70 CE, putting the Caistor Paddocks finds in the client-kingdom period. No substantial LIA settlement is yet known in the vicinity of the *civitas* capital (*contra* Davies 2011b: 103-4), despite abundant surface finds, including Icenian coins. Flavian samian ware was excavated at the town, although the formal civic layout has been convincingly re-dated to *circa* 120 CE (Atkinson 1931: 137-38; Bowden 2013b). Therefore, we would not expect many early to mid-first century CE brooches, as indeed is demonstrated by the density maps (Figure 3.4, Figure 3.5). If the Harlow brooch is characteristic of the Trinovantes (Mackreth 2011: 50), its manufacture, at *Venta Icenorum* and Old Buckenham, in the heart of Icenian territory, is unexplained. These finds have raised important questions which I will attempt to address further in this chapter.

3.5.5. Chediston

Although metal moulds are only known from Norfolk, Suffolk has several finds of ceramic moulds. At Chediston

(SHER: CHD004), bronze-casting waste, furnace and mould fragments were found (Ranson and Cooper nd: 16). The moulds were for Colchester Derivatives, several with Rearhooks.[6] This is particularly significant in light of the above discussion of Harlow production in Norfolk. Eastern Suffolk has a strong metalworking focus for personal ornament and horse harness, such as the Waldringfield terret moulds (SHER: WLD001) (section 8.10.1). Martin also mentions clay mould and crucible fragments for producing 'ornamental metalwork' from Burgh (1988: 24-25, 1999: 83).

No references to brooch production were found in the Cambridgeshire records. This is probably due to recording differences, but may also reflect the importance of specific parts of the territory in manufacturing.

3.6. Hybrids and Failed Castings

Objects which exhibit hybridity can show the assimilation and appropriation of new ideas and materials; failures can reveal experimentation and recycling processes. A brooch from Brockley has unfinished decoration and its cylindrical hinge-casing is obstructed with a compacted clay-like deposit. Both wings are truncated and chisel marks on the back of the head may signify it was a failed casting, intentionally cut up for reprocessing (PAS: SF-680F00) (Figure 3.13). Another hinged brooch from Freckenham shows damage on the head consistent with a sequence of hard blows. This may show deliberate breakage for scrap, although modern agricultural damage cannot be ruled out (PAS: SF-C6A840) (Figure 3.14). A Rearhook brooch from Methwold shows several signs of incompleteness. The semi-cylindrical wings are part-filled with superfluous metal, and the stump of a miscast hook protrudes from the head. The catchplate is unfinished: the thickened flap of metal would have been hammered out and folded to hold the pin, which was never attached (PAS: NMS-85D343) (Figure 3.15).

Some hinged brooches show evidence of a cast-in skeuomorph of the spring on the axis bar casing. The mock-spring hinged brooch is found in Britain from the Early and Middle Iron Age onwards (Adams 2013: 80). Colchester Derivative brooches with pseudo-springs come from Saham Toney (NHER: 4697), Beighton (PAS: NMS-2A0CE6) and Bythorn and Keyston (PAS: NMS-4B8E49). Mackreth discusses two unusual hybrid Rearhooks from Marham (NHER: 29189) (Figure 3.16) and Suffield, both in Norfolk. These have a pseudo-spring moulded into the rear of the wings. He regards these as transitional forms between sprung and hinged variants (2009: 137-49). A visible spring must have been an important part of the underlying 'fittingness' of a brooch. These finds demonstrate that manufacturing, reprocessing and experimentation were occurring in the region during the first century CE.

---

[5] Tylecote does not explicitly state what types of brooch the moulds were for, but one 'fits a fibula from the same area' (1969: 46). Mackreth's assertion that at least one of the moulds was for his Harlow type 1.a1 suggests he examined the finds personally (2011: 50). A search of Norfolk Museums stores has recently turned up some of these finds, although it has not yet been possible to verify the brooches or other artefacts in detail (NWHCM: 1961.150).

[6] Unpublished letter in SHER (CHD004) from J. Plouviez to J. Bayley re: samples sent for study.

Figure 3.13. Hinged Colchester Derivative brooch showing chisel marks, Brockley (PAS: SF-680F00).

3.7. 'A souvenir or a bleak survival'?

Mackreth identifies the Rearhook as a distinctively Icenian type, which ceased to be made or distributed after the uprising: 'This Icenian brooch type had become a souvenir or a bleak survival' (2009: 144). As with coin hoards, there is a risk of creating a circular argument when attempting to make the archaeology fit the classical texts. Statton (2016: 237) critiques Mackreth's reliance on 'tribal' designations and his failure to explore alternative explanations. Excavated finds may be attributed to 'Boudican' levels and those same layers dated *circa* 60/61 CE based on the

Figure 3.14. Hinged Colchester Derivative brooch with damage suggesting reprocessing, Freckenham (PAS: SF-C6A840).

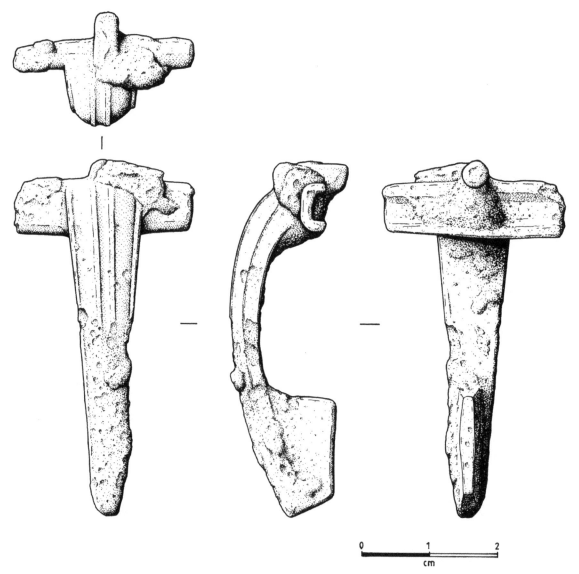

Figure 3.15. Unfinished Colchester Derivative brooch, Methwold (PAS: NMS-85D343).

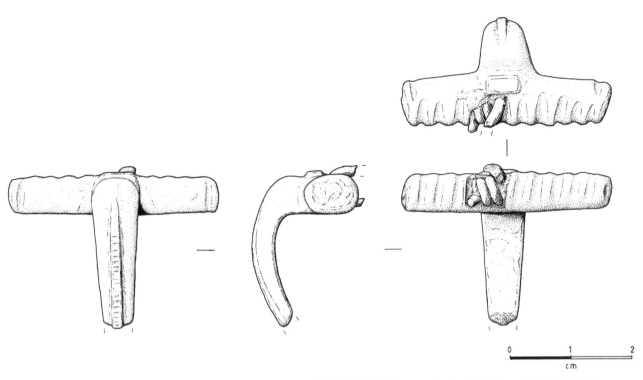

0   1   2

c m

Figure 3.16. Hybrid Colchester Derivative brooch, Marham (NHER: 29189; Illustration by J. Gibbons © NCC Historic Environment Service).

brooches deposited within them. My study shows a much more complicated picture.

The Rearhook was a particularly ineffective method of fixing the pin and soon went out of use. Although it visibly holds the spring, in reality a drop of solder was often necessary to secure it. Some brooches had multiple hooks for extra stability (Mackreth 2011: 60, 68-69) such as the triple Rearhook from Stanton (PAS: SF-885244) (Figure 3.17). The allegedly interrupted lifespan of the Rearhook may be due to this inherent design flaw and may bear no relation to the revolt (Bayley and Butcher 2004: 157; Hattatt 1982: 46). This weakness may have led to them being abandoned and hinged versions being taken up with gusto (section 3.11.3). Although, if the remains at *Venta Icenorum* and Old Buckenham (section 3.5) are correctly identified, Icenian craftspeople were fully capable of producing brooches with double pierced lugs, but chose not to wear or deposit them locally.

There is an inherent danger in mapping group identities indiscriminately onto material culture (Jones 1997: 122-23). Brooches are, of course, not directly comparable to named groups of people. Spring fixings are not especially visible, even to the wearer, so present a limited means of distinguishing one group from another, except in close proximity (Cool 2016: 415). I agree with Mackreth's observations that certain brooches had restricted distributions, but I am wary of the idea that brooches were worn as badges of ethnic identity. I am more inclined to interpret this regional patterning as reflecting local workshops, exchange networks and fashions (Eckardt 2014: 218).

3.8. What is the evidence for cultural contact?

Davies's assertion that the Rearhook indicates 'a strong tribal unity and lack of integration with other tribal peoples' no longer seems valid, although he questions whether it was 'a tribal symbol or badge' or simply 'a local way of doing things' (2014: 30-31). Based on his conclusion that the Rearhook was a homegrown brooch, Mackreth considers the Iceni to be 'relatively successful in keeping out "foreign" brooch types' (2011: 145). In this part, I use the frequency and distribution of imported brooches to examine the idea that the Iceni avoided integration with their neighbours and resisted non-local brooch types. These range from the continental *fibulae* of the late first century BCE through to British-made varieties in the early first century CE. The impact of cultural contact and change may be seen through the selective uptake of 'outsider' brooches.

3.8.1. One-piece (La Tène) Brooches

One-piece brooches are simple 'safety pin' types, hand-forged from a single piece of wire. These developed across Europe in the second half of the first millennium BCE and are designated La Tène I-III. La Tène III brooches inspired and ran concurrently with the Colchester brooch, which proliferated in Britain in the early first century CE. In turn, the Colchester gave rise to both the Harlow and Rearhook Derivatives discussed above (Bayley and Butcher 2004: 145-47).

One-pieces represent over 10 per cent of the brooch dataset (Table 3.3). Their distribution is widespread, excepting

Figure 3.17. Triple Rearhook brooch, Stanton (PAS: SF-885244).

Table 3.3. One-piece, Langton Down, Colchester and Rosette/Thistle brooches by county

Brooch Type	Cambs	Norfolk	Suffolk	Total
One-piece	188	481	465	1134
Langton Down	28	235	222	485
Colchester	119	300	317	736
Rosette/Thistle	24	159	172	355

the Fens (Figure 3.18). Concentrations occur around Coddenham (46), Freckenham (25), Oxborough (31) and Saham Toney (52) (Figure 3.19). These appear to be the main centres of population (or at least brooch deposition) in the late first century BCE and early decades of the first century CE. A comparison with the Iron Age coinage shows coins were more widespread than brooches, but with similar concentration zones, including Saham Toney and Coddenham/Baylham (Leins 2012: 170). Saham Toney presents perhaps the best case for a pre-conquest *oppidum* (Davies 2009: 124-25) (see section 3.14.10). Coddenham is said to have pre-conquest activity as well as a post-conquest fort (Blagg *et al.* 2004: 75, 87).

Walsingham is less visible in the brooch densities than coins, which could present evidence for metal-detector bias, as the site has seen little excavation. Sites like Thetford, *Venta Icenorum* and Stonea, commonly cited as probable *oppida* (Davies 2009: 120; Gregory 1991a; Malim 2005: 51) and earthworks defined as 'hillforts' in north Norfolk (Davies 2009: 95-100), are scarcely represented by the brooch mapping. These may never have been centres of occupation, or had fallen out of use by the time of the '*fibula* event horizon'.

3.8.2. Continental Imports

Early continental imports, including the Augenfibel (Figure 3.20), Knickfibel, Knotenfibel and Kräftig Profilierte (Figure 3.21), were simple one-piece brooches. These brooches are sparsely distributed from coast to Fenland: Cambridgeshire (8), Norfolk (13) and Suffolk (6) (Figure 3.22). Mackreth associates the Augenfibel ('Eye brooch') with the army and suggests it declined before 60 CE. On evidence of its absence in his *corpus*, he argues that 'Roman brooches were not generally to be seen in the lands of the Iceni before the suppression of the rebellion' (2011: 151). Indeed, Eye brooches are rare in Britain and there are only four in my database: three from Chatteris (CHER: SCB19670) and one from Woodcock Hall, Saham Toney (NHER: 4697). Heeren and van der Feijst's metal analysis puts the Eye brooch firmly in the military group, along with the Aucissa and Knickfibel types, all made from zinc/copper (brass) alloys (2017: 251-53).

Bayley and Butcher also suggest that brooches such as the Knickfibel and Kräftig Profilierte were military introductions, commonly found in the Rhine-Danube frontier forts. These are scarce in Britain, found mostly in the eastern counties. They date from the Claudian period to the later first century CE (2004: 148). My mapping shows the few Kräftig Profiliertes hug the coast and the perimeter of the 'Great Estuary' in the east. This hints at its role as an *entrepôt* for mercantile or military contact with the near continent. The presence of Colchester and derivative brooches along the Rhine *limes* (frontier) arguably shows a reciprocal movement of goods and people: British mercenaries or auxiliary troops, according to Feugère (1985: 442). This can also be seen with later

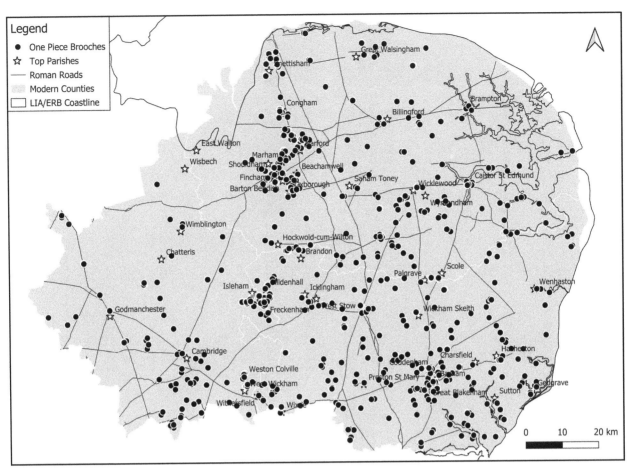

Figure 3.18. Distribution of all one-piece brooches.

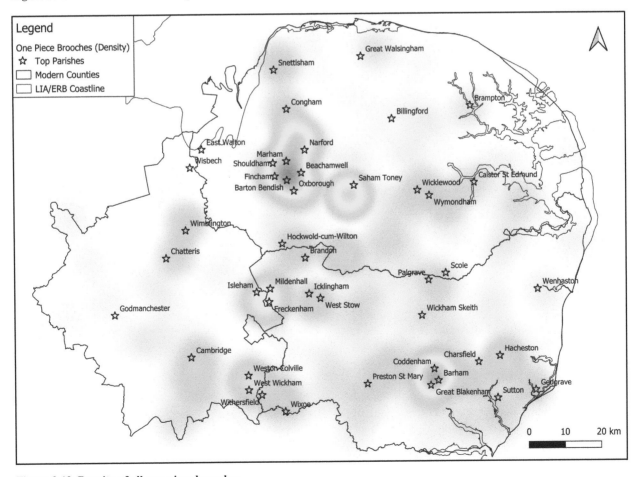

Figure 3.19. Density of all one-piece brooches.

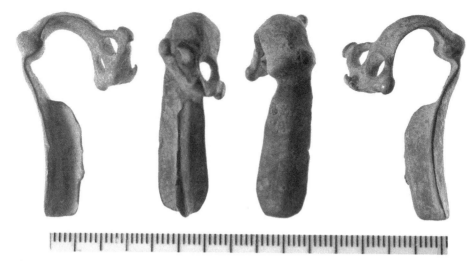

Figure 3.20. Augenfibel brooch, Kettlebaston (PAS: SF-7C5F65).

Figure 3.21. Kräftig Profilierte brooch, Gedgrave (PAS: SF-17BC30).

British brooches, such as the Trumpet and Headstud series, highlighting the continuing importance of this maritime route across the North Sea (Heeren and van der Feijst 2017: 411 and fig. 8.22).

3.8.3. *Drahtfibel, Nauheim and Derivatives*

The Nauheim has a decorated rectangular-section upper bow, which tapers toward the foot (Figure 3.23). Its date range is mid-first century BCE to early first century CE (150 BCE-50 CE on the continent). The Drahtfibel has a plain circular-sectioned bow and develops a little later (*circa* 120 BCE on the mainland). It is rarer in East Anglia than other parts of southeast England. Both have framed catchplates; derivative forms are solid (Heeren and van der Feijst 2017: 44-46; Mackreth 2011: 13-14, 21-23). My dataset contains only four confirmed examples, although there are a further 110 unspecified Late La Tène brooches.

There are very few true Nauheims or Drahtfibels in the study area, including related or possible examples (Figure

3.24). A scattering across Suffolk and Cambridgeshire is bolstered by 14 from Norfolk: Fincham, Hockwold-cum-Wilton, Snettisham, and particularly Thetford (Figure 3.25). Ten iron Drahtfibel/Nauheims were excavated at Fison Way, Thetford (NHER: 5853) hinting at an important pre-conquest centre (see section 3.14.1).

Drahtfibel Derivatives are extremely scarce in the dataset (Figure 3.26). Mackreth's Type 1.b1 includes the unfinished, forged brooch from Caistor St Edmund, evidence which suggests that casting and forging may have been taking place in the same workshop (Mackreth 2011: 21-23; NWHCM: 1961.150) (section 3.5.4). A gilt Drahtfibel Derivative was also excavated at the *civitas* capital (NWHCM: 1929.152.B17). By contrast, Nauheim Derivatives are plentiful, particularly in Suffolk; they were manufactured in large numbers in Britain in the first century CE (Bayley and Butcher 2004: 147) (Figure 3.27). The distributions reflect the overall LIA settlement pattern, with concentrations at Coddenham (10) and Saham Toney (11).

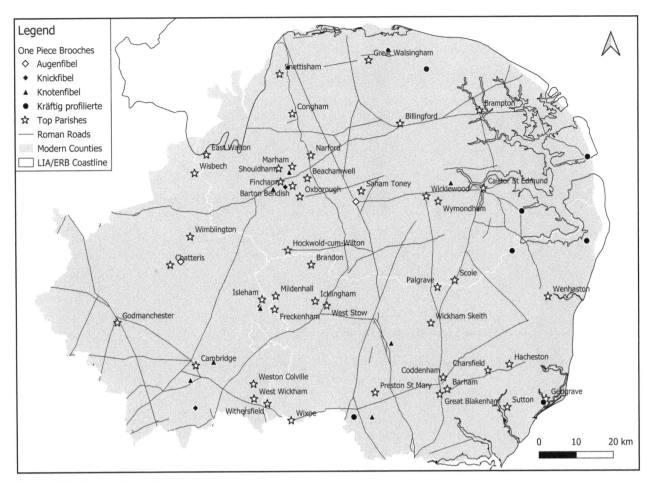

Figure 3.22. Distribution of imported one-piece brooches.

Figure 3.23. Nauheim one-piece brooch, Wymondham (PAS: NMS-FD3CB4).

3.8.4. Langton Down

The Langton Down has a distinctive, longitudinally-reeded bow, without footknob, and a cylindrical, enclosed spring cover (Figure 3.28). The distribution in mainland Europe is Gaul and the German frontier, dating *circa* 15 BCE-30 CE (Heeren and van der Feijst 2017: 85). Some arrivals may date this early, but their main period of usage in Britain is *circa* 25-60 CE (Hattatt 1982: 80; Mackreth 2011: 32-35). In Britain they focus on the southern counties, with high numbers at the King Harry Lane (*Verulamium*) cemetery. They went out of vogue by the invasion, but may have been retained, valued and deposited in burials due to their fine decoration and quality casting in brass (Bayley and Butcher 2004: 150).

Nearly 500 Langton Down brooches were recorded, approximately 5 per cent of the total (Table 3.3). There are concentrations at Coddenham (19), Hacheston (19), Preston St Mary (12), Pentney (10), Saham Toney (20) and Wicklewood (8) (Figure 3.29, Figure 3.30). The hotspot in west Norfolk again corresponds to the area of high detector use. Perhaps this brooch type is more frequently recovered due to its thicker profile, which may confirm Cool and Baxter's suspicions on morphology (2016a, 2016b). Mackreth attributes the numbers of his Type LD 2.b1 to disproportionate metal-detected collections from

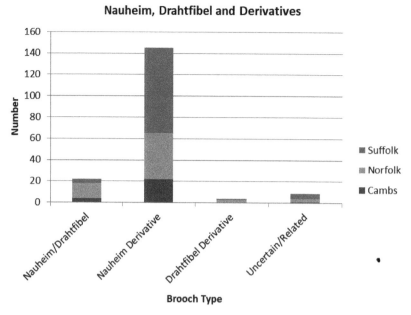

Figure 3.24. Nauheim, Drahtfibel and derivative brooches by type and county.

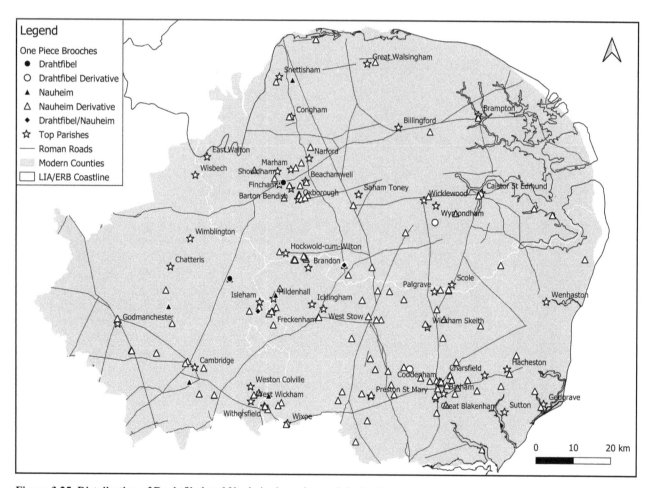

Figure 3.25. Distribution of Drahtfibel and Nauheim brooches and derivatives.

Norfolk and recommends reducing the numbers by a third to compensate (2011: 33-34). Even so, the density in the northwest would remain.

Five Langton Downs from Woodcock Hall, Saham Toney, were deliberately cut or damaged (Brown 1986) (see

section 3.14.10). An elaborate example from Melbourn, in the far southeast of the study area, has punched waves of curvilinear dots along the bow and a white metal finish (PAS: CAM-D3D5A7) (Figure 3.31). A badly miscast brooch from Great Dunham has very rough, white metal coated surfaces, molten wings and a large blob of metal

Figure 3.26. Drahtfibel Derivative brooch, Stowmarket (PAS: SF-DCADF7).

Figure 3.27. Nauheim Derivative brooch, Great Barton (PAS: SF-48E5C2).

Figure 3.28. Langton Down brooch, Great Barton (PAS: SF-78AA07).

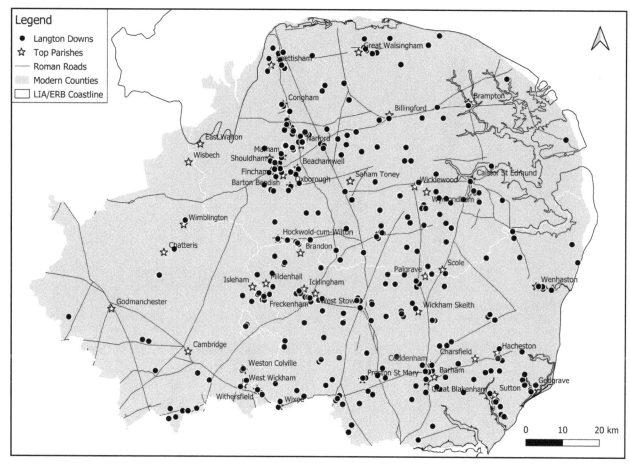

Figure 3.29. Distribution of Langton Down brooches.

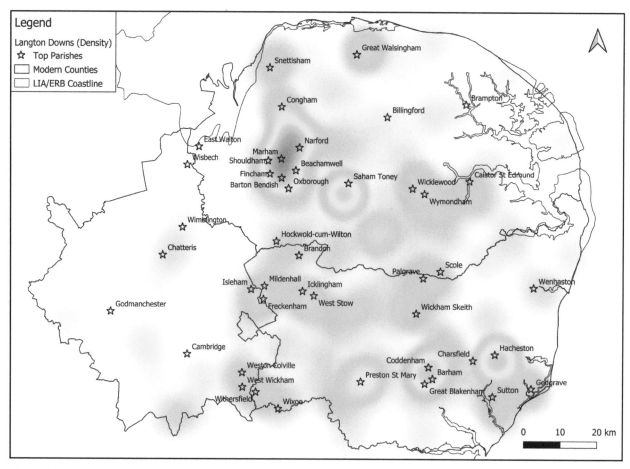

Figure 3.30. Density of Langton Down brooches.

fused beneath the spring housing (PAS: NMS-414840) (Figure 3.32). Several hybrid versions combine the Rearhook fixing and semi-cylindrical wings with a broad reeded bow (e.g. PAS: NMS-002F34, NMS-FFB395). The distribution of the Langton Down reflects pre-rebellion settlement patterns and exchange networks. The locally-made adaptations of imported brooches suggest the people of northern East Anglia were not resisting or slow to appropriate these brooches.

3.8.5. Colchester

The Colchester is a single piece brooch, with a bilateral spring held by a forward hook, and often a decorative catchplate (Figure 3.33). The type has continental origins in the late first century BCE and British copies peaking *circa* 20-60 CE. Colchester one-pieces are the standard pre-conquest brooch in the southeast and East Anglia (Mackreth 2011: 36-37). As discussed above, Mackreth claims the Colchester 'marks the lands' of the Trinovantes and Catuvellauni, whereas the Rearhook shows Icenian influence extended out from Norfolk to the Fenland margins in the west (*ibid.*: 234).

The Colchester resembles Late La Tènes in terms of its morphology and potential recovery issues. That said, over 700 Colchester brooches have been recorded, representing around 7 per cent of the total (Table 3.3). This may challenge Cool and Baxter's comments about one-piece brooches being less frequently found by detector

(2016a: 81). Concentration zones exist at West Wickham/ Weston Colville (21), Oxborough (23), Saham Toney (31), Coddenham (28) and Freckenham (23) (Figure 3.34, Figure 3.35). Notably, the towns of *Venta Icenorum* and Wenhaston have very few, presumably reflecting their later foundations. In both the Fens and Broadland, Colchesters and Langton Downs are sparsely represented. This may relate to the higher sea level and coastal flooding in the LIA, which would have restricted settlement potential.

Although the Colchester was initially imported, it found a home in Britain and was heartily embraced by the inhabitants of East Anglia, who put their own idiosyncratic twist on it. Colchesters show evidence of the transition from forged to cast brooches (Mackreth 2011: 4). There are considerable signs of experimentation and hybridity. Some present traits associated with the subsequent Rearhook or double pierced lug (Harlow) derivatives. A hinged rarity from Methwold (PAS: SF-64E224) (Figure 3.36) belongs to a group in Norfolk and Lincolnshire (*ibid.*: 26). Brooches from Beyton (PAS: SF-OFF4E3) (Figure 3.37) and Nedging-with-Naughton (PAS: SF-0A8018) (Figure 3.38) are developed forms which share decorative and structural commonalities with the Rearhook and Harlow (section 3.3.1). Their opposing-facing integral hooks show the derivation of the double lug of the Harlow (Plouviez PAS: SF-0A8018). The brooch from Brandon (PAS: SF8899) (Figure 3.39) is another step ahead, with both pierced lug and forward-hook.

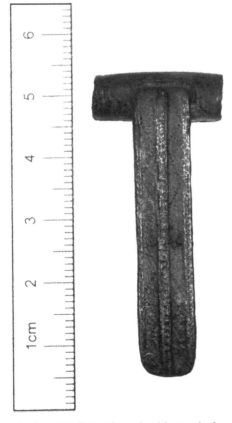

Figure 3.31. Langton Down brooch with punched decoration, Melbourn (PAS: CAM-D3D5A7).

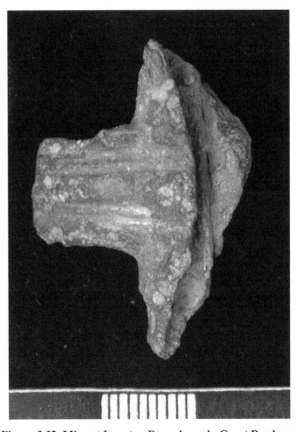

Figure 3.32. Miscast Langton Down brooch, Great Dunham (PAS: NMS-414840).

3.8.6. Rosette/Thistle

Around 350 brooches known as Rosettes, due to the decorative disc on the bow, come from the study area (Table 3.3, Figure 3.40). On the continent the Rosette is counted as a subtype of the Thistle brooch (Heeren and van der Feijst 2017: 88-90), whereas Mackreth regards the names as interchangeable (2011: 26). The PAS brooch recording guidance also suggests using 'Rosette' to cover

Thistle and Keyhole types. Here the various types are grouped together for analysis, as in many cases the dataset includes dual/uncertain identifications.

The earliest types developed before 20 BCE, probably in southern Germany, and must have arrived in Britain via Gaul shortly thereafter. Early Rosette brooches are associated with both pre-conquest settlements and Roman military activity (Bayley and Butcher 2004: 150; Hattatt

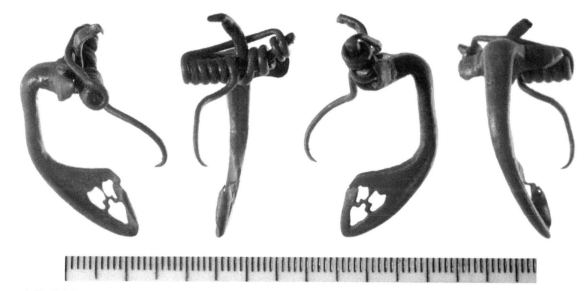

Figure 3.33. Colchester brooch with fretted catchplate, Freckenham (PAS: SF-42E064).

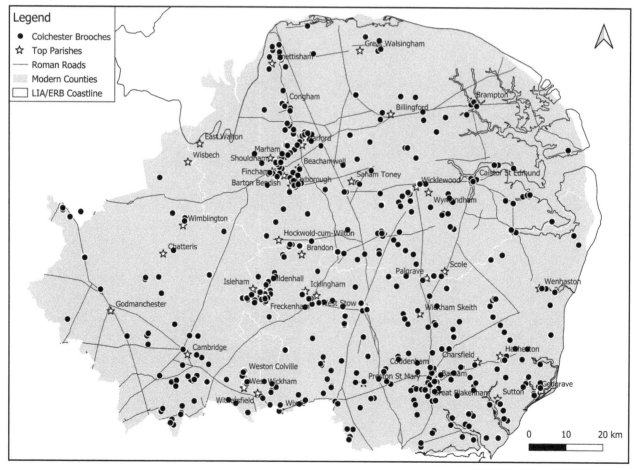

Figure 3.34. Distribution of Colchester one-piece brooches.

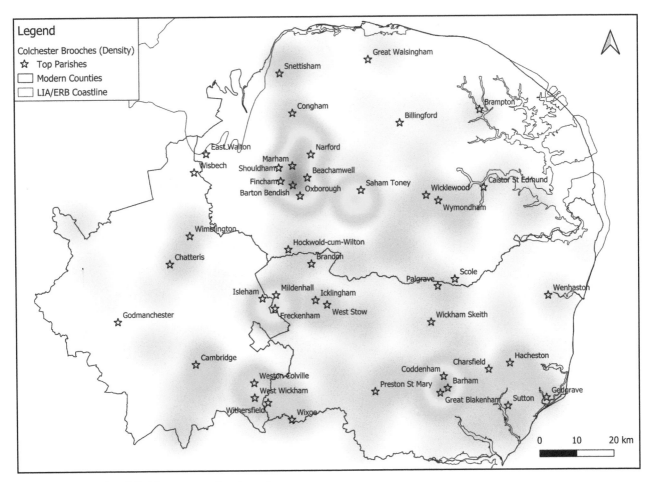

Figure 3.35. Density of Colchester one-piece brooches.

Figure 3.36. Hybrid hinged Colchester brooch, Methwold
(PAS: SF-64E224).

**Figure 3.37. Colchester brooch with double hook, Beyton
(PAS: SF-OFF4E3).**

types, demonstrating local adoption and adaptive manufacture. Rosettes are large and highly-visible, therefore morphological bias may mean they are likely to be more frequently recovered than the wire brooches.

The distribution shows the penetration of imported goods, if not actual military personnel, throughout the region. Rosette brooches demonstrate the continuity of settlements along the Icknield Way and the ascendancy of southeast Suffolk. A hotspot at Hacheston/Charsfield extends

1982: 98; Mackreth 2011: 27-28). Finds cluster in the northwest parishes and at Freckenham (9), Coddenham (8) and Hacheston (11) (Figure 3.41, Figure 3.42). A dozen from Saham Toney (NHER: 4967) includes early forms with Rearhooks, later hinged derivatives and experimental

45

Figure 3.38. Hybrid Colchester/Harlow brooch, Nedging-with-Naughton (PAS: SF-0A8018).

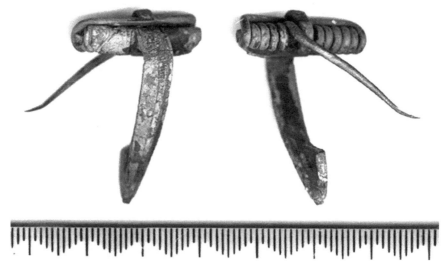

Figure 3.39. Hybrid brooch with pierced lug and forward hook, Brandon (PAS: SF8899).

Figure 3.40. Rosette/Thistle brooch, Foxhall (PAS: SF-C83122).

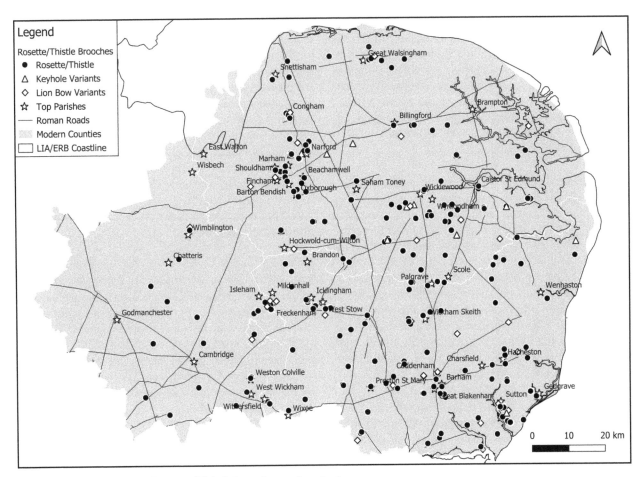

Figure 3.41. Distribution of Rosette/Thistle brooches and variants.

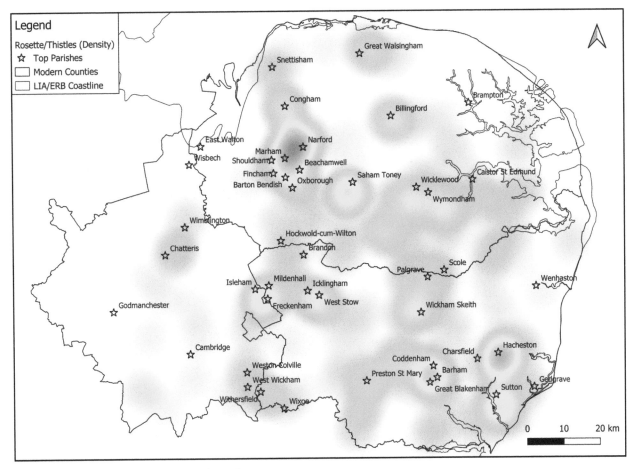

Figure 3.42. Density of Rosette/Thistle brooches.

along the northeastern bank of the Deben valley around Sutton, site of a first century CE *denarius* hoard (SHER: SUT041) and a suspected LIA to Roman settlement (SHER: SUT022). This would seem a profitable route for coastal trade and communication. Four from Walsingham (NHER: 2024/28253), three from Wicklewood (NHER: 8897/18111) and one from the Romano-Celtic temple at Caistor St Edmund (Gregory 1991b: 193; NHER: 9787) may imply votive associations.

The Keyhole variant occurs in small numbers only: Norfolk (12) and Suffolk (5) (Figure 3.41, Figure 3.43). The *Léontomorphe* type, with an applied lion on the bow, has Gaulish origins (Figure 3.44). Neither has great concentrations, suffice to note that they entered the region, and some may have been locally made. An unparalleled 'imitation' Rosette from Billingford (NHER: 7206 c.606) may be of Norfolk manufacture. The British Lion Bow is devolved: Mackreth refers to the 'decreasing skill in representing the beast' which is reduced to a bowtie (2011: 30). This schematisation is part of a key regional aesthetic (section 2.3.7). There are 46 Lion Bow brooches (Cambridgeshire 3, Norfolk 22, and Suffolk 21) (Figure 3.41). Mackreth links these to the region controlled by the Catuvellauni/Trinovantes i.e. the southeastern Cambridgeshire Fens and Essex (2011: 29-30). If anything, my distribution contradicts this, with few from either the southwest or northeast. This may be due to the use of different data sources. A peculiar example from Old Buckenham has the fully-modelled lion with a bovid head attached between its paws (PAS: SF-BA4524) (Figure 3.45). This type has its roots in late first century BCE Gaul and has been found as far afield as Turkey (Plouviez PAS: SF-BA4524). An interest in zoomorphic objects, particularly bovids, is also apparent in the later cosmetic grinders (section 5.3.2).

The association of Rosettes with temples hints at a votive aspect which continues with the later plate brooches (section 3.12.1). These complex and attractive brooches may reflect connections between the region and Gaul in the pre-invasion years. An interest in Gaulish objects and local adaptation are also evidence for Icenian openness to certain outside influences. This may have changed with the invasion, as will be discussed in relation to pipeclay figurines (section 6.8). Again, we see early adoption and selective appropriation of artefacts in the early first century CE, which contests the narrative of cultural isolationism.

3.9. What is the evidence for the Boudican revolt and military occupation?

Imported brooches show that the inhabitants of the territory were receptive to external influences and freely adopted new styles and technologies in the early to mid-first century CE. Their insularity and resistance to 'foreign' types may have been misinterpreted. The same questions can be asked of the conquest and client-kingdom period, in particular the presence of brooches associated with the military. I will now consider the discourse of the Boudican revolt and the subsequent depopulation through the evidence of brooches.

3.9.1. Aucissa and Hod Hill

Brooch-wearing was not a Mediterranean custom and only spread to the Roman military in the Augustan period due to provincial contact (Heeren and van der Feijst 2017: 361). The brooches most associated with the Claudian invasion force are the Aucissa and its successor the Hod Hill. These are often grouped together as they can look extremely similar and uncertain identifications of fragments are common. They do have different chronologies and

Figure 3.43. Rosette brooch, Keyhole variant, Shottisham (PAS: SF-B0284D).

Table 3.4. Aucissa, Hod Hill and Knee brooches by county

Brooch Type	Cambs	Norfolk	Suffolk	Total
Aucissa	15	26	31	72
Hod Hill	74	369	346	789
Aucissa/Hod Hill	16	45	82	143
Knee	7	55	69	131

Figure 3.44. Lion bow brooch, Barking (PAS: SF-7B02F4).

Figure 3.45. Lion bow and bovid head brooch, Old Buckenham (PAS: SF-BA4524).

Figure 3.46. Aucissa brooch, Wickham Skeith (PAS: SF4129).

distributions so, where possible, they are discussed separately here. In total, they form 10 per cent of my dataset (Table 3.4). Aucissa brooches occur in far smaller quantities to Hod Hills, with a ratio of approximately 10:1, which corroborates previous studies (Eckardt 2005: 150-51; Plouviez 2008: 173).

The Aucissa is a hinged brooch, with a strongly arched, D-shaped bow (Figure 3.46). It derives from the Gallic Alesia type and was widespread across the empire from the Augustan to Neronian periods. In Britain, few pre-conquest examples are known, and it is rare in the north. Aucissas are widely regarded as military brooches, perhaps distributed during the first wave of invasion. Although commonly regarded as a soldier's brooch, its frequency on civilian settlements suggests it was extensively imitated by indigenous brooch-makers (Bayley and Butcher 2004:

151; Feugère 1985: 321 and fig. 46; Hattatt 1982: 83; Mackreth 2011: 131-33).

Aucissas (and derivatives) are more common in Suffolk (50) than in Cambridgeshire (16) and Norfolk (31). There are very few in the north and east of the region. This might support the notion that the Iceni polity missed out on the 'first wave' of conquest by virtue of its client-kingdom status. Small groupings exist at sites with known or suspected early forts, including Saham Toney (6) and Coddenham (6). There is also a cluster at Hacheston (7) and in the parishes around Freckenham (9), which do not appear to have military emplacements (Figure 3.47, Figure 3.48). The PAS distribution is strong in Wiltshire, Yorkshire and Suffolk (Figure 3.49).

A numerous and diverse hinged type, the 'Hod Hill arrives, fully developed, at the conquest' (Mackreth 2011: 133) (Figure 3.50). Dating *circa* 40-70 CE, these brooches also flourished during the crucial client-kingdom phase. Not all British 'imitations' have mainland European parallels, implying that indigenous variants were rapidly

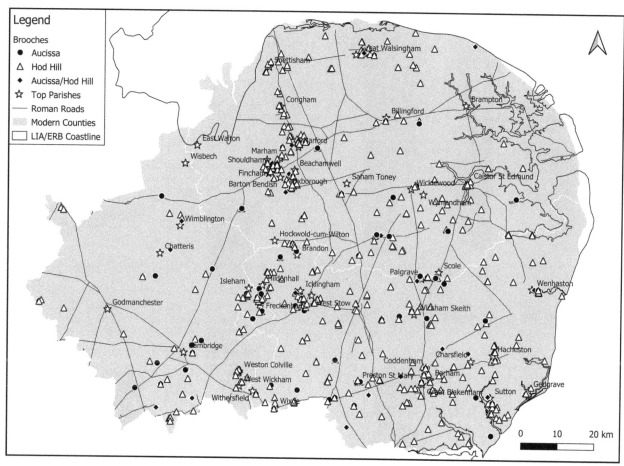

Figure 3.47. Distribution of Aucissa/Hod Hill brooches.

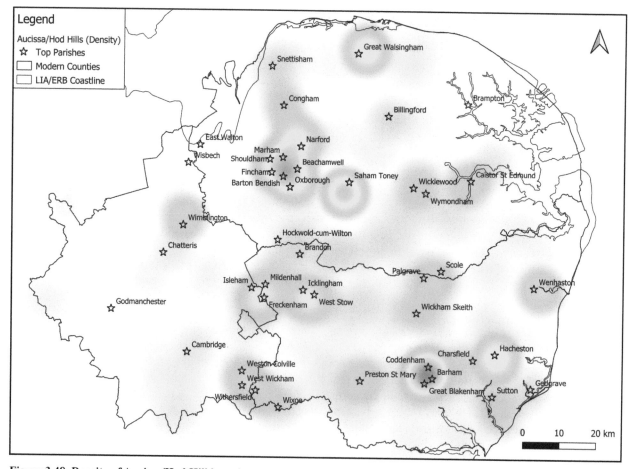

Figure 3.48. Density of Aucissa/Hod Hill brooches.

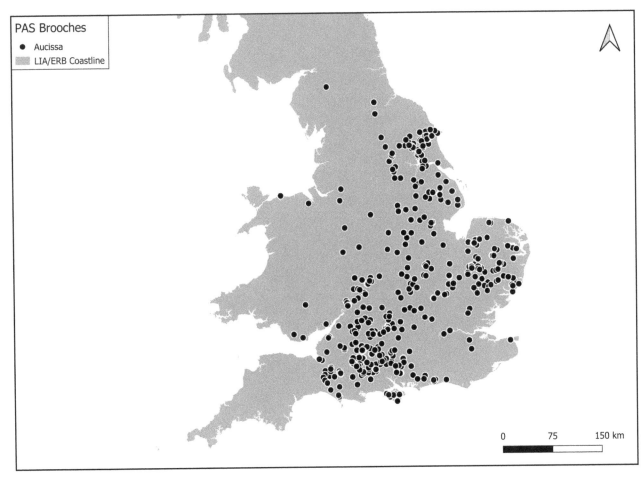

Figure 3.49. PAS distribution of Aucissa brooches.

Figure 3.50. Hod Hill brooch, Great and Little Chishill (PAS: BH-EE1C23).

Hod Hill brooches are almost equally represented in Norfolk (370) and Suffolk (361), with fewer in Cambridgeshire (75). Like the Aucissas, large groups can be seen at Saham Toney (42), Coddenham (37) and Hacheston (24), with the addition of Wenhaston (24) (Figure 3.47, Figure 3.48). In the northwestern parishes around Fincham/Shouldham and Beachamwell/Oxborough there are 77 Hod Hill brooches. This is an area of dense Iron Age settlement as well as a proposed 'marching camp' at Barton Bendish, known from cropmarks (NHER: 20130). Approximately 50 further brooches are recorded only as 'Aucissa or Hod Hill'. Nationally, the PAS shows a concentration in Lincolnshire as well as Norfolk and Suffolk, with proportionally fewer from Wiltshire and Yorkshire than the Aucissa (Figure 3.51).

Where recorded, both Aucissa and Hod Hill brooches invariably have a white metal finish. This reflective silvery shine appears essential to the design, which would have looked quite different, and perhaps desirable, to the Britons who were more familiar with iron and copper alloys. This surface similarity disguises some key differences in production between these two closely-related types. Aucissas were 'mass-produced' by die-cutting the bow and attaching a separately cast footknob and headplate, whereas all Hod Hills were cast as one. Metallurgical analysis of both British and continental examples revealed

devised. None have yet been found from a convincing pre-conquest context (Bayley and Butcher 2004: 152-53). There is a danger of making circular assumptions by allowing presence or absence to determine dating, or role, of a particular site. For instance, a Hod Hill brooch in the Santon Hoard (section 8.10.2) contributed partly to its later first century CE dating (Hutcheson 2004: 33-4).

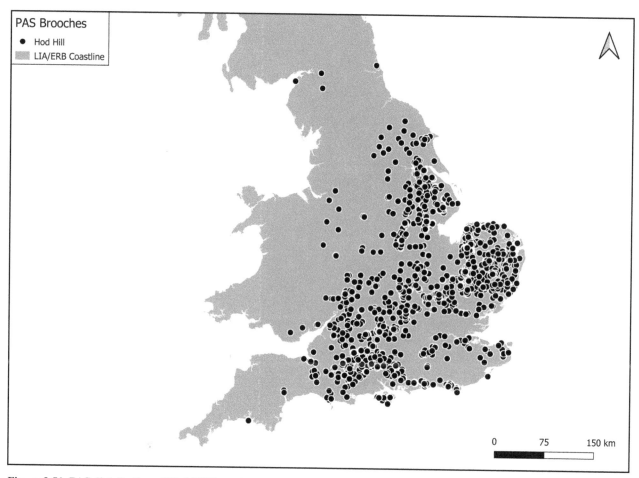

Figure 3.51. PAS distribution of Hod Hill brooches.

a remarkably homogenous brass (copper-zinc) alloy for Aucissa brooches, while the composition of Hod Hills was much more diverse (Bayley and Butcher 2004: 151-53; Heeren and van der Feijst 2017: 243-59; Mackreth 2011: 130, 134).

What are the arguments for the association of these brooch types with the Roman army? Can this dataset illuminate the client-kingdom period in the Iceni polity? In the Low Countries, large numbers of Alesia-Aucissa family brooches are found on military sites, and very few outside (Heeren and van der Feijst 2017: 362-63).[7] The highly pure and consistent brass alloy suggests an element of centralised production, perhaps controlled by the military or government, and supplied to towns and forts through official channels (*ibid.*: 358-59).

By contrast, in Pitts's correspondence analysis of Sheepen (Colchester), Aucissa brooches plotted alongside the Gallo-British material suite which included Langton Down, La Tène III, Rosette/Thistle and simple Gallic forms, which 'undermines the military interpretation frequently ascribed to this type' (2013: 239). As Eckardt noted, Aucissa brooches are surprisingly common on rural

sites and places 'where a military connection is tenuous at best' (2005: 152-53). Mapping Aucissa and Hod Hills against both known and suspected early forts in the study area confirms this divergence (Figure 3.52).[8] Evidence for local imitation and innovation also supports a potential non-military interpretation. Two very similar hybrid Hod Hills, displaying the local Rearhook spring fixing, were found at Flixton (PAS: SF-AD18F3) (Figure 3.53) and Weeting-with-Bromehill (PAS: SF3611). Likewise, two eccentric hinged and winged variants come from Brandon (SHER: BRD080) and Stradsett (NHER: 39567) (Figure 3.54).

The Boudican narrative is applied in different ways to brooches from neighbouring regions. Material culture has been used to create a distinction between the Iceni and their neighbours, as well as the military. Mackreth speculates about the movements of various legions based on brooch distributions, although he qualifies that not every Hod Hill or Aucissa 'marks the passage of a soldier' (2011: 133). He attributes concentrations from Norfolk and the Fens to the army eradicating the last traces of the Boudican revolt. In Essex, contrastingly, they belong to 'veterans left behind' at Colchester (*ibid.*: 139, 143). Why should the

---

[7] As there were very few Alesia brooches in the study area, they are 'lumped' with Aucissas.

[8] Great Chesterford is included on the 'Roman Forts' map layer although it just falls into Essex.

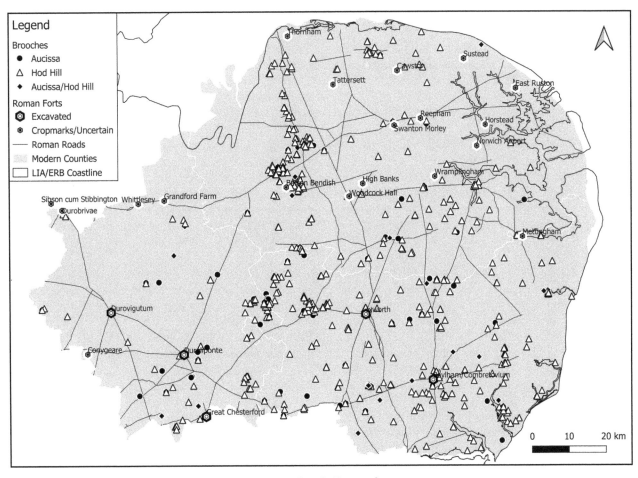

Figure 3.52. Distribution of Aucissa/Hod Hill brooches and early Roman forts.

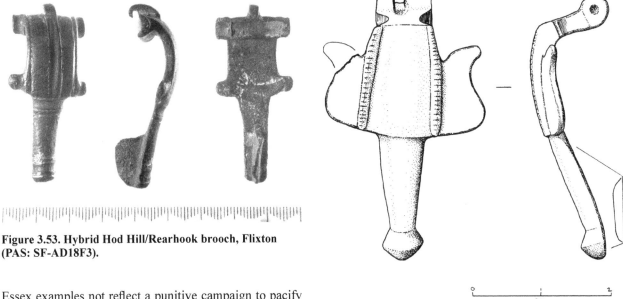

Figure 3.53. Hybrid Hod Hill/Rearhook brooch, Flixton (PAS: SF-AD18F3).

Figure 3.54. Unusual winged Hod Hill variant, Stradsett (NHER: 39567; Illustration by J. Gibbons © NCC Historic Environment Service).

Essex examples not reflect a punitive campaign to pacify the Trinovantes after the revolt in which they reportedly played a key role?

Plouviez defined first century CE East Anglian forts as sites with typically 15-20 per cent Hod Hill brooches, compared to fewer than 10 per cent on civilian settlements (2008: 176). This is explored further in the parish case studies (section 3.14). At Colchester, the proportion of Hod Hills was 19 per cent, and at Sheepen 26 per cent, reflecting the

presence of the early fort and *colonia* in that area (Wardle 2013: 198-99). Perring and Pitts consider Hod Hills part of the imposition of an 'alien material culture' at military and colonial sites with large immigrant populations.

These contrasted with the Gallo-British brooches such as Langton Down and Rosette types, preferred by the indigenous people, which may have seen a post-conquest surge in an effort to maintain local identities in the face of outright colonisation (2013: 244-45).

A relationship between early 'military' activity and sacred sites is suggested by two Aucissas and 11 Hod Hills from Crownthorpe (NHER: 8897) and 10 Aucissa/Hod Hill brooches from Walsingham (NHER: 2024). An oddity comes from the latter parish, identified as a gilded and sprung Hod Hill/Langton Down hybrid (PAS: NMS-01F393). Other temple sites like Hockwold-cum-Wilton are not greatly represented, arguably demonstrating selectivity of items for deposition, as will also be seen with seal-boxes (section 7.7). Were these items offerings made by passing Roman soldiers for success in battle? Were they taken as trophies from skirmishes or ambushes? Perhaps their silvery finish and embodied power of the invading military made them ideal votives for either side.

A cautionary tale from the continent may be told of the so-called 'Soldiers' Brooch', usually classified as La Tène III in Britain, but Roman in date on the mainland. It was previously ascribed to military dress. Recent reassessment has shown that it is common on civilian sites and exclusively found in female graves, often in pairs. Its alloy fits with the tin bronzes of indigenous brooches (Heeren and van der Feijst 2017: 123, 251-53, 363). While the presence of Hod Hill and Aucissa brooches in civilian and religious areas does not preclude their loss or deposition there by soldiers, it raises questions over the dating of known forts and the military ascription of these finds in Britain. Alternatively, their incidence in similar concentrations to civilian brooches may demonstrate a fashion for quasi-military styles among the British population, rather like the popularity of army surplus clothing today.

3.9.2. Knee

The dearth of Aucissa brooches from Iceni territory may reveal an absence of early Roman military activity. There are also few Knee brooches, so-called for their resemblance to the curvature of a lower leg (Figure 3.55), despite their prevalence in military contexts elsewhere. Initially imported from mainland Europe, where they were popular on military sites in Pannonia and the Rhine, local variants soon developed (Eckardt 2005: 150-51, 154; Hattatt 1982: 114; Statton 2016: 146). Continental versions are hinged with horizontal, often hook-like, catchplates, whereas British-made brooches were sprung, with vertical catchplates and often white metal trim. Mackreth dates them after 150 CE into the third century CE (2011: 167, 189).

Knee brooches are widespread across southern England, although there are surprisingly few on the PAS map from the northern frontier (Figure 3.56), and just 131 were recorded from the *civitas* (Table 3.4). The distribution shows groups around the towns of Coddenham (7), Wenhaston (14) and *Venta Icenorum* (7) (Figure 3.57, Figure 3.58). As some settlements developed around military bases, a correlation with Knee brooches may be unsurprising. The sprawling Suffolk small towns may alternatively have operated as market centres, connected by the expanding road network (Moore *et al.* 1988: 38). In west Norfolk, the earlier focus around Fincham is also visible, albeit lessened.

Five from Walsingham temple (NHER: 2024) include three imports. The simplest explanation is that Roman soldiers visited this shrine and deposited their own brooches. However, Knee brooches, like Hod Hills, belong to a grey area in which their military origins became blurred once they were manufactured on British shores. Most are

Figure 3.55. Knee brooch, Poslingford (PAS: SF-4A00B9).

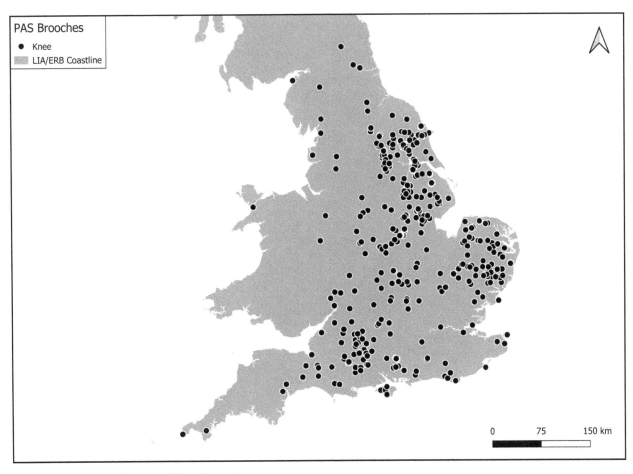

Figure 3.56. PAS distribution of Knee brooches.

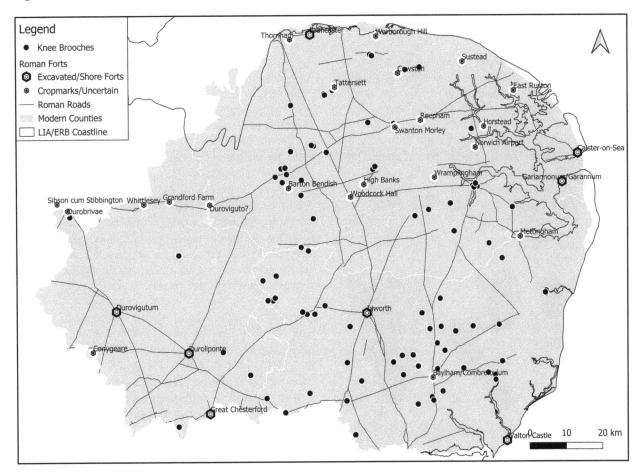

Figure 3.57. Distribution of Knee brooches and Roman forts.

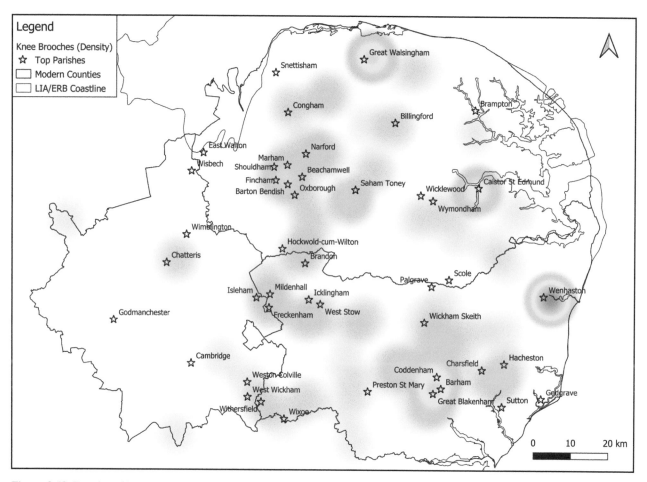

Figure 3.58. Density of Knee brooches.

diminutive and would struggle to fasten a large bunch of cloth like a cloak, but some have extended catchplates to allow for coarser fabric (Statton 2016: 147). An unusual hybrid from Isleham, probably of local manufacture; combines a Colchester Derivative-style spring fixing and enamelled spots on the bow with the sinuous profile of a Knee brooch (PAS: SF-19A3F4) (Figure 3.59). Insular variants also moved outside of the province, with occasional examples of British Knee brooches in the Low Countries (Heeren and van der Feijst 2017: 169).

Figure 3.59. Hybrid Knee brooch, Isleham (PAS: SF-19A3F4).

The Knee brooch develops into later forms which survive the '*fibula* abandonment horizon', including the Divided Bow, P-Shaped and Crossbows. These are often tinned or gilded. All have a strongly bulked-out version of its S-shaped profile, explained as a necessity for retaining a heavy military cloak (Mackreth 2011: 196-99; Statton 2016: 147). On the continent, these brooches are often found along the *limes*, resulting in the military interpretation (Heeren and van der Feijst 2017: 171-78). In Britain, like the earlier pseudo-military brooches, these later second and third century CE types do not appear to respect the known military installations of the period, including the so-called Saxon Shore Forts (Figure 3.57). This could imply that soldiers were incredibly disciplined at retaining and recycling their belongings, or these brooches were not restricted to the military.

Crossbow brooches were initially emblems of military authority, but were adopted by civic officials and their male offspring (Eckardt 2018: 165), which may echo the progression of Hod Hills. Although their later dating puts them outside the scope of this research, a cursory glance at their distribution pattern shows they were widespread but not common, with small concentrations at Caistor St Edmund and Wenhaston. Norfolk (48) and Suffolk (47) have the most Crossbows on the PAS database; such low numbers do not support a strong military presence in the Late Roman period.

3.9.3. Discussion

Several interpretations must be considered which are consistent with the evidence. An early military presence at the *civitas* capital and other key LIA sites might call into question the client-kingdom designation derived from classical sources. Were numerous soldiers stationed in the polity despite its 'friendly king' and self-governing status? Do they represent an influx of legionaries during the suppression of the Boudican revolt? If so, where are their marching camps and forts?

Davies considers Norfolk to have been garrisoned soon after the conquest, with possible forts at Ashill, Swanton Morley and Horstead and a marching camp at Barton Bendish. Irregular coinage and military fittings from the fort at Saham Toney suggest a Claudian presence in one of the major indigenous centres (section 3.14.10). Nevertheless, many of these sites are unexcavated and of uncertain date, known only from aerial photography and surface survey (Brown 1986; Davies 2009: 147-51 and fig. 122). Minimal Roman military installations in Suffolk could suggest the southern part of the polity did not oppose the invasion. A conquest period fort was constructed at Coddenham, but a Neronian fort at Pakenham (Ixworth) was short-lived. The LIA defended settlement at Burgh was remodelled and continued in use (Moore *et al.* 1988: 18). Millett also advances Scole, Godmanchester and Water Newton as invasion period forts (1990: 62). Two Roman forts have also been identified from aerial photography at Grandford on the Fen Causeway (Potter and Robinson 2000).

Rectilinear and concentric earthworks are not solely diagnostic of Roman military sites: Iron Age square enclosures (e.g. Harford Farm) and civilian triple ditches (e.g. *Venta Icenorum*) are known in the region (Ashwin and Bates 2000; Gregory and Gurney 1986; Lyons 2017: 384). Jones and Mattingly outline the risks of assigning cropmarks to temporary camps and specific campaigns (1990: 77-79). Smith *et al.* also observe a strong bias of abundant crop/soilmarks in Norfolk with 'an almost complete break' in Suffolk and North Essex which they identify as a result of different soil types and 'variable local authority records of cropmark data' (2016: 212 and map p. 389, based on Taylor 2007, fig. 3.3).

Forts established in the southwest at Longthorpe, Cambridge and Great Chesterford are interpreted as repercussions of the Boudican revolt (Moore *et al.* 1988: 25). Many civilian settlements, including *Venta Icenorum*, demonstrate a low-level background assemblage of military finds. If Knee brooches are justifiably associated with the military, their low frequency may suggest that there were few martial installations in the second century CE *civitas*. Of course, there is a risk of assuming absence of evidence here means few military sites. End-use deposition does not necessarily reflect the full lifespan of artefacts. If this *were* the case, does this sustain either the depopulation or the resettlement theory? Gambash explains the lack of militarisation as a Roman strategy

to win 'hearts and minds' post-revolt, rather than risking a military crackdown (2012: 12). This relies on a rather modern concept of warfare and although Tacitus suggests Scapula's successors followed a more 'soft-hearted' policy (*Agr.* 16.1), this is at odds with his 'harried with fire and sword' hyperbole (section 1.6).

The accepted sequence of Roman interactions with the Iceni is not supported by the brooch finds. One would expect more military trappings if the army had taken control in large numbers, or if numerous veterans were offered lands in previous Iceni-held territory. Alternatively, the paucity of martial artefacts may simply reflect better recycling of metalwork on official sites. Local manufacture and adaptation demonstrate that both Hod Hill and Knee types were being produced with indigenous or hybridised aesthetics. If the Iceni had truly been eradicated after the rebellion, who was making, wearing and depositing these brooches?

3.10. Itinerant Metalworkers and the Icenian 'Other'

Mackreth proposes that, soon after the rebellion, members of the disaffected Iceni were removed in 'a kind of enforced diaspora', developing their distinctive brooches in supervised exile (2009: 147). In an alternative storyline, he has metalworkers fleeing as economic migrants 'from a devastated and impoverished land to a more congenial area' (2011: 234). This is based on a distinct subgroup of Rearhooks clustered around Cirencester, far outside their usual distribution (*ibid.*: 64-65, Type 3.k.c). However, these brooches fall in the same area as Harlow Type 4a (*ibid.*: 58), which suggests, following Mackreth's logic, that a group capable of making both types of spring fixing moved to Gloucestershire.

Manufacture of both Rearhook and Harlow brooches has been demonstrated in the lands of the Iceni (section 3.5). This issue has previously caused some interpretive problems. The close relationship between material culture and identity means that the Iceni have been defined or even created by their brooches. Contradictory evidence has conveniently been attributed to a passing craftsperson losing his or her stock-in-trade e.g.: 'The Old Buckenham finds, with the other scraps, could be described as part of a metalworker's baggage lost in transit' (Mackreth 2011: 5). If brooches were not worn as badges of belonging, what other explanations for the observed distributions are possible? Heeren and van der Feijst lay out five models for production and distribution of brooches (2017: 358-59). These include four hypotheses combining dispersed or centralised production and distribution, plus the travelling artisan model. For example, the Aucissa brooches with their highly homogenous brass composition suggest centralised production with dispersed distribution. Either the casting and finishing of portable artefacts took place in small workshops in both rural and urban settlements (Dungworth 2016: 549) or they were produced sporadically by 'itinerant metalworkers' (e.g. Bayley *et al.* 2001). This narrative has also played its part in the construction of the Icenian 'Other'.

Bayley *et al.* are at pains to prove that the Harlow brooch moulds from Old Buckenham are aberrant. A range of speculative options is considered, including the dispersal of Icenian metalworkers after the revolt. Little Roman archaeology and a lack of any manufacturing evidence in the vicinity leads them to speculate that these isolated finds were mislaid by a travelling craftsman or even imported in topsoil during construction of a nearby airfield (2001: 97-100). Bayley *et al.* are incredulous that a simply decorated Harlow brooch was being made and even worn in Norfolk: 'The limited range of brooches using the Harlow system is in stark contrast to the Icenian metal-workers who excelled in producing decorative effects which the Rearhook family shows only too well' (*ibid.*: 110-11). I agree that the simplicity or ornateness of a brooch might have been more visually significant as a badge of belonging than the spring fixing, but the Rearhook and Harlow brooch divisions are far less clear-cut than they assume.

Bayley *et al.* attempt to fit the archaeology to the classical narrative, leading to suppositions that: 'While the Iceni maintained an independent state, and the Rearhook was the tribal type brooch, it seems unlikely that an itinerant outsider would have had much success, and even may have been barred from trade. However, with the collapse of the Boudiccan rebellion and the retaliation of the Roman army, fierce enough to ensure that no maker of Rearhook brooches continued his craft afterwards, the survivors of the tribe presented new market opportunities' (2001: 112).

This narrative has impacted on the dating of the Old Buckenham moulds: no earlier than 60/65 CE and probably not later than 80/100 CE. Mackreth's dating of Rearhooks has been questioned above. Although the army distributed equipment to soldiers and travelled with mobile workshops, a large-scale influx of continental metalworkers during the mid-first century CE seems unlikely (Eckardt 2014: 132). Rather, indigenous bronzesmiths introduced brooches and grooming implements into their repertoire of decorated metalwork, creating a 'distinctive provincial Roman style' (Cool 1983: 359).

Considering the great abundance of metalwork in this period, direct evidence for production is extremely slim (Heeren and van der Feijst 2017: 358-59). There is minimal proof of established manufactories, but equally little support for the peripatetic craftsperson, other than isolated finds of brooch moulds and occasional scrap hoards (Johns 1997; Mackreth 2011: 242; Revell 2016: 90). I explore so-called metalworkers' hoards further in section 4.7.2. Whilst manufacturing is not concentrated in any one area, there are indications that metalworking occurred right across the region. Figure 3.60 shows the distribution of moulds, miscastings and unfinished pieces for a variety of object types. This shows some patterning,

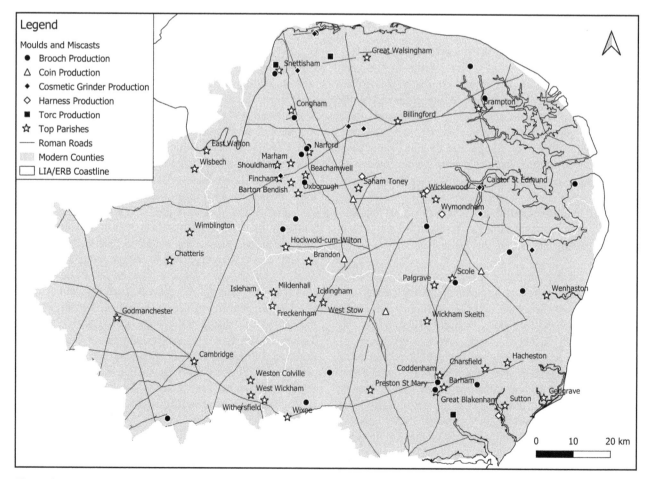

Figure 3.60. Distribution of metalwork production evidence.

such as the two groups of cosmetic grinders in northwest and southeast Norfolk, or the central placement of finds of pellet moulds.

Travelling smiths attending seasonal fairs and markets may have driven changes in style and decoration by producing certain brooches for sale. However, there is considerable risk in casting and finishing batches of brooches which might be found unacceptable to discrepant regional preferences. Producing the right material properties of moulds, crucibles and alloys was a highly technical ability (Garrow and Gosden 2012: 95). While it was entirely possible for one person on horseback to carry all the necessary tools and materials for brooch-making, and to acquire raw materials by recasting their customers' scrap metal, they would still need a range of tools, crucibles, moulds and access to a furnace.[9] Unless the maker also carried numerous different brooch moulds, those would also have to be made to order, involving further materials and tools.

Settled metalworking communities presuppose a constant flow of output and demand and perhaps aristocratic patronage in the LIA. Foster considers this system unsupported by archaeological evidence. She contributes a more cooperative parallel from a study of Andean potters in which the village provides the basic equipment while visiting craftspeople bring the tools, raw materials and expertise. In her view, the itinerant craftsperson model allows greater autonomy and diverse production within a less hierarchical social system (1995: 58). Of course, an 'itinerant metalworker' could still be part of a 'workshop' in the *atelier* sense, but not have a permanent base. It is also most likely that separate craftspeople worked iron, bronze and precious metals. Bayley *et al.* suggest that the itinerant tradition may have continued into the second century CE, based on the notion that most people lived out of range of large settlements capable of sustaining a permanent bronzeworker (2001: 116). This rather underestimates the ability of people to acquire and even commission goods through the actions of merchants, markets and middlemen. The idea that ceramics and other artefacts were made in settled workshops, particularly in urban areas, is much more readily accepted than metalwork, perhaps due to its links with coinage in the academic mindset. The changing pottery industries in the mid-late Roman period (e.g. Brampton, Aylsham) suggest increasing specialisation and centralisation away from towns (Burnham and Wacher 1990: 6; Cooper 1996: 88).

The alternative explanation is that metalworkers belonged to the community and had permanent workshops in towns and villages. This interpretation also has some problems and contradictions. Although metalworking debris is commonplace in settlements, there are limited archaeological indications of workshops, suggesting small-scale 'dispersed production' on an *ad hoc* basis (Eckardt

and Crummy 2008: 69; see Bayley and Butcher 2004: 35-40 for a summary of British and continental evidence). Cool notes the material evidence for workshop production is rarely preserved, miscastings and scrap usually being reprocessed (1983: 329). Mackreth sees a very limited spread of brooch types outside their production zones before *circa* 125 CE. He concludes that, despite the finds at Caistor St Edmund, Compton Dando and Prestatyn (section 3.4) 'craftsmen were almost certainly itinerant and travelled on a more or less fixed annual route through their market territory' (2011: 242). At Weelsby Avenue, Grimsby, large amounts of metalworking debris, crucibles and moulds for harness manufacture were concentrated in different areas on a small permanent settlement dating from the first century BCE (Foster 1995). Other workshops for portable artefacts are known at Canterbury, Keynsham, Silchester and Wroxeter (Cool 1983: 330). Mann's metalworking and brooch production site at Caistor St Edmund may have been related to a possible industrial suburb to the east of the *civitas* capital, a 'shanty town' of simple huts linked to the street grid, predating the walling of the town in the late third century CE (Myres and Green 1973: 12).

Many writers, perhaps unthinkingly, reproduce the language of capitalism when discussing Roman industrialisation and standardisation. There may be an underlying agenda which uses the terminology of materialism and western capitalism to make the Roman empire seem more 'like us'. Cool imagines 'enterprising bronzesmiths' making votives and souvenirs at temples (1983: 332). Crerar also envisages travelling craftspeople setting up shop on festival days, or having more permanent workshops near a specific shrine, making and inscribing votive plaques for dedication (2006: 78). Mackreth proposes a 'particularly successful salesman' or 'prime manufactory' producing Trumpet brooches in the Walsingham/Wighton area (2011: 125-26). The idea of 'marketing zones', 'mass-production' of brooches in a 'factory system' or pipeclay figurines as cheap commodities, churned out in continental factories, depend on modern conceptions of consumerism, which are hard to dispel (Eckardt and Crummy 2008: 68; Foster 1995: 58; Green 1976: 15, 20, 1978: 16-17; Mackreth 2011: 130).

Why were certain small finds and coins confined to *civitas* boundaries? This is an unresolved and important question. Eckardt and Crummy also pose this in relation to nail cleaners (2008: 68). Distribution patterns of small finds often show tight regional groupings which roughly correspond to *civitates*. This is unlikely to be attributable to ethnic identities and probably has its roots in the location of manufacturing or market centres in the major settlements. It may be that one of the changes during this period is from mobile production to more settled manufacture. The individuality embodied by many finished artefacts shows pieces were made to a preconceived and very deliberate aesthetic, perhaps a negotiated process between maker and recipient. Manufacturers could have been catering to local tastes, or simply the nearest providers in a 'chain

---

[9] Jason Gibbons, NMS, (pers. comm. 09/12/2017).

of suppliers'. Again the language of consumerism proves difficult to avoid. Many brooch types of the late first/second centuries CE are found with both sprung and hinged fixing methods, perhaps implying that different craftspeople (or their customers) had their own preferences (see section 3.11.4). We need a better understanding of the processes by which objects travelled from their places of origin and who was commissioning, using and depositing artefacts.

3.11. What is the evidence for change and hybridity?

In the decades after the Boudican rebellion, the area is assumed to have suffered massive depredations and repopulation with veterans (section 1.6). What happened next can be explored through later first/second century CE brooches. Were the Iceni devastated? Did their distinctive metalworking tradition continue? Brooches show evidence for changing fashions and experimentation, resulting in hybrids and new variants. This section looks at some of these changes and wider issues of identity and display.

3.11.1. Aesica

The Aesica brooch is a derivation of the Rosette (Mackreth 2011: 8). It has continental origins, developing distinctively British variants in the mid-first century CE. There are only *circa* 350 nationwide on the PAS with a noticeable absence in Kent and the southeast (Figure 3.61). Norfolk dominates the 223 examples on my database (Table 3.5)

with concentrations in the northwest and Breckland, both areas known for indigenous metalworking (Figure 3.62). Few parishes contain clusters: Beachamwell (5), Wymondham (6), Palgrave (7) and the parishes around Snettisham (7).

Aesicas are cast, rather than forged, two-piece brooches, often displaying curvilinear decoration on the bow and/ or fantail (Figure 3.63). The hotspot around Wymondham and Wicklewood is seen clearly in the mid-first century CE brooches, like Aesica and Rearhooks. My mapping repeatedly highlights this zone, suggesting an important indigenous focus (Figure 3.64). Its appearance here may relate to advances in bronze-casting technology and the development of two-piece brooches instead of single forged construction. There may also be a connection with the production of ornamental horse harness in this area (chapter eight). An unfinished casting in Mackreth's *corpus* (2011: 46, Type 2.b1) comes from Carleton Rode, close to Saham Toney and the Breckland metalworking area. The presence at Snettisham might suggest a religious focus, although the group in central Norfolk comes from Wymondham parish, not Crownthorpe temple.

The Aesica brooch, with its wide plate and fantail, lends itself to elaboration and experimentation. Several variants are mapped in Figure 3.62. The closely-related Crescent and Rearhook subtypes are centrally distributed, being absent from the extreme northeast and Fens, while Suffolk

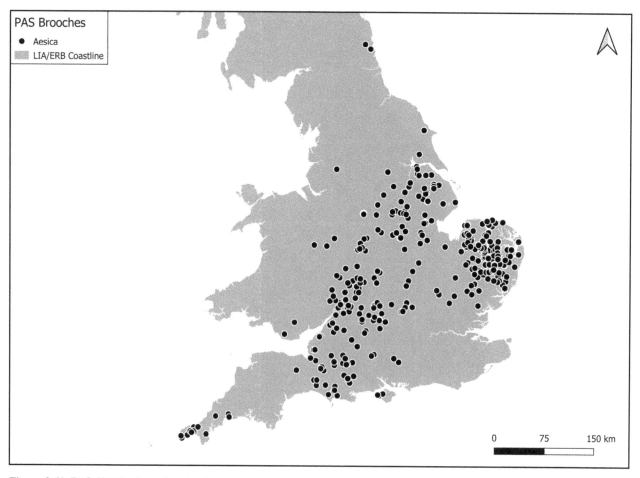

Figure 3.61. PAS distribution of Aesica brooches.

Table 3.5. Aesica, Polden Hill, Hinged, Headstud, Trumpet, zoomorphic and equine brooches by county

Brooch Type	Cambs	Norfolk	Suffolk	Total
Aesica	7	131	85	223
CD Polden Hill	16	96	179	291
CD Hinged	24	337	548	909
Headstud	20	166	139	325
Trumpet	28	239	230	497
Zoomorphic	19	133	154	306
Horse	0	2	10	12
Horse-and-Rider	5	35	14	54

has a higher incidence of Reversed Fantails. Those with the Rearhook mechanism are considered an East Anglian type (Mackreth 2011: 46-47; Statton 2016: 109) (Figure 3.65). Cool and Baxter found that Aesica brooches were highly discoverable by detectorists (2016a: 81, table 3), presumably due to their large surface area. Given the relative numbers in my dataset, it is unlikely that this has introduced a great deal of bias.

Hybrids include a Rearhook with fantail from South Elmham (PAS: SF-D0CC91), a Polden Hill/Aesica hybrid from Redgrave (PAS: SUSS-D6EB34) and, unfortunately unillustrated to my knowledge, a 'way out' variant from Ashwellthorpe (NHER: 30205)! One from Stonea Grange, Wimblington (CHER: 06057) is described as an unparalleled hinged Aesica with 'trumpet head and fantail foot both with "Celtic style" decoration'. A Rearhook variant from Tharston and Hapton has a delicately inscribed catchplate and zoomorphic bow, perhaps representing a swan or even a horse (PAS: NMS-FB0840) (Figure 3.66). Lastly, a very elaborate and devolved hinged version from Lackford has sharp-cornered enamelled triangles (PAS: SF-CF2A24) (Figure 3.67).

These brooches, like the Rosettes, were large, ornate and costly to produce (Hattatt 1982: 99-100). Their display potential means they would have been recognisable at a distance. The aesthetic choice of 'Celtic' decoration may have been deliberately conservative. This phenomenon will also be seen in the conquest period horse harness in chapter eight.

3.11.2. Colchester Derivative: Polden Hill

Polden Hills are post-conquest, British-made brooches (Bayley 1989: 180).[10] They cluster in southeast Suffolk (Figure 3.68, Figure 3.69, Table 3.5): Charsfield (10) and

---

[10] True Polden Hill brooches are a West Country type, rarely found in East Anglia. This leads to ambiguities in recording. It is impossible to tell, without images, whether the recorder meant a Colchester Derivative with Polden Hill spring or a true Polden Hill brooch. Given their rarity in the east, it has been assumed that those recorded without further elaboration are Colchester Derivatives.

Wenhaston (23), although there are fewer from nearby Hacheston (7) and surprisingly only one from Coddenham. 'Polden Hill' describes a spring system with semi-cylindrical wings, enclosed by cast on end-plates which secure the axis bar (Figure 3.70). This may have been an attempt to rectify the inbuilt flaw of the Rearhook brooch. Earlier variants have the Rearhook; on later examples the spring is held by a pierced crest. Polden Hills date *circa* 70-170 CE (Hattatt 1982: 69; Mackreth 2011: 69).

Eastern Suffolk increases in importance in the late first/ second centuries CE, perhaps reflecting the development of the East-West road network which linked coastal ports and salt production sites on the eastern seaboard to regional market towns and further afield. Plouviez's distributions of Polden Hills are heavily accented towards this area and my wider dataset corroborates her findings. A distinctive subset, with Rearhooks and folded wing-end flaps, occurs at Scole, and is potentially the work of a single craftsperson (Mackreth 2011: 78; Plouviez 2014: 35-41). Several brooches are recorded as hybrids with either lugged or hinged fixing arrangements. These include two from the Snettisham area (NHER: 23001, NHER: 1554) and one from Freckenham (PAS: SF11136). A hybrid from Wenhaston exhibits a combination of hinged bow design, Rearhook and Scole-type moulded wing-ends (PAS: SF-057E25) (Figure 3.71). Plouviez places a workshop within south and east Suffolk 'on the southern edge of the Icenian area where the rear hook type of Colchester derivative is dominant' (2014: 40).

The now familiar clusters around Fincham in west Norfolk and southeast Suffolk are persistent concentration zones in the early part of the brooch sequence. These must represent production and deposition patterns in the first centuries BCE/CE, as well as successful metal-detecting. Polden Hills are distinctly post-revolt in date and if there had been systematic depopulation of Icenian centres of settlement, these sites would not be expected to show concentrations of later first century CE brooches. Many Polden Hill brooches were still using the Rearhook spring system and co-existed with hinged Colchester Derivatives and Trumpet types. People did not abandon the Rearhook, but applied it to new and experimental variants. Mackreth's attribution of the Rearhook's decline to the destruction of the Iceni population and the redeployment of its metalworkers is not borne out. Continuity, and indeed innovation, in brooches at these sites contradicts the 'harrying of the east' narrative.

3.11.3. Colchester Derivative: Hinged

Hinged pins run concurrently with springs on certain types of brooch from the Colchester onwards (Hattatt 1982: 39) (Figure 3.72), becoming the most common fixing method in East Anglia. They belong to the second half of the first century CE to mid-second century CE. Plouviez's comparative analysis of brooch proportions from different regions shows that all the Colchester Derivative types (Harlow, Hinged and Rearhook) are concentrated in East Anglia (2008: 173, fig. 4.1.2).

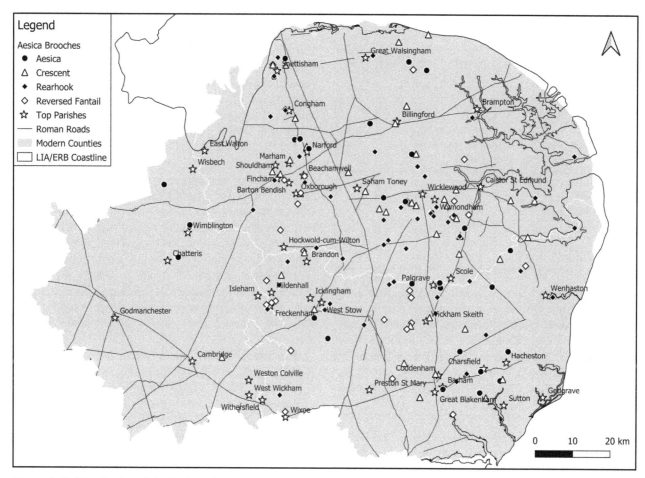

Figure 3.62. Distribution of Aesica brooches and variants.

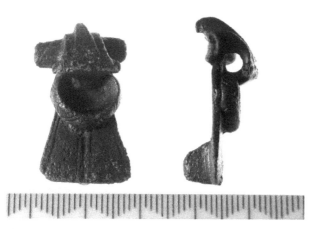

Figure 3.63. Aesica brooch, Crescent variant, Little Wilbraham (PAS: SF-15F370).

These brooches form almost 10 per cent of the dataset (Table 3.5); Suffolk is the clear focus (Figure 3.73). Hotspots include Coddenham (22), Hacheston (26) and Charsfield (46), but these are far outstripped by Wenhaston with 116 hinged Colchester Derivatives. Almost all derive from just two fields immediately on and around the Roman town (SHER: WMH004, WMH005) (Figure 3.74). The huge numbers from such a small area must surely represent a manufacturing or distribution centre (see section 3.14.7).

A second tier of parishes in Norfolk includes Beachamwell, Caistor St Edmund, Scole, Walsingham and Saham Toney. Mackreth records many hinged Colchester Derivative brooches from Norfolk – his highest proportion by county – but very few from Suffolk, which is contradicted by my findings (2011: 82-88). Mackreth calls Suffolk 'a black hole' in his catalogue, compared to Norfolk and Essex. At least half of my dataset comes from the PAS, which may explain this discrepancy, as Mackreth's data collection closed in 2004, when the PAS was in its infancy (*ibid.*: 3-4).

According to Mackreth, the Rearhook was abandoned and replaced with hinged brooches which spread into the surrounding areas (2009: 146). However, the Polden Hill brooch used a Rearhook fixing and the Harlow brooch continued into the late first century CE. Manufacturers clearly understood the weakness of the Rearhook (section 3.3.1) which was particularly susceptible to failure in use, and took steps to produce more efficient alternatives. Different pin fixings provide various mechanical benefits and drawbacks. Hinged pins were more reliable to produce, as spring coils are prone to snapping during shaping (Adams 2013: 81-84). In use, however, hinged pins are placed under less tension and liable to greater accidental loss. The makers of brooches must have weighed up the technical advantages and weaknesses of each option. Hinge mechanisms were the fitting of choice

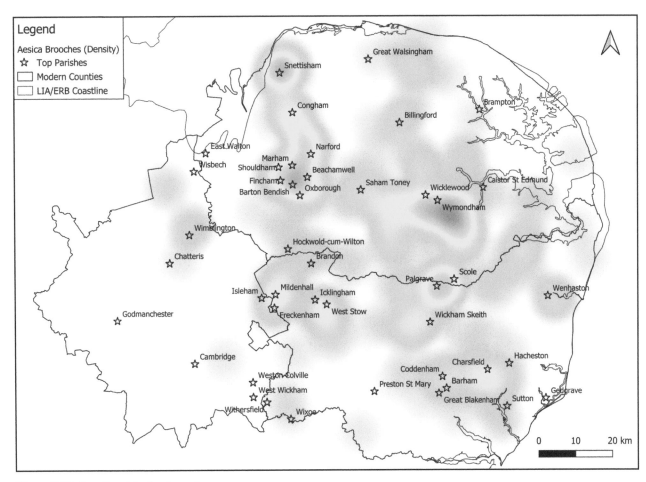

Figure 3.64. Density of Aesica brooches.

Figure 3.65. Unusual Aesica brooch with Rearhook, Wacton (PAS: NMS-459FA7).

for most plate brooches (section 3.12.1), which were more decorative and less functional. Perhaps it was driven by the preference of the wearer. Perhaps some brooches were simply 'meant' to have springs, which would fit with the simulated pseudo-spring types discussed in section 3.6. The role of the sprung bow brooch may extend beyond pure practicality as a fastener, for ornamental or even symbolic reasons.

Hinged brooches show that innovation could occur in very restricted locations, perhaps resulting from a single workshop or distribution centre. Wenhaston shows considerable evidence for development of just such a hub. Polden Hill and Hinged Colchester Derivatives improved upon the failings of the Rearhook, but retained the decorative preferences of Rearhook and Harlow brooches respectively.

Figure 3.66. Hybrid Rearhook/Aesica brooch with zoomorphic bow, Tharston and Hapton (PAS: NMS-FB0840).

Figure 3.67. Unusual enamelled Aesica variant, Lackford (PAS: SF-CF2A24).

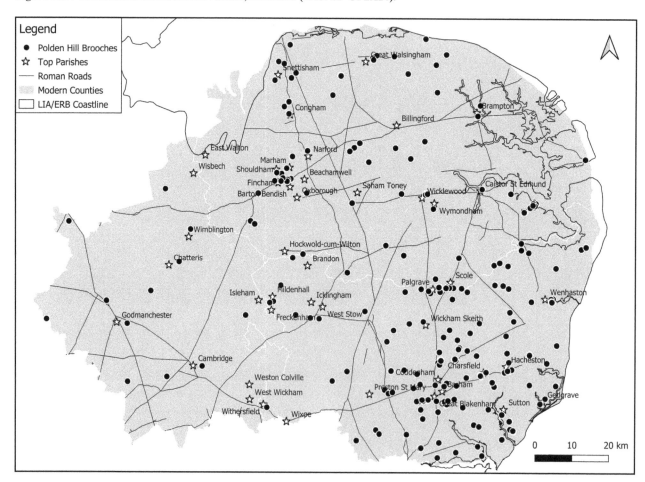

Figure 3.68. Distribution of Colchester Derivative Polden Hill brooches.

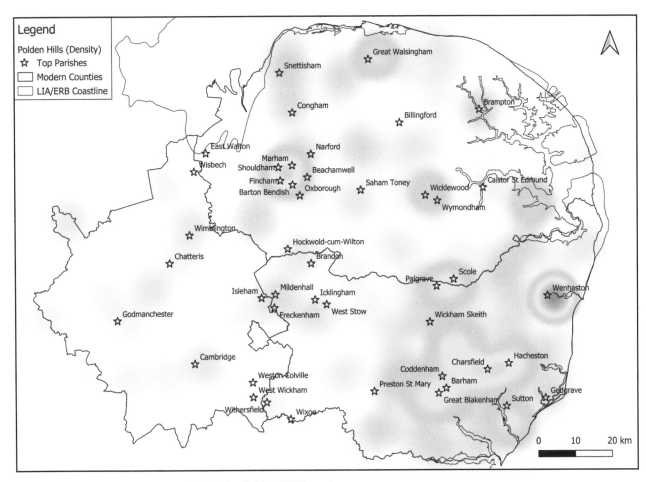

Figure 3.69. Density of Colchester Derivative Polden Hill brooches.

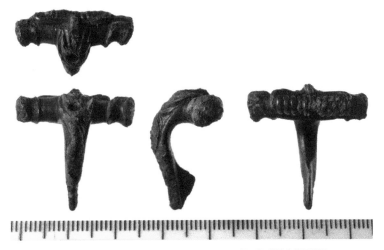

Figure 3.70. Polden Hill brooch with curvilinear decoration, Hacheston (PAS: SF-2477CB).

Figure 3.71. Hybrid Polden Hill brooch, Wenhaston (PAS: SF-057E25).

Figure 3.72. Colchester Derivative Hinged brooch, Wenhaston (PAS: SF-21FF06).

65

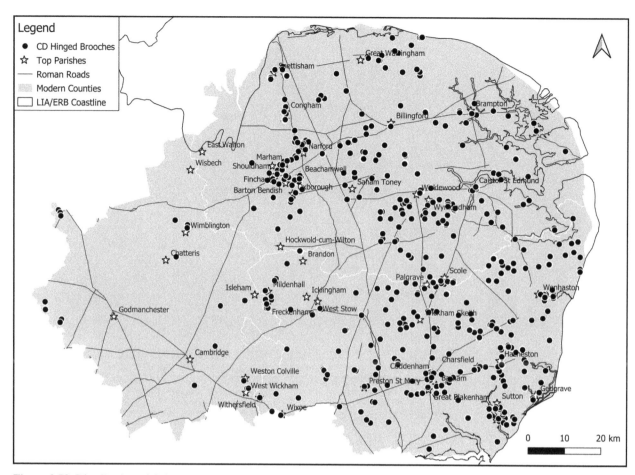

Figure 3.73. Distribution of Colchester Derivative Hinged brooches.

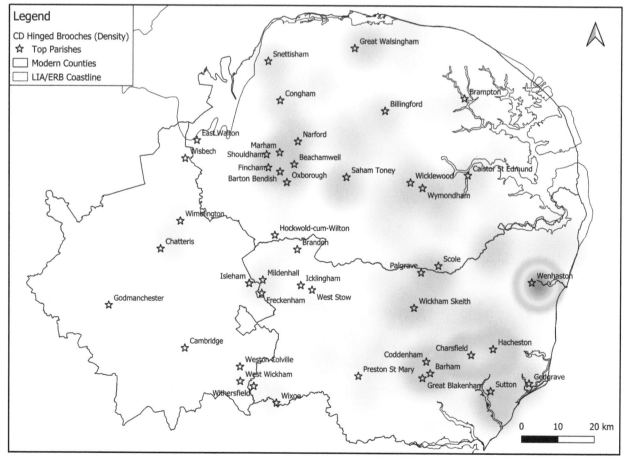

Figure 3.74. Density of Colchester Derivative Hinged brooches.

3.11.4. Headstud and Trumpet Brooches

Headstuds developed from the Colchester brooch, commonly featuring a separate spring, a cast-on headloop and an enamelled lattice on the bow (Figure 3.75). They date from the Claudian period onward, but are generally late first/second century CE, with a *floruit* 75-120 CE. Both sprung and hinged varieties are common, the hinged versions being slightly later. The distribution is wide, generally in the east and south (Hattatt 1982: 74; Mackreth 2011: 103-13).

Early Trumpet brooches were imported in the mid-first century CE. They were soon adopted and adapted by local craftspeople, flourishing in the late first/second centuries CE. The British Trumpet is a two-piece brooch, with a single spring fixing loop behind the head; occasionally hinged (Figure 3.76). The diagnostic features are the wide circular head and the mid-bow moulding, usually described as petals or 'acanthus' leaves. Trumpet brooches are often highly embellished with enamelled decoration, occasionally in curvilinear 'Celtic' swirls (Hattatt 1982: 40, 104-5; Mackreth 2011: 114-15).

For both Headstud and Trumpet brooches the county figures are similar. Norfolk and Suffolk have roughly equal quantities and as usual Cambridgeshire lags behind (Table 3.5). Concentrations of both types occur at remarkably similar locations: Caistor St Edmund, Saham Toney, Scole, Walsingham, Wicklewood, Charsfield, Coddenham and Wenhaston (Figure 3.77, Figure 3.78, Figure 3.79). These are mostly towns, some containing a religious focus. This may demonstrate a preference for wearing more elaborate ornament in urban areas, combined with population densities. As with the Polden Hill brooches (section 3.11.2), there is a shift in emphasis towards the southeast of the region in the later first/second centuries CE. Hacheston and Pakenham have more Trumpets than Headstuds. Mackreth attributes strong showings of some Trumpet subtypes in

Norfolk to recovery bias (2011: 116). Cool and Baxter point to metal-detector bias in recovery of Trumpet brooches causing a secondary peak in East Anglia in the late second/early third century CE (2016a: 86). The Suffolk figures in my dataset calibrate Mackreth's high numbers from Norfolk, and to some extent contradict this assertion.

There are some differences: of those which it was possible to identify, approximately 80 per cent of Headstuds are hinged, in contrast to only 20 per cent of Trumpet brooches (Figure 3.80, Figure 3.81). This illustrates an element of choice in the brooches on offer, but it is not one of geographical distinction. It may denote preference in the workshop traditions of the manufacturers of these two types. Headstud brooches may be creolised artefacts, combining indigenous and Roman aesthetics with colourful and ostentatious decoration. They show the decorative shift, which is also evident in horse harness, from monochrome curvilinear to geometric polychrome enamelling (Hattatt 1982: 74; Webb 2011: 13). Trumpet and Aesica brooches seem to retain pre-conquest metalwork styles (MacGregor, M. 1976: 124) and do not change to the more symmetrical decorative scheme. This suggests that some metalworkers were adapting their styles based on the prevailing fashions.

Both Headstud and Trumpet brooches often have chain-loops, suggesting they were worn in linked pairs. Cool considers these as gendered artefacts, relating to women's fashion in the later first/second centuries CE, based on art history and grave goods from elsewhere in the empire. She connects the chain-loops to wearing of a tube dress (the *peplos*) which was pinned at each shoulder. Men only wore a single brooch on one shoulder. Cool regards headloop brooches as a British response to changing costumes and the development of a 'new visual identity' for Romano-British women. Brooches with chain-loops decline (like most *fibulae*) in the mid-late second century CE, which again may reflect shifts in fashion and identity,

Figure 3.75. Headstud brooch, Lakenheath (PAS: SF-7CE16B).

Figure 3.76. Trumpet brooch, Brooke (PAS: SF-DF8AE2).

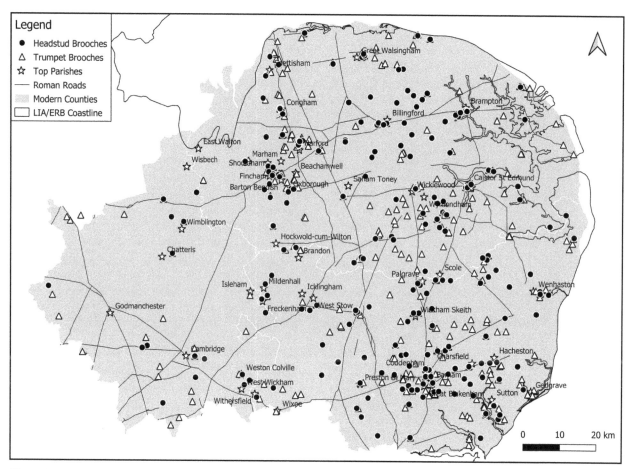

Figure 3.77: Distribution of Trumpet and Headstud brooches.

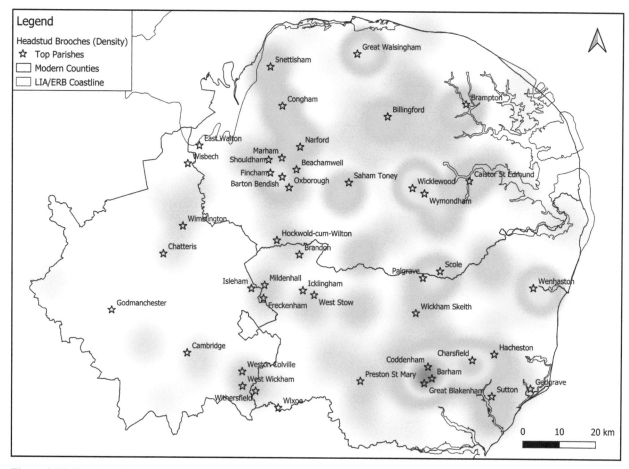

Figure 3.78. Density of Headstud brooches.

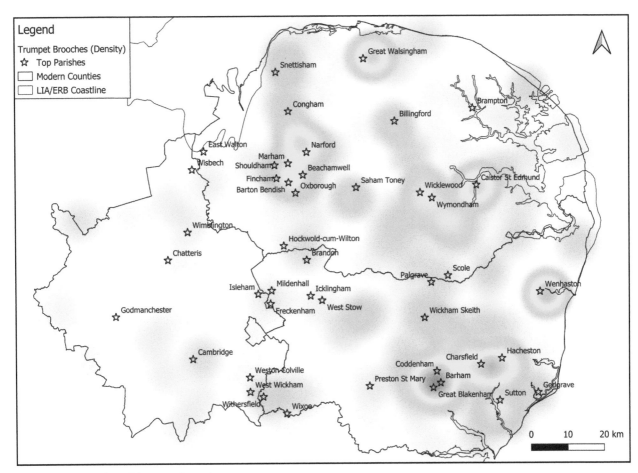

Figure 3.79. Density of Trumpet brooches.

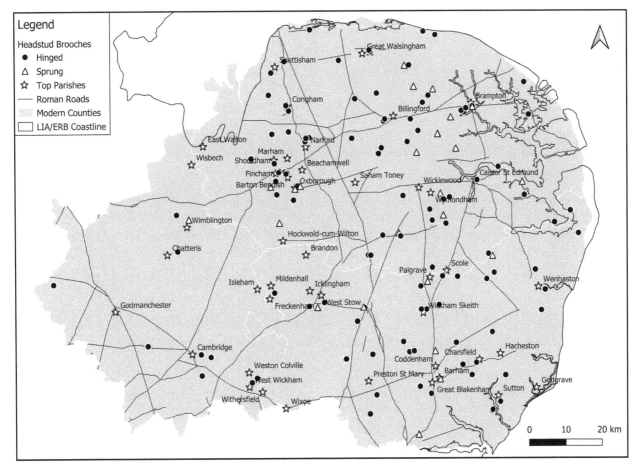

Figure 3.80. Distribution of hinged and sprung Headstud brooches.

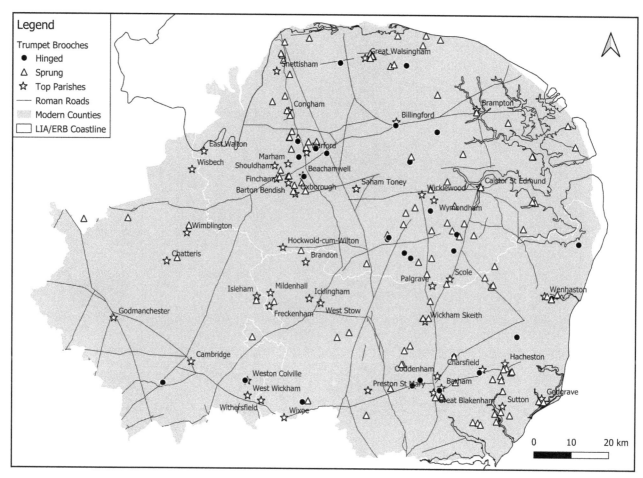

Figure 3.81. Distribution of hinged and sprung Trumpet brooches.

with women perhaps taking up the Gallic coat (2016: 413-15). Although Cool claims there is no precedent for the headloop in the LIA/early Roman period, I would argue that penannular brooches were worn in pairs and this may be a sign of continuing British practices with new material culture. Mackreth also points out that only brooches found in pairs should be attributed to women's dress, as single brooches with chain-loops may have been worn to hold a cloak and sewn to the fabric (2011: 234-35).

Headstuds and Trumpets also demonstrate the mobility of the settlement pattern. The centres around Fincham and Coddenham are still active, but a new focus emerges in Norfolk around *Venta Icenorum* and Wicklewood, with the foundation of the *civitas* capital and probable extensions to the road network in this area. The late appearance of *Venta Icenorum* in the brooch densities may have several explanations, least of all because of 'the conservative character of the Iceni' (Atkinson 1932: 42). The absence of early brooches from the town suggests that it was not an *oppidum*, although it is possible there is an unexcavated LIA centre in the vicinity (see section 3.14.11). The concentrations of Trumpet and plate brooches also fit with the archaeological evidence, which indicates the formal town developed in the early second century CE (Bowden 2013: 165). There are numerous undated and, as yet unpublished, brooches from the early excavations which may have skewed this sample (Harlow in Bowden forthcoming).

3.11.5. Zoomorphic

Zoomorphic brooches depict a veritable menagerie, dating *circa* 50-150 CE in Britain, although they can be long-lived. Mammals, avians, insects and denizens of the sea are portrayed. Some zoomorphic brooches are thought to display overt religious messages and may signal devotion to specific deities. Zoomorphic figurines and brooches may have acted as votive replacements for sacrificial animals, or signified the god in animal form. There are British variants with strongly indigenous styling. Some have an eastern distribution, although this may result from metal-detecting bias (Hattatt 1982: 158, 160; Mackreth 2011: 181-86; Marsden 2012: 58-61, 2014: 66).

The most frequently represented are birds: ducks, geese, chickens (both hens and cocks), birds of prey and more exotic species. Ducks and cockerels connect the brooches to seal-boxes and cosmetic grinders. Peacocks were associated with the goddess Juno (Toynbee 1973: 251), and while cockerels symbolised Mercury (Crummy 2011: 66), I would argue that most zoomorphics are not overtly gendered. There are 103 bird brooches from the study zone, including 48 ducks and 20 chickens (Figure 3.82, Figure 3.83). They can be depicted swimming, sitting or in flight, sometimes with three-dimensional heads and wings (Figure 3.84, Figure 3.85). A miscast chicken brooch from Poslingford demonstrates local manufacture.

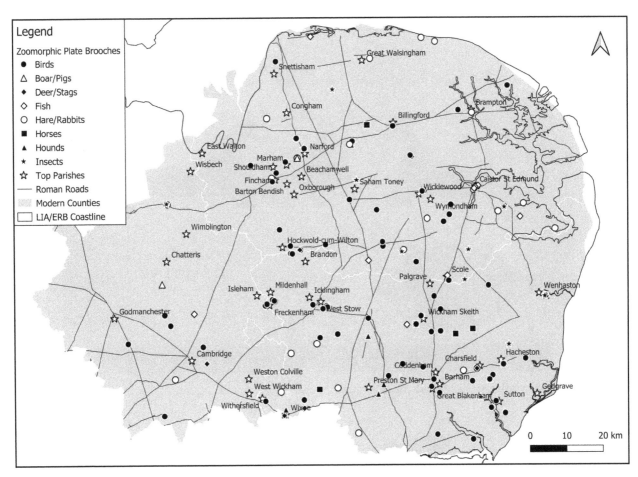

Figure 3.82. Distribution of Zoomorphic brooches by type.

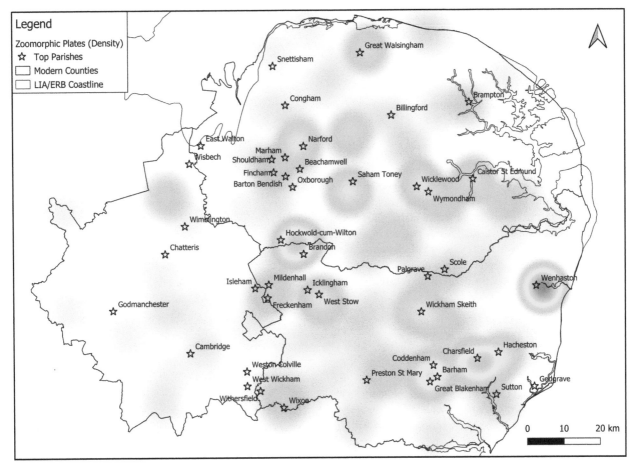

Figure 3.83. Density of Zoomorphic brooches.

Figure 3.84. 3D enamelled waterbird brooch, Brandon (PAS: SF-F3AFA9).

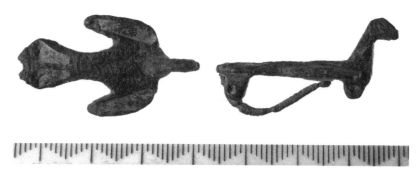

Figure 3.85. Bird in flight brooch, South Elmham St Margaret (PAS: SF-058774).

The concave underside is filled with fired grey clay, part of the original mould (PAS: SF-7821E2) (Figure 3.86). Many of these brooches have a small cast-in loop on the bird's tail for affixing to clothing or chaining in pairs, perhaps suggesting a link to female attire (Cool 2016: 413; Johns 1995: 107). Johns astutely notes that powerful animals such as rams, bulls and wild boar, often shown in both Roman and British art, rarely feature on brooches (1995: 106). This is in clear contrast to cosmetic grinders, for example (section 5.3.2).

There also seem to be rules of fittingness for different species. Ducks show evidence for continuity. Davies includes the duck and swan in his 'Norfolk menagerie' along with iconic creatures like boars and wolves which appear on Icenian coinage (2011a). Green claims that swans and ducks were associated with 'Celtic' water or solar cults (1976: 5, 1978: 24), although there is little to substantiate this idea. Waterbirds were especially popular in the eastern counties, on brooches, drinking vessels and cosmetic grinders, yet they were not sacred to any specific

deity (Marsden 2012: 60, 2014: 66). Along with bulls and dogs, they have links to healing and may represent curative aspects (Morrison 2013: 228-29). Ducks are modelled on vessels in the Crownthorpe and Santon hoards (Davies 2011a: 64-65) (section 2.3.6; Figure 2.4).

A rare owl brooch, with an enamelled 'torc' around its neck, was found at Caistor St Edmund (Gurney 2003: 360; NHER: 9791), reportedly identical to Hattatt's #1154 (1987) also from Norfolk. Owls were sacred to Minerva (Toynbee 1973: 251), the goddess of wisdom and learning. Wearing a torc or collar may perhaps symbolise the bird's domestication, or the status ascribed to knowledge. Conversely, the collar may simply be a decorative device representing feathers.

Hare brooches are found across the northern provinces and in south-central Britain. They are usually depicted running or crouching, sometimes with a pair of leverets, reminiscent of the Wolf and Twins or the *Dea Nutrix* with her paired infants (section 6.8.1). Like brooches depicting

Figure 3.86. Miscast chicken brooch, Poslingford (PAS: SF-7821E2).

a Horse-and-rider (see below), an eastern group is focussed on Norfolk, Leicestershire and Lincolnshire, 'suggesting that a hare-deity was worshipped chiefly in those regions' (Crummy 2013: 121). This may be an assumption based on Boudica's use of a hare for divination in Dio's account of the rebellion (*Hist. Rom.* 62.6.1). However, I would be wary of automatic identification of animals with deities rather than prey or as individual beings. In Roman religion, hares were sometimes sacrificed at temples and the brooches have been posited as votive substitutes (Crummy 2013: 122). Hare brooches have been found at or near temple sites at Hockwold-cum-Wilton, Walsingham, Charsfield and *Venta Icenorum*.

Hunting and prey-predator scenes were important in Roman art. Dogs were associated with hunter-gods like Diana and Silvanus and as familiars of the healer-god Asclepius. Running hound brooches may depict hunting dogs (Johns 1995: 105), famously an export of Britain, according to Strabo (*Geog.* 4.5.2). Norfolk and Suffolk have more hares than hounds, although they can be difficult to distinguish (Mackreth 2011: 182-83) (Figure 3.87, Figure 3.88). A single example of the rare 'hound chasing a hare' type is known from Wickham Skeith (PAS: SF-B857C1). These are later first century CE imports, the theme of predation supposedly having military connotations (Brown PAS: SF-B857C1).

Another predation scene is the raptor devouring its catch, usually identified as an eagle and hare. Eagles were sacred

Figure 3.87. Hare plate brooch, Ousden (PAS: SF-93372E).

Figure 3.88. Hound plate brooch, Kedington (PAS: SF-FE1338).

to Jupiter in the Roman cosmology (Johns 1995: 106). Crummy notes a concentration 'among the Iceni' (2013: 121). These are not urban finds; some derive from rural sanctuaries. There are five from the study area: Hockwold-cum-Wilton (NWHCM: 1961.199.57), Witton (PAS: NMS-116425), Worlington (PAS: SF-BAD294) (Figure 3.89), Wetheringsett-cum-Brockford (SHER: WCB048) and Papworth Everard (CHER: SCB21418). The Worlington and Hockwold examples are so similar, they may come from the same mould, and the sprung construction suggests indigenous production (Plouviez PAS: SF-BAD294). There are also two eagle brooches from Braiseworth (PAS: SF-3AB971) and Narford (PAS: NMS-56DB25).

Creatures of the waters, including fish, dolphins and the mythical hippocamp, also feature in this zoomorphic repertoire. Fish are uncommon, with eight of the 12 brooches recorded in Norfolk. Two come from northeast of

the *civitas* capital, possibly from near a spring, and a third from the far side of the extra-mural temple (Figure 3.90, Figure 3.91). A tentative fourth identification comes from within the town, on a road leading to the temple. Marsden proposes that fish brooches may be related to Neptune, named on a *defixio* from the River Tas at *Venta* (2014: 68) (section 7.3.2). Again, I would question the simple association of animals with gods and goddesses. Brooches may have represented part of a complex understanding of living beings and their roles in the natural and spiritual worlds, which were not clearly divided.

Depictions of animals and predation may also have been related to changes in cuisine. The 'creolisation of food' can be part of the negotiation of new identities (Hawkes 1999; Webster 2001: 218). Diet is one of the longest-lasting cultural attributes in colonial situations and diasporas, distinguishing locals from newcomers. Fish bones are very rare on Iron Age sites, becoming more common in post-conquest faunal assemblages, particularly on 'higher status' settlements. Taboos against fish-eating, past and present, are widespread. In Iron Age Britain, killing and consumption of symbolically 'wild' or impure creatures may have been culturally proscribed (Dobney and Ervynck 2007). Disposal of some human remains may have taken place in water; therefore, a sacred/polluted status may explain the lack of fish consumption (Booth and Madgwick 2016; Sykes 2014: 65).

Caesar (*BG* 5.11) references a British prohibition on eating hare, chickens and geese. Chickens were popularised as a food item in Britain by Mediterranean incomers (Sykes 2014: 84-88). Perhaps a change in diet and everyday exposure to these creatures was absorbed into the artistic lexicon. Wearing a chicken brooch may have been a statement of adherence to the cult of Mercury or a sign of new cuisine. Perhaps making an offering representing an impure animal lifted the taboo of killing and eating them. Hare and rabbit remains are also rare on pre-conquest sites, with little evidence of butchery, and at Romano-British rural sites and small towns, but Crummy found a high incidence in large towns and villas: 'Developing a taste for hare may have been another way in which some Britons became Roman, while others may have continued to regard the animal as taboo' (2013: 111-19).

Figure 3.89. Raptor-and-prey brooch, Worlington (PAS: SF-BAD294).

Figure 3.90. Fish brooch, Caistor St Edmund (PAS: NMS-A9F35F).

Davies's 'Celtic menagerie' (2011a) was depleted by the time plate brooches became popular in the second century CE. These share a different, more classical, iconography with the animals depicted on intaglio rings, although deities do not appear on brooches. Large, dangerous beasts like wolves, boars and bovids are infrequent. Alongside the Iron Age waterbirds, we now have more representations of chickens and hares. A different preoccupation with prey animals or the domestication of previously wild species is implied (see Sykes 2014: 84-91 on the introduction of new edible species). Changes occurred in religious behaviour, diet and the representation of animals. This fusion of old and new, indigenous and imported, indicates that the *civitas* was changing with the times.

3.11.6. Horse-and-Rider

While zoomorphic plate brooches are common, anthropomorphic representations are incredibly rare. Despite many small *personalia* (such as intaglio rings) depicting the classical pantheon, gods and goddesses never appear on brooches (Johns 1995: 104). Perhaps the exception to this rule is the Horse-and-rider. These brooches are widespread across East Anglia and the Midlands (Figure 3.92). Mackreth's Type 2.1 is the standard, usually with the applied white metal trim and bilateral spring denoting British-made brooches (Figure 3.93). Others portray the horse without its human burden

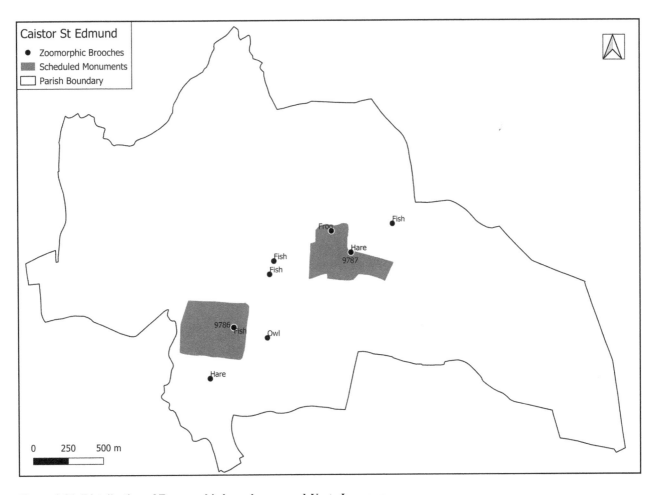

Figure 3.91. Distribution of Zoomorphic brooches around *Venta Icenorum.*

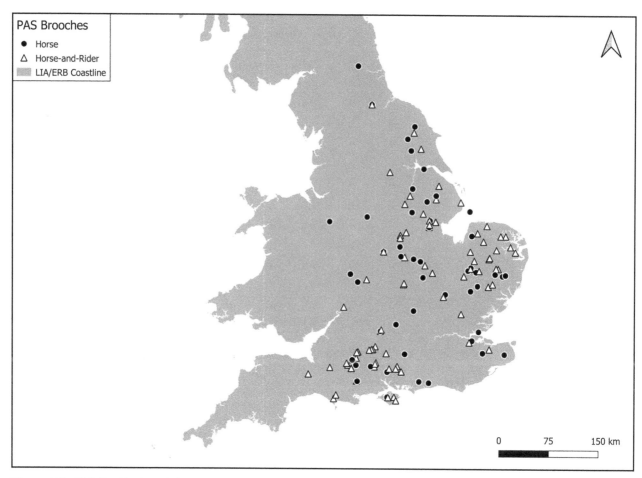

Figure 3.92. PAS distribution of Horse-and-rider brooches.

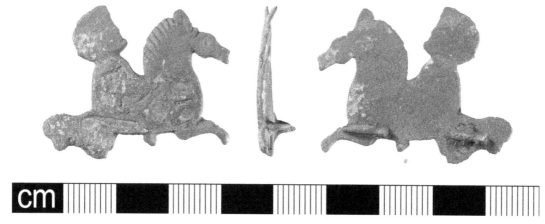

Figure 3.93. Horse-and-Rider brooch, Easton (PAS: BH-46CD64).

(Figure 3.94). The 'baton-holder' variant depicts the rider grasping an upright staff (2011: 181-82) (PAS: NMS-B9CE17). Continental variants are also found in Gaul in some numbers (Feugère 1985: 414 Type 29b1).

There are 68 equine brooches from the *civitas Icenorum* (Table 3.5) (Figure 3.95). A group of 10 Horse-and-riders comes from the religious complex at Leyland's Farm, Hockwold-cum-Wilton (NHER: 5587, NWHCM: 1961.199), with another small group from near Crownthorpe temple (NHER: 8897/18111). Three Horse-

and-rider brooches and a miniature axe were found in a hoard at Grandford (CHER: 03936) (see chapter six). These finds all evoke ritual usage in the life of these brooches.

About 34 per cent of brooches from Woodcock Hall, Saham Toney (NHER: 4697) had been 'mutilated' - crushed, broken or cut in half (Brown 1986). One of two very similar Horse-and-riders has its catchplate and pin 'crushed' (*ibid.*: 38-39, fig. 25). There is no evidence of brooch manufacture at Woodcock Hall, but bronze-

Figure 3.94. Horse brooch, Debenham (PAS: SF-D19B27).

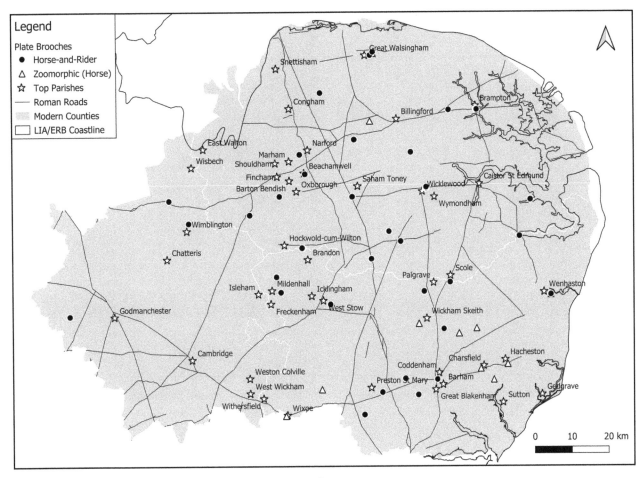

Figure 3.95. Distribution of Horse-and-rider and Horse brooches.

smelting occurred across the site. Although this might simply reflect recycling processes, Brown observed that some pieces were bigger than a standard crucible, and even the smallest brooches were seemingly 'deactivated'. It is tempting here to posit a reading of 'ritual killing' of metalwork which would fit with the deposition of many of the artefacts in water.

Although zoomorphic brooches are generally late first/ second century CE, Horse-and-rider brooches are long-lived, excavated predominantly in third/fourth century CE contexts. The short pins and tight fit between pin and plate indicate a display rather than functional role. The social distribution includes temples, small towns and rural settlements (Eckardt 2005: 148; Fillery-Travis 2012). An 'internationally significant assemblage' of equine brooches (93 Horse-and-rider and eight horse brooches) was recovered at Bosworth, Leicestershire. A high proportion were 'Baton-holders'. These may represent messengers, symbolically carrying votive communications, or a military association with Mars. Excavations in 2013 revealed a stone-built circular temple, dated second century CE to Late Roman (Scott 2017). Horse-and-rider brooches with the legend IOVIS or IOVE are associated with the military of the *limes* in the Low Countries (Heeren and van der Feijst 2017: 162).

Riders on horseback are often presumed to portray warriors or hunters. Mackreth links Horse-and-rider, raptor-and-prey and *Adlocutio* brooches to a probable hunter-god cult at religious centres like Cold Kitchen Hill and Hockwold-cum-Wilton (2011: 182, 241). The Hockwold brooches are so similar that they were possibly manufactured in the same mould, perhaps specifically for dedication (Mackreth in Gurney 1986: 65-66). Horse-and-rider and other brooches were possibly manufactured on site at 'temple service areas' (Davies and Gregory 1991: 40), which may be apparent at Walsingham and Caistor Paddocks. The Bosworth brooches are morphologically very diverse, cast in numerous moulds and enamelled with several colour combinations (Figure 3.96).[11] This might suggest that at Bosworth, unlike at Hockwold, people arrived with different brooches from multiple workshops and deposited them together. This is reminiscent of ideas about the multiple authorship of hoards of torcs and harness (Garrow and Gosden 2012; Joy 2016) (section 4.6, section 8.10). Alternatively, these could represent different moulds and craftspeople working at the site over decades or even centuries.[12]

Figure 3.96. Horse-and-Rider brooch, Bosworth (PAS: LEIC-D601A4).

Suffolk shows a higher proportion of horse brooches without riders (Suffolk 10, Norfolk 2 and Cambridgeshire 1 uncertain).[13] Unlike the rider types, these do not cluster around temples. Mackreth's emphasis on Norfolk is certainly balanced out by Suffolk in my analysis. He muses whether they reflect two distinct deities or a local horse-breeding economy (2011: 182, 241). Norfolk and parts of Suffolk are interpreted as important areas for horse-breeding and training (Davies 2014: 31), with concentrations of harness and chariot gear (chapter eight). Equine figurines from Norfolk may show 'a continued interest in the raising of horses in the Roman period' (Marsden 2014: 55).

The horse is not attributed to any Graeco-Roman deity, although Epona is portrayed as a 'Celtic' Mother-Goddess

associated with the protection and fertility of horses (Mackintosh 1995: 1, 29). Fillery-Travis is sceptical that the figure on the brooches is Epona, as the iconography is not considered female (2012: 141) and besides, this horse goddess is very rarely represented in Britannia (Mackintosh 1995: 30-31). I would argue the riders are ambiguously gendered, though some have indistinct facial markings which could denote beards. Johns makes a tenuous connection with an indigenous version of the war-god Mars, allied to agricultural fertility (1995: 105; Scott 2017). Mars is not a commonly represented god in East Anglia, which fits with other evidence for the light garrisoning of Roman Norfolk (Marsden 2012: 57) (section 3.9). The military iconography is questionable and the horse itself is clearly of importance (Fillery-Travis 2012: 142-43).

Horse and eagle brooches are often identified as badges of identity signalling affiliation to a 'provincial Rider-god', syncretised with Jupiter (Crummy 2011: 61, 2013: 122; Fillery-Travis 2012: 135-41; Johns 1995: 105; Mackintosh 1995: 20; Marsden 2014: 66-67). Green links horse and wheel symbols on Iron Age coins to figurines of the supposed Gaulish wheel-god Taranis, associating the horse with the god, thereby the 'Divine Rider' (1976:

[11] Wendy Scott, former FLO, Leicestershire County Council (pers. comm. 26/04/2017).

[12] A. Marsden (pers. comm. 09/12/2017).

[13] This may be a data collection issue. Mackreth numbers four from Norfolk: Two are unprovenanced from Hattatt's collection, the one from 'Walsingham/Wighton' is most likely the one on my database and the fourth from Fincham I have been unable to locate. The example from Cotton, Suffolk, (PAS: SF-2BE766) is broken behind the neck. As there is no sign of a rider, it has been included here.

9, 30; 1984: 40-41). Evidence for connecting this god with Taranis is 'meagre and problematical', although a mounted Jupiter is a possible candidate for the figurines (Mackintosh 1995: 21).

British rider brooches have no continental parallels or associations with any known deity, neither are they found with bronze rider figurines (Mackintosh 1995: 17), which are largely restricted to Cambridgeshire, Leicestershire, Northamptonshire and south Lincolnshire. There are at least six riderless horse figurines from Norfolk on PAS. Marsden does not favour the idea they were worn as pilgrim badges, as Johns suggests (1996b: 174), or any of the proposed identifications for the deity, simply noting the character's popularity across the Midlands and eastern England (2014: 66-67). I applaud Marsden's archaeology-first view, which resists the urge to fit the artefacts into the available pantheon. Horse-ownership or riding skill may have been more significant than any divine personification. Stereotypes that men (or male gods) are always war-like and women are forever associated with fertility, even that of animals in the case of Epona, still need to be challenged. The Horse-and-rider brooches may equally have been offerings given for luck during a rite of passage, or even a contest, for young horses and their riders.

The discovery of a new focus of religious and manufacturing activity at Bosworth changes our understanding of Horse-and-rider brooches. Their distribution and deposition around votive foci is linked to personal dedicatory practices (Fillery-Travis 2012: 135-41). The popularity of rider brooches and the absence of figurines in Norfolk may also imply regional discrepancy in devotional practice. Like the hare brooches, the distribution stretches from Leicestershire, across Lincolnshire, into Norfolk, perhaps indicating a shift in the contemporary connections of the *civitas*.

3.12. What is the evidence for cultural resistance?

In this section, I consider the evidence for cultural resistance through brooches. Which Iron Age cultural identifiers (Davies 2011b: 104) show continuity into the client-kingdom and beyond? Key issues include the selectivity of materials and choices of metals, colours and enamelling, aesthetics and the importance of decoration, ritual behaviour and votive deposition, and the role of display.

3.12.1. Plate Brooches

One of the significant differences between bow and plate brooches is the amount of fabric which could be held behind the pin. Pierced catchplates on bow brooches could also have been sewn onto the cloth for added security. Plate brooches would have been of limited use to fasten thick cloth and were probably worn for their decorative effect, more like badges than buttons (Johns 1995: 103). Despite this, their votive deposition implies they embodied more than simple ornament. Mackreth proposes that lightweight brooches were less suitable for ordinary working people,

perhaps shedding light on class differences (2011: 235). I would add that this may be evidence for the start of changes in everyday attire which eventually resulted in the abandonment of brooches (section 3.2.2).

Plate brooches are one of the most common types in my database, around 14 per cent of the total (Table 3.6). They may be preferentially recovered by metal-detectorists given their large surface area, as long as they are orientated suitably in the ground. There are roughly equal numbers from Norfolk and Suffolk, with few from Cambridgeshire and the Fens, which fits the general trend throughout (Figure 3.97, Figure 3.98). Concentrations occur at Saham Toney (44), Wicklewood (38), Charsfield (35), Coddenham (46) and Hacheston (44). Walsingham (35 per cent) and Hockwold (55 per cent) have a disproportionate number of plate brooches. Caistor St Edmund, Stonea (Wimblington) and Wenhaston all have 20 per cent plate brooches. Many of these are small towns with religious foci and early-mid Roman occupation (see section 3.14). Mackreth frequently notes a heavy bias towards East Anglia in plate brooches, which he explains is due to an uneven data collection policy (e.g. 2011: 168). When the body of metal-detected finds is considered, this issue resolves itself, with plate brooches being one of the most widely distributed types on PAS (Figure 3.99).

Plate brooches in Britain can be pre-conquest, although most are mid-first/second centuries CE. The early types are simple, unenamelled discs often with repoussé decoration, followed by lunular or flat enamelled discs (Figure 3.100). Plates are ordinarily hinged, and later examples are often elaborately enamelled or gilded. Feugère noted that in Britain, enamelling was maintained consistently throughout the Iron Age and Roman periods, with numerous enamelled artefacts being produced, though these were only rarely exported to the continent (1985: 358). Mackreth divides the numerous plate brooches into imported and indigenous types. Continental workshops rarely used the sprung pin, unlike the British manufactories. Some types of brooches are found, by this logic, to have been made both in Britain and abroad, such as sandal-sole brooches (Hattatt 1982: 148; Mackreth 2011: 154-80) (section 3.12.4).

3.12.2. Disc Brooches

Disc brooches come in a wide variety of shapes and designs (Figure 3.101, Figure 3.102). These are particularly

Table 3.6. Plate brooches by county and type

Brooch Type	Cambs	Norfolk	Suffolk	Total
Plate	134	728	714	1576
Disc	69	254	272	595
Dragonesque	1	8	20	29
Skeuomorphic	1	19	26	46

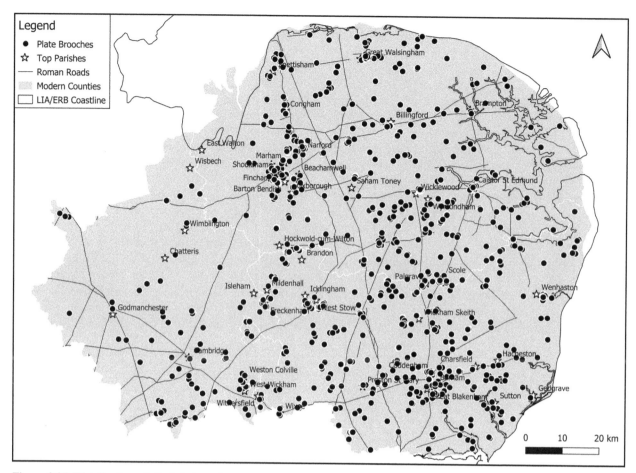

Figure 3.97. Distribution of all plate brooches.

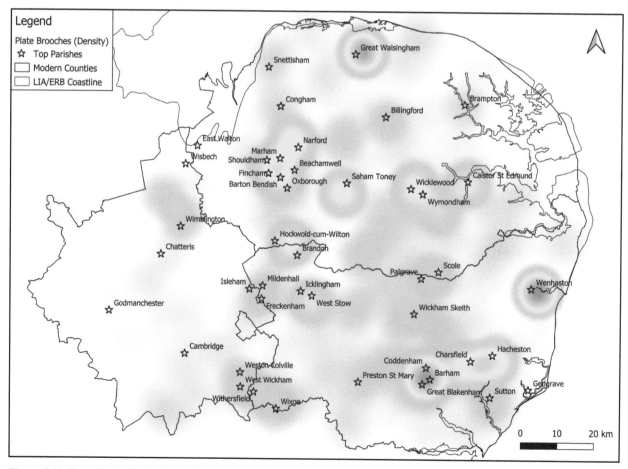

Figure 3.98. Density of all plate brooches.

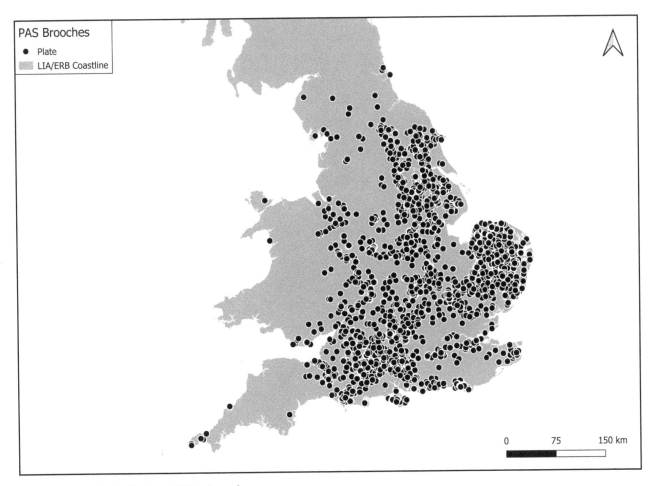

Figure 3.99. PAS distribution of Plate brooches.

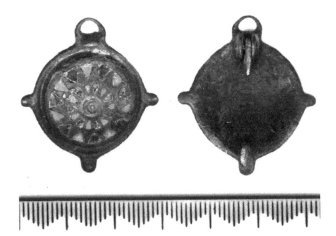

Figure 3.100. Enamelled umbonate plate brooch, Worlington (PAS: JP7277).

Figure 3.101. Disc brooch with triskele, Walsingham (PAS: NMS-974487).

difficult to quantify as similar types are often recorded under several names. The earliest flat, circular brooches are mid-late first century CE. The second century CE types have lugged projections (Hattatt 1982: 137). The 'glass centre boss' brooches, which are often gilded, date from the late second-fourth centuries CE and are mostly outside the remit of this study. These have concentrations in Wiltshire and Lincolnshire and do not have especially high numbers in East Anglia on PAS.

Approximately a third of plate brooches are described as discs (Table 3.6). Like the overall plate brooch distribution, they cluster around urban areas and temples: Wimblington (12), Walsingham (30), Saham Toney (15), Hacheston (17), Wenhaston (36) and Hockwold-cum-Wilton (13). Disc brooches were particularly suited to being repurposed as votive offerings and pierced examples are sometimes found from shrines (Figure 3.103). Walsingham and Wenhaston show particular hotspots (Figure 3.104, Figure 3.105). Most from Wenhaston are the flat enamelled type characteristic of the second century CE.

Figure 3.102. Disc brooch with 'cogwheel' decoration, Weybourne (PAS: NMS-A33796).

Figure 3.103. Modified Disc brooch, Dalham (PAS: SF-35BA47).

Why was it important to have brightly-coloured ornaments at this time? The colourful, circular designs on many disc brooches could be argued to be apotropaic. There is a decorative connection between seal-boxes, harness and plate brooches. Paites tentatively suggests that domed variants (umbonates) may be associated with women, or feminine attire more generally (2016: 20), as they regularly have chain-loops. The emphasis on gender and religious identities in the second century CE seems to outweigh any ethnic or class considerations.

There are ten examples of *Adlocutio* disc brooches, which have applied repoussé images depicting riders, soldiers and an eagle, based upon a coin of Hadrian, giving a *terminus post quem* of 134 CE. Seven of these were recovered from Hockwold (Mackreth in Gurney 1986: 64-66; NHER: 5587). These, combined with the Horse-

and-rider brooches and a raptor-and-prey type, led Gurney to draw parallels with another possible temple at Lackford. He suggests their predominance at religious sites makes it likely that they were priestly regalia, worn at the shrine as 'badges of office' possibly related to the cult of Mars. He also considers that brooches may be apotropaic, souvenir or cult emblems and observes that, as pilgrim badges, they would have moved away from temples to settlements (1986: 89-90 and fig. 41.10). I am cautious of the idea of priestly badges, but there is clearly a connection between these offerings of *Adlocutio* brooches and the coins which inspired them. Many Late Roman coins are found at temple sites, which may indicate that changes in deposition culture occurred, although the sacredness of the place remained. The ritualisation of plate brooches suggests a continuity of votive behaviour with new belongings.

3.12.3. Dragonesque

Dragonesques are one of the earlier enamelled British brooches, probably originating in Yorkshire. Mackreth suggests 'an intimate economic link' between East Anglia, Lincolnshire and parts north of the Humber (2011: 186-88). British Dragonesques are sometimes found overseas (Ivleva 2016: 15). They are a post-conquest variety (50-150 CE) which was highly-visible and distinctive in decoration, fusing the La Tène style with a Roman plate brooch and a wraparound pin similar to penannulars (Figure 3.106). The name derives from the opposing zoomorphic terminals, which might represent horses, dragons or mythical beasts. These brooches are often described as distinctively 'Celtic' or British in design, although there are no known pre-conquest examples (Croom 2004: 290; Hattatt 1982: 30, 1985: 171; Jundi and Hill 1997).

A total of 29 Dragonesque brooches was recorded: Suffolk (20), Norfolk (8) and Cambridgeshire (1) (Figure 3.107). They follow the focus of other plate brooches on Suffolk. There are two apiece from Coddenham and Hacheston and another two from Saham Toney, including an unusual 'reversed S' variant (NHER: 4697). Votive deposition has been considered as Dragonesques have been found in several caves (Eckardt 2014: 132; Jundi and Hill 1997: 131-34), although there are none obviously from shrines in my dataset and the lack of Dragonesques from Walsingham is worthy of note.

Dragonesques follow the changing decorative fashions in horse harness, seal-boxes and other plate brooches: starting with unenamelled curvilinear and circular motifs, then single rows of enamelled squares and triangles, and finally panels of geometric squares and lozenges (MacGregor, M. 1976: 127, 129). Dragonesques may reflect the hybridisation of a restricted local type into the wider plate brooch design scheme. This could derive from the integration of different groups of people or the appropriation of styles and fashions between groups (Croom 2004: 290; Webb 2011: 13). These brooches may have been used to express a non-verbal, anti-Roman

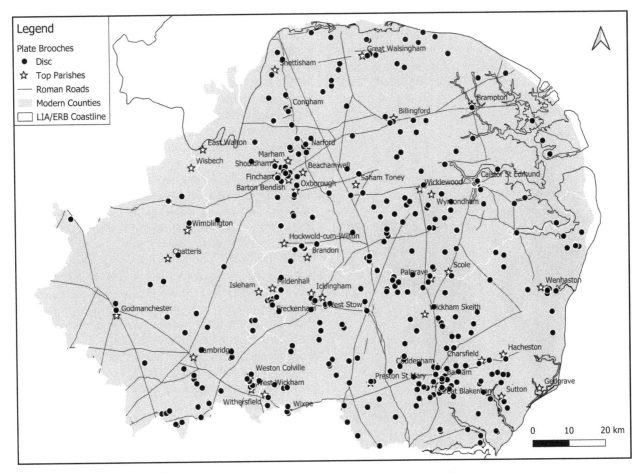

Figure 3.104. Distribution of Disc brooches.

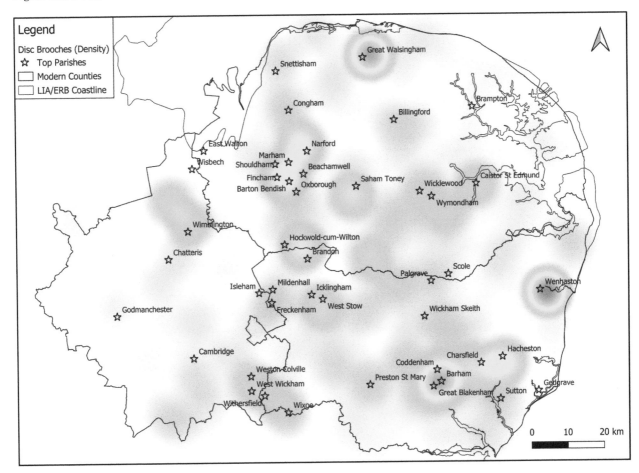

Figure 3.105. Density of Disc brooches.

message by those experiencing a loss of autonomy after the conquest (Jundi and Hill 1997; Ross 2011: 74). The lack of Dragonesques in Norfolk and from shrines shows regional discrepancies. It implies that their indigenous, northern origins and potential 'hidden transcripts' may have been less significant to people in this area than their colourful aesthetic.

Figure 3.106. Dragonesque brooch, Lakenheath (PAS: SF5191).

3.12.4. *Skeuomorphic*

Figurative plate brooches, including zoomorphic and skeuomorphic types, are frequent in East Anglia (Plouviez 2008: 173, 178). My data further refine this with a particular focus on Suffolk (Figure 3.108, Table 3.6). Concentrations on religious sites include Horse-and-rider, sandal-sole and axehead types (Bird 2011: 288). Other skeuomorphic variants include shields, tools and lamps.

I recorded nine axe brooches, eight from Suffolk and one from Norfolk. All enamelled ones have bilateral springs mounted between a pair of pierced lugs suggesting British manufacture (Mackreth 2011: 179-80, Type 1.2a). Miniature axes are also most common in south Norfolk and Suffolk (section 6.7.2). Kiernan found axe brooches were most frequently found on military sites in the northwest provinces, proposing a tenuous link between axe and Horse-and-rider brooches and the cult of Sabazius, a Phrygian Rider-god (2009: 121). Feugère regards the axe brooch as characteristic of the German *limes* (1985: 373 fn. 435). A double-bladed axe variant of the second/third century CE has been associated with a cult of Jupiter Dolichenus on the continent (Heeren and van der Feijst 2017: 160-61).

While the military link does not appear to hold true for the *civitas Icenorum*, the votive connection may have merit. Two brooches are so similar they could have shared the same mould. One comes from Crownthorpe temple

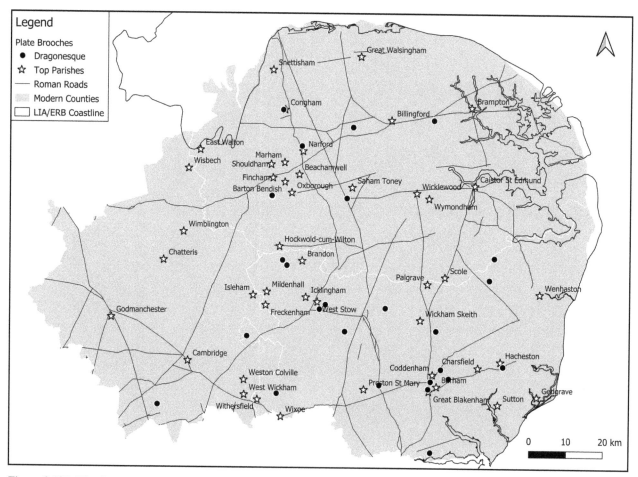

Figure 3.107. Distribution of Dragonesque brooches.

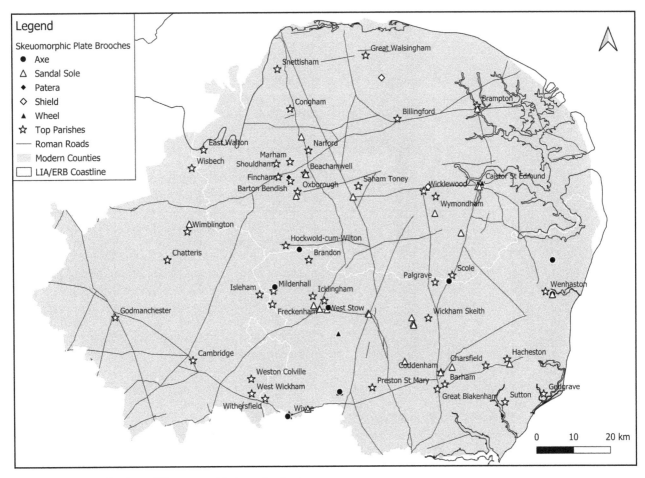

Figure 3.108. Distribution of Skeuomorphic brooches by type.

(NWHCM: 1985.380.1), the other (PAS: SF-042714) (Figure 3.109) from the same field in West Stow as the hoard of 'priestly regalia' which also contained votive leaf plaques, headdresses and staff terminals (Worrell *et al.* 2011). This parish, on the borders of Lackford, where the Cavenham crowns were discovered, also has a miniature bronze axe, a Dragonesque brooch and two sandal-sole brooches.

Hinged 'sandal-sole' brooches are the most common skeuomorphic brooches in Roman Britain (Figure 3.110). They represent the underside of a shoe, usually with enamelled 'hobnails', and sometimes a chain-loop. There are 17 from Suffolk, 12 from Norfolk and just one from Cambridgeshire (Figure 3.108). Three shoe brooches from the fields surrounding *Venta Icenorum* include one recorded as a 'double sandal-sole' (NHER: 9759, 9836). A further three are known from Hacheston, with two each from Pakenham and Wenhaston. This corroborates Statton's assertion that they are more frequently found in urban areas (2016: 146).

Sandal-sole brooches are an imported variety, ranging across the northwest provinces. Bilaterally-sprung examples show occasional British production. The earliest, non-enamelled varieties date to the mid-first century CE. Eckardt (2013) found no clear preference for depicting the left or right foot and there were none from

Figure 3.109. Axe brooch, West Stow (PAS: SF-042714).

gendered grave contexts, although the chain-loop may indicate female dress (Hattatt 1985: 170; Mackreth 2011: 179). Gender identities may have become more clearly delineated through material culture. Cool observes that women become more visible in the later first century CE (2016: 413).

Crummy's observation that sandal-sole brooches are sometimes bent, giving them a votive interpretation, is plausible, but unproven. She discusses the symbolism of the sandal and its possible relationship to Mercury/Hermes and his winged footwear (2007a: 226-27). The lack of wings is problematic, and I remain unconvinced by her examples.

Figure 3.110. Skeuomorphic sandal brooch, Ickburgh (PAS: NMS-5EA0CB).

Brooch-makers were more than capable of depicting a winged shoe in profile. Johns proposes a connection with safe travel and pilgrimage (1995: 107). Miniature votive feet and legs have been found (section 6.7.5). Eckardt concludes that shoe symbolism was apotropaic, brooches functioning 'perhaps to commemorate particular journeys or to ensure safe passage through life' (2013: 217, 230). Shoes are considered protective in much later domestic ritual practices around the world (Hukantaival 2007). Johns suspects many figurative representations, as today, derived from popular culture, well-known games or proverbs (1995: 104). This could equally apply to the hares and even the Horse-and-rider brooches.

3.12.5. Discussion

According to Hattatt, enamelled plate brooches show a strong Roman influence and a lack of 'Celtic' designs (1982: 136), although this does not account for the triskele motifs and Dragonesques. British-made plate brooches show many similarities with decoration on horse harness (Crummy 2011: 58). There was a new emphasis on multicoloured surfaces and symmetrical, contrasting ornamentation (Garrow and Gosden 2012: 29). The concentration of some plate brooches away from the main LIA centres of population in Norfolk (Figure 3.98) may reflect a general rejection of the identities and votive behaviours associated with these badge-like ornaments. The foci at temples and small towns with second century CE foundations like *Venta Icenorum* and Stonea (Malim 2005: 52) demonstrate chronological differences.

Wearing a brooch had implications for the display of identities. Different types, such as bow, plate or Knee exerted a practical influence on what sort of cloth could be worn and presented new possibilities for design and symbolism. Most people gave up wearing bow brooches, but select groups, perhaps including the military, continued to use them into the fourth century CE, which suggests their fastening function remained important. Plates did not replace bow brooches, but coexisted with Trumpet and Headstud types from the late first century CE. At this time, some people in the region were creating new religious and political identities for themselves. Plate brooches peak in popularity and then fade out in the late second/third century CE. Their waxing and waning may signify changes in lifestyle, clothing or iconography. Half a century after the Boudican revolt, did the new generation still remember or care about pre-Roman identities or are these brooches emblematic of the novel religious affiliations and familial ties which had been forged?

3.13. What is the evidence for the '*Fibula* Abandonment Horizon'?

After about 150 CE, bow and plate brooches begin to fade from the record, and once into the third century CE, a very restricted range of brooch types is being worn, or at least deposited. These include the descendants of Knee and Disc brooches, which are beyond the range of this research, dating to the third/fourth centuries CE (Hattatt 1982: 42). This '*fibula* abandonment horizon' is currently unexplained (Cool and Baxter 2016a: 94-95; Mackreth 2011: 236). Some relate the sudden decline to a sumptuary law, such as the regulation which restricted those below Equestrian status from wearing gold jewellery (Cool 1983: 15; Mackreth 2011: 237). Statton considers the abandonment horizon to be overblown. She gives examples of continued local production and importation of brooches, such as Knee and gilt plate brooches in East Anglia and the East Midlands, despite a significant decline in brooch loss. She also considers that wearing brooches in civilian as well as military contexts continued into the later Roman period (2016: 152, 260).

I am unconvinced by an edict against brooch-wearing, especially in Britain. It is much more likely, as Cool and Baxter suggest, that people stopped wearing costumes which demanded the use of brooches as a fastener (2016a: 94-95). Did new trends like wearing the Gallic coat or stitched clothing sound the death knell for the bow brooch? If multiple '*fibula* event horizons' marked the advent of shifts in social boundaries and identities expressed through material culture, then their abandonment must surely signify further changes in both objects and practices associated with personal adornment.

In Essex, the waning of brooch usage occurs earlier, towards the end of the first century CE, and continental plates and knee brooches predominate in the post-Flavian era (Wardle 2013: 203). Hattatt asserted that this was a peculiarly British event (1982: 35). By contrast, Cool and Baxter noted a drop-off in brooches in Augst and southern France, perhaps implying a regional shift specific to the northwest provinces (2016a: 88-89, fig. 6). Pitts considered the decline in iron brooches, as well as other Iron Age material culture, in burials across Gaul, Belgica and Germania Inferior as part of a tendency to increased regionalism *circa* 70-100 CE (2019: 172-75). The common female style, of paired brooches at the shoulders and a third to fasten a cloak, disappeared during the second/third centuries CE in the Treveran polity, and on urban and military settlements in the Low Countries, from the Flavian period onwards. However, it persisted on rural settlements right through to the early medieval period (Heeren and van der Feijst 2018: 360). This suggests discrepant and chronologically varied responses to changing costume in different regions, resulting in multiple abandonment horizons.

If we want to look for a historical explanation, this change in fashions may be partly related to the Imperial family, with the Emperor Septimius Severus setting up court at York in the early third century CE. The Empress Julia Domna is widely regarded as a trend-setter for hairstyles (Baharal 1992) and it follows that female fashion, and perhaps also gender identity, was undergoing a sea change at around this time. The use of jet as a material for jewellery and hairpins begins in the late second century CE at York and continues in popularity into the Late Roman period (Allason-Jones 2011: 2). This trend may have been keenly followed by some Romano-British women, much like Queen Victoria's mourning attire, which influenced the production and imitation of much jet jewellery in that era (Bedikian 2008).[14] My dataset shows that many other types of small personal belongings disappear from the archaeological record, at around this same time. I refer to this period as the Roman 'Dark Ages'. This 'object abandonment horizon' is discussed further in the final chapter (section 9.5).

3.13.1. *Penannulars*

Despite the huge changes which occurred in brooch distribution and production, from pre-Roman types, through the 'massive explosion' in imports in the first century CE, indigenous experimentation, variation and abandonment, the penannular brooch remained in use throughout (Mackreth 2011: 236-37). Were penannulars used for a different practice, or by different people, or as fastenings for something less susceptible to the vagaries of fashion?

Penannular brooches are typically divided into groups by terminal type, using Fowler's typology (1960), although Booth has recently reviewed and critiqued this system (2014). Types A and D are pre-conquest, but with subgroups extending into the third century CE. Types B and C are generally first century BCE/CE, but are often

residual (Mackreth 2011). Half of those recorded here are Fowler's Type C (Figure 3.111, Table 3.7).

Penannular brooches are one of the less-frequently recovered types highlighted by Cool and Baxter (2016a, 2016b) and Booth (2014: 72-73). The distribution and concentrations show they are found in much the same places as one-piece brooches: areas of Iron Age settlement (Figure 3.112, Figure 3.113). Groups at Saham Toney (7), Thetford (5) and Hacheston (7) are therefore unsurprising. Two examples from Thetford (NHER: 5853), in which one terminal has been cut or modified to reform the penannular into a loop, hint at the genesis of the brooch in earlier Iron Age ring-headed pins (Fowler 1960: 156). Two from Saham Toney are recorded as 'distorted', again reminding us of the 'mutilation' of brooches at that site (Brown 1986).

These brooches start early and are long lived, running throughout the LIA and Roman periods. The penannular type follows bow brooches with an intensification of numbers in the first century CE. However, it persists in use well into the early medieval period. In the Late Roman period, penannulars began to be associated with women (Cool in Booth *et al*. 2010: 285). The style of the loop and pin means that substantial fabric can be held by these brooches. It may be that penannulars were used to fasten cloaks rather than dresses. Their persistence may indicate resistance or disinterest towards changing fashions by some sectors of the population, or reflect the social status of those who could not afford to follow them.

3.14. Parish Case Studies

In this section, I have sampled parishes with substantial collections to compare proportions of brooch recovery. Some parishes are focussed on one or two key sites which have been extensively excavated or metal-detected. Others contain multiple sites or large scatters untested by excavation. However, it is useful to visualise the brooch patterns which arise from the study of individual types discussed in the preceding sections. The potential morphological bias of metal-detector finds can also be questioned (see Appendix B). I am particularly interested to compare areas which have known forts to supposed military brooches like Aucissa/Hod Hills (Figure 3.52), those with supposed 'ritual' sites to plate brooches, and those with continuing or interrupted settlement. Plouviez used Hod Hill brooches to define first century CE forts, with proportions of 15-20 per cent compared to <10 per cent on civilian settlements (2008: 176).

Pitts (2010) looked at brooch assemblages (first centuries BCE/CE) from sites in the south and east which he associated with *oppida*. This revealed that brooches such as Langton Down, Rosette and Colchester one-pieces were much more common on indigenous sites like King Harry Lane and *Camulodunum* and Colchester Derivatives and Hod Hill brooches were frequent on early Romano-British towns, villas and military sites. He interpreted this as cultural distinctiveness, defining colonised from

---

[14] My thanks to A. Marsden for suggesting this idea.

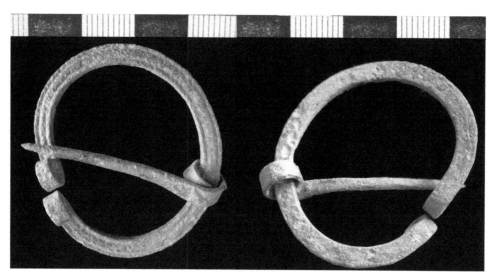

Figure 3.111. Penannular brooch, Fowler Type C, Wacton (PAS: NMS-33DDA5).

Table 3.7. Penannular brooches by county

Brooch Type	Cambs	Norfolk	Suffolk	Total
Penannular	7	38	29	74

colonisers, linked to the emergence of new political entities, as well as 'high cultural connectivity' with the near continent (*ibid.*: 50). Pitts also suggested brooches may have moved through the actions of 'independent traders' attracted to Britain as it opened up to the empire. These 'alternative "globalizing" networks' worked in parallel with the distribution of other military and indigenous metalwork (*ibid.*: 54). This approach highlights the benefits of looking at assemblages of brooches to gain an overview. These case studies also provide context for the discussion of other small finds from these parishes in subsequent chapters.

3.14.1. Thetford

Thetford is situated where the Icknield Way crosses the Rivers Thet and Little Ouse. It has a Middle Iron Age fort at Thetford Castle (NHER: 5747). Occupation continued from the Iron Age (NHER: 5756, 5738) through the Romano-British period, and a spectacular hoard of Late Roman gold and silver was found at Fison Way. Davies has suggested this was a British *oppidum*, due to evidence for contemporaneous coin minting and bronzeworking, which includes clay moulds, crucibles and pellet moulds, although occupation is slight (2009: 120, 124; NHER: 5853). The lack of settlement is corroborated by my analysis, Thetford never featuring particularly highly in any artefact category.

The important, possibly ceremonial, centre of Icenian power at Fison Way is also the origin of most brooches in this parish. The brooch percentages (Figure 3.114) show a high proportion of early types, the ten iron Nauheim/

Drahtfibels (section 3.8.3) being of particular interest. It also shows similar proportions of Aucissa/Hod Hills and Colchester Derivatives, both Harlows and Rearhooks. Thetford is one of the few parishes which exceeds Plouviez's threshold of 15 per cent Aucissa/Hod Hills relating to a military presence, at eight out of a total of 51 brooches, all from the Fison Way excavations. This is a small sample compared, for example, to the 49 Aucissa/ Hod Hills from Saham Toney. Did soldiers visit or control this indigenous ritual complex or were local people disposing of trophies or adopting incoming symbols of power?

The pre-conquest sanctuary was rebuilt at the invasion and may have been a 'symbol of native resistance to foreign rule' (Bradley 2005: 188). This potentially suffered retributive destruction as part of the Boudican backlash, although it seems the ritual centre was deliberately, but carefully, dismantled in the 60s or 70s CE (Healey in Gregory 1991a: 190). There are very few late first or second century CE brooches from this area, perhaps implying there was military occupation and civilian abandonment soon after the rebellion.

3.14.2. Hockwold-cum-Wilton

In comparison to Thetford, Hockwold has a very different brooch profile (Figure 3.115). The HER records no Iron Age settlements and minimal stray finds in this parish, close to the Fen-edge. There are Romano-British settlements and two temples with priests' crowns and pewter hoards (NHER: 5316, 5367, 5587). Hockwold is also well-known for a hoard of silver cups (NHER: 5395) (section 2.3.6). The percentage of plate brooches is extremely high (57 per cent) within such a small sample, including seven *Adlocutio* and 10 Horse-and-riders (section 3.11.6). This makes a convincing link between Romano-British shrines and plate brooches. There are very few early brooches and only a single Colchester Derivative. Figure 3.116 shows Thetford and Hockwold combined. Is it possible the ritual

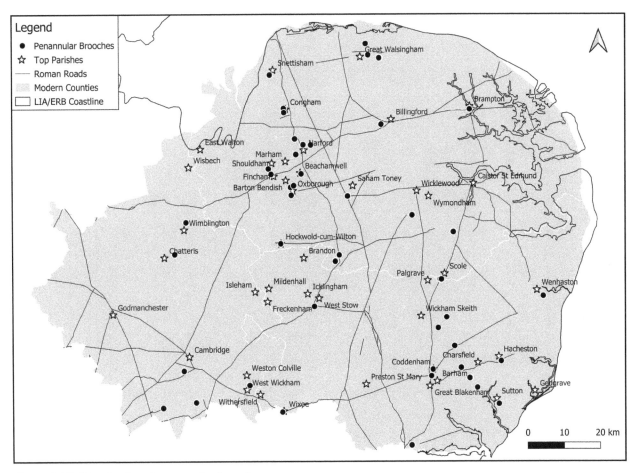

Figure 3.112. Distribution of penannular brooches.

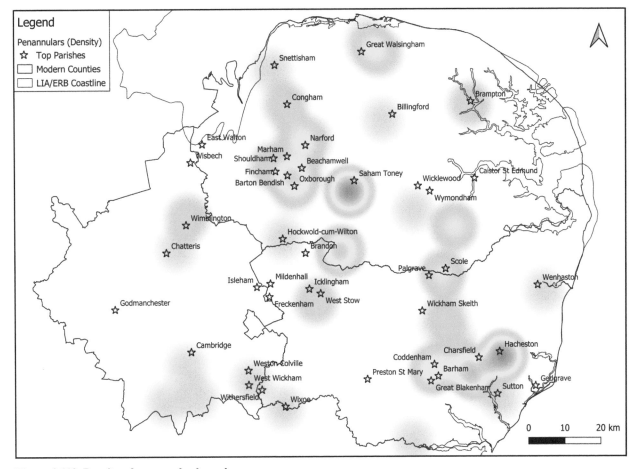

Figure 3.113. Density of penannular brooches.

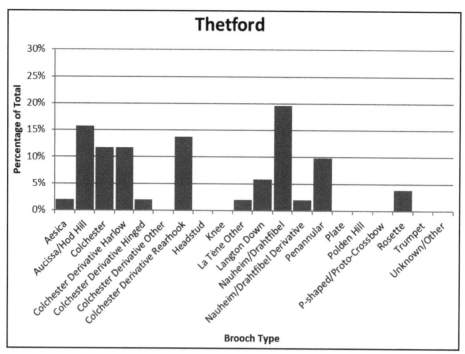

Figure 3.114. Percentages of brooches by type, Thetford (51 brooches).

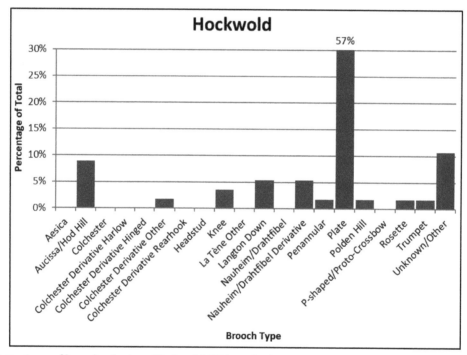

Figure 3.115. Percentages of brooches by type, Hockwold (56 brooches).

focus at Thetford moved to Hockwold, just 10 miles away? Could this be evidence for resettlement, or different populations with new gods and new masters?

3.14.3. Charsfield

Charsfield, though frequently occurring in my brooch maps, has very little Iron Age or Roman occupation recorded on the Suffolk Heritage Explorer, despite extensive Roman scatters. The profile (Figure 3.117) lacks any brooches considered pre-conquest and neither does it reveal many 'military' types. The concentrations of

Colchester Derivatives and the relatively high proportion of plate brooches could be interpreted as a post-conquest settlement, tied to the production centre at Wenhaston, with a potential ritual focus. Seeley names it as a 'probable rural temple site' (in Blagg *et al*. 2004: 87).

3.14.4. Wicklewood

Wicklewood (Figure 3.118) spans the conquest and Boudican revolt. It regularly shows high densities for both LIA and Roman brooches and other small finds, particularly horse harness, closely linked to the neighbouring parish of

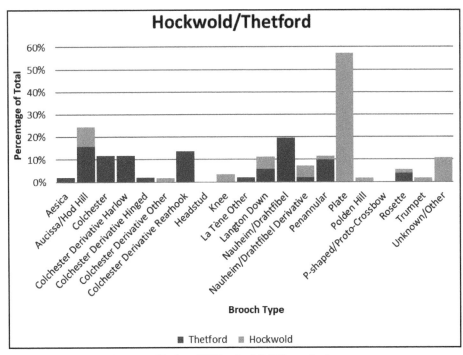

Figure 3.116. Percentages of brooches by type, Hockwold/Thetford (107 brooches).

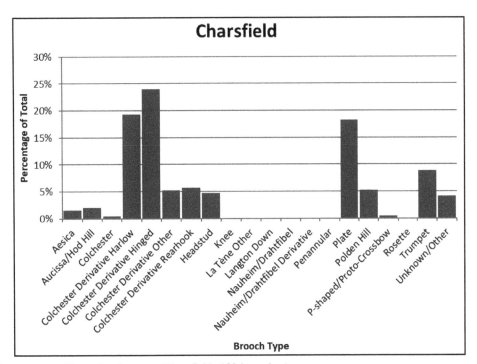

Figure 3.117. Percentages of brooches by type, Charsfield (192 brooches).

Wymondham, just east of Breckland. A large settlement is known at Crownthorpe (NHER: 8897) dating from *circa* 70-180 CE, with at least one Iron Age coin hoard and a cache of copper alloy vessels. A rectilinear Romano-British temple (NHER: 54693) was probably constructed in the second or third century CE. A metalworking area is also known (NHER: 18111), perhaps linked to the high proportion of brooches noted as unusual or unparalleled. Plate brooches, including four zoomorphics and four Horse-and-riders may represent a votive tradition, although they are not as numerous as at Hockwold or Walsingham. 'Military' type brooches are not abundant. However, there are many

unknowns in the chart, due to old HER records which simply specify 'second century brooch' or 'hinged first century' etc. This assemblage warrants further detailed investigation.

3.14.5. Walsingham/Wighton

Over 200 brooches and 6000 coins have been recovered from Walsingham (NHER: 2024), through the efforts of one dedicated metal-detectorist working in close collaboration with local authorities. Many votive items were also recorded including figurines, inscribed rings, miniature objects and seal-boxes. This points to a ritual

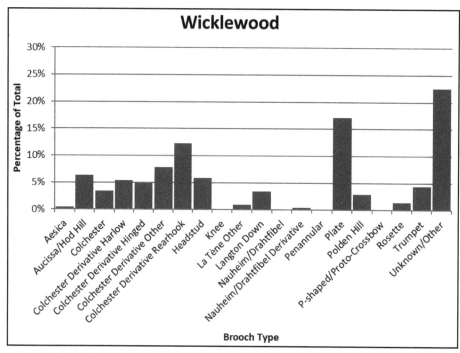

Figure 3.118. Percentages of brooches by type, Wicklewood (204 brooches).

site of some importance, although no foundations of a temple have yet been found (Bagnall Smith 1999: 22). The shrine at Walsingham may have been a location for regular markets and fairs with metalworkers possibly making offerings for pilgrims (Andrews 2012: 64).

Like Hockwold, Walsingham shows a vastly disproportionate number of plate brooches, at 35 per cent of the total (Figure 3.119). These include 30 disc brooches, mostly enamelled British types, several continental plate brooches, and six zoomorphics, including one Horse-and-rider brooch. Brooches were most probably being deposited as votives along with coins and other belongings. There are over 10 per cent Aucissa/Hod Hill brooches, but this still falls below Plouviez's 15-20 per cent for a military site. It has considerably more hinged Colchester Derivatives than Rearhooks and few early brooches, suggesting a foundation in the later first century CE. This could be recovery bias, although Marsden has suggested that the shrine at Walsingham came to replace the earlier ritual focus at Snettisham (2014: 70).

Walsingham is conjoined with the neighbouring parish of Wighton (Figure 3.120) and the two make up a Roman small town (NHER: 42850) (Figure 3.121). This is thought to date from the second-fourth centuries CE, although it is largely unexcavated. There is a small multivallate ringfort at Warham Camp just to the north (NHER: 1828) with LIA to second century CE occupation. There is LIA to Romano-British settlement at Wighton Camp (NHER: 1113) and a LIA 'fort' at Copy's Green was said to have been abandoned and then reoccupied *circa* 75-200 CE (NHER: 2072). Reoccupation by whom, whether locals, soldiers or veterans, is unknown. In contrast to Walsingham, Wighton has over 25 per cent Aucissa/Hod Hill brooches, although there is no Roman fort known to me. The majority are from

a bathhouse and metalworking area of the proposed town (NHER: 3980). There are few early brooches from this parish and, interestingly, a higher proportion of Harlow brooches than Rearhooks. This disputes the badging of Icenian identity with Rearhook brooches, especially in the most northerly lands of the territory.

3.14.6. Hacheston

The parish of Hacheston incorporates a large Romano-British town on the River Deben in southeastern Suffolk. Settlement begins pre-conquest, with metal-detector finds of a significant quantity of both Icenian and Trinovantian coins, which Martin considered evidence for 'tribal interactions' (1999: 90). Roman coins are infrequent until the late first century CE, with peaks in the Hadrianic period and the mid-fourth century CE. There is a distinction between brooches and coins here, with many more Harlow brooches than Rearhooks, despite the fairly equal numbers of Icenian and Trinovantian issues (Blagg *et al.* 2004: 75, 87) (Figure 3.122). This again contradicts the argument that brooch types were restricted to ethnic or social groups.

Hacheston also shows evidence for continuity of settlement, with Langton Down, Rosette and Colchester brooches, which Pitts used to define his pre-conquest 'political entities' at *oppida* (2010). There is no evidence for a military emplacement or post-revolt disruption (Moore *et al.* 1988: 21), although there are reasonable numbers of Aucissa/Hod Hills, again questioning the presence of these brooches on civilian sites. This is supported by the lack of indicative finds of pottery and other *militaria* (Blagg *et al.* 2004: 197). Hacheston also has a high percentage of plate brooches, including numerous discs and zoomorphics, suggesting a possible temple.

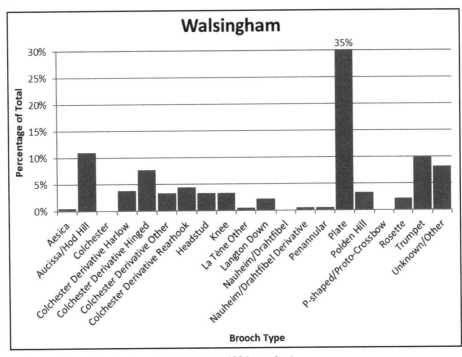

Figure 3.119. Percentages of brooches by type, Walsingham (182 brooches).

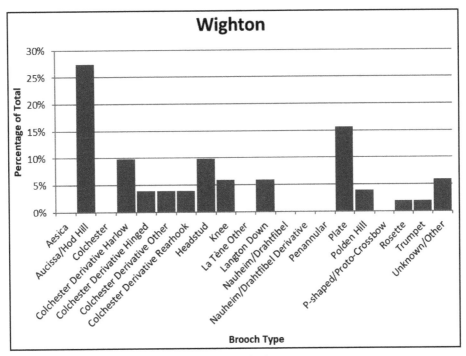

Figure 3.120. Percentages of brooches by type, Wighton (51 brooches).

3.14.7. Wenhaston

Wenhaston appears to be a Romano-British town with little previous Iron Age activity. This is confirmed by the brooch profile (Figure 3.123) which shows very few one-piece brooches. The most notable feature is the high percentage of Colchester Derivative Hinged brooches from the two fields closest to the town (SHER: WMH004, WMH005). As discussed above (section 3.11.3) this must relate to a production or market site close by in the later first century CE (Blagg *et al.* 2004: 87). Wenhaston also has a lower proportion of pseudo-military brooches suggesting either

it was not garrisoned or its population preferred Colchester Derivative and plate brooches. This also fits with Pitts's analysis of urban sites in the southeast (2010: 51). Could Wenhaston have been a new foundation in the aftermath of the rebellion? The lack of military brooches means it is unlikely to have been laid out for an intake of veterans. Towns may have been established as trading centres as much as mechanisms of control. Here we may be seeing such a nucleus for craft production and exchange, although it is important not to fall into the trap of retro-projecting a medieval market town model (Perring 2013: 4). Finds from Wenhaston also imply a religious focus, with 24

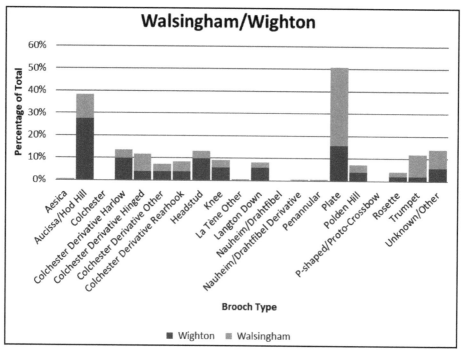

Figure 3.121. Percentages of brooches by type, Walsingham/Wighton (233 brooches).

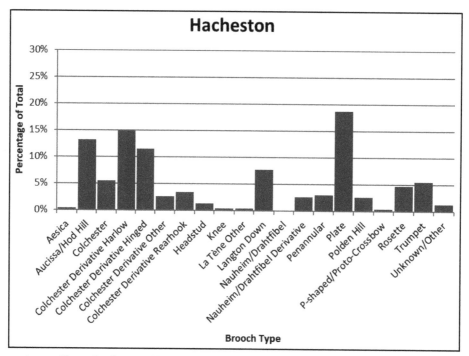

Figure 3.122. Percentages of brooches by type, Hacheston (235 brooches).

zoomorphic plate brooches, three zoomorphic cosmetic mortars (chapter five), several votive miniatures and figurines (chapter six), suggestive of a shrine or sanctuary.

3.14.8. Coddenham

Coddenham is another Suffolk small town, but with a military presence in the form of two forts (SHER: CDD016), known from aerial photography (Rodwell 1975: 92). There is LIA settlement and scatters of coinage include Icenian issues. Continuity in the brooches is evinced by the Colchesters and Langton Downs (Figure 3.124). The Romano-British settlement is associated

with *Combretovium* (SHER: CDD003). Its brooch profile shows a fairly even spread over time and type, with higher numbers of Harlow and plate brooches. Almost 15 per cent Aucissa/Hod Hills would classify this parish as a 'military' site using Plouviez's parameters, which would agree with the presence of forts. However, this is roughly equal to Hacheston which does not have military origins.

3.14.9. Wimblington

Stonea Camp, Wimblington, has been mooted as a possible Icenian *oppidum* or market centre active from the Middle Iron Age until the first century CE, although settlement

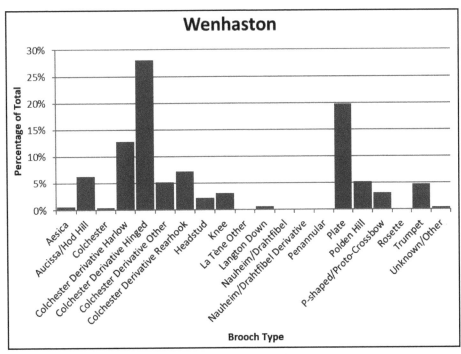

Figure 3.123. Percentages of brooches by type, Wenhaston (445 brooches).

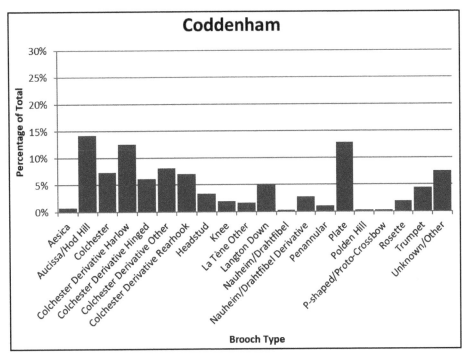

Figure 3.124. Percentages of brooches by type, Coddenham (358 brooches).

is scarce. Despite its place in the narrative of the revolt of 47 CE, there is no trace of dismembered bodies or a war cemetery, although this type of evidence is very rare. A mid-first century CE military presence is implied by Claudio-Neronian samian and surface finds of Aucissa/ Hod Hill and Colchester brooches (Malim 2005: 51-52, 77; Potter and Jackson 1982: 116). Mackreth put the relative proportion of 'military' brooches down to 'the arrival of the vengeful Roman army' (in Jackson and Potter 1996: 299). I would query this, as 12 of the brooches from Stonea Camp on my database were seized from illegal detectorists (Jackson and Potter 1996: 35-36), so it would be hard to draw any conclusions from such data. The Aucissa/Hod

Hill category stands at 20 per cent (Figure 3.125), which correlates with Plouviez (2008: 176). The only other sites which show such high percentages of Hod Hill brooches are Saham Toney and Wighton.

The settlement at Stonea Grange provided 85 of the 100 brooches. These suggest some pre-conquest activity, followed by an association with Harlow (over Rearhook) brooches in the client-kingdom period. A Romano-British town developed in the second century CE. A rectangular building excavated within the town is interpreted as a second/third century CE temple, which would fit with the 20 per cent of plate brooches recorded. These are largely

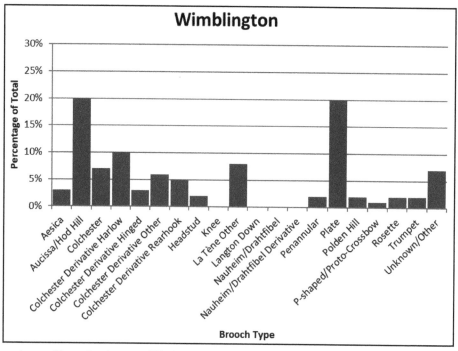

Figure 3.125. Percentages of brooches by type, Wimblington (100 brooches).

disc brooches, with one Horse-and-rider. Other religious material has been found, such as miniature axes, part of a pipeclay Mother-Goddess and a votive leaf plaque (Jackson and Potter 1996: 214-20; Potter and Jackson 1982: 112-13).

3.14.10. Saham Toney

Saham Toney and adjacent parishes show prolific Iron Age activity; it is considered a good candidate for an *oppidum*. A regionally significant cult site may have existed here in the early to mid-first century CE. There are multiple deposits of pre-conquest brooches and coins, including pellet moulds and unstruck gold stater flans (Brown 1986: 8; Davies 1999: 34-35; Hutcheson 2004: 7; Talbot 2015: 259).

A Claudian-period auxiliary fort overlooking the Iron Age settlement at Woodcock Hall (NHER: 4697) is interpreted as a response to the first Icenian uprising in 47 CE (Brown 1986; Davies 1999: 34). It oversees a meeting of rivers and a natural crossing-point on the Peddars Way. Brown envisaged a heavy military presence with its attendant infrastructure, based upon a group of 35 Claudian *aes* copies and a collection of early military metalwork. The Roman coin profile shows peaks in the reigns of Claudius (41-54 CE) and Vespasian (69-79) (1986: 5, fig. 2). Based upon this hiatus, Brown saw abandonment of the auxiliary fort by about 58 CE. A Romano-British settlement later expanded on the northern side of the river. A second, larger, legionary fort of the later first century CE has been identified from aerial photography (NHER: 8745), interpreted within the Boudican 'pacification' narrative (Bates *et al.* 2000: 204). Neither of these sites has yet been systematically excavated (Talbot 2015: 5). Strong evidence for metalworking and terret manufacture has been found at the nearby site of Quidney Farm (NHER:

29429) (section 8.10.3).

The brooches are predominantly pre-conquest types and quasi-military varieties (section 3.9) with Colchesters and Derivatives, particularly Rearhooks, numbering over a third of the total (Figure 3.126). There are substantial quantities of Aucissa/Hod Hills (although fewer than 15 per cent) and plate brooches, including four zoomorphic and two Horse-and-rider. However, only one Hod Hill came from the Claudio-Neronian fort, which makes a large-scale military occupation between the two revolts unlikely. There are few later brooch types, either military or civilian, and a solitary fourth century Crossbow (Brown 1986).

3.14.11. Caistor St Edmund

The parish containing the *civitas* capital has LIA occupation and ritual sites including the possible mortuary enclosures at Harford Farm (NHER: 9794). The parish also contains an extra-mural Romano-British temple (NHER: 9787), resulting in a mixed brooch profile (Figure 3.127). *Venta Icenorum* (NHER: 9786), while plentiful in pre-conquest surface finds, has few early brooches, although it has not been possible to track down or identify all brooches excavated in the 1930s. This agrees with the early second century CE formal layout of the town. There are more Rearhooks than other Colchester Derivatives and numerous Trumpet brooches. Aucissa/Hod Hills are infrequent, suggesting minimal 'military' contact, although there are some later brooches like Knee and P-shaped. Although over 20 per cent of plate brooches has been related to religious sites, it is important to remember these were also worn prior to deposition, except in special circumstances, like the Horse-and-rider brooches which may have been cast specifically for dedication (section 3.11.6).

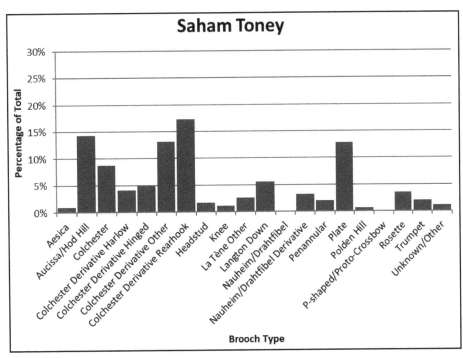

Figure 3.126. Percentages of brooches by type, Saham Toney (342 brooches).

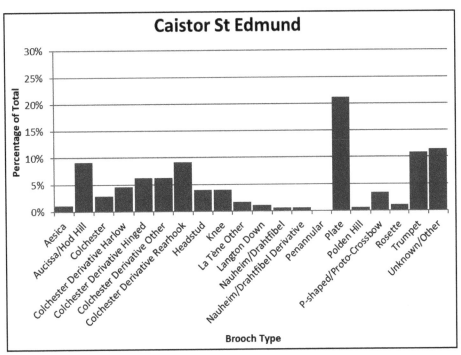

Figure 3.127. Percentages of brooches by type, Caistor St Edmund (177 brooches).

3.15. Summary

Firstly, it is important to re-state that brooches do not equal people, although we cannot divorce material culture from its social context and practical aspects of human activity. Objects find their way into the ground and are preserved into the present through various motivations and processes. Special items were selected for deposition in unusual circumstances, such as hoards. Metal was a precious and reusable resource which was hard-won, and therefore worth reprocessing numerous times. Before contact with the Roman empire, people produced a variety of brooches and

other ornaments, with technical abilities which were no less sophisticated than in the later Iron Age and Roman eras. The '*fibula* event horizon' was drawn out and episodic. Could it have resulted from the democratisation of the knowledge of production? The noticeable increase in single brooch finds at shrines, but also in settlements, may represent a change in deposition practices and attitudes towards material culture. Do these represent offerings by individuals in contrast to the group behaviour exhibited by hoards of torcs or harness? Had religion, as well as metalworking, become less exclusive and more personal? Although recycling of metalwork remained common in the Roman period, it seems that the emphasis for brooches had shifted to deposition, thus extending the practice of torc and coin hoarding to the masses.

My analysis of brooches has revealed some interesting patterns which help answer some of the key research questions. The large proportion of imported and early one-piece brooches (including Colchesters) shows the openness to outside influences in the pre-conquest period and refutes the idea that the Iceni were slow to change. Strong concentrations around Fincham, Wicklewood and Coddenham show potential centres of LIA population (with a caveat about recovery bias). Areas thought to have significant settlements, like Stonea and Caistor St Edmund, are notable by their absence. Only Thetford has a concentration of Drahtfibel type brooches at Fison Way, although the brooch profile there is unusual and suggests an abrupt end around the mid-late first century CE.

Using artefacts to subdivide the region into 'tribal' territories is problematic. As a class, Colchester Derivative brooches are high in East Anglia, some 24 per cent of the total, which agrees with Plouviez and Mackreth's work. However, the distribution of the different spring systems is somewhat ambiguous. Harlow brooches certainly have a southerly bias, in line with their 'Trinovantian' ascription. Rearhooks cluster in Breckland and central Norfolk, the Icenian core. Both types, however, extend to the settlements along the Icknield Way and are found in concentrations at Coddenham and Wenhaston. The division of these two spring types into ethnic or social groupings does not stand up particularly well. The limited evidence we do have for manufacture is contradictory, indicating production of Harlows in Norfolk and Rearhooks in Suffolk. Certainly, there is no defined boundary between them, and I would contend that the distributions are much more likely to reflect processes of production and exchange.

The interpretation of the pseudo-military brooches (Aucissa, Hod Hill and Knee) does not support the idea that the region was heavily garrisoned either before or after the Boudican revolt (Figure 3.52, Figure 3.57). The presence of Aucissa/Hod Hills at the same centres of population as the one-piece brooches (Thetford, Fincham area and Coddenham) indicates that they were probably being worn, and in some cases made, by civilians. Coddenham does have a conquest period fort, but it also seems to have suffered little disruption during the rebellion. Evidence in the brooches for the depopulation of the region and resettlement by veterans is also lacking, as the same centres of population continue with few exceptions. Although little explored archaeologically, Saham Toney appears to have been an important Icenian centre, with a cluster of Aucissa/Hod Hill brooches, although these do not come from the fort with the Claudian irregular coinage. The low numbers of Knee brooches across the region also suggests that there was not a great military presence in the second/third centuries CE, despite the difficulties of tying these wholly to the army.

Through analysis of the brooches, we can see that aspects of people's identities were changing over time. This happened gradually into the second century CE and has little relationship to the revolt. A shift in the production and deposition of brooches towards the southeast also occurs around this time. Greater changes in the material culture appear to happen earlier and later (the event and abandonment horizons). New religious foci at Hockwold and Walsingham replaced the pre-conquest sites at Snettisham and Thetford. Plate brooches also witness the development of towns, including the *civitas* capital, Wenhaston and Coddenham. Deposition of brooches, especially plates, became popular, perhaps replacing sacrifices or votive deposits of harness and jewellery. Zoomorphic brooches show animals were clearly still an important design feature, but the emphasis of the iconography shifts. Ducks remain constant, but new prey animals and scenes of predation are introduced. Wild and powerful creatures are absent, notably the characteristic Iron Age bovids, and horses are newly depicted in a medium other than coins. This may reflect changes in religious belief and prohibitions, new mythologies and folklore, animal husbandry and cuisine. Nevertheless, an emphasis on votive deposition and the related sense of appropriateness are carried through.

The evidence for metalworking demonstrates that people were keen to adopt new technologies, such as casting rather than forging, piece moulds or the two-piece spring systems. Creolisation of brooches, like the Aesica, may show the incorporation of incoming styles and the emergence of new visual identities, during the client-kingdom in Norfolk. The development of new types such as the Polden Hill/Rearhook hybrids and Hinged brooches, especially in eastern Suffolk, suggest manufacturing or market centres. Similarly, the curvilinear aesthetics of some Trumpet brooches may be evidence for persistence of Iron Age style, but this is negated by the very similar distribution of the more geometric Headstuds. Brooches with chain-loops may also exhibit a new interest in gendered identities from the late first century CE onwards.

The unexplained abandonment of brooch-wearing after 200 CE, except for certain classes possibly associated with military uniform, may relate to a return to recycling, or perhaps a shortage of metal. Were supplies of copper alloy diverted to making coinage instead of portable artefacts? There must have been a dramatic change in how people dressed and looked around the turn of the third century CE, reflecting an important shift in people's outward representation of themselves. Alternatively, archaeological dating of these objects may be due for a review. This reduction of metalwork production was not solely restricted to personal ornament, but also applies to objects relating to grooming, literacy, religion and some items of harness. This 'Roman Dark Ages' is a key phase in the territory's history, and in wider relation to Britain and the other Roman provinces, which deserves more research. In the next chapter, I consider some of the artefacts which survive and flourish beyond the 'abandonment horizon', bracelets and finger-rings, as well as other items of adornment which, like brooches, fade from the record.

4

Ornamenting the Person: Wealth you could Wear

4.1. Introduction

This chapter explores selected items of personal display, which have an ornamental aspect, excluding brooches (chapter three). These include two types of fasteners, torcs, snake-headed jewellery and wide-cuff bracelets (Table 4.1). It addresses some of the key research questions, including changing gender distinctions, the introduction of new ideas and behaviours, and the lines drawn between military and civilian identities. By investigating the distributions and concentrations of these forms of material culture, I aim to discover what these small personal belongings can tell us about status and identity, at both ends of the social spectrum. I will also consider, with a case study on hoards from Snettisham, the disciplinary discourses which have shaped the Icenian narrative.

4.2. Fasteners

Two forms of metal fasteners, distinct from brooches, are discussed here: the simple toggle and the 'button-and-loop' fastener. They date from the LIA and extend into the Roman period. Fasteners demonstrate several of the key issues at the intersection of belongings and past identities. Multifunctionality of design can be seen across artefact types, alongside a continuity and development of indigenous aesthetics. They also raise questions about metalworking, production and the flow of ideas between Britain and the wider empire.

Toggles are most commonly a cylindrical 'dumbbell' shape with a semi-circular suspension loop or simple integral slot (Figure 4.1). Examples are known from the Bronze Age onwards, but most date to the first centuries BCE/CE. It is thought that button-and-loop fasteners developed from toggles. As the name suggests, these comprise an attachment loop or shank often with decorative enamelled heads (Figure 4.2, Figure 4.3). These appear in the first century BCE and continue in use into the early third century CE. Although both types were used in parallel,

Table 4.1. Fasteners, wide-cuff bracelets and snake jewellery by county and type

Object Type	Cambs	Norfolk	Suffolk	Total
Button-and-Loop	5	49	39	93
Toggle	7	67	28	102
Wide-Cuff	16	16	43	75
Snake Bracelet	26	35	6	67
Snake Ring	9	79	12	100

Figure 4.1. Dumbbell-shaped toggle with external loop, Kedington (PAS: SF-95B8F8).

Figure 4.2. Enamelled disc-headed button-and-loop fastener, Heydon (PAS: BH-AF2E83).

Figure 4.3. Teardrop-shaped button-and-loop fastener, Lawshall (PAS: SF8242).

toggles arrive and go out of use slightly earlier. Some are distinctively British and have pre-conquest ancestors, although variants are found on continental sites. Both types of fasteners were probably designed to take leather or woven straps, which could be passed through the attachment hole and then doubled back and secured with a loop over the head. Some may have been stitched onto clothing or other fabric, to provide holds for straps. They are often interpreted as military or harness fittings (Wild 1970; Worrell 2008: 341-47).

My dataset includes 102 toggles and 93 button-and-loop fasteners (Table 4.1), with a few other items described as buttons or dress fasteners. The distribution is widespread across Norfolk and Suffolk, with Cambridgeshire being sparsely covered (Figure 4.4). There are hotspots around centres of indigenous settlement, including Snettisham and Saham Toney, but also post-conquest foundations like Brampton and the *civitas* capital (Figure 4.5). There is a group of four toggles from Barham, near Coddenham, including two from the same site as six Icenian silver coins (SHER: BRH025/027). Three button-and-loop fasteners (PAS: SF-3C8CC0, SF11039, SF9342) were found in the same field in Otley, Suffolk. A possible votive interpretation is evoked by the four button-and-loop fasteners from Walsingham temple (NHER: 2024).

There were 280 Iron Age and 93 Roman toggles, and 556 button-and-loop fasteners on the PAS (Figure 4.6). These divisions reflect recording patterns, but also remind us that small finds often do not respect modern categories. Both types are densely concentrated in Yorkshire and the East Midlands. Like East Anglia, Yorkshire is certainly well-known for its horse harness, making an equine use likely. If these were exclusively military objects, I would expect to see more on the northern frontier, although Worrell cautions this absence should not be exaggerated, considering the general pattern of PAS finds nationally (2008: 342). Like the 'military' brooches, many PAS fasteners derive from rural sites (*ibid.*: 344), which counters the military theory. This is corroborated by my density mapping (Figure 4.5). Worrell found Norfolk considerably under-represented for button-and-loop fasteners in comparison to Suffolk (*ibid.*: 342, fig. 2). This may bear out their association with the army, as Norfolk exhibits little of the characteristic military paraphernalia found elsewhere (Eckardt 2005: 150-51). It could be representative of the self-governance of the client-kingdom and the persistence of Iron Age material culture. However, my integrated database shows Norfolk has both more toggles and button-and-loop fasteners than Suffolk, demonstrating the benefit of using a combined approach.

4.2.1. 'Sitting awkwardly on the cultural fence'?

Like Wide-cuff bracelets (see below) and Hod Hill brooches (section 3.9.1), the precise function and the military or civilian attribution of fasteners remains under

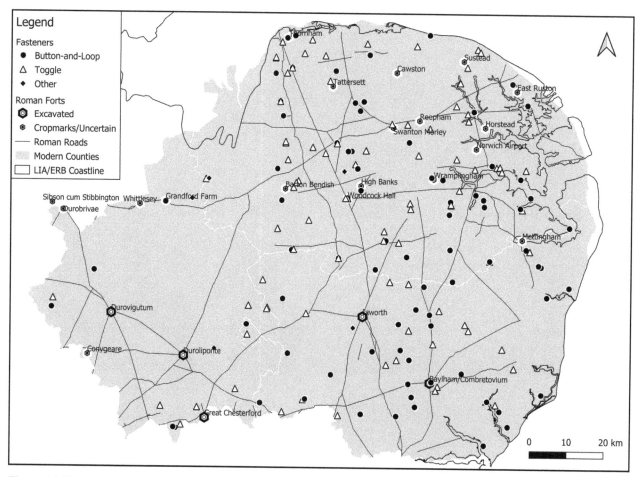

Figure 4.4. Distribution of fasteners by type and early Roman forts.

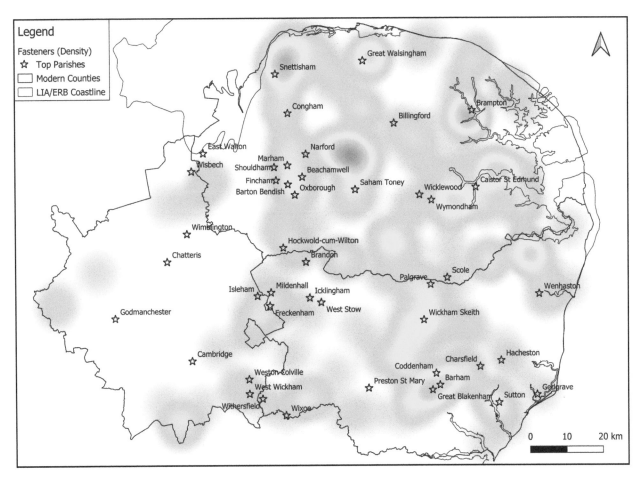

Figure 4.5. Density of all fasteners.

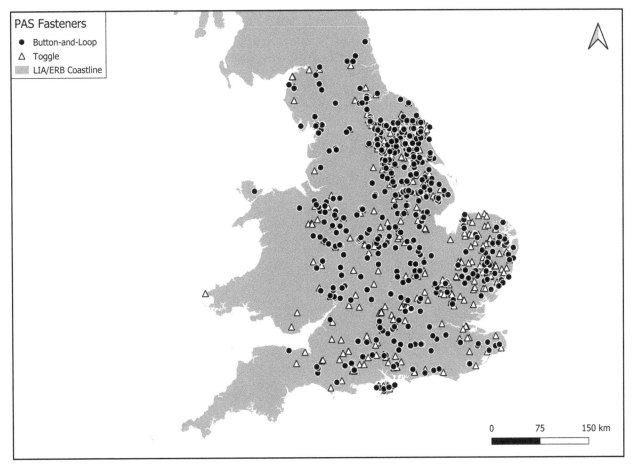

Figure 4.6. PAS distribution of toggles and button-and-loop fasteners.

debate (Davis 2014: 230; Gui 2015; Wild 1970: 146; Worrell 2008). Crummy places one example in Category 13 (*militaria*) of her Colchester catalogue (1983: 132, SF4203). Clarke describes a button-and-loop 'clasp' and associated strap union from the Ringstead hoard as fittings for a sword belt (1951: 222). Hutcheson considers Ringstead to be second/early first century BCE (2004: 33), making this an early example, possibly linked to weaponry.

MacGregor viewed the distribution of fasteners in Northern Britain as 'sitting awkwardly on the cultural fence' between Roman military sites and native settlements (1976: 130). A recently excavated group of openwork button-and-loop fasteners at the auxiliary fort at *Porolissum*, Dacia, may shed light on their continental usage. Here, at least 22 identical examples were found, closely associated with harness fittings, in a building used as a weapons store in the later second century CE. This certainly suggests a military harness function, although the flimsy construction of these examples implies a decorative rather than structural purpose (Gui 2015).

Gui notes these fasteners are very rare in Dacia and considers them to have a British Iron Age origin, adopted by the Roman army and spread across the empire (2015: 231-34). This shows that the flow of artefacts and influence could travel both ways. Nevertheless, this does not mean that they had a military function in their homeland; indeed, they may have been multifunctional. Mapping the distribution of both button-and-loops and toggles against known and conjectural military emplacements in the study area does not show any obvious correlation (Figure 4.4). Enough doubt exists over the military ascription to place them in this personal adornment section with fasteners more generally.

Limited evidence for British manufacturing of toggles and button-and-loop fasteners exists. Within the study area, an unusual toggle from Heydon has a shiny surface treatment due to high levels of tin and arsenic (PAS: BH-A973D5) (Figure 4.7). This reflects the ability of metalworkers to adapt alloys to affect colour, as seen with coins and torcs. A LIA toggle from Suffolk shows signs that it was finished and used, despite a miscasting of the loop (PAS: SF6694). Further afield, a lead alloy triangular loop from the River Tees at Piercebridge could potentially have functioned as a pattern (PAS: BM-FF1C8C). A pair of conjoined and badly miscast button-and-loop fasteners were reported in North Yorkshire (PAS: YORYM-B6D70D). Other miscast fasteners are known from Cumbria, Warwickshire and Yorkshire (PAS: LANCUM-DB854F, LANCUM-95C9B2, LVPL1553, SWYOR-64CFAB). These finds reinforce a probable northern production zone for this class of artefact, which fits with their overall distribution.

After the close of the second century CE, fasteners, like brooches, dwindle and manufacture apparently ceases (Wild 1970: 146). Does this reflect changes in costume or military uniform? Why does dress and personal ornament change at this time? While few remains of textiles exist,

this arguably demonstrates that brooches were not replaced by fasteners on clothing in this period. The '*fibula* abandonment horizon' (section 3.2.2) seems to affect other categories of material culture than simply brooches, suggesting a major shift in fashion, manufacturing or social identities took place around this time.

4.3. A Common Visual Repertoire

Toggles are often simply decorated and seldom show enamelling or other surface treatments. A few rare examples have riveted worked bone discs, in the manner of early brooches (e.g. PAS: CAM-8B6ED6). The enamelled button-and-loop fasteners share a decorative scheme with seal-boxes, horse harness and plate brooches, although this 'common repertoire' of motifs originates in pre-conquest Britain (Crummy 2011: 58; Worrell 2008: 347).

An unusual LIA toggle from Emneth (PAS: NMS-E06AC5) (Figure 4.8) is ornamented with addorsed crescents, which frequently feature on coins from this period, and which Davies equates with the Iceni (2009: 114, 2014: 27). This continuity of design can be seen in the back-to-back lunate motifs on a second century CE fastener from Strumpshaw, enhanced with red and yellow enamel (PAS: NMS-FEF246) (Figure 4.9). These designs also echo the use of 'eye' or shield imagery which may have had apotropaic associations, particularly on harness, such as the linch-pins from Colne Fen, or terret moulds from Waldringfield (see chapter eight). The triskele motif is often found on a group of objects which are usually described as 'fobs' or 'roundels'. This symbol seems particularly fluid, sometimes described as Iron Age and 'Celtic', yet at others associated with horse harness and the first century CE military (Hutcheson 2004: 31; MacGregor, M. 1976: 123).

Figure 4.7. Toggle with flaring ends, Heydon (PAS: BH-A973D5).

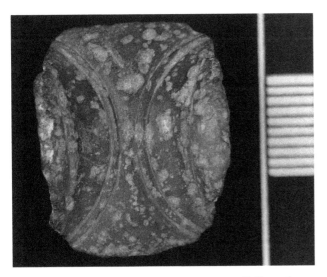

Figure 4.10. Linch-pin terminal, near Attleborough (PAS: NMS-248F38).

Figure 4.8. Toggle with addorsed crescent motif, Emneth (PAS: NMS-E06AC5).

Figure 4.9. Button-and-loop fastener with enamelled crescents, Strumpshaw (PAS: NMS-FEF246).

Other motifs which cross object types include the curved triangle or 'steering wheel' design found on Icenian coins, linch-pin terminals (PAS: NMS-248F38) (Figure 4.10) and two triple cosmetic grinders from Norfolk (section 5.3). A rare find from Great Barton, described as an Iron Age 'sword tang button', also displays this symbol (PAS: SF-D18A63) (Figure 4.11). This shape is again accompanied on the linch-pins and button by inlaid circles or 'eye'

motifs. At Saham Toney, a LIA harness roundel has a radiating pattern of enamelled triangular cells centred on the familiar 'steering wheel' motif (Bates *et al.* 2000: 226). Several objects share polychrome quatrefoil patterns, such as the platform-decorated terrets from Carleton Rode (NHER: 39434), a teardrop-headed button-and-loop from Palgrave (PAS: SF-16E8E6) (Figure 4.12), a square-headed fastener from Kenninghall (PAS: SF-34B7A4) (Figure 4.13) and a flat-ring terret, from just outside the study area at Peterborough (PAS: CAM-CFFBD1) (Figure 4.14).

4.4. Wide-Cuff Bracelets (*Armillae*)

Finger-rings and bracelets outlive the fundamental shift in the third century CE which occurs with brooches and fasteners. The majority come from third/fourth century CE contexts and are therefore outside the scope of this study. The exceptions to this rule are Wide-cuff bracelets and snake jewellery. Wide-cuff bracelets are broad penannular bands, again often associated with the military, specifically of the Claudian period (Figure 4.15, Figure 4.16). Dating is post-conquest, but pre-Flavian or 'pre-Boudican', with some stratified in mid-first century CE contexts (Cool 1983: 144-46). Crummy's data show social distribution grouped around forts, *coloniae* and large towns with a high proportion of active or veteran soldiers. She observes that most of these bracelets come from the territories of the Trinovantes/Catuvellauni (Crummy 2005). Notably there are few from Norfolk: Hertfordshire, Bedfordshire and Suffolk have the most PAS finds (Figure 4.17).

My dataset agrees with Crummy's findings, Suffolk having three times as many as the other two counties (Table 4.1). A cluster is evident in the southwest where the Suffolk, Essex and Cambridgeshire boundaries converge, within the parishes of Weston Colville (6), West Wratting (1), Withersfield (3) and West Wickham (3) (Figure 4.18, Figure 4.19). The hotspot is relatively close to Great Chesterford and Cambridge which have early military activity (Moore *et al.* 1988). A Roman road, thought to connect Colchester to Cambridge via the small town at Wixoe, runs not far from this cluster (SHER: WTH007). The proximity to the

Figure 4.11. Enamelled 'button', Great Barton (PAS: SF-D18A63).

Figure 4.12. Teardrop-headed button-and-loop fastener, Palgrave (PAS: SF-16E8E6).

road network may offer other explanations for this group, such as a *mansio* or a smaller staging post.[1] Alternatively, the concentration may be the result of a local workshop. A group of six bracelet fragments was found by the same detectorist in the parish of Combs, near Stowmarket. This area has extensive Iron Age and Roman finds scatters and cropmarks, but there is little further archaeological information available. While some finders have recorded more than one bracelet from their patch, there is no firm collection bias.

Two silver bracelets and a military armlet with a medallion were found in the Fenwick hoard (Crummy *et al.* 2015) (Figure 2.3). Crummy puts forward a good case for Wide-cuff bracelets as *armillae*, a specifically British type

Figure 4.13. Square-headed button-and-loop fastener, Kenninghall (PAS: SF-34B7A4).

---

[1] Nina Crummy (pers. comm. 02/05/2017).

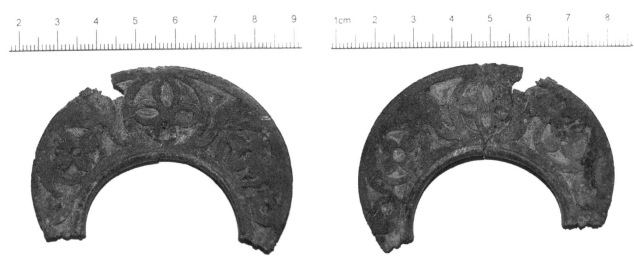

Figure 4.14. Unusual flat-ring terret, Peterborough (PAS: CAM-CFFBD1).

Figure 4.15. Wide-cuff bracelet fragment, Monk's Eleigh (PAS: SF-FE4116).

Figure 4.16. Wide-cuff bracelet terminal, West Wickham (PAS: SF-37B485).

of military award 'granted to ranks below centurion for force of arms in battle', during the conquest and early years of occupation (2005: 98). These are attested in historical sources and epigraphy. She relates the banded cable decoration to laurel wreaths, symbolising victory, and the terminal motifs to military belt plates and Aucissa/ Hod Hill brooches. Crummy asserts that these bracelets would have been 'worn with pride' by both active soldiers and retired veterans. As cherished belongings, they would have enhanced the wearer's standing within military circles, although insensitive displays in front of a hostile or resentful local populace may have been unwise. They were perhaps handed down as family heirlooms, explaining their discovery in later contexts (*ibid.*: 96-100). Crummy invokes the Boudican narrative, proposing loss by soldiers during battle, requisitioning of supplies or tax-collecting duties. Items found at shrines may have been offered 'in times of personal and family crisis' (*ibid.*: 100) or alternatively, used as votive offerings by Britons returning from the rebellion with trophies seized from Colchester or London.[2]

---

[2] N. Crummy (pers. comm. 02/05/2017).

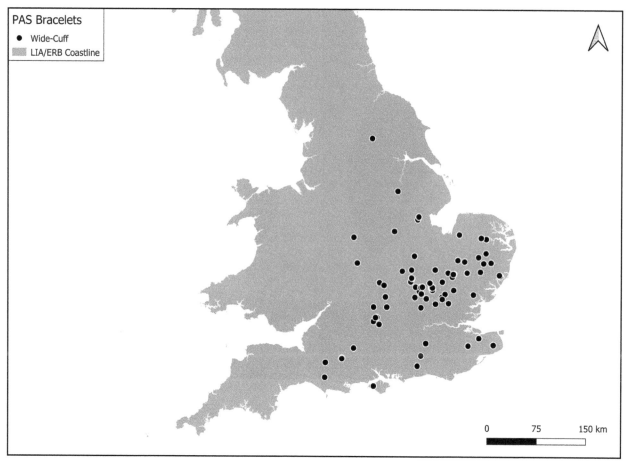

Figure 4.17. PAS distribution of Wide-cuff bracelets.

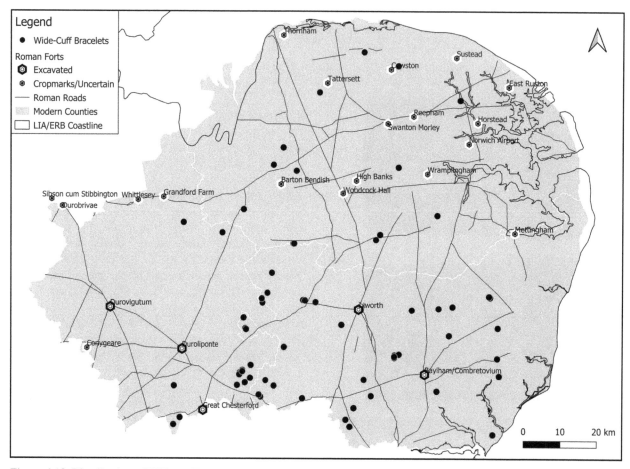

Figure 4.18. Distribution of Wide-cuff bracelets and early Roman forts.

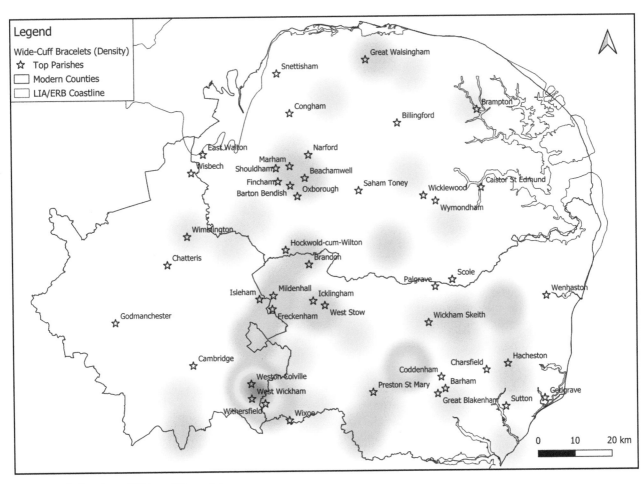

Figure 4.19. Density of Wide-cuff bracelets.

How do my findings relate to this interpretation? If Wide-cuff bracelets were military awards, we would not expect to find many in the client-kingdom before the Boudican revolt. The low number from Norfolk supports other evidence for minimal military activity in the core of Icenian territory, while the southwestern concentration raises the question of an early presence on the periphery. Was a condition of Icenian self-government that the army held back beyond the borders and took their influence elsewhere? In contrast to Crummy's forts, *coloniae* and large towns, the numerous finds from rural settlements, small towns and sanctuaries in my database do not particularly suggest military deposition (Figure 4.18). Most are fragmentary and many have been cut, folded or otherwise modified. This may indicate deliberate mutilation. Republican and early Imperial *armillae* were made from precious metals and were normally presented in pairs as awards. British versions are copper alloy, frequently with a white metal surface coating. Though these would have been a poor imitation for silver under close inspection (Crummy 2016: 100), there seems to have been an important aesthetic for 'shine' or 'reflectiveness' on certain categories of object, particularly for dedication at shrines and temples.

Do *armillae* represent redistribution of land to veterans of the conquest in Trinovantian territory and did this provoke the Trinovantes to join the revolt, as stated by Tacitus (*Ann.* 14.31)? The evidence for post-revolt continuity would suggest an influx of veterans into Suffolk is unlikely. Alternatively, were these items of military prowess adopted by local civilians? Unlike the Hod Hill brooches (section 3.9.1), I found no evidence for hybrid forms of these bracelets, nor for manufacture, although an example from Wramplingham (PAS: NMS-363A97) was repaired with four small rivets. The PAS distribution of these objects is very similar to that of the 'Baldock' style nail cleaners (compare Figure 4.17, Figure 5.27), and perhaps also the lightweight copper alloy torcs with geometric decoration which were produced in the first century CE.[3] Do these necklets, bracelets and nail cleaners form part of the output of a local production zone based in what is now Hertfordshire?

On balance, the military origin of these bracelets seems plausible; using them to visualise the movement of military personnel is less satisfactory. I would argue that the military attribution of Aucissa/Hod Hill brooches in Britain remains open to question, due to their frequency on civilian sites; such uncertainty extends to these bracelets. Finds from rural temples and the incompleteness of many bracelets would fit with a potential role as offerings or trophies. Two finds each from Walsingham and Leyland's Farm, Hockwold-cum-Wilton lend further weight to this theory.

---

[3] Michael Marshall (pers. comm. 03/06/2020).

Despite the strong association of later Roman bangles and armlets with women and girls, these bracelets may have been male items of display (Allason-Jones 1989: 123-25; Crummy 2005). Certainly, the only complete PAS examples are around 70mm in width (Kent-BCB277 at 69.8mm, NMS-FEF84D at 76mm). Although their penannular nature allows for expansion and even complete examples are often distorted, these fall into the upper end of the adult sizing range (Swift *et al.* forthcoming: fig 4.7).[4] Changing expressions of gender identity can be seen throughout the study period, whereby certain items become more associated with male or female identity or dress as time progresses. This could suggest that clearer distinctions were drawn between men and women in mid-late Roman Britain than in earlier times. Was this simply a visual expression of physical differences or symbolic of deeper social changes? Perhaps greater hierarchy or stratification was being introduced alongside these artefacts, grouping, and thereby separating, people by status, gender or allegiance.

4.5. Snake Jewellery

Finger-rings and bracelets with snake-headed terminals became popular in Roman Britain from the late first century CE. The move from realism towards abstraction on IA coins and intaglios is also seen in snake jewellery, with earlier examples being more naturalistic (Swift 2011: 196). The Snettisham Jeweller's Hoard (see below), a mid-second century CE collection of jewellery and coins, contained 46 silver snake rings and five penannular snake-headed bracelets (Johns 1996b, 1997) (Figure 4.20, Figure 4.21). Two other silver snake-headed rings are recorded from Snettisham (PAS: NMS555, PAS-C29063).[5] Excepting the hoard rings, there are only a few from each county (Table 4.1). One rare gold example is known from Little Cornard, Suffolk (PAS: SF-8A6886). The colour or shine of the jewellery seems to have been important, with many in silver, and copper alloy examples with white metal coating. Was this a means of 'dazzling' the evil eye or the forces responsible for bad luck and ill health (Andrews 2012: 102-3; Gell 1998: 83-84)?

Serpent-shaped rings and bracelets were common across the Roman empire. In the classical world, snakes were symbols of regeneration and rebirth, and wearing rings or bracelets depicting serpents was thought to be protective. Snakes appear on cult images of Isis, hands of Sabazius, and atop the *caduceus* of Mercury. Non-venomous snakes had positive connotations and were sometimes kept as pets. They were also associated with the spirits of the dead in Greek and Roman belief. The entwined snakes on the rod of the healer-god Asclepius were frequently depicted symbols of healing (Cool 2000: 33-35; Johns 1997: 35; Toynbee 1973: 223-36). Marsden (2014: 68) associates snake rings with Salus, the Roman embodiment of health.

Figure 4.20. Snake-headed ring, Snettisham Jeweller's Hoard (BM: 1986,0401.275; Image: © Trustees of the British Museum).

Figure 4.21. Snake bracelet, Snettisham Jeweller's Hoard (BM: 1986,0401.313; Image: © Trustees of the British Museum).

Cool considers the evidence for a religious interpretation of British snake-headed jewellery, proposing a link with a cult of Glycon, a popular second century CE snake god (2000: 35).

The distribution of bracelets is far less widespread than the rings, and the two rarely seem to correspond. Bracelets are a northwestern feature in the study area (Figure 4.22). Nationally, both are an eastern phenomenon, with concentrations of bracelets more tightly focussed than rings. Norfolk and Lincolnshire have the most snake jewellery on PAS (Figure 4.23). Hotspots occur at Snettisham and, for bracelets, at Stonea Grange, Wimblington (Figure 4.24). Here, 11 fragments were retrieved: nine copper alloy and two silver. One came from inside a broken jar of mid-late second century CE date. None of these are complete and

---

[4] Ellen Swift (pers. comm. 05/08/2020).
[5] These may be duplicate records. No image exists for PAS: NMS555 for comparison, but the finder and year found are the same.

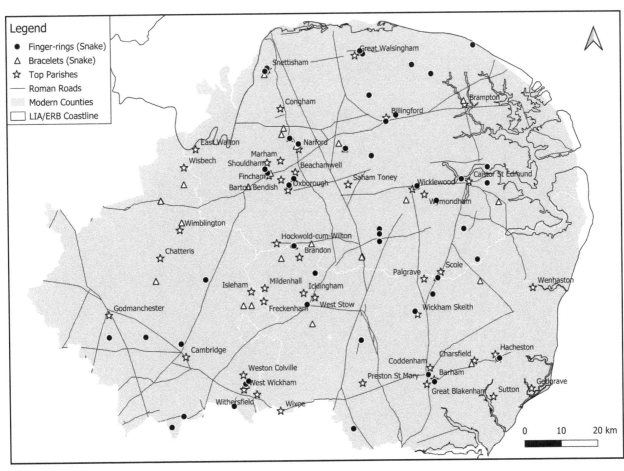

Figure 4.22. Distribution of snake rings and bracelets.

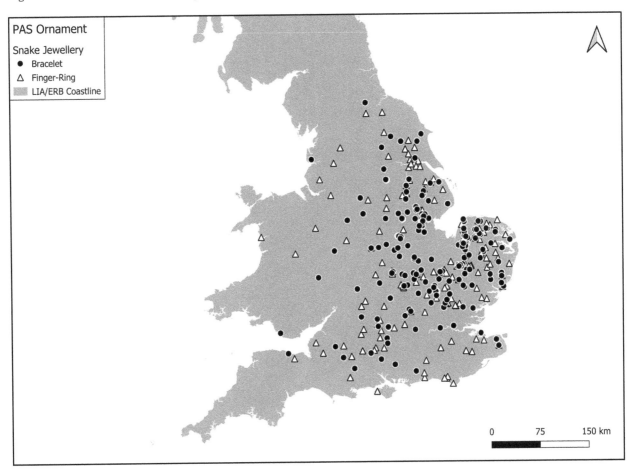

Figure 4.23. PAS distribution of snake jewellery.

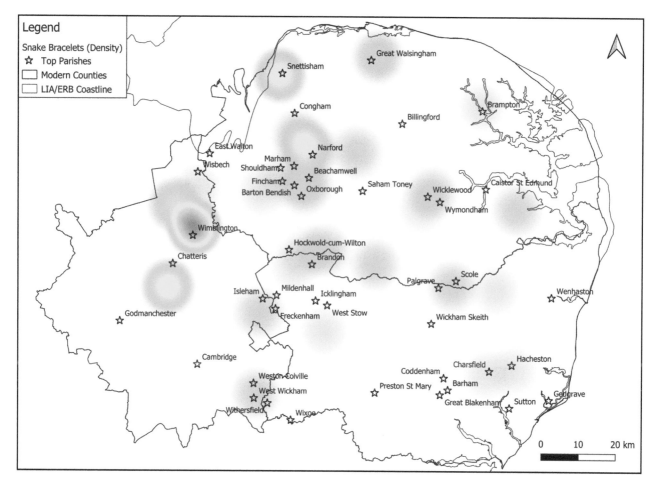

Figure 4.24. Density of snake bracelets.

no snake rings were found at this site (Jackson and Potter 1996). This may simply reflect the vagaries of recovery or a deliberate process of selection and fragmentation. A *patera* handle from *Venta Icenorum* depicts a classical Mercury holding his *caduceus*. It was reused as a plaque, possibly in a personal shrine (NWHCM: 1976.303.1, 1976.303.2) (Figure 4.25). When found, the figure had a snake-headed ring around its neck, indicating a religious connection between finger-rings and deities, perhaps even symbolising a torc (Green 1976: 31; Marsden 2014: 49 fig. 2.8; Wilson 1971: 270 and pl. 37b). A similar figure has been recorded from South Oxfordshire (PAS: BERK-F1499B).

Despite zoomorphic representations being very common on mid-Roman period plate brooches, snakes only rarely appear. This could reflect a belief that snake jewellery must encircle a part of the body for its protective powers to be effective. Cool (2000) puts the snake-headed rings from Snettisham into their wider context. She cautions against assuming the hoard was collected in the deposition area, as parallels for the less common forms come from around the Severn estuary. Finger-rings in the early-mid second century CE still had a primary role as signets, and Cool observes the unusual number of 'non-functional' rings in the hoard (2000: 31-32). If these served a quasi-medical or apotropaic purpose, this 'function' could have been just as real to their wearer.

Figure 4.25. Mercury plaque, *Venta Icenorum* (NWHCM: 1976.303; Image: © Norwich Castle Museum and Art Gallery).

110

Johns discusses 'amuletic jewellery', including the acceptance of serpent and phallic imagery in the Roman provinces (1996b: 9-12). Snake jewellery may represent the adoption of new beliefs relating to health and protection in the mid-Roman period. The concentrations at Snettisham and Stonea may relate to continuance of cult centres or even the development of healing sanctuaries in the northwest of the region. The emphasis on Norfolk and Lincolnshire has similarities with the distributions of Horse-and-rider and hare brooches (section 3.11.5). This hints at stronger connections between the northern part of the region and the East Midlands in the second/third century CE. Rippon (2018: 344) also notes that East Anglia, particularly the communities along the Fen-edge, had greater similarities with the South East Midlands than the Northern Thames basin. It may be that this area should simply be understood as the easterly edge of a focus which surrounds the wetland fringes all the way from Lincolnshire and Cambridgeshire to Norfolk.

There do not seem to be any gender preferences for snake jewellery at this time, although Late Roman bracelets, including those with snake terminals, are associated with women (Swift 1999: 134-35). The child buried with pipeclay figurines at Godmanchester (section 6.8.6) is described as a girl, based on the presence of a snake bangle (Going *et al.* 1997). The Snettisham Jeweller's Hoard snake rings fall within Swift's measurements for both adult men and women, with very few over the 20mm diameter which she associates exclusively with men (2017: 164-66).

A conquest period cremation burial at Snailwell was accompanied by a combination of homegrown and imported goods, including a spiral armlet with zoomorphic terminals, described variously as snakes or ducks. The cremation is assumed to be a male 'warrior' based on items such as a shield boss and harness cheekpieces (Lethbridge 1954). The armlet most likely originated in Scotland and travelled to Cambridgeshire, despite previous diffusionist interpretations to the contrary, which saw refugees from the invasion fleeing northwards (Hunter 1997: 109; MacGregor, M. 1976: 103). This is not the only connection between East Anglia and Scotland: recent work on the Netherurd and Newark gold torcs identified a highly technical craft tradition outside East Anglia. These techniques were perhaps imitated (or learnt) by the makers of the Snettisham and Sedgeford torcs, again countering the diffusionist interpretation and proposing contacts and workshops over long distances (Machling and Williamson 2018).

4.6. Torcs

'In stature she was very tall, in appearance most terrifying, in the glance of her eye most fierce, and her voice was harsh; a great mass of the tawniest hair fell to her hips; around her neck was a large golden necklace; and she wore a tunic of divers colours over which a thick mantle was fastened with a brooch' (Dio *Hist. Rom.* 62.2.4).

Necklaces were rare in the Iron Age. The most significant and numerous were torcs, for which Snettisham in Norfolk is duly famous. Torcs were associated with religious and political authorities in some societies (Hingley and Unwin 2005: 4). Dio's iconic description of the Icenian queen wearing a golden torc may have indicated her status and marked her out as a barbarian in the eyes of his readership in Rome (Farley 2015: 14). Or perhaps Dio was 'dressing' Boudica in the provincial costume of his day, as attested by burial goods and depictions of women wearing torcs from the Danube region in the second/third centuries CE (Carroll 2008: 295). Large, precious metal neck-rings had largely passed out of production in Britain by the first century CE, making it unlikely that Boudica, if she indeed existed, wore one.[6] If she did so, perhaps she was using the display of an heirloom to appeal to an ancestral powerbase.

In Britain, torcs are most commonly found in hoards, which may suggest they were not items of adornment for the masses, although they certainly show use-wear (Fitzpatrick 1992: 396; Rosten 2007: 39). Although torcs could be worn by either men or women in the Iron Age, many finds from continental graves are associated with female remains (Stead 1991: 459; Watts 2005: 94). The second century CE funerary depiction of Regina, the Catuvellaunian woman commemorated at *Arbeia*, shows her wearing Romano-British clothing and a twisted neck-ring and bracelets. These may have emphasised her indigenous identity and difference (Carroll 2012: 295-96). In the post-conquest period, elaborate torcs went out of fashion in eastern Britain. Hinged and beaded copper alloy torcs continued to be made and worn in the southwest and the north (Hunter 2008: 132-34; Megaw 1971). This shift could represent a renegotiation of identities as people interacted with changing gender expectations and forms of adornment. Like the *armillae*, neck-rings may have been awarded to legionaries for bravery in battle, and later became worn as good luck symbols, synonymous with crescentic lunar amulets (Allason-Jones 1989: 122; Cool 1983: 12; MacGregor, M. 1976: 93; Pudney 2010: 115).

Discoveries of numerous torcs have led to arguments for East Anglia as a principal centre of production (Spratling 1972: 328), although Machling and Williamson propose an alternative model (2018). At North Creake, a copper alloy mould for torc buffer terminals (NHER: 1913) (Figure 4.26) was found near a gold ring terminal in the Snettisham style (NHER: 1911), indicating manufacture in the area. Five of the six torcs from Ipswich were unfinished, also suggesting local production (Brailsford 1968). There is a strong emphasis on northwest Norfolk, with outliers close to major river systems (Figure 4.27). Torcs were found in great quantities at Snettisham, with groups at Ipswich and Bawsey, and individual finds from North Creake and Sedgeford (Garrow and Gosden 2012: 137). Other parishes with possible torcs or fragments include

---

[6] Although see Marshall (in prep.) on early Roman torcs in SE England.

East Walton, East Winch, Forncett, Hevingham, Holkham, Narford and Weybourne, all in Norfolk (Hutcheson 2004).

Torcs date from the third-first centuries BCE and have continental parallels. The UK distribution is sparse, but widespread, with many antiquarian examples and a significant Scottish and Irish collection which does not

appear on PAS (Figure 4.28). Torcs are commonly made from twisted wires, with cast-on terminals, although some Snettisham examples are tubular with sheet-worked terminals. They were manufactured in carefully-selected alloys of gold, silver and copper (Garrow and Gosden 2012: 134, 137; Hutcheson 2004: 23; Machling and Williamson 2018, 2020).

Several torcs share a similar aesthetic, including asymmetrical half-moons, trumpet swirls, raised dots and basket weave, defined as a 'Snettisham style' (Hutcheson 2004: 25). These include the torcs from Sedgeford and Ipswich and those from further afield at Newark (PAS: DENO-4B33B7) (Figure 4.29) and Netherurd (Garrow and Gosden 2012: 141; Hunter 1997: 113; SHARP 2014: 33). Some motifs also link torcs with horse gear and swords. Ambiguity and fluidity of design seem to be part of this aesthetic (Garrow and Gosden 2012: 59, 142). MacGregor describes torc terminals as having an 'unpredictable layout of design' (1976: 94), which is certainly true of those from Bawsey, near King's Lynn (PAS: NMS-D3BF38, BM: 1985,1204) (Figure 4.30).

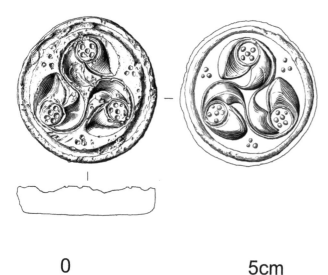

Figure 4.26. Torc terminal mould, North Creake (NHER: 1913; Illustration by S. White © NCC Historic Environment Service).

Torcs are sometimes depicted in artistic works. They may be connected with deities, such as the Hercules wearing a torc from Great Chesterford (Green 1976: 25). Two plate brooches supposedly depicting a torc-wearing owl were discussed in section 3.11.5. Similarly, the Mercury plaque from *Venta Icenorum* (Figure 4.25) may be wearing the

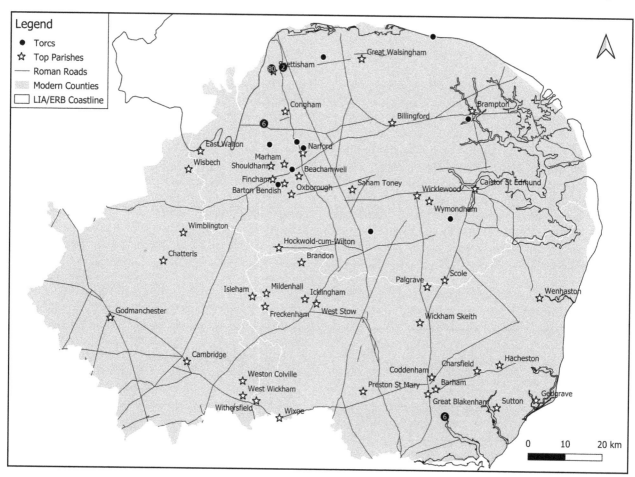

Figure 4.27. Distribution and quantity of torcs.

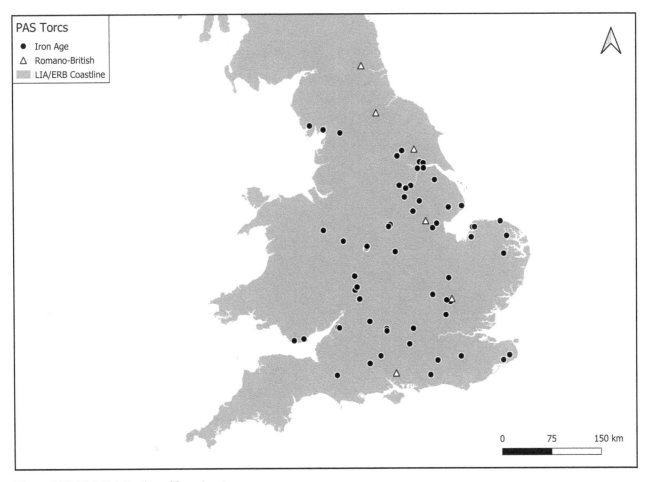

Figure 4.28. PAS distribution of Iron Age torcs.

Figure 4.29. 'Snettisham-style' decoration on the Newark torc (PAS: DENO-4B33B7).

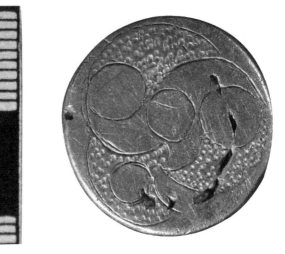

Figure 4.30. Decorated torc terminal, Bawsey (PAS: NMS-D3BF38).

snake-headed ring around its neck in imitation of a torc. I find the suggestion that torcs were made for adorning wooden statues in shrines unlikely. Wear patterns and repairs, as well as grave evidence from the mainland, suggests they were certainly worn by humans, both the living and the dead (Fitzpatrick 1992: 396; Stead 1991).

4.7. Case Study: Snettisham

The parish of Snettisham has provided us with some of the most intriguing, beautiful and technically astounding works of Iron Age art, in the form of hoards of torcs and

other personal ornament. Two hoards of jewellery deposited perhaps two centuries apart, reflect a continuity of practice, despite changing material culture. A comparison allows several of the main research questions to be touched upon: gender and regional identities, the Boudican narrative, hoarding, metalworking and continuity across and beyond the Iron Age-Roman transition. Changing archaeological interpretations and legislation also reveal how artefacts interact with modern disciplinary processes.

4.7.1. Torc Hoards from Ken Hill

Ken Hill has produced the most gold torcs in Britain and Ireland, with more than 14 separate hoards. Between the 1940s and 1990s, at least 60 torcs and over 150 fragments were found, along with bracelets, scrap metal and coins (Figure 4.31). Unfinished items, ingots and semi-molten objects provide evidence for metalworking, although the site revealed little trace of Iron Age occupation. These artefacts were carefully buried in 'nests', sometimes organised by metal alloy (Hutcheson 2004: 1, 23; Joy 2016: 243-44, Joy and Farley eds. forthcoming; Stead 1991). To gather a sense of their significance, in 2005 there were 276 torcs known from across continental Europe and perhaps 150 from Snettisham (Garrow and Gosden 2012: 138).

Interpretation of the Snettisham hoards has changed considerably over the years, partly based on archaeological understanding, but also on contemporary legislation. Under Treasure Trove law, votive deposits, grave goods and casual losses could not be declared Treasure. The criterion of 'intent to return' which was instrumental in defining Treasure Trove cases was changed in 1996, with the new Treasure Act in England and Wales.[7]

Clarke saw the tubular torcs as external objects, imported by groups of aristocratic refugees moving north following Caesar's invasions, or loot gained by Icenian raiding parties. Their rarity designated them symbols of rank amongst 'the monarchy and the priesthood', concepts derived from classical sources. The presence of gold 'cakes' and coins, and the 'dismemberment' and partial melting of many torcs led Clarke to conclude these were the stock of an 'itinerant goldsmith'. He stated emphatically that the first five hoards were deliberately buried for security, within hours or days of each other, between 25 BCE and 10 CE. Some may have been deposited in bags or boxes (Clarke and Dolley 1955: 27-86). Both Clarke and Johns (1996a: 4) consider the usage of a container evidence for 'intention to return'. Hoards A-E were duly declared Treasure (Clarke and Dolley 1955: 30-31).

After new finds in 1990, Stead reappraised the site, using repeated language of a 'treasury' of the Iceni. Drawing on continental parallels and classical texts, Stead claimed the Snettisham hoards were 'treasure assigned to the earth for safe-keeping' and 'a gradual accumulation of wealth' of a family or even an entire community. He was at pains to establish a non-votive explanation, noting that torcs are rare in British deposits in water or sanctuaries (Stead 1991: 447-65). Unlike continental finds, torcs are absent from British graves, except for a lead example from Brackmills (Garrow and Gosden 2012: 137; see discussion of lead miniatures in section 6.7.2). Stead stressed intent to return, citing the conscientious placement and secretion of the torcs. Hoards G-L were adjudged Treasure Trove (1991: 463).

The reluctance to ascribe 'votive' status to hoards may have been a political action, intended to circumvent the archaic Treasure Trove law and to claim the Snettisham torcs for the nation. This also seems to have been the case with the interpretation of the Ipswich torcs as temporarily hidden by a goldsmith or looter (Brailsford 1968). Fitzpatrick criticises Stead's reliance on classical sources and the overly simplistic sacred/profane dichotomy. Instead, he raises the social importance of hoarding and the relationships between torcs and coins. Fitzpatrick discusses the possibility that coins gradually replaced torcs as people engaged with 'different spheres of exchange' involving new concepts of wealth (1992: 395-98).

Over time the dating of the hoards has been pushed back. Clarke's dating (25 BCE-10 CE) was revised by Stead to the first quarter of the first century BCE. Hutcheson's reassessment (2004: 24) suggests manufacture in the late second century BCE, with deposition before mid-first century BCE. This removes any historically attested event, such as Caesar's abortive incursions, from the interpretation, but the sequencing is unclear and old torcs were sometimes curated before inclusion within hoards. As we have seen, archaeology has frequently been used to corroborate classical texts in the mythologising of the Iceni. The Iceni (literature, placenames) were wealthy warriors (torcs, hoards) primarily interested in horses (chariots, harness) and their 'tribal motif' was the Boar-Horse (coins) (Webster 1993: 47). Therefore, torcs are considered indicators of rank associated with warfare and individual wealth and power. Alternatively, they may have been owned and worn by generations of people, with different meanings for each. Wearing a torc could have emphasised difference rather than status, as Joy has suggested for Iron Age mirrors (2010: 76-77). As Pitts observes: 'For less hierarchical Iron Age societies, torcs could instead be used to stand for the collective wealth and power of a group, functioning as symbols of office rather than objects conferring elite status [...] While these items could have circulated in elite gift-exchange networks, their implied use in practices of communal consumption likewise cautions against viewing them as exclusively aristocratic objects' (2019: 38).

Joy (2016) rethinks Snettisham through the lens of social archaeology and object biography. He considers the cumulative aspect of hoards, the importance of practice and the longer-term actions of people (as individuals or groups) to assemble objects for deposition. Some torcs were already over a century old when they were deposited, and many show extensive use-wear and repair, raising issues of heirlooms and inheritance. Some of the coins found with the torcs were imported, others locally made. Torcs may have been made from reprocessed gold coins imported from Gaul, and later melted down to become coins again. Many objects were partially destroyed by deliberate breakage, chopping or melting; some were interlinked, especially spiral finger-rings. Joy suggests these may represent personal gifts conjoined 'to represent broader social groupings and a collective effort' (*ibid.*: 247). Garrow and Gosden draw similar parallels with

---

[7] https://finds.org.uk/treasure/advice/summary

Figure 4.31. Hoard L torcs, Ken Hill, Snettisham (BM: 1991,0407; Image: © Trustees of the British Museum).

harness hoards. The metalworking residues and pieces of scrap, along with the linked groups, suggest a connection with craft production and a preoccupation with unmaking, combining and recombining objects (Fitzpatrick 1992: 396; Garrow and Gosden 2012: 140, 176, 191).

At the time of writing, a comprehensive new volume on Snettisham is due for publication (Joy and Farley eds. forthcoming). The latest in Snettisham's long series of interpretations is eagerly awaited.

4.7.2. The Snettisham Jeweller's Hoard

Found during building work, the Snettisham Jeweller's Hoard (BM: 1986,0401) (Figure 4.32) contains over 350 objects, principally decorative personal ornaments, like the Ken Hill hoards. Yet the contents are stylistically very different, comprising silver snake bracelets, finger-rings, engraved carnelian gemstones, coins, silver ingots and scrap, buried in a small ceramic vessel (Johns 1997). Unlike the Ken Hill deposits, the Jeweller's Hoard was buried in proximity to Romano-British occupation and industrial areas, including pottery kilns and metalworking debris (Gurney in Johns 1997: 13-14).

Johns asserts that this collection was 'indisputably a manufacturer's hoard' collected for melting down

and recycling (1997: 69). She views hoards as purely practical, buried for safekeeping in times of military or political upheaval, or simply because 'the owner [...] was embarking on a long journey for business or family reasons' (1996a: 20). The latest coin is a worn *as* of Faustina I, providing a *terminus post quem* of 155 CE. The 83 *denarii* were deliberately selected for their silver content, which has led to the 'collection for reprocessing' case. However, analysis of the silver jewellery and ingots found no direct link in composition and wide disparities in purity (Burnett in Johns 1997: 16-18). Many of the objects are incomplete, which lends credence to the jeweller's hoard theory, although as we have seen with Ken Hill, fragmentation is a key component of hoarding practice. Some of the silver gem-set rings are unfinished, with hammer marks, untrimmed edges and unpolished surfaces. Many other rings are in freshly cast condition, but one or two are crushed or broken, as are the snake bracelets, which were squashed to fit into the flask. The bracelets also range from pristine condition to heavily-worn. Johns regards the snake rings as part of 'an extensive series of mass-produced, mould-made, precious-metal jewellery produced at one time in one workshop' (1997: 34-38). Several of these assumptions about the origins of this hoard have been contested. Cool puts forward a religious explanation, these items belonging to a restricted pool of ritual jewellery associated with a healing cult (2000: 37).

Figure 4.32. The Snettisham Jeweller's Hoard (BM: 1986,0401; Image: © Trustees of the British Museum).

Traces of gold alloy suggest the maker was working with other precious metals, although no finished articles were found. Local metalworkers were possibly reusing recovered torcs from Ken Hill to make new jewellery, although this is highly speculative (Pike *et al*. in Johns 1997: 58-59). Johns recognises the significance of precious metalworking in the area and goes as far as to suggest that the makers of the Ken Hill torcs were ancestors of the Romano-British jewellers. It is not beyond the realms of possibility for craft traditions to be passed down over many generations (1997: 70-73). Could this account for some of Moore's inconveniently 'tribe-sized' distributions (2011: 350)?

4.7.3. Discussion

Haselgrove observes that many LIA artefacts show uneven distributions reflecting 'preferential incorporation in certain regional hoarding or votive traditions, but not others'. Large numbers of torcs were hoarded in East Anglia, but are found elsewhere, suggesting that they were manufactured, exchanged and worn outside Icenian lands, but only deposited in exceptional, even atypical, circumstances (2015: 33). Hutcheson eschews functional explanations for hoarding due to flight or safekeeping and instead proposes hoards represent 'an ongoing, deliberate, potentially votive practice' (2004: 93). Therefore, it seems that the regional tradition of depositing portable wealth in hoards may have continued, along with a multitude of

other potentially ritualised acts, incorporating changing material culture over several centuries (chapter six).

Torcs and hoarding are seen as key 'cultural indicators' of the Iceni. The persistence of Snettisham as an appropriate location for deposition suggests an ongoing social practice, which may be associated with metalworking. The area may have been a significant, perhaps sacred, place from the second century BCE to the second century CE. Was there a healing cult here, as Cool suggests? A small Romano-Celtic temple was excavated at Ken Hill in 2004 (Hutcheson 2011). I disagree with Johns's functional explanation of the jeweller secreting his stock while going travelling or for tax purposes (1996a: 20), as too many aspects of the hoard seem to be ritualised. Additionally, the division of ritual and everyday practice is a modern construction which we should avoid applying to ancient Britain.

The overriding interest with proving the 'intent to return' of earlier hoards has clouded the interpretation of the Snettisham torcs, which has only recently been readdressed. Stead's idea of a 'tribal treasury' depended too heavily on classical and continental parallels, which did not consider the longstanding, regionally specific, tradition of hoarding. The link to Boudica and Icenian 'royalty' is untenable, given the revised chronology. The suggestion that torcs were eventually melted down to become Icenian coinage may explain the partial dismantling of some examples. Perhaps they were a form of highly decorative social currency: wealth you could wear (Fitzpatrick 1992; Joy 2016).

Joy proposes the complete torcs were associated with past generations and were taken out of 'circulation' rather than being recycled into coins. He also notes the complete size range (to fit women, men and possibly children) which demonstrates these were personal belongings and suggests torcs may have been collected when individuals died (2016: 248-50). Might hoards be proxy burials in communities which disposed of human remains in other, as yet little understood, ways? Perhaps these belongings, closely associated with individuals or lineages, were gathered and buried together as a memorialisation. The fragmentation and recombination of torcs and other jewellery in these hoards has parallels with the selection and deposition of human and animal remains in pits and in cremation burials elsewhere. The Snettisham Jeweller's Hoard may have been a late revisiting of this tradition, buried in an urn-like ceramic vessel. These ideas are discussed further in relation to hoards of horse harness in chapter eight.

4.8. Summary

This chapter has demonstrated that the people of the *civitas Icenorum* were expressing varied and multiple identities through material culture, from the simplest toggles to the ornate and precious Snettisham torcs. The distribution of *armillae* has stimulated questions about the narrative of the Boudican revolt and the potential for belongings to be deposited as war trophies. I have continued to raise doubts over the militarisation and reallocation of lands in the territory. The very restricted or concentrated distributions of torcs, *armillae* and snake jewellery may relate to local workshops and markets, but further research is necessary. Perhaps these patterns can be attributed to interconnected kin or clan-based networks of metalworkers over many generations.

Ritual practice appears to have continued, with an emphasis on hoarding and votive deposition. New material culture was incorporated into these rites. The adoption of jewellery with snake iconography, especially around Stonea and Snettisham, suggests people were expressing changing religious ideas and an interest in health and healing. Both rings and bracelets survive the 'abandonment horizon', featuring in Late Roman hoards at Hoxne and Thetford (Johns 1996b: 114-17). The emphasis on fragmentation, recombination and possible recycling of metalwork can be seen in both hoards from Snettisham. Scrap metal processing is one suggestion, but within a ritual or votive context, in which precious metals are returned to the earth.

The boundaries of function and fittingness of LIA and Roman objects were much more permeable than our restrictive archaeological categories allow. Button-and-loop fasteners may have been appropriate for clothing, containers and harness. The lines between military and civilian are also blurred. Social status and identity were most probably just as fluid. *Armillae* may have been symbolic of victory in battle, or trophies of resistance, in differing circumstances. Bracelets and torcs were worn by men, women and children, perhaps as portable displays of difference or belonging. A simple ornament could become an appropriate votive deposit, individually or in combination with other objects. Other embodied practices, relating to personal care and grooming, are more archaeologically visible in the post-conquest period. It is to these we now turn.

Personal Grooming: Display of the Self

5.1. Introduction

This chapter explores personal grooming and the relationship between the body and identity creation. The discussion moves on from decorative ornaments to the small belongings which were used to prepare the body for display and public consumption. The presence and increase of toilet implements in the Roman period represent a pervasive interest in self-presentation which matches that of personal ornaments. This 'technology of the body' was 'related to the cultivation by people of specific ideas about how to present their own identities, their well-being, and sense of their own selves. These specific new activities of caring for the body employing these objects were linked to wider changes in individuals' lifestyles, aspirations and identities' (Hill 1997: 100). The care and display of the self is tightly bound to identity and the ability of people to assimilate or stand out from the crowd.

Patterning of toilet implements, like brooches, shows a marked shift from restricted, possibly 'high-status', usage to mass consumption during the first centuries BCE/CE as part of the 'object event horizon'. This may indicate that people had greater access to objects used for grooming, that they were becoming more concerned with appearances and bodily hygiene, or that the small finds that survive represent a change in the way that these procedures were carried out. It is also possible that regional patterns demonstrate selective uptake or resistance to this incoming restyling of human appearance (Hill 1997: 98-102). Crummy and Eckardt propose a complex mix of appropriation, social change and continuity of practice. They suggest that previously 'high-status' objects became commonplace as 'elites switched to new ways (e.g. architecture, language) of expressing their superior status' (2003: 49).

This research builds on many single artefact studies, such as Cool (1990), Crummy and Eckardt (2003), Jackson (2010) and Joy (2010), by looking thematically at functional groups of objects. To Crummy's Category 2 'Toilet, Surgical and Pharmaceutical', I append the grooved mortar and pestle sets which she designated 'votive amulets' (1983: 145-46), due to their more recent interpretation as cosmetic grinders (Jackson 2010). The discussion of nail cleaners encompasses questions of social norms, grooming practice, display and appropriateness, and the division of public and private space. I have also added mirrors to this discussion, as they can equally be argued to belong within a practice of bodily preparation and modification rather than purely display. Iron Age and Roman mirrors provide insights into the recovery process and raise questions about regional burial practices (section 5.5) (Table 5.1). Several object types have reluctantly been

excluded from this discussion due to a lack of fine dating evidence, such as tweezers, cosmetic spoons, ear scoops and probes.

Grooming implements display distinctive distributions, sometimes suggesting an eastern or 'Icenian' pattern. The PAS distribution of Roman toilet instruments (including tweezers) is southeastern, extending up into Yorkshire (Figure 5.1). Combs and toilet sets (linked implements on a ring) are mostly found in excavated contexts and PAS shows low numbers of cosmetic spoons and tweezers. This disparity most probably reflects that many toilet articles and combs were made from bone, as well as the recovery bias discussed by Cool and Baxter due to the thin, wiry nature of such tools (2016a, 2016b; Appendix B).

5.2. Public or Private Grooming?

Cosmetic sets, mirrors and nail cleaners make visible the historically-situated realms of private and public grooming behaviour. Sanitary habits are often considered private or specialised acts in today's western society, although attitudes vary within and between cultural or national boundaries. Was this also the case in Roman Britain? Grooming is externally related to display of the body in the public sphere. The result of private grooming becomes one's public face, and in Roman bathhouses personal hygiene activities may have taken place in full view. This raises questions about social appropriateness and the norms governing grooming behaviour in different spaces. Was grooming carried out in public or private, and by which sectors of society? Were the tools of body modification on display?

Once public bathhouses were established in Britain, they became 'the setting for a host of activities linked to personal hygiene and well-being' (Jackson 2011: 265), one of Gardner's 'contexts of practice' (2007: 39). Hairdressing, shaving and manicures are likely to have been on offer. Age, gender and social standing would have determined the levels of access to these practices and their associated appropriate contexts of use. Taboos and

Table 5.1. Grooming implements by county

Object Type	Cambs	Norfolk	Suffolk	Total
Cosmetic Grinders	35	340	210	585
Nail Cleaners	12	74	61	147
Mirror Fragments	1	98	43	142

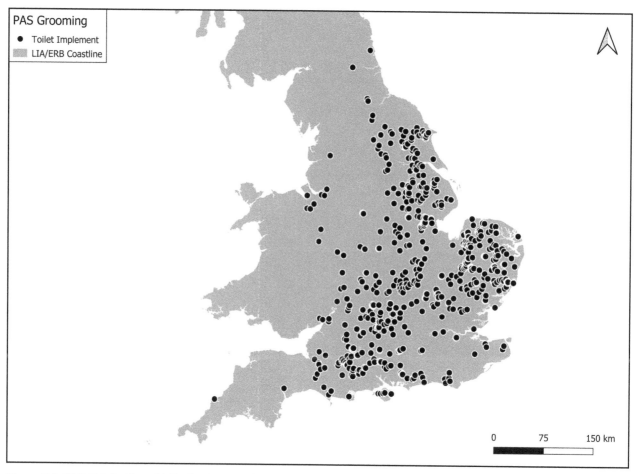

Figure 5.1. PAS distribution of toilet implements, including tweezers.

social prohibitions must have existed and changed over time. Who today would be comfortable watching someone paring their toenails beside the municipal pool? These expressions and practices would have been monitored, both from within and without.

It is unclear whether grooming sets were publicly displayed on the person. Cosmetic grinders usually have suspension loops, implying they were certainly portable, if not worn in sight. Sets of toilet instruments, usually including at least one nail cleaner, were worn suspended from Châtelaine brooches in the second century CE, suggesting they were not solely for private usage. Carr suggests that simply carrying a set or being well-groomed in public was desirable in the early Roman period (2006: 74). Eckardt and Crummy state that most small toilet implements would have been kept in private quarters. Their conclusion is based partly on the rarity of nail cleaners from bathhouses, which they argue means they were not carried or worn. The impact of grooming was nevertheless a visible sign of 'status' inscribed on the body of the individual (2008: 91-92).

This lack of nail cleaners seems strange if their purpose was for bodily grooming, an activity to be expected in the public baths. Perhaps finds from baths are rare because these grooming practices were in the hands of professionals who were less likely to lose the tools of their trade. Deposition

bias may also be at play: nail cleaners were attached to clothing by a suspension ring or brooch, unlike intaglios and finger-rings which were worn on the person, and could easily slip from the digit into the bathhouse drains, like the many examples found at York, Dover, Bath and Caerleon (MacGregor, A. 1976; Marshman 2015).

In the ensuing discussion of cosmetic grinders, palettes, nail cleaners and mirrors, I consider the role of belongings relating to grooming in creating personal and group identities. How did they act within the dynamics of appropriation and resistance during this period? Did owning cosmetic implements mark a person out as keeping up with the times, perhaps even becoming Roman?

5.3. Cosmetic Grinders

Cosmetic grinders (Figure 5.2) are two-part sets comprising a pestle and mortar. The slimmer pestle was used to crush or grind small quantities of substances in the groove of the mortar. Like Châtelaine brooches, with their conspicuous display of multiple toilet implements, cosmetic sets were multifunctional, intended to be both used and shown (Jackson 1985, 2010; Johns 1996b: 179-80). Cosmetic grinders are a southern British artefact; there are none from the forts of Hadrian's Wall and only rare examples on the continent. They are considered a strongly indigenous invention which pre-dated the conquest, but survived in

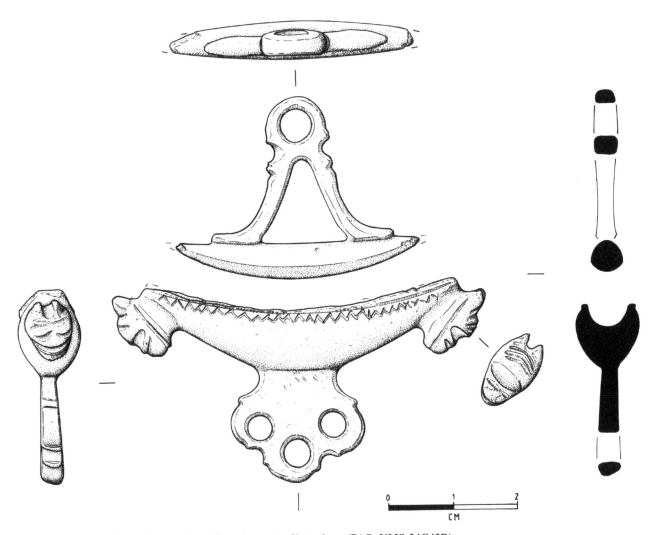

Figure 5.2. Matched set of cosmetic pestle and mortar, Shotesham (PAS: NMS-34C43D).

use into the third century CE (Carr 2006: 86; Jackson 2010: 54; Swift 2011: 209, 211). These intriguing objects show both idiosyncratic design and hybrid iconography. They are stylistically connected with brooches, seal-boxes and coins. In this section, their associations with health, fertility and gender identity are considered, as is the link between ancient Britons with the 'woad-stained warriors' of the classical writers.

Figure 5.3 shows the distribution of grinders on PAS, with concentrations in East Anglia, and *lacunae* in the extreme west, northern and upland zones. Norfolk shows a clear peak, followed by Suffolk, with Cambridgeshire far behind (Table 5.1).[1] This corresponds well with Jackson (2010), who recorded 625 cosmetic grinders from the UK up to 2004. Worrell counted 188 PAS grinders: 128 mortars and 60 pestles, with the highest proportion in Suffolk, then Norfolk (2008: 347-51). High numbers from Norfolk and Suffolk perhaps demonstrate greater usage than elsewhere

in Britain, allowing for varying levels of reporting, land-use and access (Jackson 2010: 55 and maps 1a, 1b; Worrell 2008: 348 table 4).

Jackson's dataset, which excluded PAS finds, located grinders in predominantly urban and domestic contexts, often small towns (2010: 51-52) (cf. Worrell 2008: 351). My mapping shows grinders do not respect either towns or roads, with a strongly rural distribution (Figure 5.4). This broadening of the social distribution results from my dataset of combined sources, demonstrating the value of incorporating PAS data. There are hotspots around settlements including Fincham (5), Brampton (5) and Saham Toney (9) (Figure 5.5). The concentration in Suffolk is further west than many clusters of brooches, for example, with fewer at Coddenham, Hacheston or Wenhaston.

Jackson notes a connection between cosmetic grinders and temples, especially in East Anglia. At shrines, their 'association with well-being and identity may have given them particular significance as religious gifts' (2010: 54-55). Wicklewood, particularly Crownthorpe (14), and Walsingham (13) have concentrations, as does Hockwold-cum-Wilton, with 10 finds, at least two from the temple,

---

[1] Many of the Norfolk/Suffolk grinders from Jackson's catalogue could not be matched to HER records, so coordinates are approximate, centred on parish. Some of these finds will therefore be duplicated due to insufficient information. Unprovenanced Norfolk/Suffolk collections from the BM have been excluded.

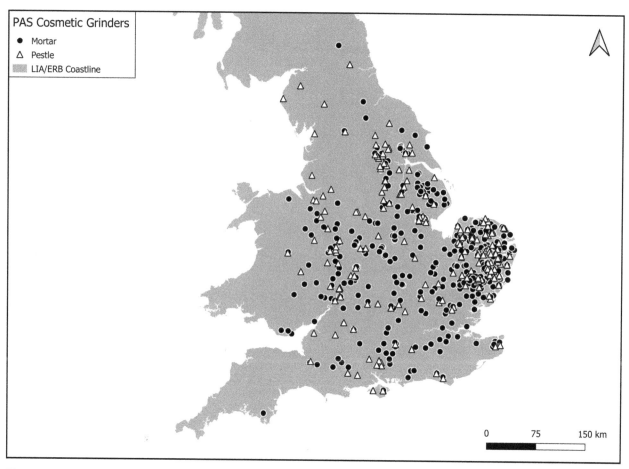

Figure 5.3. PAS distribution of cosmetic mortars and pestles.

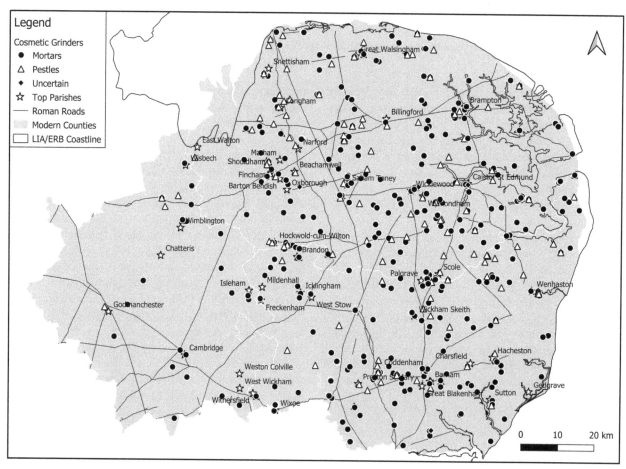

Figure 5.4. Distribution of cosmetic mortars and pestles.

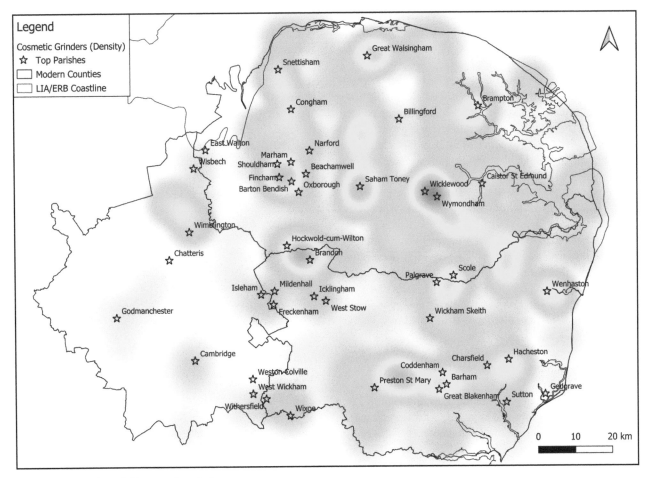

Figure 5.5. Density of all cosmetic grinders.

and a further 11 from neighbouring Brandon.[2] A previously unseen cluster in northeast Suffolk around Metfield seems unrelated to known settlement, although several scatters of Roman pottery are recorded and a Roman road runs to the west (SHER: CRT019; Margary RR55). This could signify a previously unidentified shrine in this parish.

Cosmetic mortars are typically crescent-shaped and often have figurative terminals. Both mortars and pestles can have their suspension loops either centrally placed or at one end. End-looped types are slightly earlier (first/second century CE) than centre-loops (75-300 CE). It appears that they were worn in pairs hanging from a thong or belt loop. Wear patterns show that pestles became abraded from repeated grinding against the mortar (Figure 5.6). The pointed tips may also have been used as applicators. No two examples are identical in Jackson's catalogue. This 'infinite variety' (Jackson 2010: 26) is a feature of some classes of indigenous Romano-British material culture, including nail cleaners and brooches, which goes against the perception that standardisation was necessarily part of the artefactual trend in this period.

Most complete sets come from burials of the first/second centuries CE. One cosmetic mortar was found with an adult female inhumation at Beckford, Worcs. and others

Figure 5.6. End-loop cosmetic pestle showing use-wear, Monk's Eleigh (PAS: SF-FADE94).

derive from interments gendered 'female' from other grave goods. The one exception is a possible male buried with a cosmetic set at King Harry Lane (Jackson 2010: 50-62). Cosmetic grinders may demonstrate selective displays of identity in early Roman East Anglia: 'a continuing allegiance by the Iceni to British ways after the conquest, perhaps, an acceptable, non-confrontational way of expressing a different identity, and maybe specifically by women' (*ibid*.: 52).

---

[2] Several from Crownthorpe may be duplicated with Jackson's catalogue.

Associating artefacts with gender can prove rather circular, as burial goods are not necessarily belongings of the grave's occupant. Jackson rather assumes that one person owned individual items, identity surfacing as part of a specific relationship between human and object, without considering that they could be shared or passed on. Carr considers cosmetic grinders to be creolised artefacts used for constructing identities. She infers that a pre-conquest male or gender-neutral practice of body painting changed to an expression of identity for Roman women through facial cosmetics (2006: 98).

5.3.1. *'Woad-stained Britons'? Tattooing and Body Art*

Cosmetic sets were previously known as 'woad grinders', based on classical descriptions of ancient body decoration. Caesar wrote that the Britons 'dye their bodies with woad, which produces a blue colour' (*BG* 5.14). For Ovid (*Am.* 2.16.39) and Martial (*Epig.* 16.99, 11.53.1) they were the 'green-painted' or 'woad-stained' Britons. Pliny remarks that their wives and daughters-in-law 'stain all the body' (*NH* 22.2). Propertius warns his mistress against imitating the British by painting her face blue (*Eleg.* 2.18b.23).

Carr discusses a range of potential uses and symbolism, including body-painting and tattooing. All-over colouring of the skin could be achieved by submerging the body. Woad, as an indigo dye, is activated on contact with air, resulting in a 'magical' transformation when someone stepped from the dye bath and gradually changed colour. However, the evidence for this is very limited and mostly speculative. The classical writers accentuated the Britons' otherness through barbarian practices, legitimising their assimilation into the empire. The translation of 'woad' is disputed, and it may refer to a completely different dye plant (2005: 278, 2006: 85-100).

The Iceni may have painted or tattooed their skins, like other peoples around the world past and present, for ornamental, religious or healing reasons. Body decoration and modification can reinforce group identities, both temporarily, by staining the surface of the skin, and permanently, by tattooing or scarification. Body art may also have played a part in resistance, as a 'hidden discourse' which allowed subtle anti-Roman messages to be shared (Carr 2005, 2006: 96). Jackson dismisses the connection with woad (2010: 11-12). The contents of a cosmetic grinder have never been successfully analysed and there are no known references to their use in contemporary writings. Suggestions have included body paint, facial cosmetics, medicinal herbs, drugs or other stimulants, even aphrodisiacs. Woad is perhaps the least likely due to the quantities necessary for body-painting in comparison to the small capacity of the mortars. Morrison proposes an alternative medical use for grinders in treatment for the eye disorder *trachoma* (2013: 228-29).

5.3.2. *Zoomorphic and Phallic Terminals*

Cosmetic sets can also be investigated based upon their

decorative schemes. Enamelled types (Figure 5.7) are broadly consistent with the symmetrical, geometric designs found on first/second century CE horse harness, seal-boxes and plate brooches. Type J mortars, with polychrome schemes of enamelled 'toothed' triangular cells, are most common in Norfolk and Suffolk. Zoomorphic terminals are more frequent than knobbed, which may support a regional preference for animals (section 9.6). Fusions of 'Celtic and Roman' traditions can be seen in some portrayals (Jackson 2010). Some grinders have one bovid and one avian terminal suggesting these were not mutually exclusive categories of decoration (Figure 5.8), but

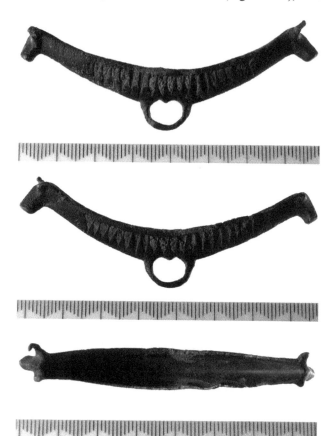

Figure 5.7. Enamelled mortar with bovid head terminals, Burgate (PAS: SF-E508C7).

Figure 5.8. Zoomorphic mortar and pestle, Hockwold-cum-Wilton (BM: 1977,0403.1; Image: © Trustees of the British Museum).

combined types are infrequent (Table 5.2). Zoomorphic grinders show clusters of bovid types in north and south Norfolk (Figure 5.9). Birds are more common on the east coast, the northern Fen-edge and mid-Norfolk. The inhabitants of the *civitas* may have been expressing their identity through these belongings.

Why do cosmetic grinders not depict horses? As discussed below (chapter eight), equids rarely feature in LIA figurative art. The dating of the grinders runs well into the mid-Roman period, by which time horses were being represented on brooches and figurines. Does this show the extension of a pre-Roman restriction? Or did bovids and waterbirds hold special significance in grooming or healing? Morrison associates the animal representations with healing deities (2013: 228-29), albeit based on Green's work which relies greatly on Gaulish parallels. Crummy also noted the lack of representations of horses, relating the bovid and phallic terminals to strength and fecundity (1983: 146). Jackson also links the presence of bull and cow terminals to fertility (2010: 21). Carr even proposes the use of semen as a binder for cosmetic preparations (2006: 97). Perhaps the sets were used for substances associated with aphrodisiacs or fertility rituals. Centre-looped mortars can appear to have a uterine form.[3] The actions of the pestle (male) and mortar (female) grinding together may have embodied this straightforward symbolism of fertility and virility. However, 'knobbed' terminals occur only on mortars, although the end-loop pestles could be seen as essentially phallic in shape (Jackson 2010: 21) (Figure 5.10). This is surely in part a practical consideration to allow the two components to fit together, but also inverts (or subverts) this interpretation, whereby the phallus becomes the vessel.

A link with temples or ritual behaviour is indicated by small groups of phallic mortars at Walsingham (4), Wicklewood (5), Saham Toney (3) and Hockwold-cum-Wilton (3) (Figure 5.11). The phallus was an apotropaic device in the Roman world (section 6.7.6). Possibly mortars were multifunctional; worn as amulets or deposited as votive offerings once their original purpose was concluded. Phallic symbolism was a post-conquest import, yet the grinders are distinctively British, and their incorporation into the iconography suggests a merging of belief systems (Jackson 2010: 21). Were zoomorphics seen as more 'local' or familiar than the 'foreign' phallic symbols? These are problematic categories which tend to divide people into 'us and them', lines which could have been drawn very differently in the past. A look at the terminal types confounds expectations: there are more knobbed grinders from the 'indigenous' settlements at Wicklewood and Saham Toney and more zoomorphics from the Romano-British shrines at Hockwold and Walsingham (Figure 5.12). This may imply that only selected mortars were considered appropriate for deposition at shrines.

Table 5.2. Cosmetic grinders by terminal type

Object Type	Cambs	Norfolk	Suffolk	Total
Knobbed	8	49	35	92
Zoomorphic	4	57	48	109
Both	4	8	4	16
Centre-Loop	18	186	115	319
End-Loop	14	81	79	174

5.3.3. Loop Types

Both end- and centre-loop types are widespread without any strong clusters. Norfolk has more of the slightly later dated centre-loops, with Suffolk closely following (Figure 5.13, Table 5.2). This agrees with Jackson (2010: 57) and Worrell (2008: 349), who both identified regional preferences in Norfolk and Suffolk for centre-looped sets. This may indicate that grinders were popular in the *civitas*, later or for longer, hinting at indigenous resistance, or at least endurance. Alternatively, like the hinged and sprung brooches (section 3.11.4), this may relate to different workshops and artistic preference.

5.3.4. Manufacture

Regional variability can demonstrate the existence of metalworking workshops, supplying specific areas with similar items. There is little manufacturing evidence for cosmetic grinders, although like brooches, they are frequently found with evidence for miscasting, repair and modification. A rare lead alloy model for a Type A mortar with bovid heads was excavated in London (Jackson 2010: 148, #318). Like most other objects discussed in this study, cosmetic sets were made in piece moulds, then finished to a high level of individuality. The aesthetic of 'similar but different' (section 2.3.7) applies. This may in part be due to the need for hand-finishing, as well as the more personal choices of the maker or commissioner. The distribution of unfinished or miscast grinders is predominantly in Norfolk (Figure 5.14), which may indicate local recording differences, but also correlates with the incidence of horse harness and brooch production in the north of the region.

Jackson considers very similar examples to share a point of manufacture and those with matching design features a common 'craft or workshop' practice. A series of matched components reveals repeat castings from the same model, if not the same mould (2010: 4, 9). Table 5.3 shows some examples from East Anglia. A rough-finished, unprovenanced Type D mortar may be evidence for a test casting of a well-made example from Saham Toney (Jackson #429).

Occasional finds show evidence of forging. Examples include a mortar from Brettenham (Jackson #51) with a quatrefoil on an open end-loop and one from Felthorpe

---

[3] My thanks to Bill Cremen for pointing this out.

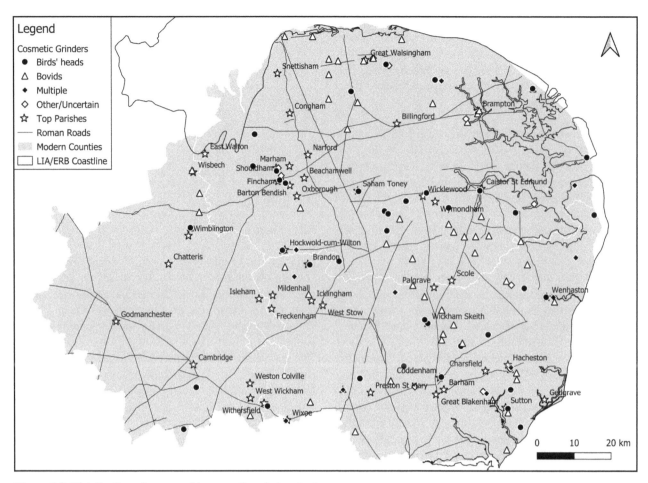

Figure 5.9. Distribution of zoomorphic cosmetic grinders by type.

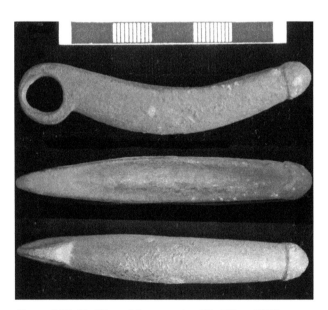

Figure 5.10. Phallic end-loop mortar, West Stow (PAS: NMS-6AD275).

(#186) which has a coiled end-loop. An unprovenanced pestle from Norfolk (#388) and a mortar (#482) from Stonea have free ends on their loops, again suggesting working rather than casting. This process is reminiscent of the integral springs on Colchester brooches which were forged after casting. These examples are all the earlier end-

loop types, which may suggest a production relationship with brooches. Hybrid or transitional manufacturing techniques have been suggested for the bronze workshop near *Venta Icenorum* (section 3.5.4).

Flawed castings were not always abandoned after production. Some poorly-cast examples were obviously well-used. Repairs and alterations were also made to several examples, including rectifying casting failures (Jackson 2010: 9-10). Other miscastings would have been recycled. On a mortar from Litcham, the snout of one bovid head terminal is considerably shorter than the other. The suspension piercing has also failed, appearing as a 'blind hole'. The central groove is smooth and unworn (PAS: NMS-82D933) (Figure 5.15). It was found close to a large metal recycling site which included lead weights, partly-melted coins, scrap metal, ingots and crucible fragments. Perhaps this object was discarded on its way to be reprocessed due to these flaws.[4] A loop may never have been intended on the knobbed mortar with the curious pedestal foot from Brome and Oakley (PAS: SF-AD6071) (Figure 5.16).

A unique, and fascinating, hybrid cosmetic mortar/brooch comes from Thelnetham, Suffolk (BM: 2010,8007.1). It

---

[4] Michael de Bootman (pers. comm. 17/11/2017).

126

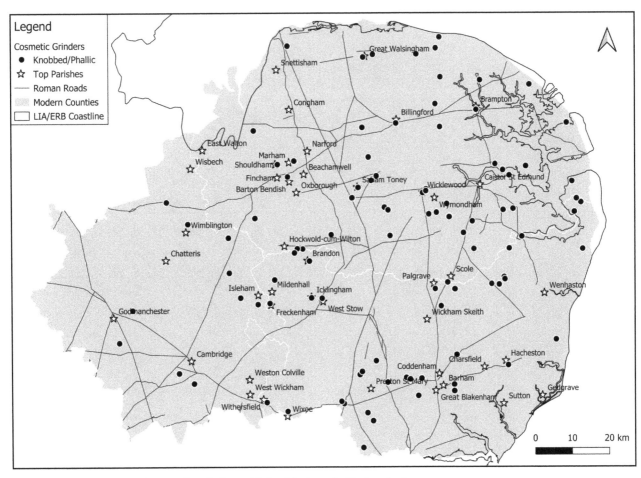

Figure 5.11. Distribution of cosmetic grinders with knobbed or phallic terminals.

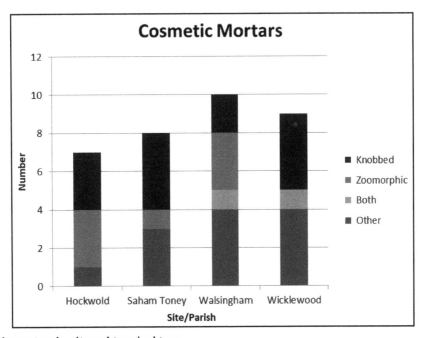

Figure 5.12. Cosmetic mortars by site and terminal type.

exhibits hybridity of form, function and ornament. It has an end-looped terminal in the shape of a waterbird's head (possibly a duck) and an opposing heavily-worn bovid head terminal. The creature's 'belly' is decorated with a 'scrolled' roundel which would have been highly visible when worn as a brooch. The reverse has an oval groove and the catchplate and lugs for a hinged pin (Jackson 2010: 193, #500). This fusion of mortar and brooch would not have been especially practical; for it to function in one capacity would negate its ability to function in the other. In this respect, it is similar to Châtelaine brooches which combine a decorative fastener with grooming implements.

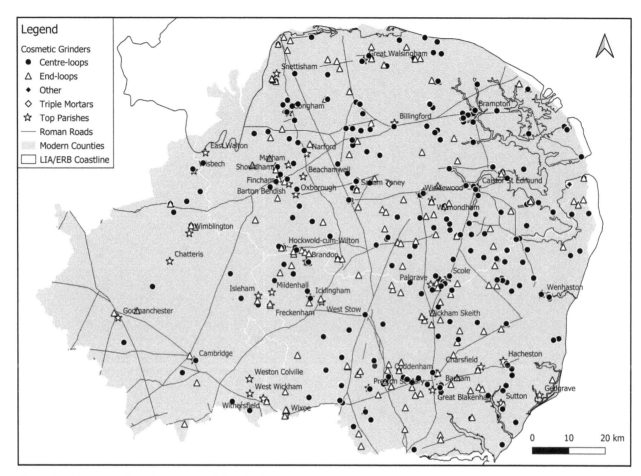

Figure 5.13. Distribution of cosmetic grinders by loop type.

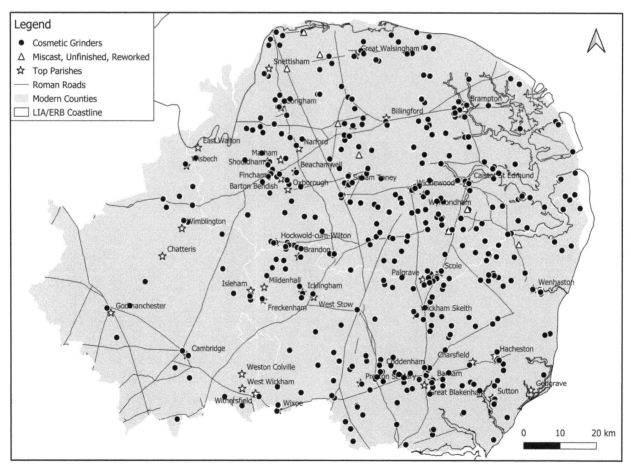

Figure 5.14. Distribution of miscast, unfinished and forged grinders.

Table 5.3. Matched cosmetic grinder components (Jackson 2010)

Jackson Cat. No. and Site/Parish	Description
#483 Stonea, #597 unprov.	Type B end-loop mortars
#53 Northants, #158 EA unprov.	Type F, Brigstock Temple; md find on antiquity market
#36 Brampton, #213 Walsingham, #510 Toftrees	3 very similar Type E centre-loop mortars
#129 ?Colchester (spurious prov.), #279 Icklingham, #578 unprov.	3 Type J mortars, knobbed terminals
#399 Oakley, #584 unprov.	Knobbed centre-loop mortars; probably same mould/model; unprov. from collector, Cambridge area
#429 Saham Toney, #582 unprov.	Type D centre-loop mortars; one well cast and finished and a very similar poorly cast and finished unprov. example, possible test casting
#134 Congham, #139 Cranworth	Type M triple mortars

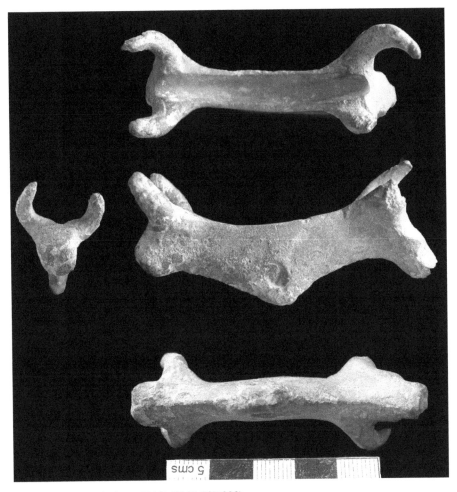

Figure 5.15. Miscast bovid mortar, Litcham (PAS: NMS-82D933).

The curvilinear pattern is reminiscent of the 'Swash N' designs on seal-boxes. However, this is a form of display which clearly references an indigenous practice, possibly as a means of emphasising the wearer's Britishness (Eckardt 2008: 126; Jackson 2010: 24, 193). Many other brooches of this period demonstrate hybrid forms and motifs, suggesting that their makers were selecting from a varied repertoire of stylistic, ornamental and functional options, which had their own sets of social and practical rules.

Lastly, two Type M oddities from Norfolk have three conjoined mortars in a curved triangular layout. This 'steering wheel' symbol is recognisable from linch-pin terminals (section 4.3) and Icenian Face-Horse coins, where it appears in an eye or shield above the horse (Figure 5.17). These triple mortars are so similar they may derive from the same mould. The inner grooves on both sets exhibit extensive wear-polish, so they were not purely ornamental. Their findspots at Congham (Jackson #134), not far from Snettisham, and Cranworth (Jackson #139), close to

Figure 5.16. Mortar with unusual 'foot', Brome and Oakley (PAS: SF-AD6071).

Figure 5.17. Face-Horse coin showing curved triangle motif, Wordwell (PAS: SF-04516E).

Saham Toney, suggest they may be products of the more experimental regional metalworkers. Jackson calls them a 'novelty', showing a 'pleasing symmetrical asymmetry', but providing no apparent functional advantages (2010: 26). They perhaps visually reference the triskele and the Icenian fondness for triplication (Davies 2014: 27). Like centre-loop mortars, the triangular shape may represent the uterus, which was conceived of as a cup in the Graeco-Roman medical tradition (Dasen 2014: 180). This finds parallels with the preference in northern East Anglia for female figurines and vulvate mounts (section 6.7.6). Were these complementary to the phallic mortars, perhaps even used to grind 'gendered' ingredients?

5.3.5. Cosmetic Palettes

Jackson proposes that cosmetic grinders were indigenous versions of the flat palettes, usually of marble, used to mix medicaments and cosmetics elsewhere in the empire. The funerary association of grinders with women may have changed with the introduction of new cosmetic items

from the continent. Importantly, grinders did not fall out of fashion in Britain once the 'cosmetic paraphernalia' of the invaders became commonplace (Jackson 2010: 11-12). Were these two categories of artefact used for the same purpose, although they were contemporaneous? Did people change from painting designs on their bodies to their faces? It is possible that both types of object were used to prepare cosmetics, the visual result being more important than the tools used to achieve it. A shift in material culture may not have been accompanied by a shift in practice.

However, Eckardt plausibly argues the flat palettes were used for mixing writing or drawing inks rather than cosmetics or medicines (2018: 28-29). No systematic residue analysis has yet been carried out. Stone palettes occur in graves with inkwells, as well as grooming or medical implements, which implies they could be multifunctional. The two forms are vastly dissimilar, in terms of material, shape, design and portability. None of the flat palettes are made from copper alloy. They may have been intended for mixing rather than grinding, with a wider working surface. The bevelled edges also provided a surface for cleaning or sharpening utensils. In terms of *praxis*, even the action of grinding differs, the linear motion of the indigenous sets contrasting with the circular wear-patterns on the stone palettes (Eckardt 2018: 214-15; Eckardt and Crummy 2008: 39; Jackson 1988: 73-74).

Venta Icenorum presents a mixture of both object types. Six 'Roman-style' palettes were found across the *civitas* capital. Two 'indigenous' cosmetic mortars and a pestle are known from the wider parish of Caistor St Edmund. Within the town, a finely-made zoomorphic mortar with swan's head terminals and a central suspension loop was excavated from inside a kiln (NWHCM: 1929.152.B136) (Figure 5.18). One stone palette (NWHCM: 1929.152. M23) came from a trench including mirror fragments, a glass bead, two pins and a needle. An unusual jet/shale palette was found in the east part of the Forum (NWHCM: 1929.152.M77) (Figure 5.19). It is oval in plan and has a smooth circular wear pattern on its upper face. There may be sharpening grooves on the underside. A refuse deposit outside the South Gate contained two 'Purbeck marble' mixing palettes (NWHCM: 1929.152.X9, X10), along with an enamelled seal-box lid, two bone counters and three pins. Two flat stone palettes were excavated in Building 4 (NWHCM: 1929.152.M66, unnumbered). This structure had a high proportion of personal ornament and grooming finds, as well as weaving tablets, needles and spindle whorls (Harlow in Bowden forthcoming). It could be argued that these are all items which tend to be gendered feminine, although we should be no more surprised to find associations of women with literacy than cosmetics. The presence of six palettes and only one grinder suggests the people of the *civitas* capital embraced some practices embodied by incoming material culture, at the expense of indigenous forms. It seems likely the stone palettes reflect more urban preoccupations, like writing and administration. Other evidence for literacy is discussed in chapter seven.

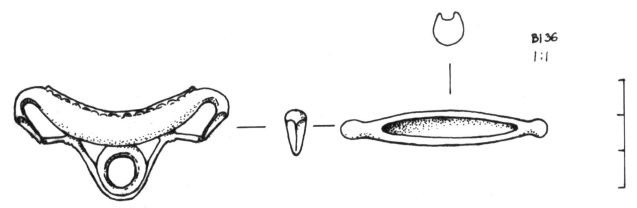

Figure 5.18. Zoomorphic mortar with swan's head terminals (NWHCM: 1929.152.B136, Image: CRP, illus. Jenny Press).

Figure 5.19. Jet palette showing use-wear, *Venta Icenorum* (NWHCM: 1929.152.M77, Image: Author).

5.3.6. Discussion

Cosmetic grinders are prone to the same collection bias as other attractive, small, portable items, like seal-boxes and terrets. Pestles are rarer than mortars, probably due to misidentification and a lack of reporting. Their small size makes them prone to corrosion and harder to identify in the ground (Jackson 2010: 4; Worrell 2008: 349). Respecting Cool and Baxter's critique of brooches (2016a, 2016b; Appendix B), it is likely that morphological bias creates differential recovery of pestles and mortars. Positive recovery bias may apply to enamelled mortars in the same way as plate brooches and terrets.

Cosmetic grinders reveal much about the post-conquest *civitas* and the identity of its inhabitants, even if their contents remain a mystery. Although they are Romano-British items in date, they are distinctly non-standardised and exhibit characteristic Iron Age motifs like bulls and birds. They persist into the third century CE, suggesting a longevity which may reflect resistance, especially in rural areas, to the incoming trend for flat and unornamented palettes. Was this related to the Icenian penchant for ornament (Mackreth 2011: 67)? Cosmetic grinders disappear after the end of the third century CE, although their use appears to outlast many of the brooches and other object types. This again reveals complex and plural 'abandonment horizons'.

Grinders are hybrid and cross-functional, with the adoption of phallic terminals and the potential for a second life as votive offerings or amulets. Grinding may have taken place in private, perhaps even as part of initiation rituals, but the sets were worn on the person, presumably in public, and sometimes in death. They are tied to the idea of the British, and the Iceni, as barbarian 'Others', tattooed or painted, a concept which holds strong in many popular reconstructions, despite the lack of archaeological evidence. Like cosmetic grinders, nail cleaners relate to ideas of display of the self, embodied identities and personal grooming.

5.4. Nail Cleaners

Nail cleaners were introduced into Britain in the LIA, with selective indigenous adoption and development. While they succeeded in southern and eastern parts of Britain (Figure 5.20), on the continent their use died out, or was supplanted by a different practice, after the Augustan period. Nail cleaners are found on settlements throughout the occupation, developing distinctive uses as strap-ends in the Late Roman period, and as Anglo-Saxon grave goods (Eckardt 2008; Eckardt and Crummy 2008: 93-96). Their social distribution in smaller habitations identifies them as a particularly 'British' artefact type (Ferris 2012: 142). This provides a good example of a sort of artefact 'naturalisation' process, which may affect the way we think of many of the supposedly 'incoming' object types during this period.

The presence of nail cleaners in British burials peaked around the invasion. The gendering of toilet implements in Britain is unknown, as there are very few from sexed grave contexts. The adult male burial from King Harry Lane, *Verulamium*, included an unusual nail cleaner, a probable ear scoop, an end-looped phallic mortar and pestle set, as well as an imported Rosette brooch. This grave is dated to

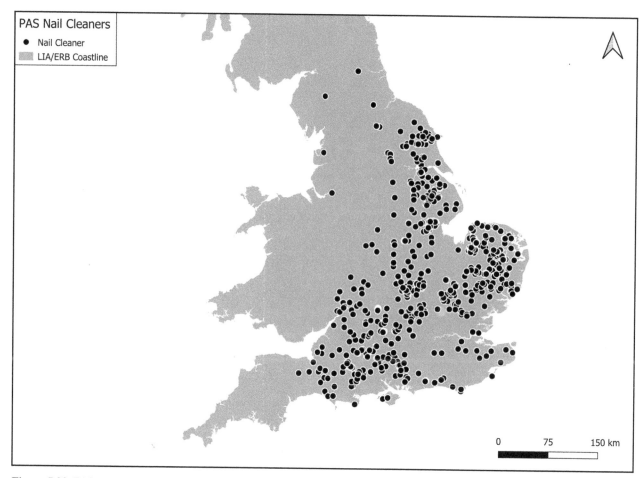

Figure 5.20. PAS distribution of Roman nail cleaners.

circa 35-55 CE, which suggests an early adopter of toilet implements or the bodily effects they created (Carr 2006; Eckardt and Crummy 2008).

Nail cleaners were often held on a suspension loop or a Châtelaine brooch with other toilet articles such as tweezers and ear scoops. It is thought they were multipurpose tools for cleaning and trimming the nails. These small copper alloy items fall into several types, the main diagnostic features being the shape of the blade and the angle at which it meets the suspension loop or handle (Figure 5.21, Figure 5.22). The ends are usually bifurcated and pointed, often showing uneven use-wear on one tip. Like cosmetic grinders, they show a wide range of decorative and formal styles and are highly individual (Eckardt and Crummy 2008; Jackson 2011: 265-66).

Norfolk has the most nail cleaners in the study area. There are minor groupings around towns including Caistor St Edmund (4), Coddenham (4), Hacheston (6) and Pakenham (4). Five come from Beachamwell on the Fen Causeway, close to Iron Age and Roman settlements at Toot Hill (NHER: 4530) and Barton Bendish. The nail cleaners seem to peak at the southern edge of the Icknield Way hotspot which includes Fincham and Oxborough. This region has strong continuity from the LIA into the Roman period. Nail cleaners are infrequent in the Fens and northeast Norfolk (Figure 5.23, Figure 5.24).

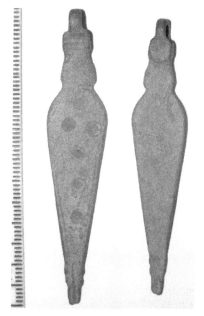

Figure 5.21. Nail cleaner with loop in same plane, Stapleford (PAS: CAM-1736C2).

In comparison to cosmetic grinders, deposition of nail cleaners from known shrines is low. There are none recorded from the area around Hockwold. Four examples come from Walsingham, one each from temples at Crownthorpe (NHER: 8897) and Scole (NHER: 30650)

Figure 5.22. Nail cleaner with loop at right angles, West Stow (PAS: SF-70F507).

and another from Fison Way, Thetford (NHER: 5853). Deposition of toilet instruments at Romano-British shrines may have been part of the wider tradition of devoting personal belongings, such as brooches or hairpins. Some nail cleaners are described as 'bent' or 'damaged', but this could be post-depositional. Toilet implements are rare in hoards, unlike personal ornaments (Eckardt and Crummy 2008: 103-4), which suggests an element of appropriateness for deposition. Crummy proposes the weapon-like shape of toilet implements represents dissent, a 'quietly subversive imagery' which followed Roman disarmament of the British. The popularity and longevity of nail cleaners in Britain depended on 'their similarity to forbidden weapons' (2016: 290-92). Could this explain the high concentration in the indigenous settlements of northwest Norfolk?

Eckardt and Crummy looked at the social distribution of toilet implements. Although significant numbers of nail cleaners occurred at military sites, large towns and *civitas* capitals, most of their examples came from small towns, rural settlements and villas. This counters the expectation that nail cleaners were associated with 'an incoming, highly Romanised population'. Instead 'the social distribution pattern of nail-cleaners is biased towards the "native" end of the settlement hierarchy' (2008: 97). While I am uncomfortable with the idea of a native/Roman settlement hierarchy, my distribution agrees that nail cleaners are widespread in rural parts and clustered in an area of LIA

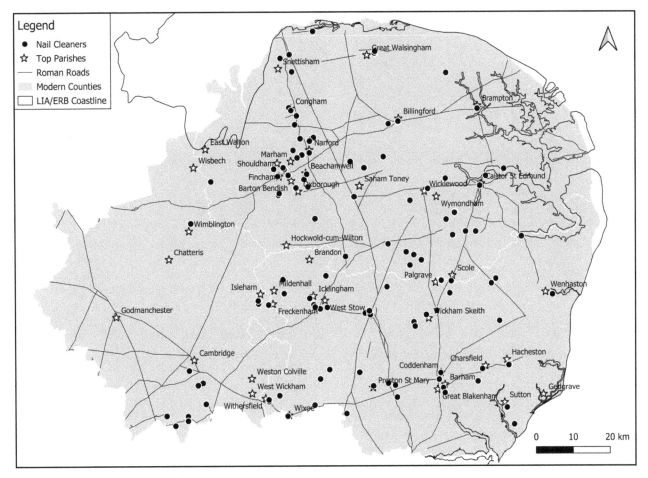

Figure 5.23. Distribution of nail cleaners.

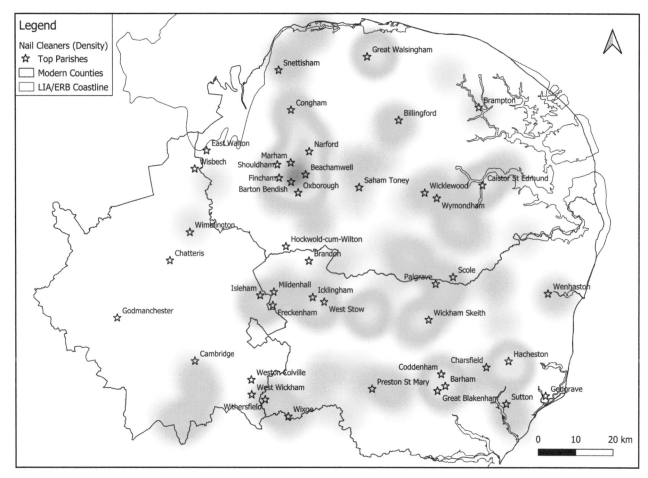

Figure 5.24. Density of nail cleaners.

activity. Eckardt and Crummy's study only used PAS as a supplementary, rather than primary, resource (2008: 16). Worrell's appendix of PAS finds (*ibid.*: 177-81) added many rural sites to Eckardt and Crummy's distribution. This demonstrates the value of PAS finds for filling in distributions, despite the problems of context.

5.4.1. Loop Types

Substantial regional preferences were found for these artefacts. Norfolk has more nail cleaners with the blade and handle in the same plane. Right-angle types are more common in Suffolk, and the Baldock types (which have a distinctive groove running parallel to the blade edges) are wholly absent in the north of the region (Figure 5.25, Figure 5.26). Baldock nail cleaners are tightly concentrated in Hertfordshire and Essex, corresponding with the supposed Catuvellaunian territory, or the manufacturing zone which includes penannular copper alloy torcs and Wide-cuff bracelets (Marshall in prep.) (Figure 5.27). I agree with Eckardt and Crummy that these do not represent group identity, the distributions more likely reflecting production zones and individual or local aesthetic choices (2008: 67-69 and fig. 29). These regional preferences are at odds with the cosmetic grinders discussed above; where nail cleaners appear strongly localised, the grinders showed a widespread distribution of both end-loop and centre-loop types (Figure 5.13).

5.4.2. Châtelaine Brooches

Châtelaine brooches were designed to hold a set of toilet implements on a bar suspended between two projecting lugs (Figure 5.28). These replaced sets hanging on suspension loops in the late first century CE. They are very occasionally found in burials (Eckardt and Crummy 2008: 74, 81-82). Clearly intended to be worn and displayed, the implements may have been non-functional for grooming (Eckardt 2008: 126).

There are 34 Châtelaine brooches in my dataset: Cambridgeshire (2), Norfolk (12) and Suffolk (20), Coddenham and Barham being the only parishes with two examples each (Figure 5.29). Mackreth includes Châtelaines with his British 'petalled boss' series (2011: 166), although Hattatt says they were probably imported (1982: 149). The geometric enamelling, often blue and yellow, links them to Dragonesques, umbonate brooches and horse harness, and an indigenous, post-conquest origin, related to the mass uptake of grooming implements. The strong Suffolk emphasis in distribution echoes the Dragonesques (section 3.12.3) and other plate brooches, but there is only one from Essex, and few from Yorkshire (the homeland of Dragonesques) on PAS. By contrast, the concentration of individual nail cleaners is focussed on the Icknield Way settlements (Figure 5.24). This makes sense if the bifid nail cleaners were seen as a wholly indigenous

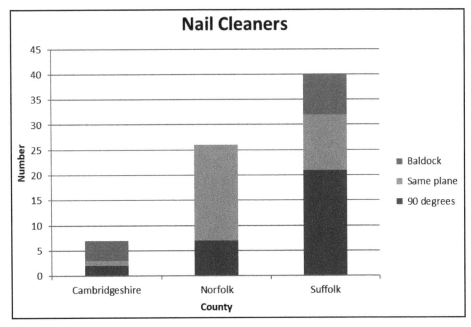

Figure 5.25. Nail cleaners by type and county.

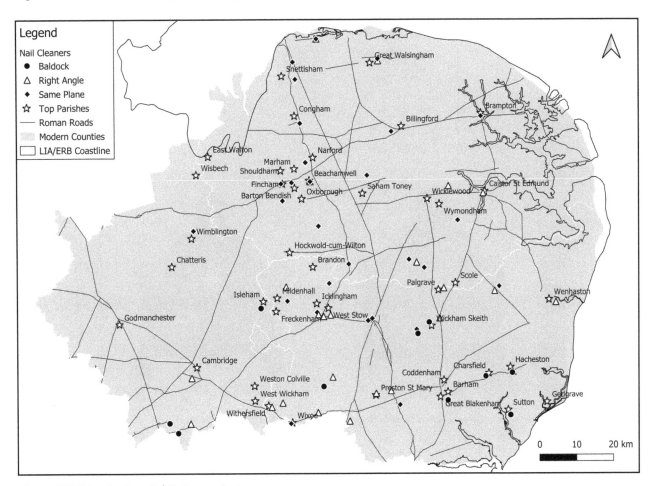

Figure 5.26. Distribution of nail cleaners by type.

form by this period, showing the way in which external items can become completely embedded within a new cultural milieu.

Eckardt and Crummy assert that these implements were purely decorative and symbolic, privileging display over function, expressing status through 'the well-groomed body' (2008: 173). Nevertheless, occasional implements on Châtelaines do show use-wear. The tips of a nail cleaner from Croft, Leicestershire are unevenly broken off (PAS: LEIC-8572C4) (Figure 5.30). Hattatt (1985: 169, #603) illustrates a Châtelaine brooch from Epping Forest, Essex, with a nail cleaner, ear scoop and tweezers. The nail cleaner shows characteristic wear on only one point

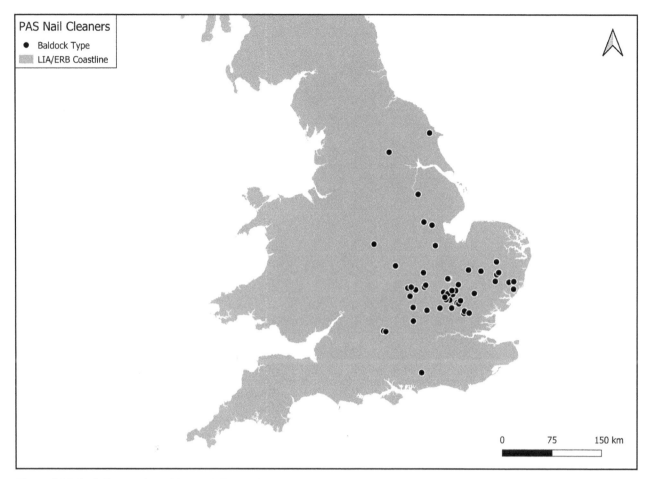

Figure 5.27. PAS distribution of Baldock Type nail cleaners.

Figure 5.28. Châtelaine brooch showing suspension fittings, Melbourn (PAS: CAM-F66342).

of the bifurcated end, suggesting that it saw functional use at some time in its life. Although toilet instruments could have been purely for show, a set of tools carried on the person could have been utilised when necessary. The nail cleaner would not need to be detached from the suspension bar to be functional, rather like a Swiss Army knife.

The proliferation of enamelled geometric decoration in the second century CE on items including seal-boxes, harness, brooches and cosmetic grinders suggests a widespread, if not blanket, aesthetic. Two oddities are noted from Norfolk.

One is a brooch from Narborough which shows no evidence for the horizontal bar for hanging implements (PAS: NMS-FFD942); it also displays a quatrefoil enamelled motif which references the platform-decorated terrets from Saham Toney (section 8.10.3). In my view, this object has had its attachment lugs removed and filed down at the corners, which are unusually rounded. The display component of this brightly-enamelled brooch may have had more significance to its wearer than the attached grooming implements. Perhaps during the object's life history, the bar was broken, its toilet implements lost, but it was still considered worthy of reuse.

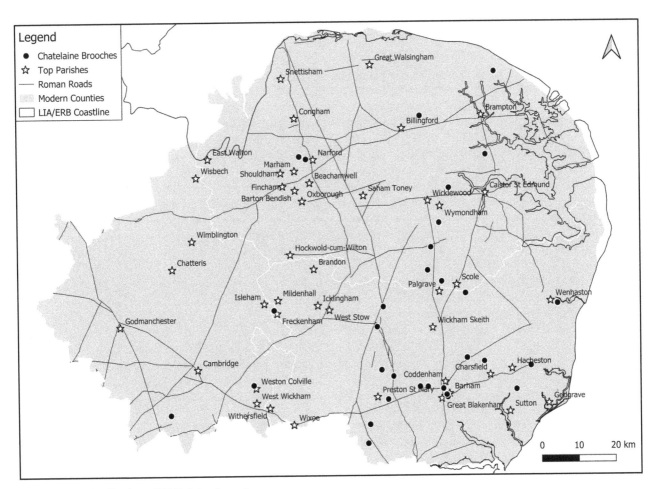

Figure 5.29. Distribution of Châtelaine brooches.

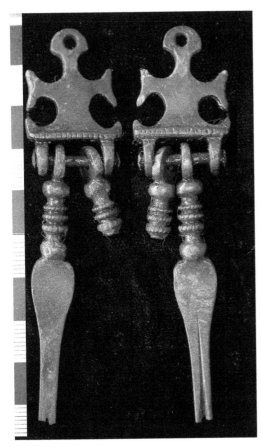

Figure 5.30. Châtelaine brooch with broken nail cleaner, Croft (PAS: LEIC-8572C4).

The second is a heavily-modified brooch from Themelthorpe, apparently cut down into a triangular shape and pierced (Figure 5.31). Rogerson suggests reuse as a mount (PAS: NMS-F66332), to which I would add the potential for it to have been nailed up in a shrine, like two disc brooches from Hockwold (section 6.6). These modifications hint that people in the north of the region may not have always used Châtelaines to display toilet implements, but adapted them accordingly to fit their own practices. This shows how the same artefacts may cross boundaries between display and practice or practical and votive uses.

Figure 5.31. Modified Châtelaine brooch, Themelthorpe (PAS: NMS-F66332).

5.4.3. Negotiated Identities and Creolisation

No two nail cleaners are exactly alike, and their decoration is variable and idiosyncratic. The diversity of design noted by Crummy and Eckardt (2008: 179) parallels the cosmetic grinders, which 'probably represents the customising of a very intimate possession' (Jackson 2011: 266). Although the distribution of these two artefacts is similar (Figure 5.32), the grinders are more widespread in rural areas, and the densities and 'rules' for loop types do not synchronise. The scarcity of nail cleaners from bathhouses suggests that some Britons avoided these places of observation and self-monitoring, carrying out indigenous grooming practices in other locations. Crummy and Eckardt regard Britain's incorporation into the Roman empire as 'the catalyst for the large-scale production of small *personalia* [which] removed the barriers of privilege' from personal artefacts (2003: 61). This may represent a democratisation of the body, a new ability to procure, personalise and use items within the renegotiation of identities occasioned by the conquest.

Carr proposes that unusual nail cleaners are better represented at small settlements, villas and religious sites than large towns. She sees these as deliberately equivocal 'creole' artefacts which expressed post-conquest counter-cultural identities (2006: 81-83). Identifying 'unusual' examples in my dataset proved difficult, due to the overall individuality of the objects. The distinctiveness of nail cleaners and cosmetic grinders raises questions about the commissioning process, the aesthetics of 'similar but different', and the potential for both normalising and subversive uses in different contexts, from bathhouse to burial. My data indicate a clear distinction between single nail cleaners and Châtelaine brooches, possibly between usage and display. This may be an example of the ambiguous negotiation between Roman domination and British resistance in which 'provincial artefacts in the Roman world can sometimes appear "Romanised", but can in fact operate according to a different, indigenous, set of underlying rules. As creole artefacts, they can negotiate with, resist, or adapt Roman art styles to serve indigenous ends, and ultimately, they are part of the emergence of a creole society' (Webster 2003: 42).

5.5. Iron Age Mirrors

Iron Age mirrors were discs of highly polished metal, usually with handles (Figure 5.33). They often display elaborate, curvilinear decoration, in the La Tène style. Joy catalogued 58 from Britain, predominantly in southern-central England (2010). The earliest mirrors from East Yorkshire are *circa* 400 BCE, but most others date to the first centuries BCE/CE. Many items of material culture span the conquest in this way, which reveals the artificiality of the division between LIA and Roman in Britain.

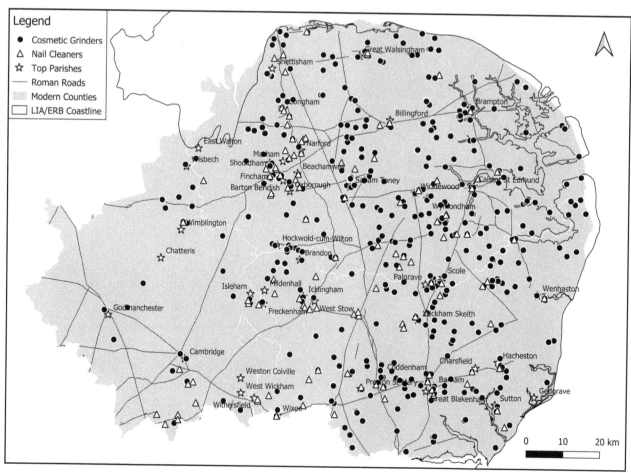

Figure 5.32. Comparative distribution of nail cleaners and cosmetic grinders.

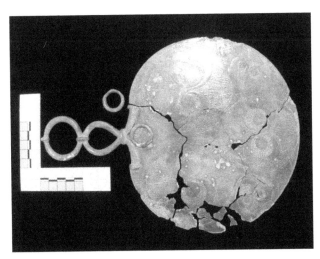

Figure 5.33. Decorated Iron Age mirror, Portesham, Dorset (PAS: DOR-F12EF3).

Iron Age mirrors are rare and special items, like torcs. They are virtually absent in northern East Anglia and the Midlands. Only one mirror handle is known from Fison Way, Thetford (NHER: 5853), which may instead be a tankard or bucket handle (Gregory 1991a: 132; Joy 2010: 87, 143). Three handle fragments have been found in eastern Suffolk: at Akenham (SHER: AKE006), Westerfield (PAS: SF6712) and Badingham (SHER: BDG033). This may reflect not collection bias, but the lack of burials, generally the most common context for mirrors. Davies notes non-burial as characteristic of the Iceni (2011b: 103-4). By contrast, Essex, which is rich in Iron Age burials, has at least ten mirrors (Joy 2007; Whimster 1979). There are none from Cambridgeshire, which contradicts other findings which show that county tends to follow the southeast in burial practice. Joy takes a post-processual approach, using grave contexts and assemblages to construct object biographies (2009, 2010). This is not easily achieved with surface finds. Mirrors have greater interpretive potential when they are contextualised as part of burial practice. To extend Joy's metaphor, we are often faced with only an object's afterlife, with little information as to its biography-in-use.

The conventional assumption that mirrors were prestige cosmetic items, buried with high-status women for the afterlife, is problematic. Burials with mirrors have usually been gendered female. Some mirrors have been found in graves that also contain weapons, considered a masculine trait (Jordan 2016). No mirrors have yet been categorically associated with a male individual, but many 'female' burials were poorly recorded in antiquarian excavations. Gender is just one of the intersecting identities which finds expression in material culture. Joy (2010) regards mirrors as part of a negotiated process between the individual and the community, and as indicators of 'difference' not status. Given the intensification of interest in bodily adornment and grooming in this period, a natural response is to look at one's own reflection. Monitoring of bodily presentation in this way may have affected power relations between

people, reproducing or disrupting social norms and ideals. Clearly, these were not simply passive cosmetic objects.

Mirrors may have had uses beyond personal grooming, playing an active role in social situations. A mirror can be used to see behind or beyond one's person. It can catch and reflect light outwards, even to signal and communicate over large distances. They were perhaps used in ritual practices for scrying or divination (Joy 2007, 2010). Mirrors may also replicate the otherworldly, shimmering boundary of water, possibly relating to the deposition and burial of both artefacts and humans in wet places. Iron Age mirrors could be part of both private acts of grooming and public performance, rendering them a cross-functional artefact.

Joy sees mirrors as active objects reinforcing social relationships in times of cultural contact and change (2009: 552). Regional and chronological differences are evident. The use of large, elaborately-decorated mirrors was abandoned by people in the southeastern core in the first century CE, yet continued in more westerly parts of Britain. Joy notes that a few Roman mirrors were already in use during the LIA, suggesting that certain people could pick and choose at this time. These deliberate choices of material, size, style and decoration perhaps signalled identity, group allegiance or exchange networks (2010: 48, 57). The absence of Iron Age mirrors reminds us that the people of the Icenian polity may have been selective about adopting their near neighbours' cultural types, as well as Gaulish or Roman artefacts.

5.6. Romano-British mirrors

Romano-British mirrors were small, circular or rectangular, sometimes fitted into ornamental cases. They often have moulded decoration or punched patterns of ring-and-dot around the outer edge of one face. Representations of women on tombstones are often holding a mirror (Allason-Jones 1989: 9-10). Unlike Iron Age examples, Roman mirrors are widespread in the *civitas Icenorum* (Figure 5.34). Mirror finds on PAS are highly concentrated in the Eastern counties (Booth PAS: SF-2ADBD7) (Figure 5.35). PAS gives a broad 'Roman' date range, whilst Eckardt and Crummy date those with handles from the mid-first/early second century CE (2008: 32). Like many other forms of material culture, mirrors fade from the archaeological record in the third century CE (Eckardt 2018: 214).

Roman mirrors were made from '*speculum*' metal: a brittle, highly-tinned, copper alloy. This material fragments easily and is often found in small straight-edged chips. It is thought that all Roman mirrors were imported, suggesting indigenous manufacture ceased post-conquest. This may relate to their superior efficacy (Eckardt and Crummy 2008: 31-32). Perhaps they were less valuable and/or more available than the ornate, one-off Iron Age types, or they may have belonged in a different social context. This temporal shift arguably demonstrates a change in practice or appropriateness, from a role in funerary deposition in the Iron Age, to a more everyday and widespread usage.

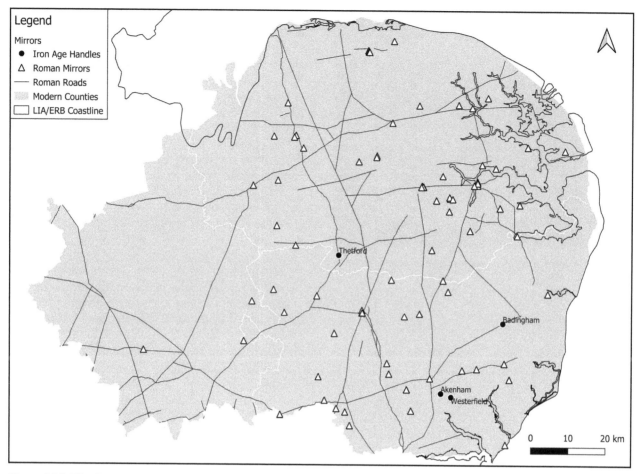

Figure 5.34. Distribution of Iron Age and Romano-British mirrors.

There are 98 Romano-British mirror fragments from Norfolk (Table 5.1). The lack of Iron Age mirrors in the region makes this concentration even more unusual. It is worth remembering that one mirror can shatter into many fragments, so the numbers of whole mirrors would be considerably smaller. Clusters come from parishes which have temples and/or towns, including Walsingham/Wighton (27), Wicklewood (26), Scole (6) and Caistor St Edmund (5). In Suffolk, there were finds from the small towns at Pakenham (6) and Wixoe (5). Does this represent a connection with the increased nature of personal grooming and etiquette in more urban 'observed' spaces, or a continuity of ritual practice? We may again be seeing a preference for the power of reflectiveness and shine at religious sites. At the extra-mural temple at *Venta Icenorum* (NHER: 9787), a hinged bronze mirror was excavated in 1957, which may suggest ritual usage.

Recovery bias is an important factor here. During data collection in Norfolk, I noted that a small number of key detectorists regularly reported *speculum* fragments. Plotting findspots confirmed this: the distribution is skewed heavily in favour of three detectorists (Figure 5.36). Almost one third of mirror finds reported in Norfolk were made by Finder 1, another third by Finder 2, and Finder 3 recorded seven pieces from the same parish. The concentrations reflect their search areas and ability

to recognise mirror fragments (usually by their distinctive sharp 'snapped' edges and the highly-tinned metal). This pattern, while unusable for distribution analysis, other than to confirm that people were using Roman-style mirrors in Norfolk, is telling of the processes of recovery for metal-detected finds. It may also have a bearing on excavated and museum assemblages, if mirror fragments are hard to recognise. The ability and knowledge of individual metal-detectorists have an important effect on the artefacts recovered and reported. Unlike Norfolk, the Suffolk finds did not show any notable bias, although several were antiquarian finds.

The Iron Age association of women with mirrors appears less significant in the Roman period. At Coddenham an urned cremation was buried with a copper alloy lid-mirror, consisting of two circular cases containing convex tinned mirrors (BM: 1838,0331.1) (Figure 5.37). These are rare in Britain, largely found in Gaul. On the outside are motifs based on a coin of Nero. One case shows his laureate head, and the other an 'imperial *Adlocutio*' (Lloyd-Morgan 1977: 235). Although the cremation was not sexed, this symbolism may indicate 'male', perhaps military, identity. Its inclusion in a cremation shows the continuing tradition of mirrors and burials and perhaps ritualised behaviour, akin to the deposition of the *Adlocutio* brooches at Hockwold-cum-Wilton. It appears that the use of mirrors

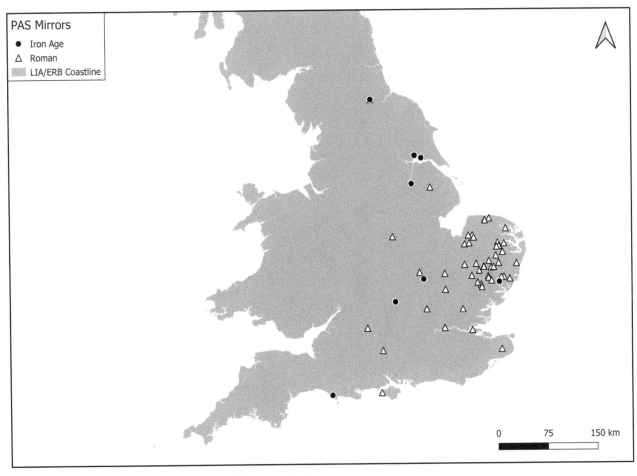

Figure 5.35. PAS distribution of Iron Age and Romano-British mirrors.

was not solely a female preoccupation in the Roman period (Eckardt and Crummy 2008: 32), although we must remember binary gender norms are not necessarily applicable to the LIA and Roman periods.

5.6.1. Stanley Avenue, Norwich

Two cremation burials from Norwich (NHER: 550), dating to 65-70 CE, provide 'good evidence against the cultural and economic retardation of the Iceni in the wake of the Boudican rebellion' (Gurney 1998: 23). In one, the cremated remains of an adult human (interpreted as female) and bones from the right-hand-side of a pig were accompanied by *asses* of Nero (64-66 CE), a blue glass bead, and a circular copper alloy mirror. The latter had a highly-polished white metal surface, a decorative border and handle, and was found with the remnants of its wooden case (*ibid.*: 25 pl. 3). The mirror had been deposited while the bones were still hot from the cremation pyre, and the case, despite being charred, retained traces of Pompeiian red paint. The second cremation also included adult human and pig bones, along with a fragmentary Thistle brooch, dating from the early to mid-first century CE. With both cremation burials were flagons and platters. Gurney maintains that these 'richly furnished' burials 'point to the rapid re-emergence of a new and probably pro-Roman Icenian aristocracy' (Anon 1951: 132; Gurney

1998: 23-27). In this scenario, it is plausible to apply Joy's object-centred approach and see the mirror as an indicator of difference rather than status (2010: 76-77). This woman and her companion were individuals being marked in death by their community, for despite the introduced materials, there is nothing to suggest that they were not local. The appearance of imported objects and coinage may represent an appropriation of 'other-ness' for those individuals, or part of the community's rationalisation and integration of the political turbulence around them.

These interments may represent a hybridised rite incorporating elements of LIA and Roman traditions. The combination of the mirror in a cremation burial with pig bones seems to be a particularly Iron Age practice (Davies 2014: 33), but the material culture is distinctively Roman and possibly imported. The burials date to the period when the client-kingdom was hurtling towards its violent end, shortly after the Boudican uprising, but embody the opposite of the post-revolt destitution that we are led to expect by classical sources.

5.7. Summary

Material evidence for bodily grooming shows significant post-conquest changes. Some items, like cosmetic grinders, were widespread in town and country, similar to

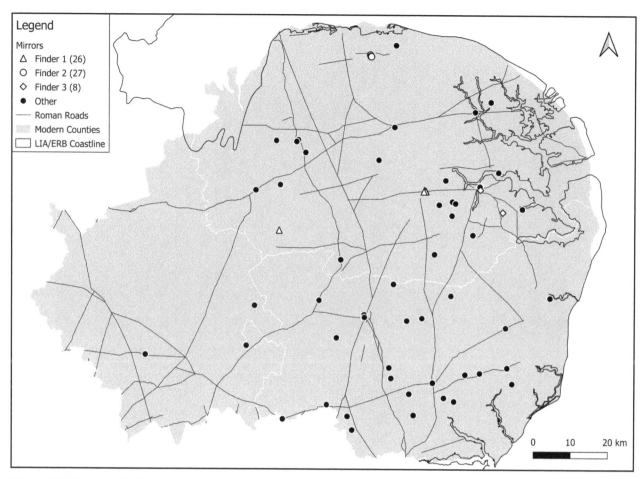

Figure 5.36. Romano-British mirror finds showing detectorist hotspots.

Figure 5.37. Elaborate mirror case, Coddenham (BM: 1838,0331.1; Image: © Trustees of the British Museum).

toggles and fasteners. Cosmetic grinders were distinctively British, but most post-date the invasion. The creatures represented, predominantly bulls, cows and waterbirds, were favourites of Iron Age craftspeople, although these are not the animals represented on Icenian coinage. These also differ from the more classical zoomorphs on the plate brooches and seal-boxes. The 'outsider' symbol

of the phallus (Johns 1996b: 12, 62; Plouviez 2005) was incorporated. Representations of different animals were clearly appropriate in different circumstances, although their meanings remain intangible.

The hotspot for cosmetic grinders around Wicklewood/ Wymondham echoes the Rearhook and Aesica brooches and horse harness, all considered indigenous artefacts. This area must surely have been a powerbase and manufacturing centre during the client-kingdom period, perhaps focussed on a shrine which developed into the Crownthorpe temple (NHER: 54693). The idiosyncratic finishing of the grinders reveals a distinct local aesthetic and the lack of standardisation in some Roman-period objects. Grinders may also show shifts in practice, running concurrently with the marble palettes. Palettes were not displayed on the person, unlike grinders and Châtelaines, and may have served a completely different purpose, such as mixing writing ink (Eckardt 2018: 28-29, 214-15).

Nail cleaners also reflect changes in display and identities. They may show a division between appropriate behaviour in public and private. There is regional variety, with a concentration around Fincham and the Icknield Way settlements which have strong LIA to Roman continuity, reflecting their 'naturalised' status. The loop types are clearly split between the north (same plane) and south (right angle) of the region, with Baldock types only in the far south. This may show regional preferences or the availability of certain types due to local manufacture. Again, a shift in visual, and possibly gender, identities was occurring. While Iron Age mirrors are rare and Roman examples suffer from collection bias in Norfolk, mirrors possibly became less strongly gendered during the Roman period. It is pertinent to remember that presupposing gender dichotomies based on binary sexing of remains can preclude other narratives (Jordan 2016: 888).

After the second century CE peak, most grooming implements decline, perhaps replaced by other means of personal and group expression, such as religious adherence or literacy. Artefacts like nail cleaners and finger-rings are important indicators which continue through the 'abandonment horizon', although their usage seems to change from functional to decorative. The need to display a strong identity through a groomed exterior may have become less significant once the initial upheavals of conquest had receded (Carr 2006: 79). Cosmetic grinders survived somewhat longer into this period, perhaps as a result of their rural distribution or their use as offerings. The sense of appropriateness and votive deposition seen in the pre-conquest period continue well into the 'Roman Dark Ages'. This period, the second/third centuries CE, is a time when little is written about Britain and there are few well-dated excavation sequences to distinguish small finds.

This point marks the end of part one, dealing with the individual body and personal adornment. Through items of bodily modification, hygiene and decoration, we have seen how the body became a 'symbolic source', personifying the fluctuating social and economic power structures which impacted on status, rank and gender identities (Hill 1997: 101). In part two, I investigate artefacts relating to broader group activities and identities, such as religion, literacy and transport, beginning with material culture associated with magical and ritual practices.

Making an Offering: Votive Miniatures and Figurines

6.1. Introduction

This chapter investigates the connections between people, things and concepts through votive objects, with specific reference to miniatures and pipeclay figurines. Although 'Celtic' religion is often referred to, there is minimal concrete evidence for it in Britain, with few inscriptions or known deities; much of the comparative material comes from very different European cultural contexts. Using my dataset, I consider evidence for continuity of practice, hybridity and syncretism within the material record.

Familiar terms need constant questioning and re-evaluation. A 'votive' is a ritually deposited gift or devotional offering, technically a fulfilment of a vow to the deities (Bagnall Smith 1999; Kiernan 2009: 2). A 'hoard' is a collection of objects buried together, often seen as a temporary cache. This contrasts with 'offerings' which are seemingly part of a one-way transaction. Haselgrove proposes the alternative *dépôt* which strives to be less value-laden in terms of the original motivation (2015: 27). Broken and incomplete artefacts, often deposited in water, render obsolete the idea that hoards were for 'temporary safekeeping' (*ibid.*: 36). 'Ritual' is broadly defined as a habitual action, 'a kind of practice - a performance which is defined by its own conventions' (Bradley 2003: 12); it need not be synonymous with religion (see Bradley 2003 for a deconstruction of its use in archaeology; Insoll 2004: 10-11). A 'deposit' is something deliberately placed, unlike a casual loss. This is notoriously difficult to substantiate archaeologically without contextual evidence for a hoard or deliberate concealment. Brudenell and Cooper (2008) have questioned the concept of 'structured deposition', although I use it here as a less loaded alternative to some of the above.

Studies of religious artefacts and ritual practices have been carried out by Hutcheson (2004, 2007) and Marsden (2012, 2014) for Norfolk, Derks (1998) and Henig (1984) on religion, Talbot (2011, 2015, 2017), Chadburn (2006) and Creighton (1995) on coins. Green's (1976, 1978) oft-quoted compilations of Roman religious items are now in need of modernisation. Jenkins's catalogue of pipeclay figurines (1977) remains a valuable source of information, currently being updated by Fittock (2015, 2016). Farley (2011, 2012) discusses miniature objects from neighbouring Lincolnshire, while Kiernan (2009) provides an overview of the northwestern provinces.

In the study area, the tradition of hoarding endured the fluctuating political situations of the Roman occupation. Devotion and deposition are fascinating practices which involve giving or putting something away. Therefore, they can give us a glimpse into the intersection between *praxis* – ritual and habitual action – and material culture. Objects can be interpreted differently depending on their use in varied contexts, e.g. temples, hoards or structured deposits in settlements. Small finds from hoards, burials and religious sites can tell us about the multitude of public and private acts of devotion, although belief is very subjective and hard to assess.

Crummy includes figurines and other ritual items, such as amulets and votive plaques, in Category 14 (Objects associated with religious beliefs and practices) (1983: 141-48). Due to the lack of good chronology for statuettes in bronze, such as the Mercury figurines from Walsingham, these artefacts have only been included on maps for comparison, based largely upon Durham's online 'Depicting the Gods' database (2012). Some brooches may also have been votive offerings, e.g. the concentrations of horse-and-rider brooches around small towns and rural shrines in East Anglia and the Midlands (section 3.11.6). The votive interpretation of model objects is also evaluated, excluding miniature terrets which are discussed alongside horse harness (section 8.9).

6.2. Magical and Ritual Practices

If objects acquire meaning through exchange, ritual and performance (Joy 2009: 544), this surely encompasses exchanges of artefacts between humans and the numinous realm (Insoll 2004: 19-20). Moretti notes the lack of distinction between magic and religion in the ancient world (2015: 107). Parker and McKie (eds. 2018) set out to address the lack of attention to the materiality of magic and the limited theoretical engagement and definition of the field, particularly in contrast to religion. They attempt to reduce reliance on classical literature, instead taking a 'post-functional' turn, in which multiple agencies, functions, practices, uses and meanings can coexist.

Metalwork, especially weaponry, was deliberately damaged and deposited in rivers, lakes and bogs throughout the Bronze and Iron Ages (Garrow and Gosden 2012; Haselgrove 2015: 36; Wells 2001: 91). Prehistorians often use the term 'ritual killing' (Joy 2011: 410-11), but this is less frequent as a discourse in Roman studies. Generally interpreted as a means of putting items beyond human use, Garrow and Gosden reassess some of these ideas in their wider discussion of fragmentation in 'Celtic art' (2012: 174-78). Deposits in water may remove objects from the community, similar to grave goods. Watery places were perhaps understood in prehistory as permeable borders between life and death, liminal zones linking the world and the underworld. Human remains from peat bogs across northern Europe lend weight to the idea that wetlands were places of sacrifice or suitable locations for the dead (Glob 1971). The possible Iron Age taboo on fish consumption was discussed above in relation to zoomorphic brooches (section 3.11.5).

Modern conceptualisations draw convenient territorial lines using waterways. However, water is a connective medium. Rivers are in constant motion; before the development of wheeled transport and passable roads, they connected the living with each other, not just the dead or the spirit world. Offerings when crossing water were made in the Roman period. At Piercebridge in County Durham, many thousands of finds were made by divers searching the bed of the River Tees, including coins and brooches dating from the first-third centuries CE. A military explanation has been proffered for this particular crossing, although objects relating to women and children have also been found (Walton 2011: 263-86). Indigenous Britons were likely no less superstitious.

6.3. Ritualisation as Power and Practice

Anthropological studies show there is often no explicit distinction made between the everyday lived world and the supernatural dimension (Bradley 2003; Insoll 2004). The static concept of religious activity is being replaced with an idea of 'ritualisation' as a form of practice (Bradley 2003: 12). This concept allows for the fluctuating status of sites and objects, their ability to be both ordinary and special, at different times, to different people. Ritualisation can also be part of power relationships; it can empower and control, promote social cohesion or distinction. Power, and thereby ritual, operates through the body (Bell 1992: 197-223). Bradley questions the separation between Iron Age public/private and domestic/ritual worlds at Thetford, concluding that these spheres moved gradually apart as a response to increasing contact and centralisation (2005: 165-90).

What evidence is there for magical and ritual practices in the Iceni territory? Did they approach the world differently to their neighbours and Roman rulers? Can we retrieve anything of their attitudes, their beliefs, their rites? Classical accounts refer to the strange behaviours of the Britons: their priests, the 'Druids', worshipped in 'groves consecrated to their savage cults' (Tac. *Ann.* 14.30). The Gauls and Britons are said to have practised human sacrifice and taken heads as gruesome trophies, although there is little evidence for this in Britain either in literature or archaeology (Frere 1991: 320; Henig 1984: 18-19; Salway 1981: 681). These have been rejected as propaganda, intended to exaggerate barbarian difference from the Roman incomers (Wells 1999, 2011).

Dio's (*Hist. Rom.* 62.6.1) tableau of Boudica's ritual behaviour on the brink of battle names a female British war deity, Andraste. Dio describes the Icenian queen releasing a hare, not sacrificing it, which goes against the bloodthirsty image painted elsewhere. Perhaps the key issue is difference. The ritual practice of seeking auguries in the passage of animals is a Roman behaviour, transposed here onto the leader of the Iceni. Assumptions have also been made that the Britons worshipped nature, not anthropomorphs like Roman deities, based on the lack of representational art (Watts 2005: 132). This 'aniconic stereotype' has been questioned (Green 1998), although Webster notes that many 'Celtic' representations of deities occur post-conquest (2003: 43-44). The idea of religious syncretism has also been problematised. This fusion of belief systems was far from a 'neutral process', but embodied the power relationships of the colonial situation. The adoption of the classical pantheon was not a progressive move towards Rome, but a sequence of negotiated and contested political actions between different indigenous class strata, as well as military and other incomers. In this light, the pipeclay figurines discussed in this chapter become an 'alternative indigenous pantheon' (Webster 1997).

6.4. Deposition and Intentionality

Hoards have often been interpreted as valuables secreted in times of stress, with the intention to return. This was previously a key criterion of Treasure Trove legislation, which was removed in the 1996 Treasure Act.[1] Single finds are usually deemed 'casual losses' unless specifically associated with other objects, such as ploughed-out hoards. Nevertheless, clusters of individual objects are found at shrines, perhaps representing personal moments of devotion (Garrow and Gosden 2012: 31). How can we establish whether hoards were permanent offerings or temporary caches? We might look for 'purposefulness in deposition', but context is rare (Wason 1994: 109). Identifying intentionality in the past is problematic and similar assemblages could have been hoarded for different reasons.

The importance of place and appropriateness are central to votive deposition (Fitzpatrick 1992: 396; Hutcheson 2007: 369; Osborne 2004: 7-8). Material interactions with objects shape whether things are perceived as in their rightful place and time, or are rejected or changed. Ritual practice often stands upon notions of 'fittingness' and the human tendency to seek out coherence (Hodder 2012: 113-37). Many deposits show a strong sense of suitability in selection, arrangement and location, such as the deliberately arranged 'nests' of torcs from Snettisham (Joy 2016; Stead 1991) (section 4.7.1). Bronze Age hoarding involved placing metalwork, often weaponry, into rivers and other watery places. Iron Age deposition in water is rarer, suggesting a shift in appropriate location or medium (Garrow and Gosden 2012: 69, 97). Hoarding practice was transformed with the increase, and perhaps 'reorganisation of control', of metal artefacts in circulation in the LIA (Hutcheson 2004, 2007: 369).

---

[1] https://finds.org.uk/treasure

6.5. Religious Regalia

It is often assumed that a 'priestly caste' gained material wealth and status through officiating at ritual sites. There are occasional finds of religious regalia: staff terminals, headdresses and crowns, sometimes in hoards. These are most common in the lands ascribed to the Iceni and Catuvellauni (Bird 2011: 276; Green 1976: 49, 75). At Hockwold-cum-Wilton, a cache of crowns and diadems was found in 1956-7 (NHER: 5367; BM: 1957,0207). Another group formed part of the Felmingham Hall hoard (BM: 1925,0610), which also included a miniature wheel and two corvid staff terminals. In Suffolk, a chain-crown and two diadems were found at Cavenham Heath, Lackford (SHER: LKD003) and a recent hoard discovered at nearby West Stow (PAS: SF-D4D044) contained chains, disc and lunular pendants and a crest which may have come from a cult image of Minerva (Worrell *et al.* 2011). These finds are interpreted as priests' ceremonial headwear and may have been deliberately deposited near shrines. The headdresses are often associated with votive leaves or feathers (section 6.7.4) and curse tablets (section 7.3.2). Dating is poor, but not usually earlier than mid-second century CE (Gurney 1986: 49, 90-92; Marsden 2014: 46).

Religious concepts are expressed in material culture and are both 'confirmed and renewed' by ritual behaviour (Derks 1998: 19). Status acquired through spiritual practice is another archaeologically invisible rank. Religious hermits or ascetics may have been highly-regarded in social terms, but conspicuously eschewed material riches (see section 2.3.3). Hoards of 'priestly regalia' may be seen in a similar light to the torcs and harness hoards, for the safe disposal of personal belongings associated with potent magical practices and occupations. Could these caches be substitutions for burials of important and powerful individuals? Post-conquest, Romano-British cult behaviour was pantheistic, with temples providing more formalised opportunities for worship. Literacy also became ritualised through amulets and curse tablets. Later, mystery cults and exclusive sects such as Mithraism and Christianity gained popularity (Creighton 1995: 300; Eckardt 2018: 26; Moore *et al.* 1988: 73).

6.6. Votive Jewellery

Osborne observes that votives stand apart as objects transformed by human agency through the process of dedication (2004: 1-3). Small personal belongings may have been offered in this way. Dragonesque brooches are sometimes found in caves, and Horse-and-rider brooches are commonly found at rural sanctuaries. Rings inscribed 'TOT' (to the god Toutatis) have a strong regional distribution in Lincolnshire, and Minerva wax *spatula* handles may have doubled as offerings (Daubney 2010; Eckardt 2014: 132) (section 7.4). Bronze, rather than bone, pins were preferred as funerary and votive offerings, perhaps having 'greater symbolic value' (Perring and Pitts 2013: 248). Some may have been deliberately bent or 'ritually killed' (Carr 2006: 67). A third of the brooches

recovered at Saham Toney had been 'mutilated' in some way (Brown 1986: 11), perhaps for recycling purposes or as a ritually-motivated termination practice (section 3.14.10).

Enamelled plate brooches (usually disc and zoomorphic types) are often found at temples. Two pierced second century CE disc brooches came from the Sawbench temple at Hockwold-cum-Wilton (NWHCM: 1962.396.37, NWHCM: 1962.396.47). Plaques, brooches, discs and letters may all have been ceremonially nailed onto the walls of the temples themselves or onto trees, sacred posts or wooden panels. Not all plaques have holes, so were perhaps propped up on shelves or laid on altars for display (Bird 2011: 287; Crerar 2006: 80). Iron nails are often found in structured deposits and other votive contexts, such as the *amphora* with pipeclay figurines discussed below (Dungworth 1998). Was the process of affixing by nailing associated with the permanence of the vow being made, a continuation of the prehistoric 'ritual killing' practice, or simply a means of putting one's religious beliefs on display to the gods, religious officiants and other members of the community?

Miniature brooches have been included in the personal ornament category, unless specifically identified as votive. A minute copper alloy rendition of a bow brooch (length 10mm) from Cambridge illustrates this point concisely (PAS: CAM-26D033) (Figure 6.1). This must have been made either as a votive or a casting pattern, as it has neither a completed spring housing nor catchplate. Another is known from Beachamwell in Norfolk (NHER: 4530). When brooches are fully-modelled but diminutive, it is hard to divide function from intention. These factors all influence recording and interpretation. The brooches recorded as 'tiny' are not the enamelled discs and zoomorphics found at shrines, but typically bow brooches in familiar regional styles, such as Colchester Derivatives and Hod Hills, including one from Worlington which appears fully-functional (PAS: SF-ADD6C5) (Figure 6.2). A plausible alternative suggests they were for fastening children's clothing or fine undergarments (Kiernan 2009: 181). This implies there could be appropriate scales and designs for votive models.

6.7. Votive Miniatures

Deposition of votive miniatures in northwest Europe begins in the LIA.[2] A range of miniature objects is known from northern Gaul and Britain, from the first century BCE into the Roman period (Kiernan 2009). Votives are found at both settlements and temples, such as Walsingham (Bagnall Smith 1999). They are made from iron and copper alloy, lead and bone, most often representing tools or weapons. Other miniaturisations include parts of the body, symbols and animals. Chariot gear or horse harness, other than miniature wheels, is very rarely found.

---

[2] The PAS database gives search options of either 'votive model' or 'miniature object'. Some objects are found in both categories.

Figure 6.1. Miniature brooch, Cambridge (PAS: CAM-26D033).

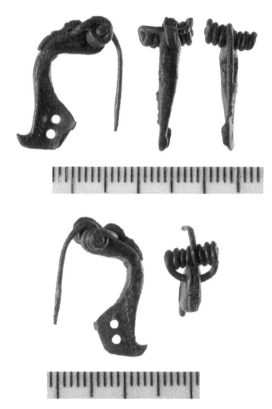

Figure 6.2. Diminutive Colchester brooch, Worlington (PAS: SF-ADD6C5).

Figure 6.3. Miniature bridle-bit, Southery (PAS: SF-691092).

A miniature Roman bridle-bit from Southery (PAS: SF-691092) (Figure 6.3) and a mini prick-spur from Mattishall (NHER: 25729) are the only examples on my database. Miniature terrets may have been deposited as offerings, although they appear to have been originally produced for a functional purpose (section 8.9).

Stewart's theoretical art-historical view of the microcosmic may help us think about archaeological miniatures. She describes the miniature as a discourse of the self, as opposed to the gigantic, which is a discourse on the world, the collective. Miniatures are cultural artefacts which have no parallels in nature (1993). Through miniaturisation, large-scale concepts can find material expression. Farley found varied regional deposition of miniatures in the Midlands, with a focus on shields and swords in Lincolnshire (especially at Nettleton). Neighbouring areas favoured model axes and *defixiones*, which she attributes to the powerful influence of Roman votive practice (2011, 2012).

For Kiernan, models must replicate full-size, everyday objects, produced specifically for dedication. For a miniature object to be considered votive, it must not be functional. His narrow definition excludes representations of divinities, people, animals and anatomical parts, as well as functional objects and decorative fittings. I would argue our options for archaeologically retrieving this sort of intentionality are limited and use broader criteria in my discussion. Kiernan's rather linear interpretation considers miniatures as sympathetic magic: farmers' tools for fertility of the land and a successful harvest, weapons for success in battle, or shields for protection. A celebrated group of axes from Allmendingen, Switzerland, carry inscriptions with the names of gods, confirming their votive nature, at least in that area (Kiernan 2009: 7, 114).

A miniature axe will not fell a tree or a model wheel transport any goods. The idea that miniature replicas were being offered up instead of real tools and weapons implies a certain credulity on the part of the divinities, but the devotee may indeed believe that these things are causally linked. As Henig observes, in 'the spirit world, token-coins and other objects become real' by the process of substitution (1984: 22-23). In this instance, objects have agency to effect belief in people as well as engage in perceived interactions with deities.

The miniature impacts upon perceived time as well as space, transcending everyday experience (Stewart 1993: 65). Although Stewart's perspective is a long way from the LIA, it raises issues about the perception and impact of small votive items, which may relate to their production and deposition. Like their larger-scale counterparts, miniature objects are frequently found bent or broken (Bird 2011: 288; Green 1976: 42-43). To perform a 'ritual killing' on non-functional objects is surely unnecessary if the intention is to remove them from human use and make them more acceptable to the deities. One of the constants of ritual behaviour is that it is complex, erratic and often illogical.

6.7.1. Weapons and Tools

This group includes knives, swords and spears as weapons, and tools such as sickles, chisels, hammers and anvils. Despite Kiernan's assertion that model weapons were the most common in the northwest provinces, my study shows that miniature axes and anatomical votives are most frequent in eastern England (Figure 6.4). The numbers are small, but Norfolk has the bulk of tools and weapons with eight of each type. Cambridgeshire has one tool and two weapons, Suffolk two of each (Figure 6.5). No records of miniature shields (or cauldrons) were found in East Anglia, despite having much the same date range as axes, *circa* 200 BCE-50 CE (Kiernan 2009: 45).[3] This concurs with Farley's study (2012: 315) showing regional selectivity in production and deposition of miniature artefacts.

In several cases, identification is ambiguous, for example the two copper alloy sickles are potentially toilet implements (NHER: 8675; SHER: SUT022) although the iron example from Swaffham Prior is perhaps a less likely candidate. A miniature spear from Walsingham (NHER: 2024) is possibly from a figurine and a double-ended fork from Brampton (NHER: 1124) could have several interpretations. An undated small bone shovel from the *civitas* capital may have had multiple uses including as an incense scoop (NWHCM: 1929.152.18). None of these alternatives would preclude these small belongings being offered at shrines. Only one example is identified as lead: a votive hammer from Walsingham (NHER: 2024). A miniature silver sword from Bracon Ash has two small holes near the hilt, either for affixing a lost handle or for suspension (PAS: NMS-F2D1B2) (Figure 6.6).

Kiernan dates model weapons from the first century BCE to the end of the first century CE (2009: 109). There are large assemblages from Romano-Celtic sanctuaries in Gaul. The site of Flavier, near Mouzon, France, yielded 309 swords, 213 shields, 33 spearheads, five axes and two possible arrowheads. The peak in deposition dates

from the early first century CE. These generally copy Iron Age rather than Roman prototypes. They were all of iron except one copper alloy shield, which again reminds us of how much has been lost to rust. Many were pierced, presumably for display in the shrine, like the plaques and brooches mentioned earlier. Two of the swords had been deliberately bent in the middle, perhaps as some form of ritual mutilation (*ibid*.: 47-63).

Farley discusses the assemblage of over thirty miniature weapons from Nettleton Top in Lincolnshire (2011), adjacent to my study area. An important LIA centre, with parallels to Thetford, was found during excavations. This hilltop site yielded ritual and settlement activities dating from the Bronze Age into the Roman period. The miniatures mostly comprised shields, with swords, spears and axes. There were also brooches which may have been votive offerings, which has parallels with the shrine at Walsingham.

Farley suggests that the deposition of miniature weapons was a response to the major social changes in Britain in the first centuries BCE/CE. Miniatures may have reduced ritual display and deposition of full-size weaponry to a more appropriate and controlled (or controllable) form (2011: 111, 2012: 315). Kiernan regards miniature representations of arms and armour as part of a 'substitutional rite' which replaced offerings of real weapons. This ritualisation may be linked to the supposed confiscation of arms by Roman officials from rebellious Britons (2009: 40, 111; Tac. *Ann.* 12.31.2). The tools on toiletry sets are sometimes modelled as weapons, which links the iconography to personal appearance and grooming (Crummy 2016; Kiernan 2009: 85). Symbolic weaponry is worn today by Sikh men in the form of the kirpan, which may also be miniaturised into a turban pin or pendant.[4]

6.7.2. Axes

One frequent motif in miniature is the axe. Kiernan asserts that LIA axes were not commonly used as weapons and are rarely found in burials or martial contexts (2009: 144-45). In Roman iconography, they may represent the axe used in animal sacrifice (Henig 1984: 149). Axes are also depicted on plate brooches, sometimes associated with temples (section 3.12.4).

Kiernan's catalogue lists 16 votive axes from East Anglia, within a cluster in southern and eastern Britain (2009: fig. 4.9). This distribution is confirmed and enhanced by more recent PAS records (Figure 6.7). My combined dataset numbers 116 axes: Norfolk (49), Suffolk (45), while Cambridgeshire has a larger proportion than in other categories (22) (Figure 6.8). There is a slight southern trend, with minor concentrations at Great and Little Chishill (4, three from the same field), Hockwold-cum-Wilton (4) and Scole (4), including one from the temple.

---

[3] My thanks to Andy Lamb (University of Leicester) for raising this question.

[4] http://www.sikhcoalition.org/documents/pdf/kirpan-factsheet-oct2014.pdf

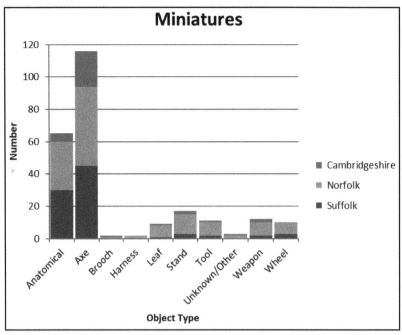

Figure 6.4. Miniature objects by type and county.

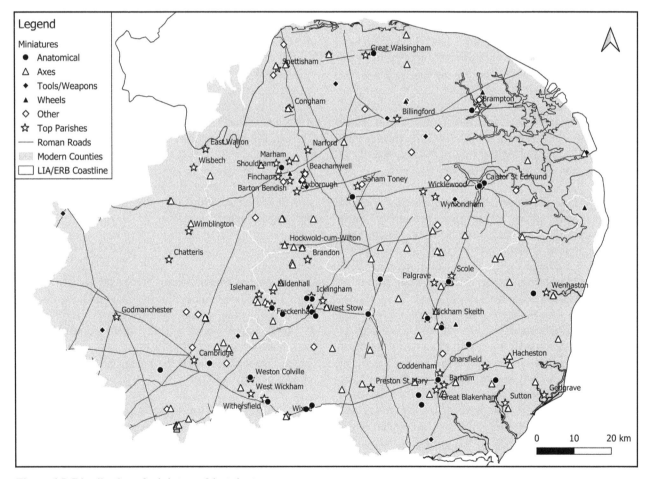

Figure 6.5. Distribution of miniature objects by type.

Another comes from the Roman temple at Cottenham (CHER: 05523) and an unfinished bronze model axe, reportedly still in its mould, from a metalworking area at Walsingham, suggests manufacture for deposition at the shrine (Bagnall Smith 1999: 48).

Thirteen examples have incised markings on the blade, usually in the form of a saltire and interpreted as bindings which secured the blade to the handle on a full-size axe (Figure 6.9). Some 'binding marks' are mislocated, and others have parallel lines, open V-shapes, mouldings or,

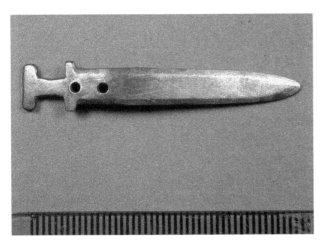

Figure 6.6. Miniature silver sword, Bracon Ash (PAS: NMS-F2D1B2).

in the case of one from Kenninghall, a + symbol (PAS: NMS-CB4D75). Does this mean their makers were unfamiliar with axe construction or did these symbols have another meaning? An alternative reading considers these inscriptions as part of the ritual practice of marking which predated common literacy (section 7.3). These markings are also sometimes found on nail cleaners. From Melton Warwick, Leicestershire, is an elaborate example with inscribed symbols (possibly a wheel and a lyre) on either side of the blade (PAS: LEIC-88ADC3) (Figure 6.10).

Miniature axes are usually less than 50mm long and found in Romano-Celtic sanctuaries across Gaul and Britain. They date between 50 BCE and 200 CE, with a focus on the first century CE. Kiernan is keen to substantiate the pre-Roman origins of miniatures. He sees 'an abrupt cessation' in the tradition of high-value precious metal offerings following the Claudian conquest. Instead, smaller, lower value deposits began to be made, perhaps reflecting a shift to personal rather than group devotion. The 'extreme paucity' of miniature votive axes from military sites suggests an indigenous custom rather than a Roman import (Kiernan 2009: 114-52).

Miniature axes pose two intriguing puzzles regarding both form and practice. The first relates to material. Kiernan states miniature axes are almost always made of copper alloy (2009: 115). Yet approximately a third of the miniature axes from the study area are made from lead (where recorded), particularly in Suffolk, with a concentration around Coddenham (Figure 6.8). Recovery bias does not appear to explain this difference.[5] All the miniature Pb finds were made by different detectorists, which rules out an individual being particularly vigilant in one area, or Suffolk detectorists setting different parameters.[6]

Lead in the ancient world was associated with the 'unlucky' planet Saturn and the underworld. It was certainly used for coffins and baptismal tanks, especially in the later Roman period. The predominance of lead for curse tablets, from ancient Greece into the Medieval period may be significant (Merrifield 1987: 142; Moretti 2015). Lead may have been a material metaphor for death: heavy, cold, incompatible with life (Sánchez Natalías 2018: 11-12). Green notes that it was used for all the model tools and weapons from Chesters, and more prosaically, was a commonly available, malleable metal, easy to work and inscribe (1981: 260-62). Crude pot mends on samian vessels demonstrate lead's domestic availability.

If there were similar proportions of lead miniatures across the board, I could accept this, but when other materials are considered, the axes are clearly set apart (Figure 6.11, Figure 6.12). The proportion of other lead model objects is much lower than axes (Table 6.1). There are only six, including two lead phalli from Suffolk, a miniature hammer, a phallic pendant and a model finger from Norfolk, and a model foot from Cambridgeshire. This suggests that axes/hammers and anatomical models were disproportionately and deliberately made from lead, unlike other miniatures.

The second question concerns model socketed axes, which appear to copy Late Bronze Age originals, but sometimes come from Iron Age and Roman contexts (Figure 6.13). There are socketed miniature axes from all three counties (Cambridgeshire 1, Norfolk 2, Suffolk 5) (Figure 6.14) including examples from Snettisham (PAS: NMS-CBCB34) and Saham Toney (PAS: SF-838F44). These are all copper alloy and come from different parishes. Three have attachment loops (PAS: SF-632655, SF-631D32, SF698), perhaps for veracity to the original design of the axe, or for suspension as an amulet. Robinson's catalogue of bronze miniature socketed axes (1995) showed they are mainly found in Wiltshire and range in date between Late Bronze Age and Late Roman, although few are well-stratified. Miniature axes are not found in metalwork hoards predating 600 BCE. The Iron Age assemblages from Netherhampton (Salisbury) and Nettleton Top both included socketed axe models (Farley 2011: 98).

Some PAS records date miniature socketed axes as Bronze Age, while others suggest that they may be Iron Age or Roman copies (e.g. PAS: SF-9398D2, SF-F97721, NMS592). By this period, full-size axes were made of iron, not bronze, and were hafted through a shaft-hole, rather than socketed. This would suggest they did not replicate objects in contemporary practical usage. Robinson found little evidence for unearthing or veneration of Bronze Age socketed axes in LIA and Roman Britain, although this was not ruled out (1995: 60-61). Certainly, prehistoric stone and flint axes appear to have been curated in later periods, such as at Ivy Chimneys, Essex (Turner and Wymer 1987) and perhaps at the Forum of *Venta Icenorum* (CRP: SF7055). Bliss (2020) has recently updated the chronological framework and distribution of miniature socketed axes, with PAS providing numerous additions to Robinson's

---

[5] A. Marsden (pers. comm. 09/12/2017) observed that detectorists do recover lead axes, but because they are often small and unattractive, they are relegated to the scrap box.

[6] I asked interviewed participants if they regularly discriminated against lead, and none did, partly because it would exclude medieval seals and other objects.

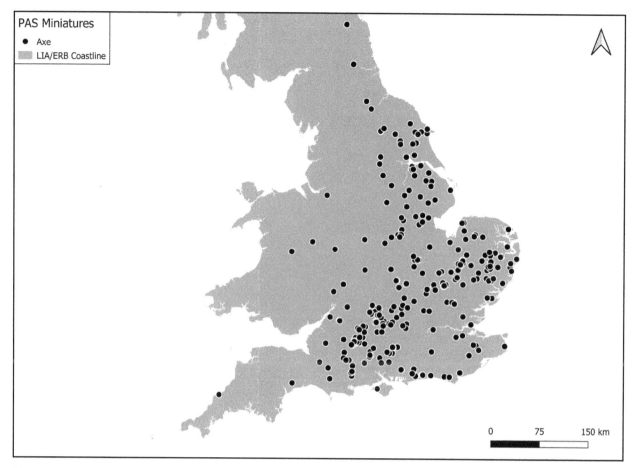

Figure 6.7. PAS distribution of miniature axes.

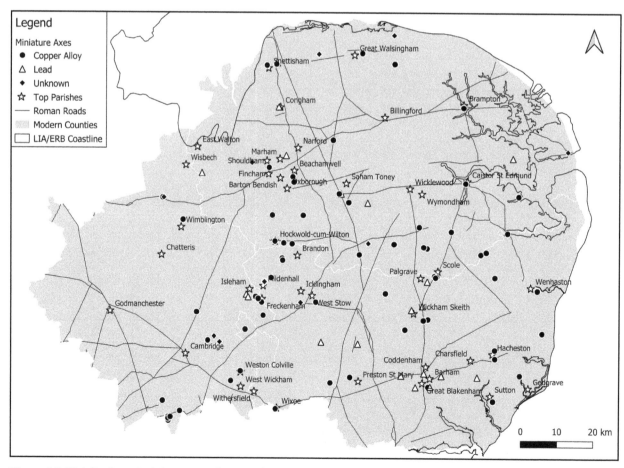

Figure 6.8. Distribution of miniature axes by material.

Figure 6.9. Miniature axe with 'binding' or saltire, Freckenham (PAS: SF-77FA41).

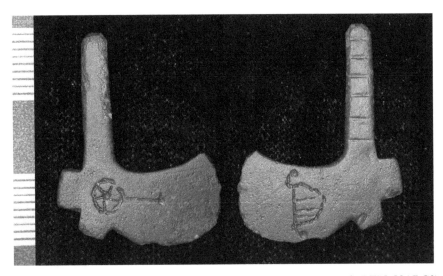

Figure 6.10. Miniature axe with inscribed symbols, Melton Warwick, Leicestershire (PAS: LEIC-88ADC3).

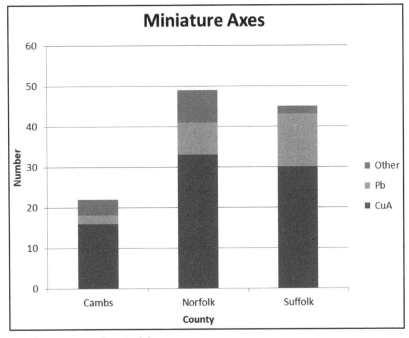

Figure 6.11. Miniature axes by county and material.

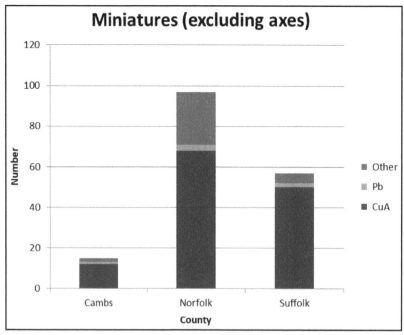

Figure 6.12. Miniatures (excluding axes) by county and material.

Table 6.1. Miniature lead objects by county

Object Type	Cambs	Norfolk	Suffolk	Total
Anatomical	1	2	2	5
Axe	2	8	13	23
Tool	0	1	0	1

Figure 6.13. Socketed miniature axe, Sutton (PAS: SF-631D32).

corpus. The main centre of deposition remains Wiltshire and Hampshire. Bliss concludes that miniature socketed axes were contemporary copies of several different types of Late Bronze Age/Earliest Iron Age functional axes, with a strong possibility that they were either found, curated or copied and redeposited in later periods (*ibid.*: 22).

Davy looked at miniaturisation as resistance in the material culture of the American Northwest coast (2016). Despite either being rendered obsolete by colonial contact, or by technological advances in boat-building, some groups continued to make miniature models of 'traditional' canoes. This revival of forgotten vessels in miniature is nostalgia and loss made material. It also evokes a sense of pride and resilient community identity (*ibid.*: 143). The 'fittingness' or conceptual presence of *canoe* may have had similar resonance in the curation and production of archaic socketed miniature axes in the Roman era.

6.7.3. Wheels

Deposits of wheel models at LIA shrines in mainland Europe can number in their thousands (Kiernan 2009: 16-20). Miniature wheels are also known from Gaulish graves and tombstones (Green 1976: 10). The wheel motif is found on brooches, pendants and necklaces, and chain-crowns (Bird 2011: 276; Cool 1983: 305-6). These symbols were worn and displayed in a variety of situations, perhaps as apotropaic amulets. An Early La Tène burial of a young girl from Dürrnburg contained a necklace made of charms, including a wheel, triangle and an axe (Kiernan 2009: 14, 120 fig. 4.5i).

By contrast, miniature wheels are not known in great quantities from Britain. This prompts us to keep in mind the geographical differences in ritual behaviour throughout this discussion. Kiernan's chronology is LIA

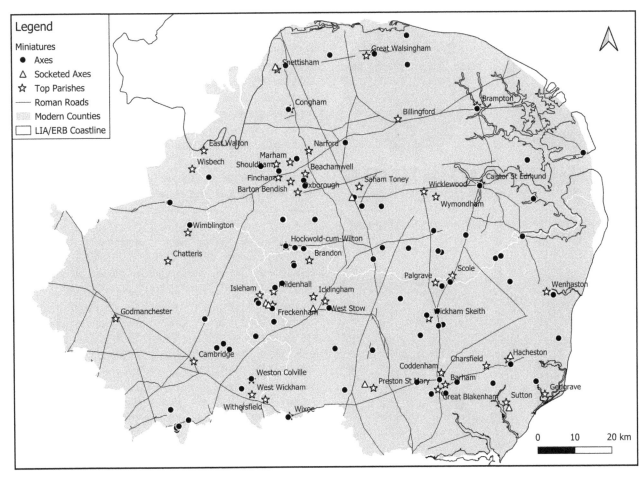

Figure 6.14. Distribution of miniature axes by type.

to late first century CE, although the Felmingham Hoard example was found with a coin of 260 CE (2009: 23, 29), suggesting they remained in use for some time, perhaps being curated like the model socketed axes discussed above. Kiernan discounts the idea that miniature wheels were parts of model or toy chariots or that they could be substitutions (*pars pro toto*) for full-size chariots in graves. He also considers the possibility that model wheels could have been used as currency or voting tokens (2009: 29-32, 39). An amuletic function seems probable given the aforementioned pendants and brooches, but the most likely explanation is as votives, which could be dedicated for a range of reasons, 'from casual piety to a very specific request' (*ibid*.: 39). Miniature wheels, like the axes, seem to have been specifically produced for dedicatory purposes.

Wheel symbols are common on Iron Age coins, usually above or below the horse on Icenian issues (Figure 6.15). This makes the paucity of miniature wheels stand out: Norfolk (7) and Suffolk (3) (Figure 6.5). Two six-spoked examples from different moulds from Walsingham (Figure 6.16) are discussed by Bagnall Smith (1999: 34); a third with three spokes is registered on the HER.[7] A fragment comes from Woodcock Hall at Saham Toney and one from

the Felmingham Hoard, which also included 'priestly' crowns and staff terminals in the form of corvids. There is seemingly little patterning, but this is unsurprising given so few examples.

The one regularly-cited parallel from Cambridgeshire is the bronze 'mace' from the Willingham Fen hoard. This odd object, found in 1857, resembles a Hercules club, decorated with a bull, dolphin, eagle, a six-spoked wheel and a 'Taranis and chthonic giant' (CHER: 05784). Its function is unknown, but it is unlikely to have operated as a sceptre or mace, even symbolically (Alföldi 1949: 16-22, pl. 1). Despite recording no model wheels from Cambridgeshire, the combination of a wheel and other religious imagery on this object show that the symbolism was recognised in the Roman Fens. Cambridgeshire also has fewer full-size horse and vehicle fittings (chapter eight), probably due to its large areas of wetlands. The low quantities of votive wheels in the *civitas* shows selective uptake of religious material which was popular in Gaul.

Green attributed wheels to the syncretic 'Jupiter-Taranis', supposedly the lord of the sky and sun, symbolised by the wheel and thunderbolt (1976: 9, 1978: 18-19, 1981: 255). These connections rely rather heavily on antiquarian studies and ethnographic parallels. In Britain, there is no epigraphic mention of a combined indigenous deity

---

[7] Possibly a duplicate as it was the same finder, but in a different year and location in the field than the other two.

Figure 6.15. Boar-Horse coin with wheel motif, Whepstead (PAS: SF-729FDD).

Figure 6.16. Miniature wheel, Walsingham (NHER: 2024; Image: © Norwich Castle Museum and Art Gallery).

sharing attributes with Jupiter (in the mode of Sulis Minerva or Mars Nodens). The closest inscription, to 'IOM Tanarus' from Chester, has a rosette, not a wheel, motif. Some military altars with wheel symbols in northern Britannia were devoted to Jupiter, but dedicated by Dacian and Spanish troops (Green 1984: 218-47). Admittedly, in Gaul there are numerous male figurines holding wheels, although the 'solar' wheel is not held aloft, but tends to rest by their side, or be held like a shield. A link between wheel models, a sky-god and a Jupiter cult in Britain is entirely conjectural, although often repeated (Allason-Jones 1989: 122; Bagnall Smith 1999: 34; Johns 1996b: 92). Spoked-wheel pendants have also been speculatively associated with the supposed sun-cult and Taranis (Green 1984), but I share Paites's reluctance to associate solar symbols, wheels and deities in Britain (2016: 20).

6.7.4. Leaf/Feather Plaques

Repoussé plaques, in the shape of leaves or feathers, were made from thin sheet metal, sometimes silver-gilt or gold. Occasionally found in the *civitas*, they are considered a 'stock votive offering' in the northwestern provinces. They are interpreted as ornaments from priests' headdresses (section 6.5) or as votive plaques dedicated at temples. The symbolism of the leaf may refer to Jupiter (oak), Apollo (laurel) or Victory (palm). It is unlikely that these were feathers although, as we have seen, birds were revered in both Iron Age and Roman religion (Crerar 2006; Henig 1984).

Examples are known from Cavenham (Lewis 1966: 125), Walsingham (PAS: NMS-9BC376) and three from *Venta Icenorum*: one from north of Temple A within the town (NWHCM: 1929.152.B6), one from the Caistor Paddocks 'workshop', which also produced evidence for brooch manufacture (section 3.5.4) and another from the extra-mural temple (NHER: 9787). There are four from Hockwold-cum-Wilton (NWHCM: 1961.199.105, 1962.396.70, PAS-D29168). A fine gold example from Stonea is inscribed to the goddess Minerva (Potter and Jackson 1982: 112-13). Finds near Bury St Edmunds revealed three votive leaves in a cache of objects which included chain-headdress fragments and staff terminals (Worrell *et al.* 2011; PAS: SF-D4D044). Dating is difficult. The plaques range from the second century CE to the post-Roman period. They are therefore at the edge of my study range, but worthy of mention, as they add to the picture of a long-continued pattern of votive deposition which sometimes embraced the classical pantheon.

6.7.5. Anatomical Models

Kiernan excludes anthropomorphic and zoomorphic representations from his discussion (2009: 2). Although there are few from the region and dating is poor, I have chosen to include phallic mounts and pendants as well as 'votive models' (following Plouviez 2005). My dataset contains 39 anatomical models of which 35 are phallic. The other four miniature body parts are a finger from Shouldham (NHER: 28645), a foot (PAS: CAM-6C84E2) and a leg (CHER: SCB20969) from Cambridgeshire, and an eye from Caistor St Edmund (PAS: NMS385, NHER: 9815). The foot and finger are cast in lead alloy, already noted above in the discussion of metals and materials of miniature axes. The eye is interesting in the light of a collyrium stamp for eye remedies from the *civitas* capital (Jackson 1990: 278). Another possible copper alloy model eye is among the metalworking debris at Caistor Paddocks (NHER: 9816). This may have been part of a 'temple service area' (Davies and Gregory 1991: 70) producing and reprocessing offerings for the extra-mural temple (NHER: 9787).

Jackson (1988) relates offerings of model body parts to the cult of Asclepius, the primary Graeco-Roman healer-god. Some shrines specialised in certain ailments, attracting offerings of model eyes, feet and hands, or genitals, breasts and wombs (*ibid.*: 160). Such votive reliefs and anatomical *ex-votos* present us with an interpretive problem: were they consecrated as a prayer for help, or in gratitude for divine intervention to cure an illness? Perhaps both. This interpretation is rather reliant on our modern understanding of Christian healing shrines such as Lourdes.

At Lydney near Chepstow, a Romano-British cult centre developed associated with the syncretic god Mars Nodens. Finds included votive plaques, offerings of coins and small metalwork 'trinkets', a miniature bronze arm and an engraved bone plaque of a naked woman pressing her hands against her belly, interpreted as a childbirth votive. By contrast, at Bath the temple and healing springs dedicated to another syncretic deity, Sulis Minerva, produced numerous curse tablets, metal artefacts and coins, but no anatomical votives. Jackson (1988) proposed that the curative nature of bathing in hot springs was more important here than petitioning the deity for health, suggesting appropriateness of location or association. Finally, as a salient reminder of what time has taken from us, several hundred wooden carvings were found in waterlogged conditions, near the source of the Seine, along with stone and bronze *ex-votos* and coins. This was the site of a Gallo-Roman spring shrine, dating from the mid-first century BCE onwards, dedicated to the goddess Sequana (Deyts 1983).

6.7.6. Phallic Amulets

Phallic objects are concentrated in Suffolk (Figure 6.17). There are six very similar pendants from Lackford (PAS: SF-5B3285, SF-760A21, SF-75EC55, SF-75CF48, SF-75B574, SF-660C05), which may be the site of a temple (Gurney 1986: 89-90) (Figure 6.18). They are reminiscent of cosmetic mortars which often have phallic terminals (section 5.3.2). Similarly, the pendants have either end or centre suspension loops, although casual observation suggests they have not been used for grinding. *Venta Icenorum* has three copper alloy phallic pendants – one from the town, and two from the extra-mural settlement (NHER: 9786, 9759), as well as several other crudely carved phallic objects. Three lead examples are recorded from Scole (SHER: OKY005), Clare (SHER: CLA018) and Saham Toney (NHER: 4697).

Phallic amulets may have been fertility charms (Green 1976: 47) or military harness pendants (Johns 1996b: 108; Plouviez 2005). Whitmore (2018: 25) states that surprising, improper or amusing uses of imagery could be distracting and thereby deflect the evil eye. Small apotropaic phallic pendants were worn by Roman children, as well as soldiers, although whether these customs applied to Britain is debateable.[8] Swift discusses the predominance of the phallic motif on very small finger-rings, presumed

for wear by children (2017: 168-73). Ferris notes the frequency of Priapus images and phallic ornaments from rural Suffolk (2012: 152-53). Small towns with examples include Icklingham, Coddenham and Pakenham, which has three almost identical phallic mounts. Plouviez endorses their Roman nature and considers them indicative of new cultural forms which penetrated the rural hinterland from the towns in the region (2005: 161-62).

Plouviez reported a PAS trend of phallic amulets towards the North and Midlands, a reversal compared with many other artefacts. She links their presence in the military north with serving or retired soldiers, referring to the redistribution of lands after the Boudican revolt as a possible explanation for their appearance in Suffolk (2005: 163). While this may be the case, I would add a reminder that if phallic amulets were worn by children in Britain as well as in Rome, their presence on military sites could be indicative of soldiers' families, rather like pipeclay figurines. The lack of phallic amulets in rural Norfolk differs from the widespread distribution of knobbed cosmetic grinders (Figure 5.11). This may imply a resistance to this type of imported symbolism, which was more acceptable in Suffolk and at the *civitas* capital than elsewhere. If Plouviez's hypothesis regarding soldiers is correct, this may also demonstrate the lack of militarisation in the Icenian heartland.

A comparative look at the findspots of 26 'vulvate' or 'coffee-bean' mounts (usually recorded as harness fittings/ mounts) shows they are largely distributed in northwest Norfolk and around the Great Estuary. These objects are generally associated with the military and are broadly dated, but were perhaps also used as votives or amuletic charms (Figure 6.19). They may indeed have been intended to represent (and ward off) the evil eye (Parker 2020: 96, 102). Neither form of anatomical mount appears to respect the known military sites in the region (Figure 6.20). It is unlikely that two different military units using separate anatomical harness mounts and pendants were in residence in the north and south of the *civitas*. As we shall see with the pipeclay figurines, there is a preference for female symbolism in Norfolk.

6.8. Pipeclay Figurines

Representations of humans, animals and deities in pipeclay are common in the northwest provinces, but rare in Rome itself, where terracotta statuettes were popular. Large quantities were manufactured in central Gaul and the Rhineland during the first/second centuries CE (Bird 2011: 287-88; Crummy 1983: 141; Jenkins 1977; Rouvier-Jeanlin 1972). Pipeclay statuettes were made in piece moulds and finished by burnishing and painting. In parts of Gaul, manufacture was closely related to samian production. The figurine industry is likely to have suffered the fate of the samian workshops, exports from which declined severely at the end of the second century CE (Jenkins 1977).

---

[8] Pliny (*NH* 28.39) states that infants (not gendered) were at particular risk of the evil eye and required the protection of the god Fascinus, the embodiment of the phallus.

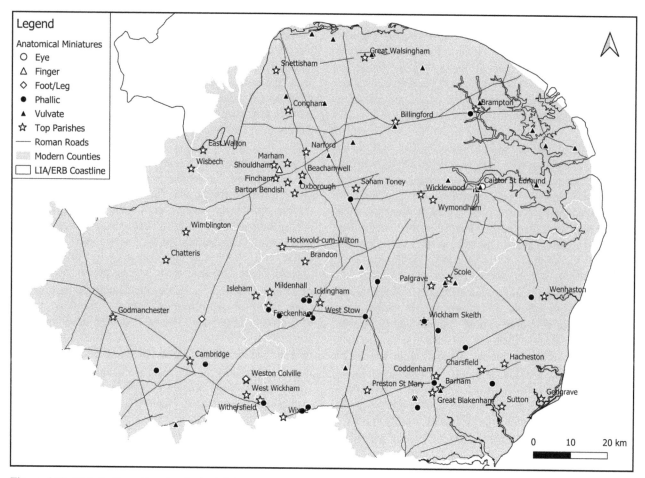

Figure 6.17. Distribution of anatomical miniatures.

These artefacts are not found in pre-conquest Britain and are generally considered cheap imports for an entirely 'Romano-Celtic' market (Crerar 2006: 79; Green 1976: 20, 1978: 16). The range of types in Britain is restricted compared with Gaul. This may suggest that only certain forms were offered for export, or demanded for import. Fittock found no evidence to suggest that pipeclay figurines were ever made in Britain. They are distributed widely, with a trend towards southeastern settlements and shrines, as well as military *vici* in the North. Fittock notes the lack of pipeclays from military installations and temples in *Londinium*, an odd distribution which he tentatively explains as related to private, domestic worship (2015, 2016).

Forty-two pipeclay figurines were identified (Figure 6.21): Cambridgeshire (19), Norfolk (14) and Suffolk (9). The distribution shows a general trend towards the south. There are no PAS records for pipeclay figurines in the region, perhaps unsurprisingly, as they are non-metallic and unlikely to be recovered by metal-detection.[9] The most common type (17) are female figures identified as Venus, the Roman goddess of fertility. There are 10 zoomorphic statuettes and five Mother-Goddesses, known as *Matres* or *Deae Nutrices* (Figure 6.22).

Figure 6.18. Phallic pendant, Lackford (PAS: SF-75CF48).

Although metal figurines (most commonly bronzes, with a few lead examples) are rarely convincingly dated, many are likely to date from the same period as the pipeclay figurines. I have included them here as comparative material, always bearing in mind some may be considerably later. HER and PAS records were checked against, and supplemented by, Durham's online database (2012). The overall distribution is similar to the pipeclay examples, with a general southerly bias (Figure 6.23). There are few around the northwestern parishes, while Cambridgeshire boasts more

---

[9] There are only eight individual PAS records of pipeclay figurines, plus a group of thirteen from Nornour in the Scilly Isles.

Figure 6.19. Vulvate mount, Scole (PAS: NMS-827A54).

than its usual slim proportion. Of the 277 metal figurines, there are groups at Willingham (10 from the Fen hoard), Brampton (8), Caistor St Edmund (7), Walsingham (9) and Icklingham (7). Remarkably, in the light of the preference for lead miniature axes (section 6.7.2), most Pb figurines are also found in Suffolk. The most popular deities represented are Mercury (38), Hercules (15), Minerva (11), Mars (7), Cupid (7) and Jupiter (5). There are also just over 100 zoomorphic renderings in metal.

6.8.1. *Venus and the Mother-Goddess*

Venus figurines depict a youthful woman, standing with the folds of her drapery held at one side, sometimes touching her hair with the other hand. She is described as a provincial 'pseudo-Venus', based upon the classical Venus Pudica. Despite her 'Romanised' appearance, Venus figurines may be part of an alternative pantheon reflecting discrepant indigenous beliefs (Webster 1997: 332-33, 2003: 46-47). The Mother-Goddess is seated, often in a basketwork chair, with various attributes on her lap, including nursing infants as the *Dea Nutrix*. Venuses date *circa* 70/80-200 CE and the *Deae Nutrices circa* 150-200 CE (Barnard 1985: 237; Jenkins 1977: 161-62).

Two Venuses are recorded from the settlement and temple at Hockwold-cum-Wilton (NHER: 5587). One (a truncated 'bottom', almost certainly a Venus) came from a chalk

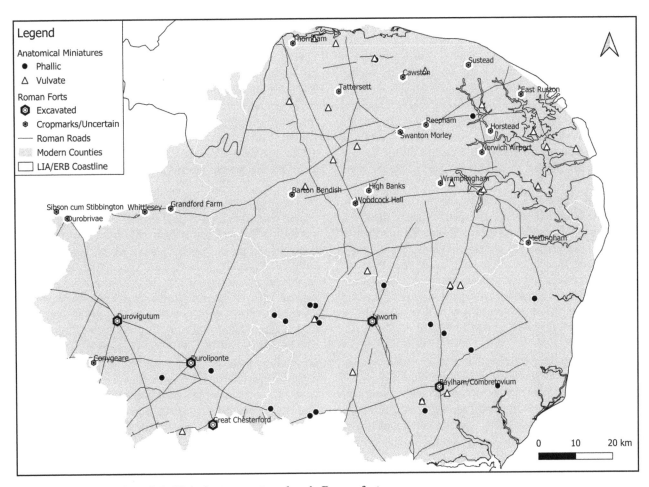

Figure 6.20. Distribution of phallic/vulvate mounts and early Roman forts.

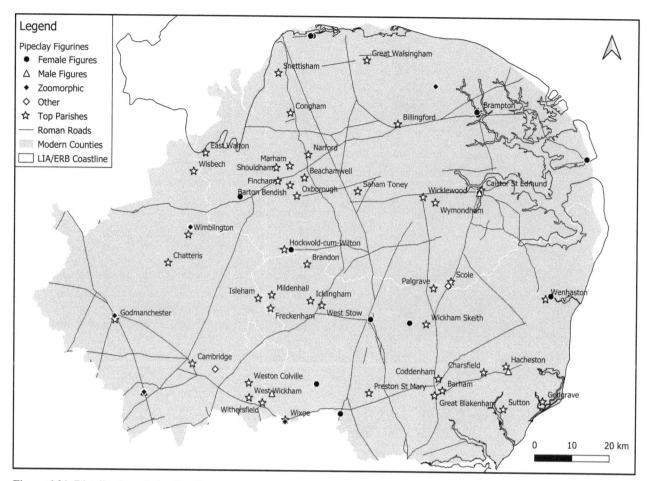

Figure 6.21. Distribution of pipeclay figurines by type.

floor which also yielded an assemblage of coins, jewellery including Horse-and-rider brooches, crown fragments, votive leaves and letters, and the foot of a model bird (Gurney 1986: 56, 73 fig. 45). This building is thought to be a temple or related structure dating to the later second century CE (*ibid.*: 88). Another Venus fragment, found in 1931, was reported by Clarke, although details are sketchy (Jenkins 1977: 346).[10]

A second century CE Spanish olive oil *amphora*, containing iron nails and two fragmentary Venus figurines, was found at a possible temple at Hawkedon. The vessel may have been reused as a cremation urn (Jenkins 1977: 353).[11] Three pipeclay Venuses are also recorded from the town of *Durovigutum* (Godmanchester). Two came from second century CE rubbish pits at the *mansio* or inn and the other was found at the gateway of a possible shrine (CHER: 00927, 00961; Green 1977: 17-18).

Two Venus figurines were excavated at the small town of Brampton. The first was found in mid-late fourth century CE occupation, on the site of an earlier kiln field. This sculpture was missing its head, feet and base (Jenkins 1977: 346; Jenkins in Knowles 1983: 26). The second, complete and virtually undamaged, came from a complex of third/fourth

century CE pits. Their fills included animal remains (one pit contained four dog skeletons and an ox skull, another had horse and dog bones), a small wooden box represented by *in situ* nails and a bronze pin depicting a hand holding an apple. A disturbed male inhumation on the site was also covered by fragmentary ox skulls and other faunal remains. These finds have clear ritual connotations (Knowles 1981: 12, 1983: 20-26; Rankov 1982: 370 and pl. 36).

In Gaul, pipeclay figurines, especially Venus and *Dea Nutrix* types, were often deposited in shrines and burials (Green 1976: 20). In Britain, figurines are found in domestic religious contexts, as well as in burials of children. Pipeclay Venuses are also found in military establishments (Green 1978: 16). If directly related to women, this supplements other evidence for women's presence in forts, usually defined by personal ornament (e.g. Allason-Jones 1989: 61; Allison 2008; Cool 2016: 417-18; Mattingly 2007: 170-76). These women are rather predictably assumed to be soldiers' unofficial wives, daughters, prostitutes or servants. By the conquest, military wives were commonplace, although ordinary legionaries were not officially allowed to marry until after 197 CE (Watts 2005: 26-27). Venus figurines are widespread in London, especially in and around the Walbrook, implying a possible import and/or cult centre (Fittock 2015: 119), although many Walbrook finds come from a washed-out cemetery (Pearce 2017).

---

[10] Matt Fittock (pers. comm. 18/01/2017).
[11] M. Fittock (pers. comm. 18/01/2017).

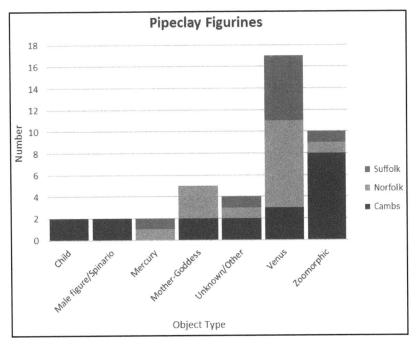

Figure 6.22. Pipeclay figurines by type and county.

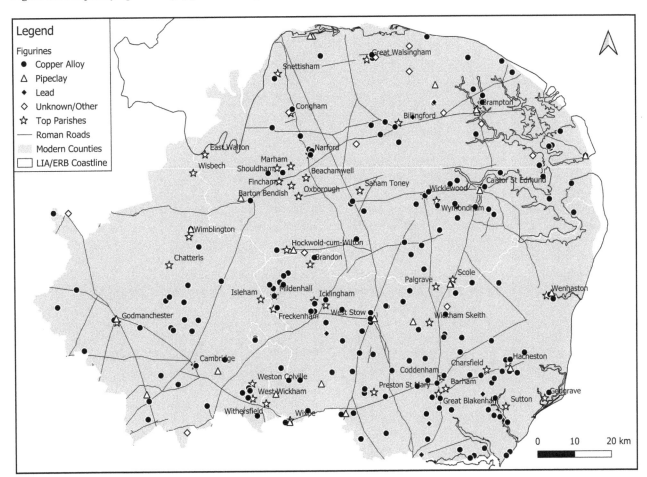

Figure 6.23. Distribution of all figurines by material.

The distribution in northern East Anglia is temples and towns, with little penetration into rural settlements (Figure 6.21). In Norfolk, 12 of the 14 pipeclay figurines are female, either Mother-Goddess or Venus, and another is a fragment of a pigeon or dove, often associated with Venus. However, this does not hold true with the metal figurines (Figure 6.24), which shows clusters around Brampton and Coddenham/Charsfield areas and a gap in the parishes along the Icknield Way. This may point to a change in the perception and social currency of gender between the earlier and later Roman occupation.

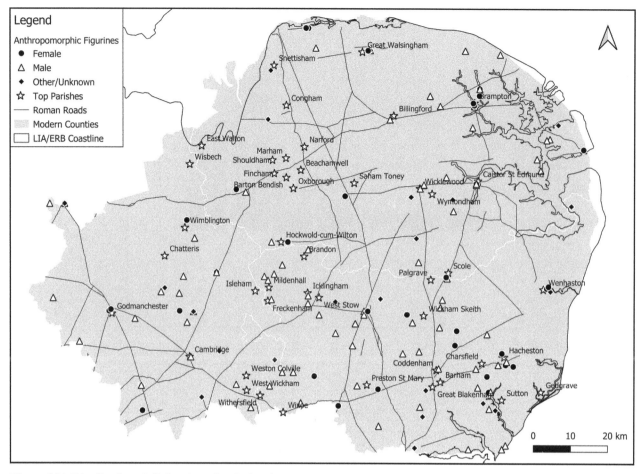

Figure 6.24. Distribution of all female and male figurines.

A Romano-Celtic cult of the *Matres* has been deduced from epigraphy, material culture and so-called 'Celtic Mythology', despite a lack of literary references. Images of *Matres* have been found in *Mithraea*, begging the question of who was worshipping them, given that Mithras's cult was supposedly restricted to men. The cult of the *Matres* was also popular in what is now Lincolnshire: a temple to the Mother-Goddesses has been posited at Ancaster; reliefs are also known from Lincoln. The *Matres* often appear in groups of three. Instances of 'triplication' seem to have symbolic importance in LIA art, perhaps suggesting that the *Matres* slotted into a pre-existing indigenous belief system (Barnard 1985; Davies 2014: 27; Green 1975: 13, 1976: 20; Lewis 1966: 124).

The Mother-Goddess is often subject to the same kind of woolly mythologising as the Taranis-Jupiter and Rider-God characters. She is described as 'a symbol of protection in death and rebirth in the Otherworld', and as a symbolic parent or guardian for 'the journey to the afterlife' in child burials (Green in Taylor 1993: 196). Barnard claims that goddess worship ensured the fertility of the earth, animals and women (1985: 237). Green suggests that these female figurines were private, domestic representations of the 'Celtic' Mother-Goddess rendered in a cheap material. She proposes that they were *ex-votos* designed to bring luck to women for fertility and childbirth (1978: 16-17). The stereotypical association of women with the domestic sphere, low-status materials and

fertility has been widely debunked (Butler 2006; Gilchrist 1999; Sweely ed. 1999). Derks notes that Rhenish cults of the Mothers were based on pre-Roman ancestral beliefs in local communities. Their sanctuaries were modest in appearance and size, suggesting a low rank in the cult hierarchy (1998: 122). This perhaps supports a class distinction rather than a gender split in their adherents.

Votive anatomical models found at shrines include breasts, genitalia and uteri, which would comfortably fit with a medical devotion or healing interpretation (Jackson 1988: 91, 160). Venuses and Mother-Goddesses are also often too simplistically connected with fertility and motherhood. Burials accompanied by *Deae Nutrices* have sometimes been interpreted as mothers or babies who died in childbirth (Allason-Jones 1989: 148; Laurence 2012: 147-52). The *Dea Nutrix* is regarded as a goddess of childrearing, depicted nursing one or a pair of infants (Bird 2011: 287-88; Green 1976: 20), although she has numerous other attributes including small animals, baskets of fruit and loaves of bread. Tacitus makes a distinction between Roman children and those of barbarians, whose 'own mother suckles each at her breast; they are not passed on to nursemaids and wet-nurses' (Laurence 2012: 149; Tac. *Germ.* 20). Whether this was also the case in Gaul or Britain is a matter for debate. This demonstrates how meanings can intersect between Roman ideals and provincial practices, expressed through figurines.

Interpretations of figurines range from children's toys to votive objects. Pipeclay is fragile. Although sometimes packed in wooden boxes, most are broken, which may be accidental in the former use and intentional in the latter (Fittock 2016: 4-5). Several explanations are put forward for this: Allason-Jones (1989: 148) suggests they were purposely smashed to free the spirit of the object to accompany the deceased. Cool proposes that figurines from cremation burials may have been damaged on the pyre (2011: 296).

Fittock experimented with fragmentation analysis of pipeclays from London. He states that the heads, particularly of Venus and *Dea Nutrix* figurines, were selectively kept, whether deliberately or accidentally parted from their bodies. They may have been a source of impromptu anatomical votives, broken up for deposition in healing rituals, or linked to the 'cult of the head'. Unfortunately, caches of pipeclay heads are yet to be discovered and broken heads remain scarce. Complete figurines are seemingly reserved for burials (Fittock 2015). Two finds from the second century CE outer ditch at *Venta Icenorum* support the deliberate breakage theory. One is a Venus fragment, broken at the waist and knees (CRP: SF5141) (Figure 6.25), and the other is a headless torso of Mercury, wearing his characteristic cloak (*chlamys*) across one shoulder (CRP: SF5139, SF5140) (Figure 6.26). Both seem to have been intentionally fragmented before deposition, close together in the enclosure ditch (Harlow in Bowden forthcoming).

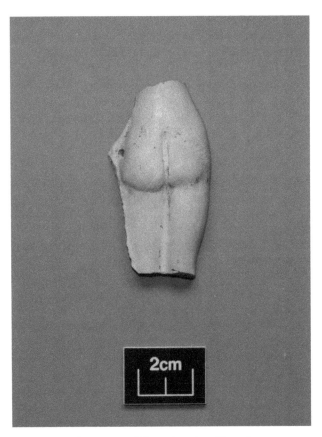

Figure 6.25. Fragment of Venus figurine, *Venta Icenorum* (CRP: SF5141, Image: CRP/Ian Jackson).

6.8.2. Mercury

Mercury's popularity in Roman Britain is attested by numerous inscribed rings, bronze figurines and other references (e.g. goats and cockerels) (Marsden 2014: 50-55, 65). There are 38 metal figurines portraying Mercury; however, depictions in pipeclay are extremely rare. The Mercury figurine from *Venta Icenorum* is certainly part of a suite of finds which allude to a cult at the town, including a seal-box and a pan handle (see section 7.6). A good continental parallel shows the *chlamys* draped over the opposite shoulder (Rouvier-Jeanlin 1972: #490). The only other examples are from Corbridge and York (Green 1978: 11). There are no Mercury pipeclay figurines in Fittock's recent study of Roman London (2015: 115). This could suggest that Mercury figurines were less common products of the Gaulish workshops, although they were undoubtedly made there, or that they did not appeal to British tastes.

6.8.3. Apollo and the Thorn-Puller 'Spinario'

Some characters from the Graeco-Roman pantheon or Gaulish folklore may have appeared more 'alien' to the people of the Iceni polity. An unusual find is a pipeclay Apollo from Hacheston. The god holds his five-stringed lyre (*cithara*) and a large plectrum which identifies him as a provincial copy of the classical 'Apollo Citharoedos' (Jenkins in Blagg *et al.* 2004: 140). The clay is very fine

Figure 6.26. Two joining fragments of Mercury figurine, *Venta Icenorum* (CRP: SF5139, SF5140, Image: CRP/Ian Jackson).

and typical of central Gaulish fabrics. It is close in style to a second century CE clay statuette of Apollo from Bedford (Blagg *et al.* 2004: 140-41, fig. 100 and pl. 13).

Based on a Hellenistic prototype of the third century BCE, the 'Spinario' depicts a young man seated with one ankle drawn up on his other knee, removing a thorn from the sole of his foot (Jenkins 1977: 386). Thorn-pullers were only produced in the central Gaulish workshops, based on finds of moulds and wasters (Fittock 2016: 4). Jenkins dates this type, in Britain, to the Hadrianic period. Two examples from London bear traces of a dark red pigment, perhaps imitating samian. The Thorn-puller does not have any known mythological or religious symbolism (1977: 8, 163, 507), although later anecdotes and legends have been attached to him.

What did this symbolism achieve during the client-kingdom and early years of occupation? Did owning it confer a means of distinction, the power of being 'in the know', or was it viewed as a curiosity or souvenir? Were these artefacts seen as Gaulish, Rhenish, Greek or Roman? Male figurines, like the female representations, are almost absent in the northwestern parishes, considered one of the cores of pre-Roman settlement. This absence of anthropomorphic depiction may be evidence for deliberate resistance to the classical pantheon. In contrast, the southern and northeastern regions are well-populated with statuettes, along with several in central Cambridgeshire (Figure 6.24). Even by the later Roman period, there is very little Romano-Christian material culture from Norfolk, unlike Suffolk and Cambridgeshire, suggesting an area 'rather unreceptive to the new religion' [...] 'even as Roman authority was collapsing in Britain, most of Norfolk's inhabitants stuck stubbornly to the gods of their ancestors' (Marsden 2014: 70). Is this further evidence that change happened slowly in the Iceni heartland or that paganism was more firmly rooted in the hearts of its people?

6.8.4. Zoomorphics

The other main class of pipeclays from Britain are representations of animals and birds. Frequently, these portray bulls and oxen, dogs, horses, goats and sheep, chickens, doves and pigeons (Fittock 2016: 3). This is a remarkably similar list to the zoomorphic plate brooches (section 3.11.5). A pipeclay horse was excavated at Stonea Grange, Wimblington (CHER: 06057), from the early third century CE fill of a pit shaft adjacent to the temple *temenos*. From the same site came a *Dea Nutrix* fragment found in a third/fourth century CE well fill (Jackson and Potter 1996: 486, fig. 177). A pipeclay ram comes from the curious context of inside a metalworking 'oven' in an industrial area at Wixoe (SHER: WIX003; Chapman *et al.* 2012: 324), reminiscent of the cosmetic mortar placed in the kiln at *Venta Icenorum*.

Bulls are frequent characters in Graeco-Roman mythology and art, linked to Jupiter and Mithras among other deities

(Toynbee 1973: 135, 151). Rams, goats and cockerels were associated with Mercury. Marsden considers goats, rams and lambs to be ideal sacrifices to Faunus, in his role as guardian of flocks (2014: 55). In Roman tradition, sheep were sacrificed to many gods including Jupiter and Mars, and cockerels were offered to the *Lares*. Doves and pigeons symbolised Venus. Dogs and horses were the companions of Epona, who herself was sometimes associated with the *Matres* (Toynbee 1973). Caches of pipeclay horses are known from Belgium and at healing-spring sanctuaries in Gaul (Green 1976: 12).

Zoomorphic figurines, both metal and ceramic, are widespread and include a few finds from the Icknield Way parishes (Figure 6.27). There may be a slight tendency towards deposition along roads and around coastal waterways. There are 16 sheep/goats, 39 birds of various species and nine horses. Some clusters may be seen around Brampton and Caistor St Edmund. The latter appears to be a focus for sheep/goat figurines, likely to be associated with a cult of Mercury at the *civitas* capital, and there are three dogs, sometimes related to healing cults, from southeast Suffolk (Bird 2011: 287-88).

The figurines' function is debated. Bird concedes that while both pipeclay and copper alloy figurines of animals could feasibly be children's playthings, they only seem to depict creatures associated with cults and healing (2011: 287-88). There are no wild boars or wolves to appeal to the indigenous mindset, although animal representations may have provoked a sense of familiarity, unlike the classical pantheon. Some zoomorphic figurines are found in grave contexts and at shrines. They may have been produced as proxies for the sacrificial animals which usually accompanied rituals of devotion and burial (Taylor 1993: 199-201). While pipeclay animal figures are mainly found in Cambridgeshire (Norfolk 1, Suffolk 1, Cambridgeshire 8), their metal counterparts are proportionally rarer in that county (Norfolk 48, Suffolk 44, Cambridgeshire 15). This may be related to their selection for deposition in children's graves (see below) or differences between status and materials. Is this another sign of local selectivity regarding imported artefacts or practices? Was the ritual of animal sacrifice, and therefore its symbolic counterparts, alien to the people of early Roman Norfolk and Suffolk, in contrast to those inhabiting Essex and Cambridgeshire?

6.8.5. Arrington

The earliest pipeclay figurines known in Britain come from Colchester, dated around 55-65 CE. A 'child's grave', excavated under antiquarian circumstances in 1866, contained 13 figures, including a triple-horned bull, a Hercules and a set of 'comic old men' characters. The figurines were thought to represent toys, and a small vessel, possibly a lamp-filler, was considered a 'feeding bottle' (Jenkins 1977: 155-59). Green proposed the grave instead belonged to a 'high-ranking woman' (in Going *et al.* 1997: fn. 254). The poor preservation of skeletal remains means age and gender remain inconclusive (Eckardt

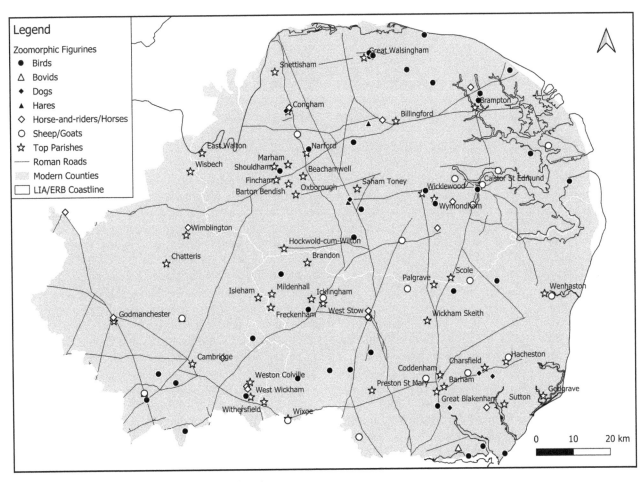

Figure 6.27. Distribution of zoomorphic figurines by type.

1999). This very unusual early Roman burial is paralleled in two examples from Arrington and Godmanchester in Cambridgeshire.

A grave was discovered in 1990 at Arrington (CHER: 09955). The small lead coffin (1m long) and surviving fragments of the cranium and hair are convincing evidence that this was the burial of an infant, aged six months to a year old at death. The pipeclay figurines were probably contained in a wooden box which sat atop the coffin. The pipeclay grave goods are dated to *circa* 130-160 CE (Taylor 1993).

The group comprises an unusual Rhenish-type *Matrona* figure wearing a distinctive large, round headdress (Green 1998: 26), a seated male, probably a Thorn-puller, a figure wearing a cloak and Phrygian cap, two images of children (an infant and an older child), a male bovid, and two complete and two fragmentary rams. The Mother-Goddess holds a pile of fruit in her lap, and the rear of her seat is inscribed with faint markings (Taylor 1993), illegible but possibly in cursive script. This relates to the role of magical literacy and the connection between writing and votive deposits, which will be discussed below (section 7.3). Green tends to mystify these objects in their role as grave goods: the rams and bullock may symbolise fertility, strength, Mercury, or substitutes for sacrificial offerings

'to the gods of the underworld'. The busts may represent the dead child and a sibling, or perhaps its unrealised future self, 'in a kind of wistful hope that it would grow up in the Otherworld' (in Taylor 1993: 197).

The coffin also contained red-dyed cloth and an aromatic resin. Along with the imported figurines, these have been interpreted as components in an 'exotic' burial for a 'cosmopolitan family', passing through the area along Ermine Street from one urban or military location to the next (Green in Taylor 1993: 208). While this may be somewhat pejorative to the local inhabitants, the inclusion of Rhenish and Gaulish statuettes may indicate genealogical associations with the continent, an important reminder not to lose sight of the numbers of Gauls who may have been resident in Britain during this period.

6.8.6. Godmanchester

Godmanchester is the site of Roman *Durovigutum*, at a strategic crossing point of Ermine Street over the River Ouse. In 1991, a mid-second century CE cremation burial was discovered (CHER: SCB21040). A samian jar contained the cremated remains of a child, aged three to eight years at death, with two bangles, box-fittings, three pots and pipeclay figurines of a bull and a horse. One of the bangles had snake-headed terminals and both were small enough to fit a child, 'probably a girl' based on the presence of these bracelets (Going *et al.* 1997), although not confirmed scientifically.

The horse figurine has a mane and wears neither saddle nor bridle. Its sex is not indicated, which may mean it is a mare or gelding. The pipeclay bull portrays an uncastrated bovid wearing the *vitta* or sacrificial 'body-belt' around its waist. The triple-horned bovid from the Colchester burial also has this band. Both bulls and horses were considered appropriate for sacrificial rituals. The placing of the figures either side of the cremation vessel suggests a guardianship role over the deceased child (Eckardt 1999: 66; Green in Going *et al.* 1997). The dedication of pipeclay animals as proxies for sacrificial victims finds parallels with the shift from deposition of full-size to miniature weaponry (section 6.7.1).

6.8.7. Discussion

When discussing objects of potential veneration and devotion, it is easy to fall into the trap of reading too much into too little evidence, or attempting to layer the known rites and beliefs of other communities onto an unknown one. The arrival of pipeclay figurines, representing alien deities, sacrificial practices and mythological allusions, must have seemed mysterious or simply irrelevant to some local populations. Were they seen as Gaulish, Roman or simply different? Similarly, Gosden asks if imports of Gaulish samian were regarded as 'Roman', or from near neighbours across the sea, or even as novel indigenous objects arriving through 'well-known local exchange networks' (2005: 207). The later Roman dates of some deposits suggest a lag between the figurines' manufacture and subsequent use and discard in some parts of the region, with early adoption and usage, especially in funerary contexts, in other areas.

The high proportion of pipeclay Venuses and *Matres*, against zoomorphic and masculine representations, in the northern and eastern range, perhaps relates to an interest in the feminine aspect, fertility or the cult of the Mother-Goddess, although this remains speculative, and it must be remembered that these are the most common types across Roman Britain. The Venus from Hockwold temple is associated with a collection of votive objects, including numerous brooches and coins dating from the mid-second century CE onwards (Gurney 1986). The pipeclay horse and Mother-Goddess from the Roman temple at Stonea may emphasise this as a place where different traditions interacted: 'The fens appear to have been a border land, with Stonea and perhaps March islands as western outliers of Icenian power' (Malim 2005: 39-40, 93).

The presence of (primarily zoomorphic) pipeclay figurines with child burials is incongruous with the lack of early burials in Norfolk and Suffolk. Cambridgeshire fits into a very different funerary distribution, allied with Essex and Hertfordshire, attributed to the 'tribal territory' of the Catuvellauni/Trinovantes. Going *et al.* regard figurines as

indicators of the importation of Gallo-Belgic traditions into this area (1997: 391-93), and Martin claims the urned cremation at Elveden and the Snailwell burial represent the 'outer limits' of this polity (1999: 70-72). Although this may lend some credence to the idea that the Fenland was divided between different communities, I doubt the relationships were as strongly defined as these 'tribal' ascriptions suggest.

One important observation about pipeclay figurines is how they differ from many other categories of objects studied, even the bronze and lead figures. Firstly, we are dealing with a limited number of imported objects which are rarely, if ever, retrieved as surface finds by detectorists and therefore are not subject to the recent explosion in numbers of other PAS finds. This discrepancy presents a rare opportunity to talk about context and discovery circumstances, as most of the finds come from excavations. Although many are either antiquarian or development finds, there has been enough information to discuss the role of figurines in temples, domestic contexts and burial rites. These finds may relate to a post-conquest tradition of structured deposition of objects and animal/human remains in pits, which is also a practice seemingly carried out at the *civitas* capital (Bowden 2017: 22). Despite their fragility, pipeclay figurines are long-lasting, appearing in contexts dated centuries after their production. Their similarity to samian ware in terms of production centres may also extend to their longevity, and perhaps even curation, within the domestic sphere.

Secondly, the distribution of figurines is very different to other small finds. The parishes with the usual highest densities (along the northern Icknield Way, around Saham Toney and Wicklewood in Norfolk) are barely represented. These areas lack anthropomorphic representations in both pipeclay and bronze, arguably supporting the pre-conquest non-depiction of humans (*contra* Green 1998). The pipeclay figurines present a very small sample of the non-British material culture which was finding its way into the country in the decades after the invasion. Imported brooches were accepted into the pre-conquest inventory (section 3.8), so the preference for figurines is not related to resistance of all 'alien' objects, but perhaps more closely associated with the burial traditions of each local community. These imported goods, along with *amphorae* and other continental trade items, may have been selectively rejected by those in the Iceni heartland, where practices of devotion and burial followed older customs into the early Roman period. This is in marked contrast to second century CE brooches, for example, which seem to cluster around the traditional areas of settlement. The difference between these two categories is that local manufacturing of brooches is evidenced, bringing up the questions of disparate markets, distribution and demand.

6.9. Summary

The idea that the Iceni were combining old ways and new gods agrees with the hybridity of personal ornamentation and horse gear. Some of these practices and events may have been used to reinforce group identity, at the level of a family or a community. One of the qualifiers mentioned in the introduction of this section was the complexity of recovering past beliefs through material culture, and the potential for large-scale concepts to be materially expressed through miniaturisation. The sheer volume of finds seemingly associated with ritual behaviour invites interpretation, although our attempts will inevitably fall short. We can endeavour to surmise past people's activities, if not their actual philosophies.

My investigation of votive and miniature objects shows intra-regional differences. The burials with pipeclay figurines suggest that the people at the core of the polity were still 'Doing Different' to their Cambridgeshire, Essex and Hertfordshire neighbours in the post-conquest period. Such interments are rare, special deposits across Britain, so Norfolk and Suffolk may simply lack evidence. I also suggest that different iconography was chosen regionally, with female representations in pipeclay particularly favoured in Norfolk. A clear geographical division was noted between the phallic and vulvate mounts, which may have been used cross-functionally on military and civilian harness and as votives.

Assumptions about female deities and fertility need to be thoroughly interrogated for implicit gender bias, as do the views on phallic symbolism and other anatomical votive miniatures. Votive miniatures and figurines reveal gender bias in both classical and modern interpretations. This is based on double standards in which classical medical texts are read as fact, despite their inherent prejudice against women. Images of female figures or anatomical parts are assumed to represent fertility and a preoccupation with reproduction. The presumption is that infertility was understood as an ailment which could be corrected by petitions to the gods. Phallic votives and amulets, conversely, are rarely used to suggest that men deposited these as part of ritual behaviour to ensure healthy children or relief from STIs. Votives of vulvas or other parts of the body are referred to as miniature anatomical models designed for healing, yet both vulvate and phallic mounts are recorded as military charms.

The pipeclay figurines prompt questions about the relationships between adults and children in the past (Crawford and Shepherd eds. 2007; Millett and Gowland 2015). What were people's attitudes towards the physiological dangers and rewards of childbirth and rearing? How did people feel about losing a child? What symbolic or spiritual dimensions did they imagine? Clearly some of the children who died young were enormously important to their families and were buried with care, attention and distinctive material culture. Marking people out through objects may have been a way of emphasising difference, social distinction, rather than status, part of the production of the body in life and death (Bourdieu 2010; Fowler 2004: 38-39; Joy 2010: 76). Cremation was also a way of fragmenting and rearranging the bodily remains (Cool 2011: 295; Pearce 1997: 177), in some senses a similar process to the selective destruction and reintegration of objects like torcs and harness, which were then buried. There is scope to consider figurines in terms of group and individual, public or private identities. Were burials private events? Did domestic shrines contain objects only for the family's use? Were dedications to deities part of a discreet and personal rite or on full show in temples?

There are also similarities and differences outside the immediate area. Miniatures show continuity of indigenous practice, deposition and appropriateness in terms of scale and materials. The few model wheels show that not all Gaulish *comparanda* are appropriate, and the lack of shields is notable, given the concentrations in Lincolnshire and elsewhere. The use of lead for miniature axes and figurines in Suffolk is also intriguing. This indicates that very local practices could occur within wider trends. There is a lack of distinction between what is 'votive' or 'ritual' and what is functional. As with miniature terrets, seal-boxes and brooches, the use of everyday objects in different contexts is what marks them out. Again, the persistence of hoarding is seen throughout the period. Special or structured deposits, hoards, however categorised, form part of a long-standing ritual practice which absorbs changes in material culture. There is a strong argument for this behaviour continuing well into the Roman occupation, with pits, shafts, wells and other features being used for deposition, such as the two figurines from the enclosure ditch at *Venta Icenorum*.

Religious practices were changing with the institution of formal temple complexes, often linked to developing towns in the second century CE onwards. Priests may have become more visible, perhaps wearing crowns and brooches as exterior signals of their office. This again challenges the idea of the material elite, with a concept of spiritual capital. The inhabitants of the Icenian *civitas* seem to have followed wider trends, with increased deposition of miniatures, but continued to develop distinctive regional tendencies during the move to Roman administration, such as the absence of model shields or the use of lead. This may be a sign of resistance to Roman rule, or rather an evolving process which incorporated new materials, beliefs and belongings into existing practices. Miniature objects and other votives reveal changes in ritual behaviour over time. Mark-making on miniature axes prefigures the introduction of magical literacy, through cursing and amulets, incorporating the symbolism of writing into ritual. The next chapter considers the personal and public expression of these activities.

Writing and Sealing: A New Lexicon of Power

7.1. Introduction

The following chapter examines written communication and mark-making in the Icenian polity. It argues that certain displays of status, power and control were implemented through literacy and its accoutrements. As 'a set of social practices' (Eckardt 2018: 5), literacy became necessary for engagement with the Roman administration. Aside from written texts and inscriptions, the main paraphernalia of literacy are wax *spatulae*, *styli* and inkwells, with the possible inclusion of seal-boxes and signet rings (Andrews 2012; Derks and Roymans 2002; Eckardt 2014, 2018; Henig 1974; Marshman 2015). Their distributions may tell us about how people reacted to the introduction of literacy (Figure 7.1). They may also shed some light on the 'Roman Dark Ages', the second/third centuries CE, when so much existing material culture disappears, and little is known historically about what was happening in East Anglia. In the post-Boudican generation, the material culture and architecture of the *civitas Icenorum* was becoming more like other provinces of the empire. This echoes work by Roymans (1996), Fernández-Götz (2014b), Pitts (2019)

and others which shows the 'standardisation' process at work, and the concomitant reforging of new and diverse identities.

Evidence for literacy in Britain begins with coin legends, around a century pre-conquest (Williams 2001). Writing was therefore familiar to Iron Age Britons, although comprehension is another matter. Legends on Roman coins would have been sources of information, power, or frustration depending on one's level of literacy. The potency of writing would have been a daily reminder of a person's place in the hierarchy of empire (Creighton 2000: 146-73; Williams 2007). Exposure to Roman administration may have demanded an increasing need for personal identification and a desire to demonstrate the ability to read and write.

Woolf sees the spread of writing as parallel processes of local adoptions, adaptations and rejections. Imperial expansion was accompanied by 'widespread cultural change which destroyed writing practices and changed their meaning as well as spreading new ones' (1994: 97).

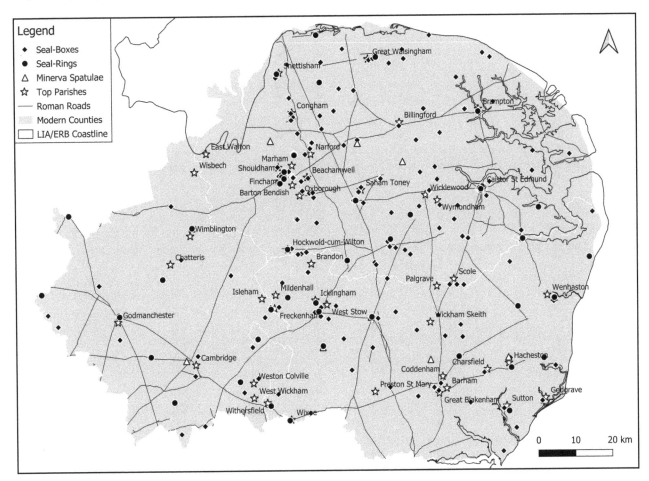

Figure 7.1. Combined evidence for literacy and sealing.

At this time, oral and visual traditions may also have been lost or downgraded. Is this a fundamental part of such 'globalisation' or was there indigenous resistance? Nash Briggs (2011, 2017) claims Icenian coin legends use a language closer to West Germanic than Celtic. Williams proposes that the Iceni may have deliberately resisted using Latin on coins until the SVB ESVPRASTVS issue (section 2.3.5). He also notes that the East Anglian coin series retains its traditional symbolism and aesthetics until quite late, which 'suggests strongly that this was a conscious expression of preference, rather than the outcome of ignorance' (2007: 8-9).

Some objects continue to function over many centuries with limited innovation, which gives us insights into long-standing practices. *Styli* are too similar to date tightly, especially without a full survey of published and unpublished data (Eckardt 2014: 187). Inkwells are relatively rare finds in Roman Britain, with a peak in the late first/early second centuries CE. They were clearly valuable possessions, perhaps expressing status through literacy, and in some cases, were interred with the dead. Samian inkwells are biased towards military sites and urban centres, suggesting a predisposition towards places requiring day-to-day record-keeping (*ibid.*: 193-204). Eckardt has recently published a comprehensive survey (2018).

Seal-boxes were introduced in the late first century CE. They peaked in popularity, along with wax *spatulae*, in the second/third centuries CE. The engraved or inscribed surface design of an intaglio ring was pressed into the soft wax contained within the seal-box. Dating of signets covers the Roman period, with a peak in the third century CE, mostly falling outside the range of this study. The distribution across the research area is heavily skewed by the large group of 127 intaglios from the Snettisham Jeweller's Hoard. Therefore, only selected seal-rings are discussed below as part of the case studies on Walsingham and *Venta Icenorum*.

Other evidence comes from the actual practice of writing: inscriptions, graffiti and curse tablets. Personal names were often scratched on pottery vessels, especially finewares and plain samian tableware. This may point to individual ownership of vessels and the ability, at the very least, to write one's own name. The occurrence of graffiti is higher at forts and *vici* than small towns and rural sites, which may suggest lower levels of rural literacy, although *styli* occur on all site types (Cool 2006: 35-36). Below, the relationships between writing, sealing and the wider practice of mark-making are explored to weigh up the responses to the occupation across the *civitas*.

7.2. Writing Power

A shared spoken language is more fundamental to feelings of belonging or otherness than other elements of costume or material culture. Repetitive activities, like writing, are normalised or subverted as part of the performative action of identity. Routine activity becomes internalised, producing and reproducing social norms and the sense of self-identity. These performances also allow for demonstrations of difference - to choose to comply with the norms or adopt different routines, to make an 'Other' of oneself (Revell 2016: 10-11). Indigenous Britons were presented with opportunities to become literate and multilingual, or could have been doubly disadvantaged by the lack of a written mother tongue, meaning even dictation to a scribe would be difficult. Refusal to adopt Latin and literacy could also be seen as resistance, as Williams suggests for coin legends (2007: 8). Bowman and Woolf describe writing as 'a transferable technology' which could be turned to multiple ends regardless of the power structure in which it was taught (1994: 6).

Eckardt has looked at the power relationships embedded in literacy, which is part of the domination of the Roman occupation. She considered how material culture reveals the impact of literacy on Britain, looking at socio-spatial distribution and materials. The practices of reading, writing and speaking in a new language would have been part of the internalisation of power structures and the rules governing social order. Literacy could also be an empowering skill-set, providing aspirations within certain social strata and the ability to engage with the prevailing power structure. The new skills of writing and reading involved 'culturally laden' front-stage artefacts (2005: 142, 2014: 177-207, 2018: 3-20). The physical actions of smoothing, sealing, inscribing, and the use of materials such as ink and wax in a new context would all have given opportunities for people to identify and belong, or to resist and stand apart.

7.3. Magical Literacy

Repeatedly chosen motifs on material objects have cultural meaning. In the absence of a written language, symbolism was used to reinforce group identity. Later Icenian coin issues feature names, possibly of leaders, moneyers or trade organisations (Talbot 2015: 310-11, 2017: 148). The multivalency of Iron Age coins as tokens in an economic sense, and as votive offerings, may put these legends into the realms of magical literacy. Davies suggests that certain animals and designs may have distinguished the Iceni from their neighbours. The Iceni avoided the classical imagery used by the Trinovantes/Catuvellauni and were the only issuers to depict a wolf on their coinage. There is a preference for back-to-back crescents on both gold and silver issues, especially the Pattern-Horse and later inscribed series. This addorsed crescent motif, which is also seen on other Iron Age metalwork, could represent a 'tribal emblem' (Davies 2009: 114-15, 2014: 27-29). Talbot suggests the addorsed crescents were a quality control mark which gave 'confidence and the assurance of authenticity' (2015: 302) (see section 4.3). Triplets are another Iron Age motif found on objects across Europe. The triple pellet, usually arranged in a triangle, is found on Iceni coins and other artefacts, such as linch-pins and button-and-loop fasteners (Davies 2014: 27-29). Nash

Briggs proposes that the tripartite motifs on coins and the architecture at Fison Way reflected the kingdom's subdivision into three *pagi* or districts (2011: 85, 2012).

Eckardt notes that cult writing was important, in the form of inscriptions and devotional records. Inkwells are rarely found at shrines, but wax *spatulae* with a handle in the shape of the goddess Minerva may have been used in devotional writing practices and deposited as offerings (Crummy 2002; Eckardt 2014: 187-93, 2018: 127). Roman religious literacy included personal dedications on wood or stone at temples enhanced by metal letter-plaques, such as the two from Hockwold (NWHCM: 1961.199.27, 1962.396.19). Ritual literacy was an important means of communicating with the gods. *Defixiones* (curse tablets) and *nuncupationes* (ritual vows) were written on lead and wooden tablets respectively (Bagnall Smith 1999; Crerar 2006: 80-81). Analysis of handwriting on *defixiones* demonstrates that these were written by individuals, rather than scribes, and many bear local British names, often female (Eckardt 2014: 180; Watts 2005: 139). Perhaps there was an appropriate and intimate connection between the petitioner marking the curse or charm in her/his own hand. Women also wrote letters, famously including some of the *Vindolanda* tablets (Bowman and Thomas 1987: 137-40; Eckardt 2018: 157).

7.3.1. The Billingford Lamella

Occasionally, we are fortunate to discover the names of dedicants and the intention of magical writings. In 2003, a gold amulet (*lamella*) was discovered in Billingford (PAS: NMS-7BEED8) (Figure 7.2). The thin rectangular plaque was originally rolled into a tube, worn around the neck in a small cylindrical pendant. The sheet is faintly incised with a mixture of Greek and Latin characters and magical symbols, written *circa* 60-150 CE. The Latin inscription reads: 'Iao, Abrasax […], ablanathanalba, give health and victory (to) Tiberius Claudius Similis whom Herennia

Figure 7.2. Gold *lamella*, Billingford (PAS: NMS-7BEED8).

Marcellina bore'. Naming matrilineal relationships is the norm for these inscriptions, unlike other epigraphy. Greek magical symbols make up the first two lines, with others appearing in the third and fourth lines. The names of the gods Iao and Abrasax are written in Greek characters. The strange, almost palindromic, 'ablanathanalba' was a magical word like 'abracadabra' (Tomlin and Hassall 2006: 481-82; Marsden 2012: 52-53).

Gold *lamellae* are extremely rare, with fewer than 70 known across the Roman empire. They were worn as charms for luck or talismans to ward off evil. Mark-making was essential for the success of mystical formulae: 'the precise form and arrangement of the words and characters was critical in investing the object with its protective magical powers' (Hinds PAS: NMS-7BEED8).

7.3.2. Curse Tablets

As well as amulets for personal protection, Roman Britons used magical inscriptions to petition the gods for justice, almost always in matters of theft. This is in distinct contrast to their continental neighbours, who also frequently mention affairs of the heart and business. Curse tablets (*defixiones*) were normally made of lead sheet, allowing the curse to be scratched into the soft metal. Many were then rolled, folded and/or pierced (Mattingly 2011: 230; McKie 2017: 109-10). The 'cold, poisonous metal' may have invoked a 'sympathetic magical association' between the curse and the accused (Moretti 2015: 107). Lead or pewter may be associated with shrines, springs and ritual activity (Eckardt 2018: 131) and a symbolic connection with the underworld (see section 6.7.2). This reminds us of the preference for silvery or reflective metals at temples in the region.

One curse tablet was found on the bank of the River Tas, not far from *Venta Icenorum*, dedicated to Neptune (NWHCM: 2005.600). The inscription is somewhat formulaic, requesting divine intervention to punish a thief. The *defixio* itemises a long list of missing belongings, and promises: 'If you, (Neptune) want the pair of leggings they shall become yours at the price of [the thief's] blood' (Bagnall Smith 1999: 49; Hassall and Tomlin 1982: 408). This sort of contractual arrangement with deities is typical of Roman religion. Marsden (2012: 51-52) links the rather unusual appeal to Neptune to the position of *Venta Icenorum* on one of the tributaries of the Great Estuary. Caistor St Edmund also has an unusual concentration of brooches depicting fish (Figure 3.91). This may hint at the association of Roman gods with earlier sacred watery places. Other evidence from the parish is discussed in the case study below.

Two lead tablets are known from near Hockwold-cum-Wilton temple. One was dredged from the Little Ouse in Brandon. It was also addressed to Neptune, in a fourth century CE script. Dating of *defixiones* is problematic, often stylistically based on the handwriting. The other came from Weeting-with-Broomhill, an adjacent parish just west of Hockwold. The characters on this *defixio* were in mirror-writing, another common manifestation of ritual literacy (Hassall and Tomlin 1994; McKie 2017: 107). Curse tablets were particularly popular in Britain and are usually associated with sacred sites. The finds from dredgings and riverbanks hint at a persistent connection between the divine and the liminal boundary of water. McKie identifies springs, wells and rivers as common contexts for curse tablets across the northwest provinces (2017: 31). Perhaps Neptune was appropriated as the embodiment of the local spirit of the waters.

Watts notes that *defixiones* were regularly written by, or on behalf of, women (2005: 139), perhaps signifying a practice which did not have gender restrictions. Additionally, some Britons, including women and slaves, who did not have the personal wherewithal or legal status to petition the court system for redress, may have resorted to appealing to the gods through cursing. Almost a quarter of named victims and petitioners on *defixiones* had female names (McKie 2017: 131-35, 192). The colloquial Latin and stolen belongings itemised imply the enactors of curses were not highly-educated or materially wealthy (Moretti 2015: 113). The study of handwriting suggests they were lettered by individuals rather than scribes (Cool 2011: 36). Even if the person who commissioned the amulet or *defixio* were themselves illiterate, the importance and power of marking may have created a symbolic dialogue with the gods. This may also be a consideration in votive deposition of coins.

Deposition of inscribed metalwork continues into the later Romano-British period, including the Thetford Treasure (Marsden 2014: 48). There are traces of nascent Christian cults, including the Water Newton Treasure (Jones and Mattingly 1990: 295-97), culminating in several late hoards of pewter and silver tableware with Christian inscriptions and symbolism, such as the Mildenhall Treasure (BM: 1946,1007) and the Hoxne Hoard (BM: 1994,0408). A recent find of a gilded disc with a *Chi-Rho* at *Venta Icenorum* (CRP: SF17125) demonstrates that, by the very end of the Roman period, some people were adopting the magical literacy of a new faith.

7.4. Minerva Wax *Spatula* Handles

Spatulae are generally found at or near urban centres, reinforcing the view that the need for written documentation and literacy was higher in small towns and *civitas* capitals than the countryside. These objects were used for smoothing out the waxed surface of a writing tablet and are therefore associated with the spread of literacy in the provinces. *Spatula* handles in the shape of a bust of Minerva, recognisable by her crested helmet (Figure 7.3), are found in small numbers across Gallo-Belgica and the Rhineland. Minerva was the Roman goddess associated with wisdom and learning. They were particularly popular in Roman Britain and 39 are recorded on PAS; by contrast, only six examples of the plain *spatulae* are known, although this may result from under-reporting. Dating

Figure 7.3. Minerva wax *spatula* handle, Middleton (PAS: SF-3292E6).

is second/third century CE (Božič and Feugère 2004; Crummy 2002; Eckardt 2018: 24).

Nationally these finds occur in a broad swathe across the southern counties from Suffolk to Somerset, with hotspots in Wessex and outliers moving north into Yorkshire. Lincolnshire, Wiltshire and Hampshire have the highest PAS concentrations, albeit in single figures. My database has just 10 Minerva *spatulae* (Table 7.1). With such a small sample it is unwise to generalise about their distribution. Suffice to say the Cambridgeshire and Suffolk *spatulae* occur at or near urban sites and roads, whereas the Norfolk ones do not; there are none known from the *civitas* capital (Figure 7.1).

Minerva *spatulae* do not coincide exactly either with the distribution of seal-boxes. Eckardt's study (2014: 187-93) showed a more rural distribution than other finds involved in literacy, perhaps related to their reuse as votive objects. Representations of Minerva, in her capacity as a goddess of healing, are often found at Romano-British temples and shrines. Once detached from the blade, the handle bearing the goddess's likeness could function independently as a votive offering or amulet (Crummy 2002). Two finds from Lincolnshire show potential hybridisation of classical and provincial stylings (PAS: NLM-9E4586, LANCUM-55B647). It is likely that a British workshop existed to cater to the demand in the province (Božič and Feugère 2004: 33). As we shall see with the seal-boxes from Walsingham, the association of *spatulae* with writing may have become

Table 7.1. Number of seal-boxes and Minerva handles by county

Object Type	Cambs	Norfolk	Suffolk	Total
Seal-Boxes	18	189	107	314
Minerva	2	3	5	10

less significant when these objects were repurposed in a votive role, perhaps used as offerings by those whose cultural mode remained oral rather than written.

7.5. Seal-boxes

Seal-boxes are small copper alloy containers used to hold wax impressions. The ornamental lids often display zoomorphic symbolism and enamelwork similar to plate brooches and cosmetic grinders (Figure 7.4, Figure 7.5). The bases are connected to the lids via a simple hinge and generally have three or four attachment holes. Wax tablets or a leather bag could be tied shut with string, which was knotted inside the base of the seal-box. The knot was covered with beeswax, impressed using an intaglio ring. This seal was protected by the lid and served as a means of guaranteeing identity and security during transit (Andrews 2012; Bagnall Smith 1999: 40).

Debate continues over their function, whether for certifying documents written on wooden tablets, or sealing

Figure 7.4. Enamelled geometric seal-box, Watton (PAS: WAW-0B6AD4).

Figure 7.5. Circular seal-box lid with zoomorphic decoration, Weasenham St Peter (PAS: NMS-5DF6D5).

coin sacks. Research by Andrews (2012, 2013) means it is no longer possible to categorically associate them with writing and correspondence (Eckardt 2018: 23-24; Marshman 2013: 759). Nevertheless, seal-boxes represent an 'incoming' form of material culture, a new focus on personal ownership of possessions and mark-making relating to individual identity and personhood. As objects which may have had multiple functionalities, I include seal-boxes here with the artefacts of literacy, with the caveat that while they may not be proof of writing, they are evidence of identifying and mark-making, which were actions of power and knowledge in early Roman Britain.

What can these portable objects reveal about identity and belonging in the *civitas*? Seal-boxes do not have a known LIA predecessor, suggesting they were part of a new post-conquest lexicon of belongings related to literacy and administration, alongside wax *spatulae*, *styli* and inkwells. In Eckardt's study (2014: 184-86), seal-boxes are interpreted as part of the language of literacy and power, with a marked bias towards military sites and major urban centres, including *civitas* capitals. However, she has more recently dismissed seal-boxes as certain indicators of literacy due to their ambiguous function (2018: 23-24). Seal-boxes worked in tandem with intaglio rings, although the dating is not entirely synchronous. In some cases, they were incorporated into votive practices, like the Minerva *spatulae* handles. They can be read as an assertion of individual identity and ownership, crossing boundaries of financial, informational and devotional transactions. These ideas are discussed further below.

Like terrets and cosmetic grinders, seal-boxes are small, attractive, often brightly-coloured artefacts which appeal to collectors; this ensures they are regularly recorded and included in museum collections. In the field, they may also be differentially recovered in comparison to other less ornate objects, in the same way as has been suggested for plate and bow brooches (Cool and Baxter 2016a, 2016b). This may skew their distribution and their proportional relationship with other types of material culture.

7.5.1. Distribution and Chronology

Andrews (2012) recorded 871 seal-boxes from the province, finding them largely absent from the southwest and Wales.[1] Norfolk, Suffolk and Lincolnshire have the most seal-boxes nationally on PAS (Figure 7.6), although it should be reiterated that these counties also have the most overall finds of all periods. They were used by a range of people across various site types. Substantial numbers were recorded from the northern frontier, major civilian towns and rural roadside settlements, places where 'activity associated with the Roman occupation is most visible' (Andrews 2013: 428).

---

[1] Andrews does not give grid references, but itemises the parish or site for each seal-box. Cross-referencing his catalogue with mine has left some queries, therefore, some locations may be approximate, centred on parish.

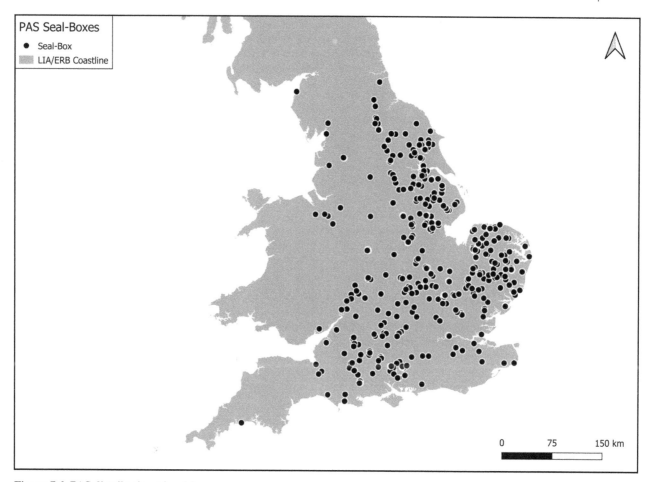

Figure 7.6. PAS distribution of seal-boxes.

My dataset contains over 300 seal-boxes, with the highest number in Norfolk (Table 7.1). This confirms Andrews's observations, which he felt could not simply be explained by the arable nature and long history of metal-detecting in the county (2012: 57-59). Clusters are apparent around urban and religious foci, including Caistor St Edmund (17), Walsingham/Wighton (37), Saham Toney (6) and Hockwold (6). There is also a group in the Icknield Way parishes around Fincham. The towns of Wenhaston (10), Coddenham (18), Wixoe (6) and Pakenham (9) in Suffolk are well-represented (Figure 7.1, Figure 7.7). There are also numerous finds away from the major centres of occupation, along the coast, Fen-edge and in the countryside. A noteworthy absence can be observed in the area around Wicklewood (4), which shows such strong concentrations for manufacture and deposition of 'indigenous' brooches and horse fittings. This may mean that these 'incoming' items were considered unnecessary, useless or otherwise inappropriate to the people living here.

Cambridgeshire is typically quiet, with an obvious blank area reaching deep into the Fenland around the Wash. This is further evidence against the idea of an Imperial estate here (Catling 2014), where surely a greater presence of administration and officialdom would result in more seals being lost, whether from wax tablets or coin sacks. An uneven distribution between sources was noted, with all PAS finds in western and southern Cambridgeshire

and HER finds clustering along the eastern border with Norfolk, with the exception of one near Cambridge. This again confirms the benefit of expanding my research beyond a single resource, with the effect that PAS fills in the gaps left by HER and excavated sites and *vice versa*.

Seal-boxes are rarely precisely dated on PAS, often described as 'Roman' and dated 43-410 CE. Simple unenamelled types occurred on the continent from the first century BCE. Square and circular forms, including variants with zoomorphic lids (Figure 7.5), arrived in Britain at the conquest. From the second century CE onwards, all seal-boxes had enamelled lids. The geometric designs of the second/third century CE have aesthetic links to cosmetic grinders and Dragonesque brooches. Square and rectangular seal-boxes with short hinges and curvilinear 'Celtic Swash-N' motifs may have British origins (Andrews 2012 Type D5). These are rare in the *civitas*, with only four each from Norfolk and Suffolk. Leaf-shaped seal-boxes date from the later first century CE onwards. The most common type in Britain is leaf-shaped with an enamelled 'heart' motif (Type P3D3) (Figure 7.8). This had a slightly later date range, mid-second to mid-third centuries CE. The latest are the enamelled lozengiform varieties (Figure 7.9). Seal-boxes fell out of use by the mid-third century CE, like many other portable artefacts discussed in this study (Andrews 2012; Derks and Roymans 2002: 91-92).

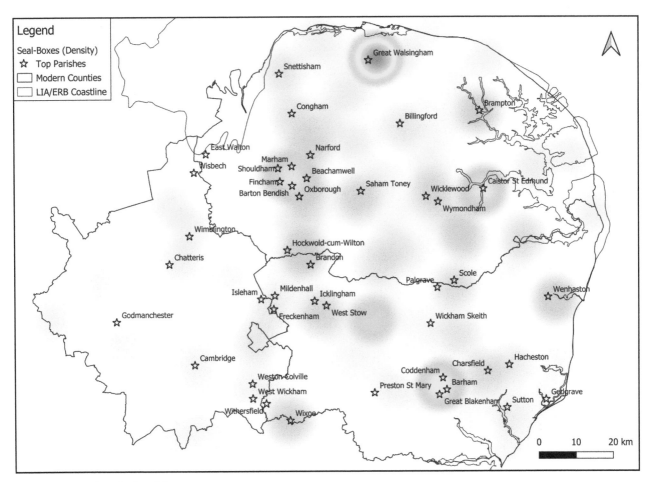

Figure 7.7. Density of all seal-boxes.

Figure 7.8. Leaf-shaped seal-box lid with enamelled heart motif, Weston Colville (PAS: CAM-8904D3).

Figure 7.9. Lozengiform seal-box lid with enamelled leaf motif, Bacton (PAS: LON-E001C0).

Twelve examples of seal-boxes with riveted zoomorphic attachments were recorded, with most in Norfolk (Figure 7.10), suggesting a few cases of early adoption, perhaps in the later first century CE. Birds are most frequent, including a cockerel and two eagles, and there are two frogs. These animals are said to represent specific deities, for example Eagle/Jupiter, Cockerel/Mercury and Frog/ Diana (Andrews 2012: 64-65). Andrews considers the frog among apotropaic symbols. Many seal-box designs may have had a protective function, intended to avert

the 'evil eye' from the private contents of a letter, or to protect valuables from theft (*ibid.*: 102-3). Frogs, while frequent on seal-boxes, are rare on brooches. Horses are not represented on seal-boxes or cosmetic grinders, but are relatively common on brooches (section 3.11.6). Like the plate brooches, anthropomorphic representations of deities on seal-boxes are unknown (*ibid.*: 99). Some rare early boxes depict the emperor, possibly referencing coin portraits or an official function (Andrews n.d.: 3). The regional preference for zoomorphic imagery has already been noted and may have had more resonance than classical associations with deities in the late first/second century CE *civitas*.

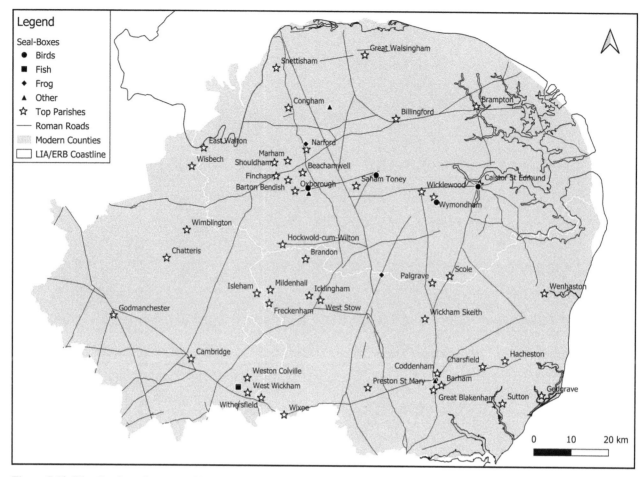

Figure 7.10. Distribution of zoomorphic seal-boxes.

Andrews observed significant regional differences over time. My dataset corroborates his assertion that the later enamelled lozengiform seal-boxes are particularly common in Norfolk (2012: 29, 45, 64-65). Leaf- and lozenge-shaped boxes are the most prevalent in the parish of Caistor St Edmund (section 7.6). Did the 'cultural backwater' of the client-kingdom hamper growth and imports or was this a conscious choice? Does the popularity of later types mean people here were slow to adopt sealing (or whatever was being certified) as part of resistance to Roman identity?

7.5.2. What did Seal-boxes do?

What was being protected or guaranteed by these seal-boxes? Derks and Roymans (2002) proposed that seal-boxes were used to protect private documents, written on wax tablets and sealed with the author's personal signet ring. Andrews refutes this function, providing persuasive evidence that seal-boxes could equally have been stitched to cloth or leather pouches, containing money or small valuables, rather than wooden tablets. Andrews cites the seal-box found in the pot containing the Snettisham Jeweller's Hoard (section 4.7.2) which may have been affixed to a cloth bag of carnelian gems by the flax string still attached to its base. A seal-box found *in situ* sealing a leather pouch of gold *aurei* in a hoard at Trier bolsters his claim (2012: 80-92, 2013).

Andrews sees a need for tamper-evident seals on coinage moving throughout the province. Therefore, seal-boxes should be found at places associated with trade and administration, where cash transactions occurred, or valuables were stored. Apotropaic motifs on seal-box lids may have been intended to avert the 'evil eye' – the covetous or envious gaze – perhaps well-suited to ward off potential thieves from amounts of cash in transit (2012: 97, 102-3). That seal-boxes are rarely found with coin hoards remains problematic, considering the numbers recorded across Britain. Perhaps hoards were multi-authored, communal events or performances, at odds with the individuality of sealing.

Seal-boxes may also have protected wooden tablets on which supplications to the gods were written. The contract of the *votum* involved a request to the deity (*nuncupatio*) and a vow in return for its granting. The *solutio* was the fulfilment of this vow. Both parts of this transaction were recorded with inscriptions. Much like sealing day-to-day correspondence, a pair of writing tablets containing a private *nuncupatio* could be tied with a cord fastened within a seal-box for protection (Bagnall Smith 1999: 48-50; Crerar 2006: 80-81).

As these artefacts are regularly found at temple sites, with or without other evidence for writing tablets, it is highly likely that they were also independently deposited as votives (see section 7.7). An oddity comes from Lackford in which part of the enamelled lid of a circular seal-box has been cut away (PAS: SF6731) (Figure 7.11). This may represent ritual mutilation, as Lackford parish contains the findspot of the Cavenham crowns, possibly the site of a rural shrine (Moore *et al.* 1988: 70). By itself, this might seem unusual, but a parallel from Cheshire (PAS: LVPL-6C9BA5) implies there was something worth removing from these lids. Perhaps a riveted zoomorphic appliqué was detached to be used as a votive, as we have previously seen with the Minerva *spatulae*. This may have been considered an appropriate ending for an object with multiple meanings and purposes.

Seal-boxes and signet rings went out of use in Britain after *circa* 250 CE. Like the '*fibula* abandonment horizon' (section 3.2.2), this has yet to be fully explained. Bagnall Smith theorises that the ritual formalities of the *votum* changed character, losing the necessity for written and sealed vows (1999: 51). As Andrews observes, it is unlikely people stopped writing letters, so perhaps the practice continued, but the material culture changed. His alternative theory, that the mid-third century CE monetary crisis and debasement of silver currency restricted the movement of coinage, is less convincing (2012: 97-98, 2013: 436). The abandonment horizon extends here to objects other than personal ornament, showing that it was not merely fashion which changed, but other practices. Either there was a seismic shift in material culture at this point, or perhaps our chronologies and typologies are erroneous.

7.5.3. What do Seal-boxes want?

Seal-boxes are problematic artefacts if we only want to think about them in terms of their function or association with written language. To paraphrase Gosden (2005), what do seal-boxes want? How did they act upon people? Was their decoration novel and surprising, or familiar and comforting? Does this explain why boxes with appliqué birds are more common in Norfolk, where waterbirds are an enduring symbol, and there are only six phallic seal-boxes in the dataset?

Were seal-boxes recognised and interacted with as a 'Roman' object in this area or did they reflect connections with Gaul or the Low Countries? These objects are found in large numbers across town and countryside, suggesting they were not restricted or rare. Did seal-boxes impose a hierarchy between courier or messenger and sender? Did using, and being seen to use, seals reinforce some people's sense of security and rank? The widespread use of keys and locks also appears during this period (Mould 2011: 176-78), indicating a growing preoccupation with individual ownership and possession, rather than belonging. This arguably suggests a breakdown in trust and an increase in crimes against property as people increasingly interacted in 'alien' urban spaces.

Figure 7.11. Unusual circular seal-box lid with 'cutout', Lackford (PAS: SF6731).

The lack of overt religious imagery on seal-boxes implies they were not specifically made for devotional purposes, but could be reinterpreted and reused in votive contexts. The emphasis is instead on decorative motifs and those associated with good luck or protection. This contrasts with the regular appearance of deities and other personifications on seal-rings. Was making the mark of the divine symbolic, within the more prosaic wax of the apotropaic seal-box? An occasional votive deposit of a zoomorphic appliqué may have led to a snowball effect of seal-boxes being seen as appropriate gifts to the gods, but only at certain temple sites.

Seal-boxes and intaglio rings brought together metal, glass, enamel, thread or leather and beeswax. By the nature of their mixed materials, and role in transactions, whether for business, religion or correspondence, they would have influenced everyday *praxis*. Certain new physical actions, of wearing a signet ring, of handling and impressing wax, of tying and sealing would have become commonplace. They may have been worn in public view, attached to the outside of a coin purse. Like the cosmetic grinders and palettes (chapter five), these objects played an active role in materialising and changing identities.

If Andrews's theory holds true, seal-boxes may demonstrate the use of individual sigils to safeguard shipments or payments of coins in the mid-Roman period. If Derks and Roymans and Bagnall Smith are correct, these artefacts may signify the spread of literacy and the language of conquest into the polity. In this case, the Iceni, like other provincial subjects, were powerless to resist literacy as both a useful skill and a way to claim and display authority. Alternatively, sealing may reflect an interim approach which allowed non-literate people to dictate a message to a scribe (Eckardt 2018: 42-45) and still authenticate it with a personal mark.

7.6. Case Study: *Venta Icenorum*

Literacy at the *civitas* capital is attested by graffiti and inscriptions, mostly on ceramics, with occasional letters and numerals on bone gaming counters; these may also have been used as accounting tokens (Eckardt 2018: 201; Harlow 2019). There are also about 70 *styli*, although these lack close dating. There are two samian inkwells: a central Gaulish example from a pit in the northern part of the walled town and a south Gaulish inkwell from the early Forum (CRP: CRT10 4101; Frere 1971: 24).[2] A badly crushed copper alloy receptacle with separate lid, found in the 1933 Forum excavations, has also recently been identified as an inkwell (NWHCM: 1929.152.B217a, B217b). No wax *spatula* handles have thus far been identified.

There are several partial, literate graffiti including two on samian (CRP: CRT10 2315, 3137), the 'IQVINI' example mentioned above (Figure 1.4), and an undeciphered 'IKOSVRRVIIII' on an early second century CE greyware vessel (Atkinson 1932: 45-46 and pl. 12). The *defixio* dedicated to Neptune, from the River Tas, is discussed in section 7.3.2. Monumental stone carving is limited to one inscribed fragment 'ADAT SVPE' (NWHCM: 1929.152. M94), probably due to the lack of freestone as a building material and the impracticality of carving on local flint. Many wooden inscriptions must surely have been made which no longer survive.

7.6.1. Seal-boxes

Seventeen seal-boxes were recorded from Caistor St Edmund parish. Two were found in the Forum and another near an intramural road (NHER: 9786). A Type P3D3 from a rubbish deposit near the South Gate has the white metal trim which Mackreth associates with indigenous brooch production (NWHCM: 1929.152.X5). Two more came from Dunston Field across the River Tas (NHER: 9759), four from the east side of the town, with another from the nearby Romano-Celtic temple (NHER: 9787). Another seal-box was found near the Late Roman villa in neighbouring Stoke Holy Cross (Bowden 2011). Some of these may be residual in contexts post-dating the second/third century CE.

One circular seal-box has a riveted attachment in the form of a cockerel (Andrews Type C2D6). This noisy, watchful bird was part of the apotropaic menagerie and may reference the worship of Mercury as herald of the dawn. It was excavated in a posthole in the Forum (NWHCM: 1929.152.B215), which evokes a potential offering or foundation deposit. Here we have an association between the administrative heart of the town, the deity of merchants and trade, and a seal-box, perhaps used for closing correspondence or payments of coins.

My recent re-evaluation of the finds from *Venta Icenorum* brought to light two new seal-boxes. A simple circular base with four holes (in Andrews's C2 layout) was found with metalworking debris from Mann's 1938 excavations at Caistor Paddocks (NWHCM: 1961.150). It may have been a product of the bronze workshop or collected for reprocessing. The second, recorded as a fragmentary hinged brooch, was excavated in 1929 inside the town. The hinge and shape strongly resemble Andrews's P1 ovate lids, although the copper alloy is corroded, and no decoration is visible (NWHCM: 1929.152.B49). If so, it may have an official origin, usually with an applied Imperial portrait on the lid. P1 seal-boxes are Flavian imports and are very rare in Britain (2012: 18); Andrews has only five examples in his *corpus*.[3] Moulds for numerous artefacts were found at Caistor Paddocks, but further work is necessary to fully identify these finds. Manufacturing evidence for seal-boxes is extremely limited, with the only mould known from *Dura-Europos* (Andrews 2013: 427). Only three miscast or unfinished seal-boxes were noted from the study area (PAS: NMS-1A71A2, BH-2868AF and CAM-8A9EA3 found at Balsham) (Figure 7.12).

One hybrid or creolised artefact is an enamelled leaf-shaped seal-box lid which bears a stylised phallus and crescent motif (CRP: SF4483) (Figure 7.13). The lunula and phallus are not rare designs on seal-boxes (Andrews type P4D15, 2012: 13, 26), but they are always separately cast and riveted attachments, like the cockerel discussed above. The phallus and lunula were potent symbols considered to ward off bad fortune (*ibid.*: 102-3). As discussed previously, phallic symbolism was not a feature of Iron Age Britain (Plouviez 2005: 161). The phallus had a long tradition in Roman culture, where it was not directly sexual, instead inviting good fortune and averting evil. Johns sees its appearance in the provinces as indicative of 'Romanisation' (1996b: 12, 62). The crescent motif is frequently found on Icenian coins and other metalwork and may represent lunar symbolism, associated with the feminine and protection (Creighton 1995; Davies 2014; Johns 1996b: 143). The mingling of the iconography on this artefact hints at a convergence, or even parity, between male and female elements, as well as blending indigenous and incoming styles. This has parallels with the symbolism of the cosmetic mortars and pestles.

7.6.2. Intaglios and Seal-rings

Three intaglio rings from the first/second centuries CE show the early practice of sealing at the *civitas* capital: a silver ring (Henig Type II) set with an oval carnelian depicting a standing figure was found close to the River Tas (PAS: NMS-9D9633). An engraved red jasper intaglio set in an iron ring (Henig Type II) was found in dredgings, perhaps a votive offering. The design features three conjoined heads arranged as a triskele (Henig 1974: 55,

---

[2] Samian ware information from Gwladys Monteil (pers. comm. 12/06/2017).

[3] A similar hinge is known on a seal-box from London, but the heavily-corroded example from *Venta* may not be a seal-box owing to its flat profile (Colin Andrews pers. comm. 21/10/2016).

Figure 7.12. Unusual seal-box with miscast base, Balsham (PAS: CAM-8A9EA3).

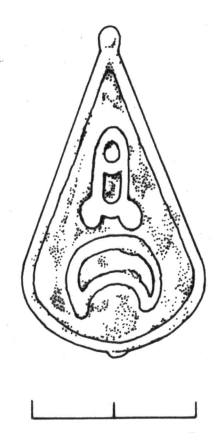

Figure 7.13. Seal-box lid with enamelled phallus and lunula, *Venta Icenorum* (CRP: SF4483, Image: CRP, illus. Jenny Press).

112-13, cat. #380). Combinations of multiple human or animal heads are recurring symbolic motifs (Marshman 2015: 123). Around the heads is inscribed 'CEN' in retrograde, erroneously thought to be an abbreviation of 'Iceni', but demonstrating its potential use as a signet ring (Allen 1970: 24; Frere 1972; Ross 1972). I would add a reminder of Davies's symbolic code which sees triplication as a key marker of Icenian material culture (2014: 27).

A silver ring with a cockerel intaglio was found near the extra-mural temple (PAS: CORN-7384FE). Marshman notes chickens are common subjects on rural intaglios, perhaps an appealing (if prosaic) symbol for the farming community (2015: 178). The imagery of the cockerel has been discussed in relation to seal-boxes. Its association with Mercury further strengthens the likelihood of a cult at *Venta Icenorum*, along with the pipeclay figurine and the *patera* handle. Several undated rings from the area also have 'MER' inscriptions. Mercury was one of the more popular deities in Britannia, as in Gaul (Caes. *BG* 6.17; Marsden 2012: 53, 2014: 68-69). These three rings demonstrate that, at an early stage in the *civitas* capital's development, displays of both personal adornment and literacy were important, along with a possible ritual focus of deposition in the River Tas and links to the cult of Mercury. Mercury was also the patron of travellers and merchants (Crummy 2011: 65-66), perhaps appropriate for the market centre of the new *civitas*.

Two rings and an intaglio date from the second century CE. A worn copper alloy finger-ring with an oval bezel showing engraved lion, star and crescent motifs was found in the northwest corner of the walled town (Figure 7.14). Parallels include intaglios with lions which may relate to the astrological sign of Leo, and the stars and crescent motif symbolising *Aeternitas* (Henig 1974: 59, #409, #627-640). The motifs are also reminiscent of symbols on the Icenian horse coins. Another zoomorphic ring was found in the south wing of the Forum. The heavy silver band holds a carnelian intaglio depicting an animal kneeling below a palm branch. Marsden identifies this as a goat, again emblematic of Mercury (PAS: NMS-FAC7E2). This subject is unknown in the Snettisham Jeweller's Hoard. Marshman sees depictions of familiar farmyard animals evoking 'an atmosphere of rustic abundance', although intaglios of sheep and goats are more frequent among military communities (2015: 119, 121). Nevertheless, the context may place this object into the practical realm of

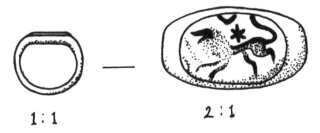

Figure 7.14. Engraved lion, star and crescent ring, *Venta Icenorum* (CRP: SF1620, Image: CRP, illus. Jenny Press).

179

either mercantile trade or administrative documentation at the *civitas* capital.

The third example is an engraved carnelian of a ship and lighthouse, a chance find from inside the western (riverine) end of the town (Henig 1974: pl. XVII #538). Merchant ships are not a common motif on intaglio rings (Marshman 2015: fig. 4.30). This may relate to *Venta Icenorum*'s growing importance in the East Anglian trade network, and its central role as the marketplace of the Iceni. If intaglios were used not just to seal correspondence, but also coinage and as a form of quality control, rather like medieval seals (Furger and Riha 2009: 22), this could reflect the presence of merchants at the town.

Finally, two metal-detector finds dating to the second/third centuries CE were also found near the town. A silver finger-ring with a blue glass gem depicting cupid on a dolphin came from the south field. A copper alloy ring with 'PIA' engraved on the bezel (Frere 1984: 344) may be the owner's name or more likely a religious reference meaning 'pious'. Inscribed personal names are rare on signets (Henig 2002: 56), which is intriguing given their assumed connection with literacy and sealing. This may be evidence that seals were intended to be recognised by more than just the literate few, perhaps those who carried the message or coin purse.

7.7. Case Study: Walsingham

Walsingham/Wighton is a large Romano-British settlement with a clear religious emphasis, to date mainly unexcavated (section 3.14.5). Metal-detector finds from the area around the temple (NHER: 2024) indicate a cult of Mercury, including three figurines and statuettes of goats and cockerels, among other deities (Andrews 2012; Bagnall Smith 1999; Marsden 2012).

The Walsingham collection comprises around 30 seal-boxes and components.[4] The wide date range suggests the boxes were deposited over a long period, not as a hoard or single votive incident. Leaf-shaped and circular forms are the most common (Andrews 2012: 63-65), many with brightly coloured enamelling (Figure 7.15). There are no zoomorphic lids and the only phallic example was not found in the 'temple' field (PAS: NMS-985BE7) (Figure 7.16). The paucity of these earliest boxes agrees with the proposed foundation of the site in the late first century CE. Colour and repeated pattern seem to have been appropriate choices for deposition here, perhaps related to Gell's idea of apotropaic 'demon-traps' (1998: 83-84). Two seal-boxes recorded as having 'Celtic' motifs suggest a fusion of indigenous depositional practices and aesthetics with Roman votive offerings and religious concepts (Bagnall Smith 1999: 48, 51). A silver finger ring, also from this site, shows a 'Celtic-style' head in low relief (NHER: 2024).

Finger-rings with engraved gems or inscriptions to Ceres, Neptune and Mars were found at the site. Other rings from Walsingham/Wighton carry symbolism associated with Jupiter (including a double axe, a thunderbolt and Leda and the Swan), Toutatis and the Mother Goddesses. At least three finger-rings reference Mercury (Bagnall Smith 1999). While some of these artefacts could have been used in association with seal-boxes, some lack the mirror-writing which would produce a legible impression on wax, and should perhaps therefore be considered separate devotional offerings in this context. These finds imply a votive practice, perhaps to seal dedications or vows to the gods, or to fasten bags of coins or other offerings. As no writing tablets or inkwells have yet been found at Walsingham, the seal-boxes were possibly appropriated for ritual behaviours unassociated with writing or sealing. They also evoke a link between transactions of money and transactions with the gods. The emphasis on local discrepancy is also notable in the restricted numbers of seal-boxes from other temples, with few from Hockwold, Wicklewood, Lackford or Charsfield, which was also noted with Hod Hill brooches (section 3.9.1).

7.8. Comparative Material from the Netherlands

A comparison can be made between the *civitas Icenorum* and the *civitas Batavorum*, homeland of the Batavian people, a key supplier of auxiliary troops to the Roman army. Like the Iceni polity, the Batavian territory consisted of a 'non-villa landscape' of traditional rural settlements. There may have been a direct connection in the form of a sea route between the Rhine Delta and the so-called Great Estuary. Derks and Roymans (2002) connected seal-boxes with correspondence between literate serving soldiers and friends and relatives in their homelands. Seal-boxes may reflect the impact of the army, with high concentrations from military sites along the German *limes*, in the hinterlands of the frontier zone (mainly from *civitas* capitals and rural centres) and at sanctuaries. They concluded that military service meant informal literacy training for lower ranks, which then extended into rural areas with returning veterans. The influence of Latin (both written and spoken) must have 'brought about a radical transformation of the native spoken language' although this change did not persist into modern Dutch (*ibid.*: 102). If Andrews's coin purse theory is correct, then perhaps Derks and Roymans's findings relate to the sending and receiving of payments between military personnel and their homelands. This negates the requirement for literacy in the rural population, although mark-making remains an important means of guaranteeing identity and security.

Could the numbers of seal-boxes in rural Norfolk reflect a strong military presence, perhaps garrisons or resettled auxiliaries? The social distribution of seal-boxes changed over time in the *civitas Batavorum*: earlier ones are restricted to military sites, extending to the *civitas* capital and the cult site at Empel during the Augustan-Tiberian period. This rural temple complex, like Walsingham, produced numerous seal-boxes (26) (Bagnall Smith 1999;

---

[4] At least two of these I believe to be duplicated with PAS records, but I cannot completely discount them based on a lack of precise information in Andrews's catalogue.

Figure 7.15. Assemblage of seal-boxes from Walsingham (NHER: 2024; Image: © Norwich Castle Museum and Art Gallery).

Figure 7.16. Seal-box with riveted phallus, Walsingham (PAS: NMS-985BE7).

Andrews applied the Boudican model to the concentrations along the Icknield Way, suggesting that the villas which cluster in this landscape may reflect the confiscation and reallocation of Icenian lands, with 'almost complete native depopulation followed by repopulation by officially sanctioned incomers, such as auxiliary and legionary veterans' (2012: 57, 63). Conversely, these rural villas date from after seal-boxes fall from use and this area was the focus of LIA and early Roman activity, as seen in prior chapters. Continuity of settlement and little evidence for a replacement population indicate that indigenous people were engaging with the material culture of communications. They may also have been using seal-boxes for other purposes, beyond their intended function.

7.9. Summary

Becoming part of the Roman empire meant adopting a new language, practices of speech and the habit of written communication. Literacy would have started as a symbolic indicator of authority and an exclusive activity. People would have been familiar with the symbolism and legends on coinage and other forms of mark-making, the 'symbolic code' of the Iceni (Davies 2014). Becoming Romano-British involved learning a new shared symbolic language. This would have developed with the spread of literacy and increasing familiarity with classical mythology, seen in the fine mosaics from other parts of Britain. These stories could also have been transmitted through a common visual currency, like the figures and

Derks and Roymans 2002). In Suffolk, some parishes with known forts have more earlier seal-boxes, such as Ixworth/Pakenham and Coddenham/Baylham, which have twice as many circular and square variants than the later leaf- and lozenge-shaped examples. Caistor St Edmund has only three circular/square boxes and 11 leaf/lozenge forms, perhaps reflecting the lack of an early military presence and the later development of the *civitas* capital (Figure 7.17). This trajectory broadly follows that of the *civitas Batavorum*, although there are too many undated or uncategorised examples in the dataset for this to give more than an impression. Further comparison between the two *civitates* is made in chapter eight.

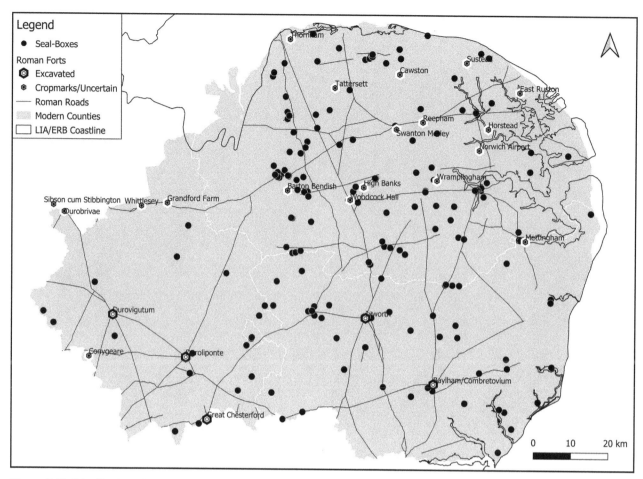

Figure 7.17. Distribution of seal-boxes and early Roman forts.

deities represented on intaglios and wax *spatulae* (Revell 2016: 34-36). The social distribution of sealing in the Iceni territory appears to have been limited during the client-kingdom period, expanding in the second/third centuries CE. If seal-boxes indeed represent the movement of coinage around the *civitas*, they could manifest the shift from collective ownership and power expressed through livestock and hoards, towards individual wealth changing hands as people increasingly engaged with a monetary economy.

In the early Romano-British period, most people sealed documents or valuables with images of gods or animals rather than words. This arguably demonstrates that literacy was for the select few. It is possible that people used seal-boxes and intaglios precisely because their level of literacy was low, and they engaged with writing through the services of scribes (Eckardt 2018: 9-10). Placing their personal mark on a transaction authenticated the written words, while being recognisable to a wider part of the population. As the importance of sealing declined, rings became increasingly ornamental (Cool 1983: 284). Later intaglios became divorced from the practice of sealing altogether and may have been reused as amulets or miniature personal shrines (Henig 2006: 3). Excluding the ambiguous seal-boxes, the emphasis on magical literacy is deceptive and results from the poor dating of *styli*, the lack of epigraphy and the end deposition of items at temples.

When considered together, the evidence for literacy shows it was a widespread and not purely urban phenomenon. Rural areas show plenty of evidence for accompanying changes in practice and display: wearing rings, sealing and writing. Some of the material culture may have been subverted by incorporation into indigenous ritual practices, such as the votive seal-boxes from Walsingham. The *civitas Icenorum* was clearly embracing material culture relating to literacy by the second/third centuries CE. There is a lack of obvious evidence for resistance here to the power exercised through a new language and practices of reading and writing. For the post-Boudican generations, literacy was adopted as a necessary, desirable skill.

Engaging with Latin may have been a beneficial way to integrate with new power structures. However, the ability to switch back and forth between modes depending on the social circumstances may have presented opportunities for 'hidden transcripts' and subversion (Revell 2013; Scott 1990). In the following chapter, we return to the dynamic between individual and collective identities, and the potential for resistance, through analysis of the many horse and vehicle related artefacts found in the region.

Icenia: The Kingdom of the Horse

8.1. Introduction

This penultimate chapter takes a side-step from personal belongings to examine the relationships between horse harness and group identities. Horse and chariot fittings are one of Davies's 'cultural indicators' of the Iceni. He calls the Icenian territory 'The Kingdom of the Horse' (2009: 109). Davies sees a special affinity between the Iceni and horses: a persistent motif, along with the boar and wolf, on their coins (2011b: 103-4, 2014: 27-34). 'Icenia' has a predominance of finds of horse equipment and has been identified as an important production area.[1] The continuity of hoarding practice for jewellery (section 4.7) also applies to the deposition of harness. Pudney explores human-animal-object relationships, noting the 'powerful associations of the horse and of metalworking in regional Iron Age societies [...] as an integral fragment of personhood' (2018: 3). For these reasons, I consider horse trappings as portable artefacts, items of display, and therefore 'belongings', though I acknowledge that they are not personal possessions like brooches.

Possible horse ornaments such as button-and-loop fasteners and anatomical mounts were examined above (section 4.2, section 6.7.6). Here, I present the artefactual evidence for both horses (bridles and harness fittings) and vehicles (terrets and linch-pins). These finds have a similar collection profile to brooches including surface finds, hoards and manufacturing evidence. They are key artefacts for investigating chronological changes (see Appendix D: Harness Date Ranges). Many of these harness fittings continue into the Roman period in East Anglia, which suggests that the equine economy remained important and people continued to display this aspect of their identity and heritage (Hutcheson 2004: 98).

MacGregor (1976) and Palk's (1984) catalogues provide useful background, even if the interpretations are now in need of refreshing. More recent research by Davis (2014) and Lewis (2015) complement these studies. The subdiscipline of ethnozooarchaeology also provides a different perspective on the subject (Argent 2016; Bendrey 2010; Sykes 2014). Hutcheson's work on Norfolk (2004, 2007) has been particularly influential. She utilised comparative material from PAS, showing the easterly pattern of horse gear, and noted that enamelled and highly-ornamental harness pieces are concentrated in this region (Figure 8.1, Figure 8.2). This preponderance of horse gear shows the wealth and connectedness of the territory. Harness and chariot fittings may also reveal potential

collection bias as identified by Cool and Baxter for brooches (2016a, 2016b). Many are large, attractive pieces, often brightly enamelled and therefore highly-collectable. Hutcheson discounts the East Anglian metal-detector bias; although the region has more finds overall, there is no particular bias towards any one period and therefore the distribution is likely to reflect actual Iron Age practices (2004: 19-22).

Attitudes towards accumulation of portable wealth, especially metalwork, across the Iceni territory changed under the occupation, but within distinct cultural conventions. Hutcheson has suggested that rather than leaving the region stranded in a 'cultural backwater', the changing political and economic arrangements 'facilitated the extensive use of a new material language' (2004: 98). Analysis of the role of horse and vehicle fittings during the transitional period can reveal a potentially alternative social structure which set the Iceni apart from their neighbours and enabled their resistance to Rome (Harlow 2018). As Davis observes 'horse gear seems to symbolise a conflict between the old and the new [...] in areas of Britain committed to resisting Rome' (2014: 247).

8.2. The Ancient Horse

Horses are native to Britain, becoming extinct during the Mesolithic, with small numbers probably reintroduced in the Bronze Age. These animals were sometimes given special burials suggesting they were highly valued. The arrival and spread of horses was 'transformative, bringing new mechanisms for the negotiation and legitimization of power'. A horse was 'an animal having the capacity to genuinely change human life and worldview' (Sykes 2014: 81-84). From the Late Bronze Age, horses were used to manage livestock, control territory and transport people and goods over large distances with relative speed. People also turned this to their advantage for raiding and warfare (Bendrey 2010: 16).

Classical authors wrote of the Britons' abilities with horses. Caesar mentions the enemy's cavalry tactics and use of chariots to close in on Roman infantry (*BG* 5.16). In Tacitus's depiction of the Boudican revolt, the insurgent forces are 'disposed in bands of foot and horse' who 'brought even their wives to witness the victory and installed them in waggons' (*Ann.* 14.34). During her protest to the 'clans', Boudica was 'mounted in a chariot with her daughters before her' (*ibid.*: 14.35).

Special animal deposits including horse bones are found on many Iron Age and Roman sites. Hill's discussion of skeletal remains in Iron Age Wessex revealed that horses

---

[1] A rather charming term used by Rainbird Clarke, based on antiquarian predecessors, to refer to the LIA territory (1939: 3, 84).

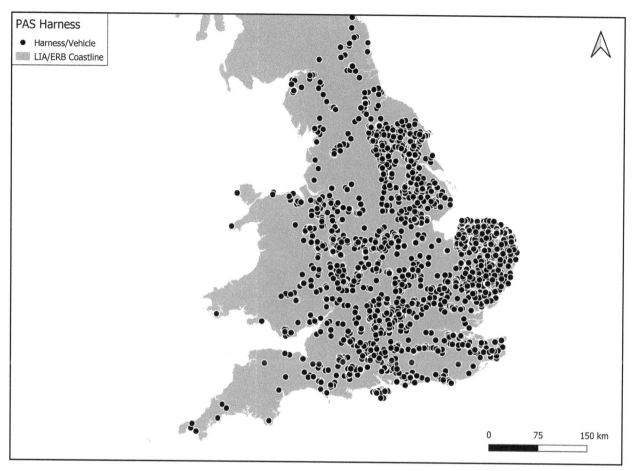

Figure 8.1. PAS distribution of harness and vehicle fittings.

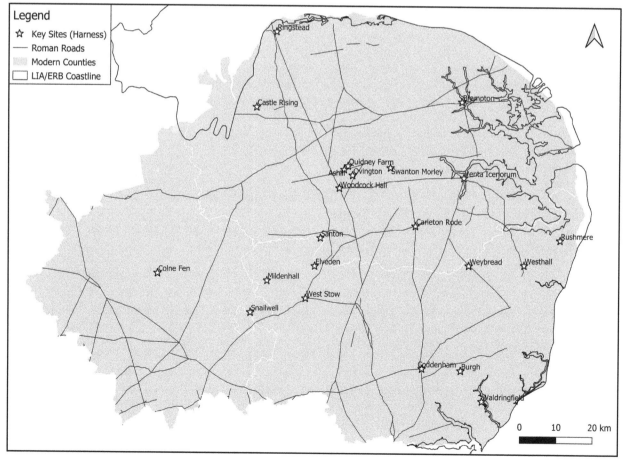

Figure 8.2. Sites relating to harness mentioned in the text.

and dogs were treated differently to other animals, but human and animal remains were treated in similar ways in structured deposits (1995a: 103-5). Martin reports deliberate placement of horse jaws at the possible ritual enclosure at Barnham, Suffolk, suggesting a religious or supernatural intention (1999: 61-62). At *Venta Icenorum*, excavation of the second century CE perimeter defences revealed a partially-articulated horse skeleton accompanied by a broken greyware vessel at the base of the ditch (Bowden 2017: 22). Hoards of horse harness, like torcs, may have represented the dead and stood in for their mortal remains which were disposed of in other ways. Pudney has also related horse harness and coin hoards to death and burial of humans: 'The horse-gear deposited in the ground, just as the coins, become totemic objects of the human-horse person' (2018: 18-19). Hoarding and manufacture of decorated horse harness at Westhall (northeast Suffolk), Santon (Norfolk) and Waldringfield (Suffolk) are discussed further below (section 8.10).

8.3. The Symbolic Horse

Imagery of horses is common on Iron Age coinage, thought to be based upon gold staters of Philip of Macedonia depicting a charioteer. This was replaced on most British types by a solitary horse. It seems too straightforward to relate the ubiquity of horses on LIA coinage simply to their importance in the regional economy. Creighton describes the horse as a potent symbol and an 'icon of kingship'. He considers that horses had cultural significance which pre-dated the advent of coinage 'rather than merely representing a Celtic artistic abstraction' (1995: 286-87). Many Icenian issues have a horse on the reverse, with a boar, wolf or human face on the obverse. On some coins, the letters of the legend are deliberately fused with the zoomorphic imagery, the inscription becoming part of the animal and *vice versa* (Allen 1970; Creighton 1995; Talbot 2015: 214-16 appendix 3). Talbot also describes encoded faces on Icenian coins (2017: 90). This merging of creatures with other design elements is similar to the 'hidden faces' on the characteristic 'La Tène' style enamelled harness, some of which Foster suggests may be very stylised horses' heads (2014). These enigmatic designs continue during the occupation on items such as the Westhall terrets (section 8.10.1).

The horse is rarely depicted on other LIA material culture, as though its symbolic use was restricted (Creighton 1995: 289; Davies 2014: 31). This may suggest a prohibition or taboo on the representation of horses other than on coins. The Aylesford bucket is one of a very few non-numismatic images of certain Iron Age date (BM: 1886,1112.3-7). Two creatures with 'pantomime horse' legs perhaps depict mythical rather than natural beings (Stead 1971: 266). Garrow and Gosden note that this mixing of representations, like on the coins, may reflect 'a blurring of boundaries', an absence of distinction between people and other types of animals (2012: 146). Another exception is the horse-head mount from the Stanwick

(Melsonby) hoard (BM: 1847,0208.82). Not only is it a rare appearance of an equine head in the art of the period, but its full-face (rather than profile) representation is remarkable (MacGregor 1962: 26-27).

A cache of pipeclay horse figurines is known from Belgium and others come from Gaulish healing spring sanctuaries (section 6.8.4). Green associated horses with pre-Roman 'solar cults', along with a range of other animals. She described horses as one of the 'divine animals' and the companion of Epona, the Romano-Celtic horse goddess attested by epigraphy (1976: 5, 12, 30; 1978: 25). However, Epona is virtually unknown in Britain and I am cautious of the uncritical use of parallels from Gaul to extrapolate ideas about Romano-British religious beliefs.

There are important questions regarding social hierarchies and elites to be investigated. Herds of livestock can form a key part of a group's collective wealth and express social status through a complex set of values invested in their ownership (Giles 2012: 58-62). Horses and related gear could have been owned and maintained by communities rather than individuals (Davis 2014: 249). Equestrian prowess is a common feature in societies which place high value on the interaction between humans and other animals (Argent 2010, 2016). An emphasis on highly-visible, decorative horse gear may be part of the wider preference for marking difference through displays of material culture in the *civitas*. Ambivalent attitudes suggest that horses held a special status which may have been enshrined in everyday practice as well as art. This has also been seen in my discussion of cosmetic grinders (section 5.3.2) and other zoomorphic artefacts. The abundance of Horse-and-rider brooches in the East Midlands and East Anglia in the second/third centuries CE shows a change in attitudes, or perhaps differing responses to the idea that horses were sacred (section 3.11.6).

8.4. Breeding and Training

The Iceni people have been described as experienced equestrians who trained ponies for daily transport and warfare. Norfolk appears to have been an important area for horse-breeding (Davies 2014: 31; Marsden 2012: 61). Martin estimates the sizes of Iron Age ponies from settlements in Suffolk: West Stow (11-13.5 hands) and Burgh (11-12 hands). Small by today's standards, they accord well with the diminutive varieties of other livestock including sheep and cattle (1999: 47). Palk disagreed with the idea that wild herds roamed the landscape. She regarded animals as commodities, with horses ranking above other domestic livestock as important resources to be exploited in Iron Age economies (1984: 98). In Wessex, Hill states that horses were probably selected from managed semi-wild herds, rather like New Forest or moorland ponies today (1995a: 104, 107). Absence of breeding on settlements is based on the scarcity of neonatal horse bones compared to cattle, sheep and pig. Alternatively, young horses may have received greater nurture and care, meaning more survived to adulthood (Bendrey 2010: 14-15).

Hill envisages the process of bringing in wild horses: capturing, domesticating, 'breaking', taming and controlling activities, which may have held similar resonances to the training of dogs and even young humans (1995a: 107). This raises questions about the actual process of living and working with horses, the power structures exercised during the lifetime of these animals and the bonds which surely developed between humans and horses, not just the artefactual record of their ornaments and shackles.[2]

Not only must horses have been ridden and worked, but fed, groomed with a range of implements, treated for ailments, possibly eaten and certainly buried. Recent interest in care and presentation of the human body as social *praxis* could be extended to non-human animals. There is little room to deviate into the realm of human-horse interactions here, but much as we are often reminded to keep people in mind when discussing their accoutrements, it is essential to reflect upon the beasts of burden themselves when considering their harness.[3]

8.5. Horse and Chariot Equipment

Harness gear spans the LIA-Roman divide, with many artefacts dating from the first centuries BCE/CE, peaking with highly-ornamented equipment in the mid-first century CE. Other than the well-known Arras-style burials from Yorkshire and the recently discovered Pembrokeshire chariot (Halkon *et al.* 2019; Krakowa 2019), physical evidence for vehicles is extremely rare in Britain, although indirect traces in the form of wheel-ruts in roads are abundant. Some Roman examples have been identified, such as the complete wheels and other components found in pits at Newstead fort (Crummy 2011: 53, 55; Curle 1911: 292). Chariot burials are almost unheard of in East Anglia, with only one reported antiquarian find at Mildenhall (Clarke 1939: 43). Two iron wheel hubs, together with several other ferrous objects which may have been part of the same vehicle, were excavated at the Forum of *Venta Icenorum*, although the dating is probably Late Roman (NWHCM: 1929.152.F150-5). In many cases, these finds are poorly documented or long lost, as they were discovered during antiquarian excavations, Victorian civic projects or ploughing.

What can finds of vehicle and harness fittings tell us about group identity in the region? Was riding or driving horses a reactionary or revolutionary act in the client-kingdom? Iron Age carts or chariots contribute to the Iceni 'cultural backwardness' narrative. Webster regarded the British war chariot as 'outmoded', long since given up by their continental neighbours (1993: 29). Clarke certainly saw the Santon and Westhall hoards as preserving the 'vitality

of the chariot tradition in Norfolk and Suffolk' (1939: 43). Even if war chariots were unwelcome, unfashionable or even prohibited in the *civitas*, carts surely had an essential place in everyday life for both indigenous Britons and their occupiers, and their innumerable passages are worn into many of the region's roads and trackways.

Martin attempted to plot the geographical boundaries of the Iceni and Trinovantes using 'tribal indicators', including ornamental horse harness. He saw the fine metalwork, especially round the Fen-edge, as an inheritance from the Bronze Age, re-emerging as conspicuous consumption in the later Iron Age. In the early to mid-first century CE, northern Suffolk was a focal point for harness which stylistically references the curvilinear designs and red enamelling of tankard and mirror handles (Martin 1999).

There are approximately 700 finds of harness and chariot gear in total. Norfolk is best represented for horse equipment, particularly terrets (Table 8.1). Horse harness is widespread, reflecting both the broad pattern of settlements and the coverage of metal-detecting (Figure 8.3). There is a strong showing along the northern Icknield Way, Saham Toney and a cluster around Brampton. The small towns of Suffolk also show concentrations. The density map (Figure 8.4) shows the northern and eastern bias, with an intense hotspot in the area around Wicklewood/Wymondham, with its settlement and temple complex. The strong concentration is partly due to several hoards from the vicinity of Attleborough in mid-Norfolk. This area shows concentrations (and probable manufacture) of several object types considered to have indigenous origins: Aesica, Rearhook and Headstud brooches, terrets, cosmetic grinders and fasteners.

As far back as 1939, Clarke observed that much enamelled horse harness was concentrated in Breckland, long considered to be the heartland of Iceni territory. He dated much of this metalwork to the mid-first century CE, disparaging its 'degenerate Celticism', but noting the development of a 'rigid symmetry' derived from Roman influence (1939: 68). Despite the outmoded language, Clarke's perception was accurate: as we shall see below, the decorative schemes of northern East Anglian harness show the change in fashion away from asymmetric curvilinear ornament. Crummy also proposes a link between the geometric designs on harness pendants,

Table 8.1. Harness/vehicle fittings by county and type

Object Type	Cambs	Norfolk	Suffolk	Total
Bridle-Bit	2	18	5	25
Cheekpiece	7	3	3	13
Linch-Pin	5	44	16	65
Terret	15	304	111	430
Other	5	112	49	166

---

[2] In the hoard from Quidney Farm was a pair of broken Roman iron shackles (Bates et al 2000: 228, 230). Could there be an association with power, ownership and control over another being, human or animal, at work behind this assemblage?

[3] See, for example, Argent's interesting take on the Pazyryk human-horse burials from the perspective of a working rider (2010, 2016).

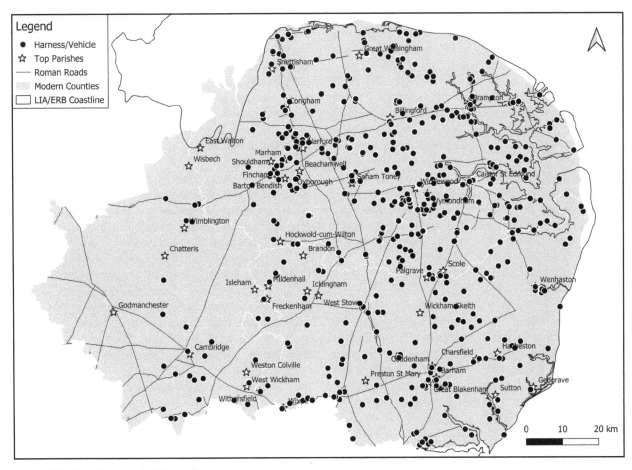

Figure 8.3. Distribution of all horse harness.

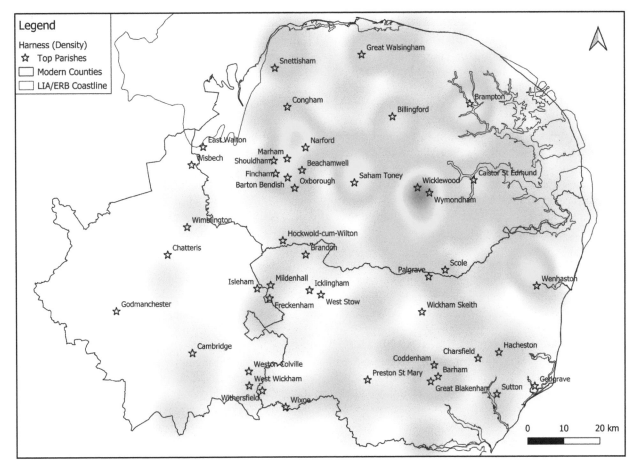

Figure 8.4. Density of all horse harness.

seal-boxes and plate brooches, many of which date from the second century CE (2011: 58), demonstrating that aesthetic preferences can also cross boundaries between species and function.

The following sections present an analysis of horse gear including bridle-bits, linch-pins and terret rings, which are necessary for harnessing a team of ponies to a cart. Miscellaneous fittings and harness mounts are only discussed in relation to hoards, as they are seldom closely dated. Hipposandals have been excluded as they are broadly dated; there is doubt whether horseshoes were used in this period (Crummy 2011: 61). There are no hipposandals from *Venta Icenorum*, despite other significant towns, such as Heybridge and *Verulamium*, having large numbers (Wardle 2013: 220).

8.6. Terret Rings

The most numerous finds in the transport category are terret rings: small, often decoratively-moulded or enamelled rein guides. Norfolk and Suffolk have the highest number of Iron Age and Roman terrets recorded on PAS, and this is reflected in my data. Approximately two-thirds of horse harness finds are terrets, with few in Cambridgeshire.

Each pair of draught ponies would require a set of five terrets: four similar-sized terrets across the yoke and one larger ring fixed to the central pole of a chariot or cart. As will be discussed, miniature terrets may also have been used to secure wheels onto vehicles. While Davies described most Norfolk terrets as 'relatively plain' (1999: 21), Hutcheson noted a concentration of elaborate and ornamental harness in Norfolk and north Suffolk (2004: 22). Davies's distributions show a major hotspot around the parish of Saham Toney (see section 3.14.10), clusters of lipped and knobbed terrets in west Norfolk, simple terrets in the south, and miniatures in the south and east (1999: 21 and map 2.4). These essential items for draught horses are found in both urban and rural locations. Terrets may also have been used to yoke oxen for ploughing, which may explain the rural nature of many finds and the frequent, but undateable, simple iron rings (Crummy 2011: 57), although Foster asserts that oxen did not need reins (1995: 59).

Terrets came into general usage in the first century BCE, but with a focus in the first century CE. There are numerous stylistic varieties, although their basic function is broadly agreed. Miniature terrets present an anomaly: some interpret them as votive, others as fasteners for fine straps or linch-pins (Hutcheson 2004: 29, 34-35). Lewis exempted these from her study of rein-guides (2015: 57-58). They are included here as part of horse and vehicle trappings as I consider this the most likely explanation. Protected-loop (skirted) and dropped-bar terrets are post-conquest imports, with a later first/second century CE range (*ibid.*: 76, table 4.1). These differences permit us to look at terret usage chronologically, as well as spatially.

Lewis's study recorded 596 terrets from her research area, which included Wales, central and western England, but excluded Scotland, East Anglia and the southeast of England (2015: 55 fig. 3.1, 65 table 3.1). Hutcheson's (2004) catalogue of horse harness included 88 terret rings from Norfolk. My database comprises 430 examples, including hoards and miniatures (Table 8.1). There are over 300 from Norfolk, a dramatic increase in numbers since Hutcheson's study, partly due to the success of PAS.

The distribution of terrets (Figure 8.5) shows widespread coverage in Norfolk and Suffolk, sparser in the Fens, as would perhaps be expected in a marshy landscape with few surfaced roads. The usual Norfolk hotspots around Saham Toney and Pentney/Fincham are also seen in the terrets, though this may reflect heavy metal-detector use (Figure 8.6, section 2.4.5). The Brampton group arguably represents a connection between the large ceramic industry at the town and the need for transportation. Hutcheson observed that many terrets are found in close proximity to routeways (2004: 86-87, map 28). The flat-ring terrets from Weybread and Westhall (see below) were found near Roman roads (Martin 1978: 140 and fig. 18). While this may not be unexpected for chance finds associated with transport, the correlation is slight in my distribution. There are numerous 'linear' terret findspots which do not relate to known routes, but may respect long lost tracks and bridleways across the countryside.

The following sequence maps the distribution of the different forms of terret. In East Anglia, certain forms are rare or non-existent, including the early ribbed varieties and the 'massive' terrets found in northern England and Scotland (Hutcheson 2004: 30).

8.6.1. Simple Terrets

Simple terrets are plain and undecorated, usually with a collar either side of a bar for the strap to pass over (Figure 8.7). They date from the third century BCE to 100 CE, although PAS generally gives a first century CE date. Figure 8.8 shows they are nearly all clustered in southcentral and eastern Norfolk, with a few outliers in Suffolk.[4] This agrees with Davies's assessment of the Norfolk patterning (1999: 21). This distribution may relate to centres of settlement and production. The wide river valleys and heathlands of the Brecks may have made ideal rough pasture for herds of horses. The scattering around the Great Estuary may also be explained by coastal grazing marsh, or the transhipment of goods coming in by sea. As the simplest form of terret ring, numbers would be expected to be greater and the distribution wider. Hutcheson states that Norfolk is lacking in early forms of terret (2004: 30). However, this may be explained by variations in recording nomenclature and the lack of tight dating. Miniature terrets (section 8.9) are most often of this simple design.

---

[4] Unclassified rings recorded only as 'terret' have been represented on the distribution map as they are most likely to be of this simple type.

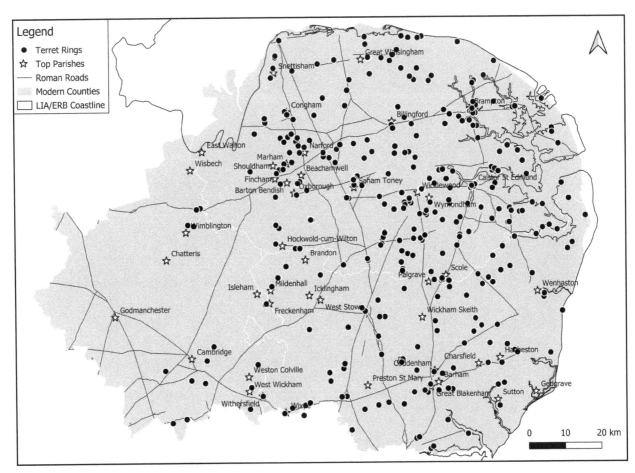

Figure 8.5. Distribution of all terrets.

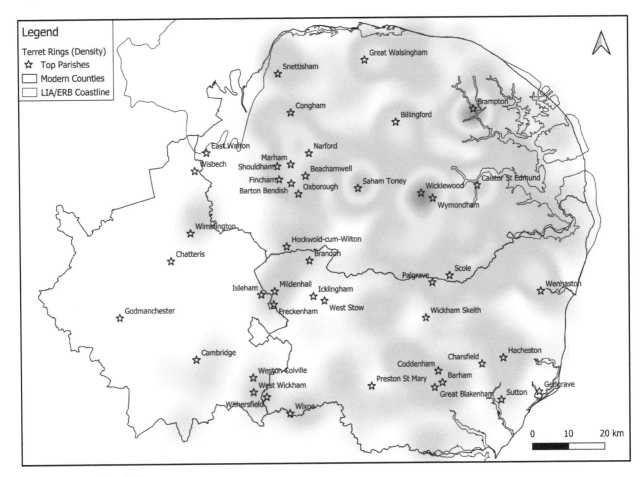

Figure 8.6. Density of all terrets.

8.6.2. Knobbed and Lipped Terrets

Davies (1999: 21) describes regional distributions of lipped and knobbed terrets in west Norfolk.[5] New finds in the intervening period have rewritten this distribution pattern. While my research supports Hutcheson's conclusion that lipped terrets are fairly evenly distributed across Norfolk, not just in the west (2004: 66 and map 18), extending my search into Suffolk and Cambridgeshire reveals a stark absence in the southwest (Figure 8.9). Again, there are several around the periphery of the Great Estuary. Lipped terrets have a first century BCE/CE date range and are considered Iron Age artefacts (Figure 8.10).

Hutcheson dates knobbed terrets (Figure 8.11) to the post-conquest era, from the mid-first century CE onwards, although she highlights examples from Hingham and Gunthorpe which appear stylistically more Iron Age than Roman, suggesting a hybrid form (2004: 30). The distribution of knobbed terrets (Figure 8.9) shows a wide dispersal, with several from the southwest, unlike the lipped types. This also contrasts with Davies's statement that knobbed terrets are a western feature in Norfolk (1999: 21). Could this be explained by a post-conquest increase in demand for transport in this district?

These two types of harness fitting demonstrate regional and chronological variations and how the increased reporting of metal-detecting finds is changing our interpretations. Nonetheless, several issues should be noted here as potential recording bias. Better identification and dating are necessary. PAS records are particularly variable, with a lack of consistency over formal differences between knobbed and lipped terrets (e.g. the 'knobbed' terret from Stapleford, PAS: CAM-5D7F05, which would elsewhere be classified as a lipped example) (Figure 8.12). The vocabulary is certainly inconstant, although it would be unlikely that the same finds recorder used different terminology for east and west Suffolk.

8.6.3. Flat-Ring Terrets

Flat-ring (or 'crescentic') terrets are usually decorated with red enamelling in characteristic swirling patterns on both sides (Figure 8.13). They are given a very wide date range on PAS: anything from 200 BCE to 100 CE. Hutcheson (2004: 29) considers a date in the mid-first century CE most likely. The distribution (Figure 8.14) is similar to lipped terrets: Norfolk and eastern Suffolk, with few in the south and west. As far back as 1973, Moore suspected a production centre for these terrets in Norfolk and Suffolk (1973: 153). The discovery of the Waldringfield terret moulds in the 1980s confirmed this expectation (section 8.10.1). This type is completely absent from the Wicklewood area and the *civitas* capital.

Figure 8.7. Simple terret ring, Shudy Camps (PAS: CAM-D62140).

A group of two enamelled flat-ring terrets and one plain harness ring were found at Castle Rising, near King's Lynn. The enamelled examples have similar decoration to the terrets from the Westhall hoard, with S-shaped swirls in a 'moustache' around the flattened crescent. The third object is hesitantly called a terret (PAS: NMS-30AC24). Although no parallels have been found, it would seem to be another piece of harness paraphernalia, which perhaps prefigures the divided dropped-bar terrets, such as the one from Sutton (PAS: SF-E4B59A) (Figure 8.21). A harness mount decorated in the Westhall style was found less than half a mile away, suggesting they could have been part of a single deposit (Hutcheson PAS: NMS-30AC24).

8.6.4. Platform-Decorated Terrets

Platform-decorated terrets have three ornamented projections spaced around the ring, which are decorated with geometric polychrome enamelling (Figure 8.15).[6] Hutcheson argues that the blue and yellow enamelling, like on some plate brooches, justifies a post-conquest date, probably mid-late first century CE. She records that all single finds of platform terrets from Norfolk come from Roman sites (2004: 30). My distribution (Figure 8.16) strongly locates them in the north of the region, with a group around Brampton and only one outlier in Suffolk.

The five terrets reported in 1838 from Ovington/Saham Toney (section 8.10.3) are platform-decorated types (Norfolk Archaeology 1849; NHER: 15050). Three are decorated with polychrome quatrefoil enamelling on disc-shaped platforms. By remarkable coincidence, in 2004, an almost identical terret was found as part of a small harness hoard by a metal-detectorist in Carleton Rode, approximately 13 miles away (NWHCM: 2006.349)

---

[5] Some terrets are recorded simply as having 'triple projections', which could be lipped, knobbed or winged, and are included on the maps as such.

[6] Platform-decorated terrets are also sometimes recorded as having 'triple projections'.

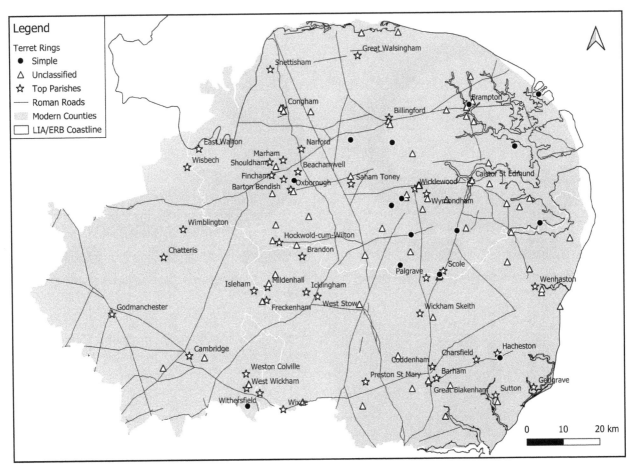

Figure 8.8. Distribution of simple terrets, including unclassified.

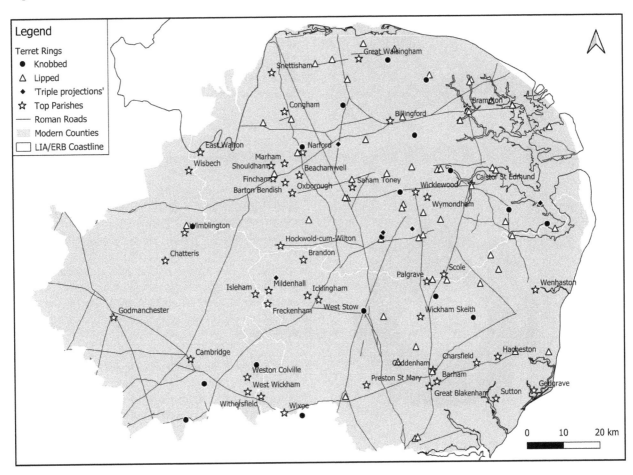

Figure 8.9. Distribution of lipped and knobbed terrets.

Figure 8.10. Lipped terret, Suffield (PAS: NMS-D36060).

Figure 8.13. Westhall-type flat-ring terret, Sporle (PAS: NMS-6599B4).

Figure 8.11. Knobbed terret, Lyng (PAS: NMS132).

Figure 8.12. Knobbed terret, Stapleford (PAS: CAM-5D7F05).

(Figure 8.15). This shares the enamelled blue and yellow geometric petalled design. They are so closely matched that they must have been manufactured in one workshop (Pestell in MODES News 2015). Also found were a lipped terret and a harness mount with red enamelled lobed decoration, similar in style to the Polden Hills and Santon hoards. The group is dated towards the mid-late first century CE, based on the presence of multicoloured enamel which, as mentioned above, is possibly a post-conquest innovation (Hill and Hutcheson 2004: 47). A hoard of three linch-pin terminals was retrieved from near Attleborough (PAS: NMS-41A985) by the same finder in 2007. Subsequent to the data collection for this project, a fine enamelled cheekpiece (PAS: NMS-5983B3) and a delicate openwork fob or 'dangler' (PAS: NMS-AC2BD4) were also recorded from the same parish.

Platform-decorated terrets are extremely attractive and would have been conspicuous items, ornamenting the chariots of the client-kingdom period. Forged in the heat of the conquest and revolt, were they used to brighten and attract attention to the vehicles used in warfare? Did the eye-catching decoration on horses signal their value to the community? These finds are good evidence for manufacturing centres in the Saham Toney and Attleborough areas. Their deposition in hoards hints at a religious or funerary role at these important places. The adoption of polychrome enamelling shows the local bronzeworkers' habit of appropriating new technologies and design elements and applying them to a very localised material culture.

8.6.5. Parallel-Wing and Transverse-Wing Terrets

Parallel-wing and transverse-wing terrets date from the first century CE. These are distributed in the central region, with one ornate example found in the extreme northwest at Snettisham, which confirms Hutcheson's findings (2004: 73) (Figure 8.17). The parallel-wing types, while admittedly a small sample, are decidedly easterly finds.

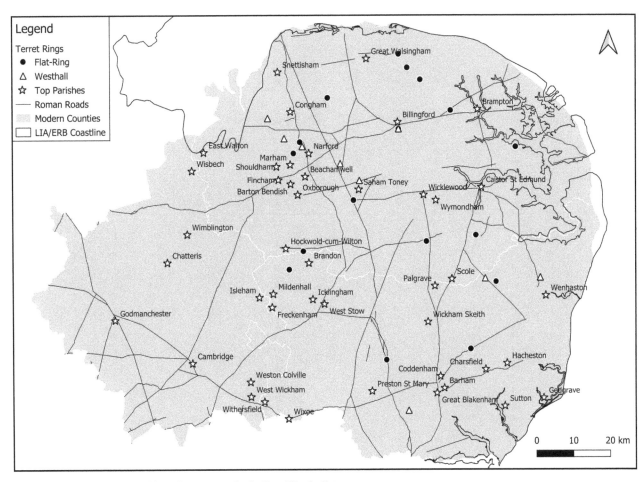

Figure 8.14. Distribution of flat-ring terrets, including Westhall types.

Figure 8.15. Very similar platform terrets, Saham Toney and Carleton Rode (NWHCM: 1847.66.3, 2006.349.1; Image: © Norwich Castle Museum and Art Gallery).

Six of the terrets from Saham Toney (section 8.10.3) are transverse-wing types, adding to the mounting evidence for an experimental workshop of metalworkers in this area. Two of these show hybrid forms, one which has some similarities with an unusual example from Clare (PAS: NMS-D5E6F4) (Figure 8.18). A fragment of a large terret from Oulton (PAS: NMS-C18B95) is described as having mouldings which combine the transverse and parallel-winged types.

8.6.6. Dropped-Bar and Protected-Loop Terrets

Figure 8.19 shows the distribution of dropped-bar and protected-loop terrets. These forms date from the later first-second centuries CE and are thought to be Roman imports, although a miscast example from Marham (PAS: NMS-F747B6) implies local production. The later terrets lack the colourful enamelling of the client-kingdom examples, which typifies the Icenian style, but one is described as having 'a stylised ox-head on each face of the skirt' (PAS: LANCUM-9BD5B6), which would fit within the local aesthetic. Display and differentiation were clearly of utmost importance during the upheavals of the mid-first century CE, perhaps lessening as the occupation progressed.

Dropped-bar terrets have an extended bar, as the name suggests, which may have allowed for a more secure

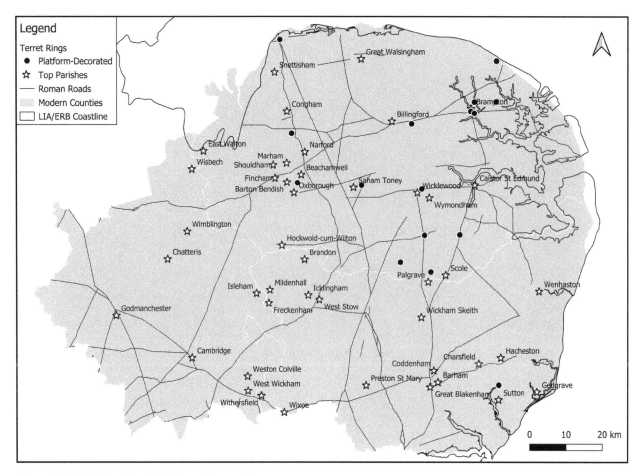

Figure 8.16. Distribution of platform-decorated terrets.

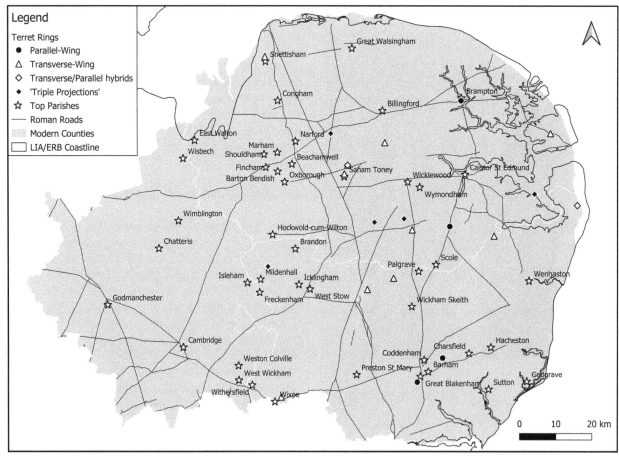

Figure 8.17. Distribution of parallel and transverse-wing terrets.

Figure 8.18. Unusual transverse-wing terret, Clare (PAS: NMS-D5E6F4).

fixing to the yoke (Figure 8.20). There is a dearth of this type in north Suffolk and northeast Norfolk. A late example from Sutton is dated second/third century CE and shows heavy wear to one side of its projecting loop. It also has a central dividing feature which was perhaps intended to prevent a pair of reins from becoming twisted

together or for securing a looped strap (PAS: SF-E4B59A) (Figure 8.21). Protected-loop terrets are concentrated in the north and east, with very few from the Fenland. The *civitas* capital (7) and Walsingham (6) have the only concentrations. The protective 'skirt' creates a cover for the lowered bar or loop. In an example from Offton, the skirt has been decoratively moulded into petal shapes (PAS: SF-CE0736) (Figure 8.22). Dropped-bar types are also recorded as 'projecting loop' terrets, which could be a recording issue, as there is often some confusion between the dropped-bar and protected-loop types, the latter also inconsistently known as 'skirted' or 'covered loop' terrets. Better guidance for recording could improve the definition between these items.

8.6.7. Discussion

Norfolk (69) and Suffolk (15) have a much higher concentration of the later protected-loop and dropped-bar types than neighbouring Cambridgeshire and Essex. This probably reflects an ongoing tradition of horse usage, perhaps using imported material culture. Yorkshire and Lincolnshire also show higher proportions of later terrets on PAS, areas which have a tradition of Iron Age chariot burials. These later terrets are decorated differently and less conspicuously to the earlier enamelled types and do not feature highly in hoards. The functional purpose of these terrets seems to have persisted, but the modes of display and disposal changed.

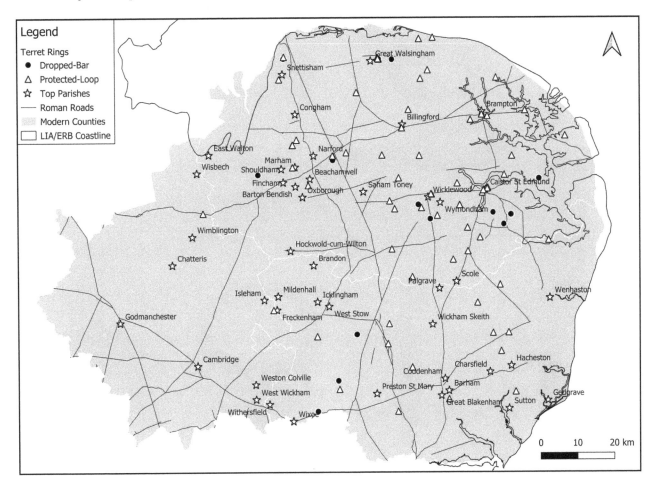

Figure 8.19. Distribution of dropped-bar terrets and protected-loop terrets.

Figure 8.20. Dropped-bar terret, Holbrook (PAS: SF-5565A1).

Figure 8.21. Dropped-bar terret showing wear to attachment loop, Sutton (PAS: SF-E4B59A).

Figure 8.22. Protected-loop terret, Offton (PAS: SF-CE0736).

Following the discussion of restricted depictions of horses (section 8.3), we may speculate why equines are not more frequently represented on terrets or other harness trappings. A rare exception is a double horse-headed skirted terret from Buckinghamshire, dated first/second century CE (PAS: BUC-F16307). There are also several broadly 'Roman' dated horse-head mounts on the PAS database, including one from Scole (PAS: NMS-78F017). Figurines in bronze and pipeclay are also known. This suggests there may have been changing attitudes towards (representing) horses after the conquest.

Hutcheson's observation (2004: 30) of the striking abundance of later-dated terrets in Norfolk would seem to hold true for the wider study region. There are large numbers of flat-ring and the protected-loop/dropped-bar types which flourished from mid-first century CE onwards. To divide the terrets into Iron Age and Roman types seems unnecessary, as the likelihood is that people and their horses were very much embedded in the landscape throughout. This could be taken as evidence for the continuity of settlement, industry and metalworking in the region, again contradicting the story of the great depopulation after the revolt. If anything, transport seemingly became more important from the mid-first century CE onwards. Whether this was related to increased military manoeuvres, road-building projects or overland trade is hard to say.

8.7. Bridle-Bits and Cheekpieces

Without terrets there are no chariots; without bridles there are no riding ponies. Davis suggests that riding was relatively common in the LIA, but its impact has been underestimated by the prevalence of vehicle fittings and the lack of positive identifiers for single riders (2014: 81). During the contact period in southern Britain, 'the adoption of the horse by an individual, and the act of riding rather than driving a cart or chariot could be seen as a way of legitimising and empowering the position of influential and controlling individuals' (*ibid.*: 252).

Bridle-bits are generally classified into three-link (double-jointed) and two-link (single-jointed) snaffle forms. Three-link varieties are slightly earlier and are the common Iron Age type, dating from as early as the fourth century BCE to the conquest. Two-link bits are later, generally first century CE, including 'Polden Hills' types, such as those from Santon and Elveden (Hutcheson 2004: 31; Palk 1984: 3).

Bridle-bits are much rarer than terrets. Norfolk has by far the most bridle-bits of both three- and two-link types (Table 8.1). My mapping shows absences in most of Cambridgeshire, much of southeast Norfolk and, unusually in comparison to terrets, eastern Suffolk (Figure 8.23). This may simply represent a lack of close dating, or other

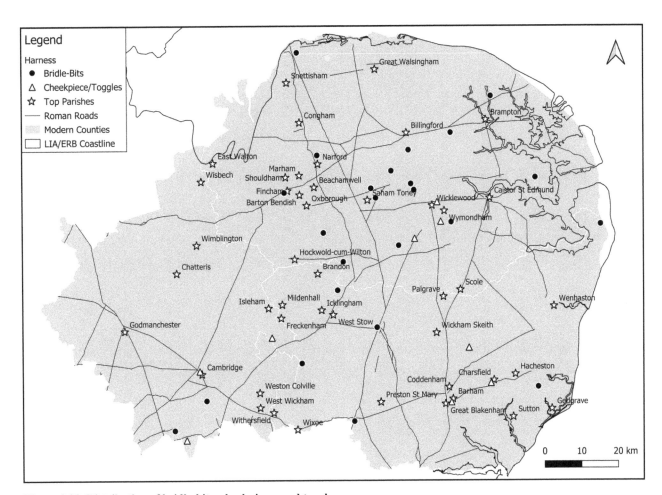

Figure 8.23. Distribution of bridle-bits, cheekpieces and toggles.

recording bias. Some bridles were found in hoards which will be discussed further below. MacGregor mapped major clusters in Yorkshire and Wessex (1976: 24-31), with PAS records for Iron Age bits showing a similar distribution. Only 12 Roman bits are recorded on PAS, most of which are not given a date range (Figure 8.24). Like the terrets, Roman snaffle bits are much plainer than their Iron Age counterparts, suggesting display through decorated metalwork became less important. Unlike the explosion of terrets in the later first century CE, there appear to be more (earlier) three-link than two-link bits. However, this is probably due to the number of bridles which are not dated to a specific century. Bridles are often composites with iron components which may also impact on survival and preservation.

Two three-link bridle-bits are known from Swanton Morley in central Norfolk. One is a simple, robust, undecorated bit and the other is a unique, highly-ornamental enamelled example, with asymmetrical castings within each ring (PAS: NMS213) (Figure 8.25). Davies observes that bridle-bits 'of such high quality are exceptionally rare', suggesting that the latter was owned by 'a high-status individual of the Iceni' (2009: 11). Rarity is certainly a factor, although status may have been attached to the horse who wore it, and by association its owner, if indeed individuals had a sense of private ownership in the LIA. The same person may have used both bridles in different social contexts, or to mark out different vehicles.

Two other three-link bits came from the Ringstead hoard in northwest Norfolk, which also included a strap union, two 'shield plates', a button-and-loop fastener and a bronze 'ingot'. These two bits are very closely matched in shape and decoration, suggesting they were made as a pair for a team of ponies. The decorative scheme is a delicate relief pattern draped over the bulbs of the bridle, differing at each end. They share aesthetic similarities with some of the Snettisham torcs (Garrow and Gosden 2012: 179-84; Hutcheson 2004: 33; Palk 1984: 37) (section 4.7.1).

Although the Ringstead decorative style is very different from the Swanton Morley bit, asymmetry seems to be an important part of both designs, perhaps revealing an emphasis on the different sides of the horse or chariot. When worn by a pair of horses, the undecorated inner ring would be hidden from view (Blockley *et al.* 1989: 188; Giles 2012: 195). One of the paired bits from Ringstead had its mouthpiece purposely broken prior to deposition, as had selective examples from Garton Slack and Polden Hills (Palk 1984: 71, 93). It is tempting to relate this to the longstanding cultural practice of bending and breaking other metal items such as swords, especially given that these examples are from harness hoards or funerary contexts.

The shape and decoration of horse bits find parallels with Iron Age mirror and tankard handles (Joy 2010: 46). Like other metalwork, the decorative style on bridle-bits

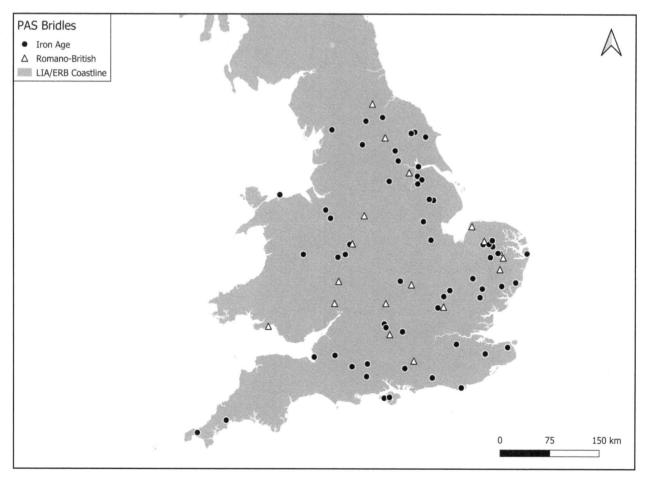

Figure 8.24. PAS distribution of bridle-bits by period.

Figure 8.25. Asymmetrical three-link bridle-bit, Swanton Morley (PAS: NMS213).

changes over time from swirling, asymmetrical patterns to more geometric, polychrome designs. Early opaque red glass is followed by red and dark blue enamelling post-conquest, with turquoise and yellow in regional variations (Davis 2014: 157; MacGregor, M. 1976: 30).

A comparison of the bits from Ringstead (Palk 1984: fig. C20) and Saham Toney (MacGregor, M. 1976: 26) illustrates this different aesthetic well. The geometric enamelled square and triangular cells on the Saham Toney harness can also be seen on seal-box lids, button-and-loop fasteners and cosmetic grinders, which became popular in the later first-third centuries CE. It is also closely paralleled by some of the harness from the Seven Sisters hoard (Davis 2014: 160). MacGregor's assertion, based on the annihilation theory, that it is 'unlikely that the Saham Toney trappings could have been manufactured after the Icenian revolt' (1976: 26) seems unfeasible. If anything, this shift to geometric enamelwork is exactly characteristic of this period.

The fittings usually described as cheekpieces or toggles are often found as components of harness hoards and sometimes in pairs, although there is debate over whether they were attached to bridles (Spratling 1972: 122). There are only three examples apiece from Norfolk and Suffolk (Figure 8.23). The number from Cambridgeshire is skewed by the five decorated bone toggles from the Snailwell burial (section 4.5). Lethbridge suggested that they were handles for a bier used to lift the body onto the cremation pyre (1954: 32). Regardless of whether the Snailwell artefacts were part of horse harness, they remind us that many portable artefacts were made from perishable

materials, not just leather straps, but also bone, antler and wooden components which may not survive.

8.8. Linch-pins

Linch-pins are the mechanism by which the wheel of a cart or chariot was secured to the axle. These composite iron and copper alloy objects often have highly-decorated terminals, gilding and enamelwork (Figure 8.26, Figure 8.27). The shape of some linch-pin feet resembles a horse's lower leg and hoof (Spratling 1972: 58), which is interesting in light of the possible disinclination to represent horses in the Iron Age (section 8.3). There is an echo of this form in the recurved heads of trumpet brooches. Linch-pin terminals may have had an apotropaic function, protective of the vehicle or its occupants, in the crescentic shape of the heads and zoomorphic imagery such as dogs, waterbirds and rams. A phallic example is also known from Chesham, Surrey (Crummy 2011: 67).

The distribution shows few linch-pins in Suffolk (16) and Cambridgeshire (5) (Figure 8.28), despite the Colne Fen hoard (section 8.10.4). In Norfolk (44), the findspots are mostly southcentral (Breckland) and northwestern (Icknield), with a cluster around Wymondham. As previously mentioned, a decorated linch-pin head and two matching feet were found near Attleborough, dating to the first century BCE/CE (Figure 4.10). All had the enamelled curved triangle or 'steering wheel' motif. Very close by, a symmetrically-enamelled harness mount (Figure 8.29) and two terrets were found, suggesting a dispersed hoard. Two further Iron Age linch-pin terminals have been recorded since 2017 in the parishes around Wymondham

Figure 8.26. Baluster-headed linch-pin, Fressingfield (PAS: SF-1007C4).

Figure 8.27. Crescent-headed linch-pin, Wymondham (PAS: NMS-F36EDA).

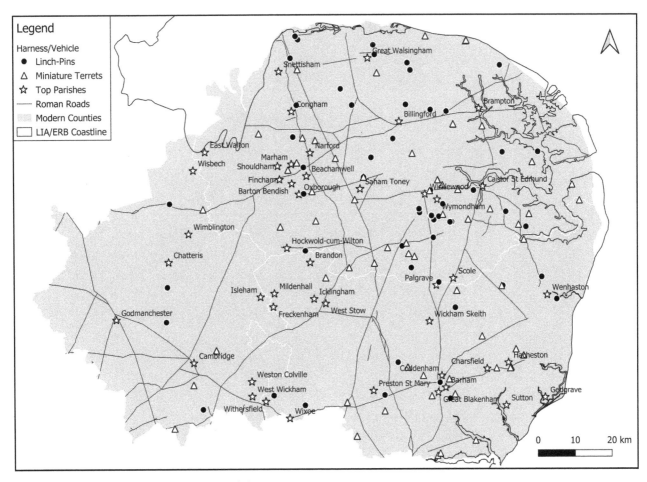

Figure 8.28. Distribution of linch-pins and miniature terrets.

Figure 8.29. Curvilinear enamelled harness mount, Attleborough (PAS: NMS-EE8B03).

and Attleborough, where so many harness finds have been made (PAS: NMS-78884E, NMS-DC7F9C). Evidence for production also includes a casting failure found at Sedgeford (PAS: NMS-AE1963) and a distorted, molten example from Oxborough (PAS: NMS-6FFAD9).

Nationally, Norfolk, Suffolk and Lincolnshire have the highest numbers of linch-pins (Figure 8.30). These are the areas which also show a predominance of Horse-and-Rider brooches and figurines (Figure 3.92). This adds to the emerging trend of artefactual connections between northern East Anglia and the East Midlands in the mid-Roman period. There are very few recorded as Roman by PAS (10 as opposed to 102 Iron Age), which suggests a change in modes of transport, recording bias, or a change in materials with all-ferrous linch-pins becoming much more common and therefore less likely to survive in the ground.

8.9. Miniature Terrets

Miniature terrets are frequently recorded as 'votive', and although the weight of evidence falls towards their use for fixing vehicle wheels, this does not preclude them from being used for religious deposition. Unlike full-scale terrets, miniatures are usually plano-convex in shape (Figure 8.31). Their D-shaped cross-section suggests a slightly different function to their unreduced

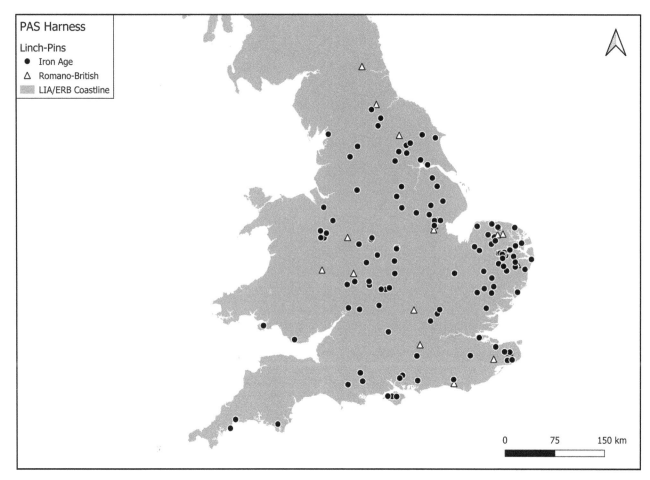

Figure 8.30. PAS distribution of linch-pins.

relatives. Occasionally circular-section examples are recorded; others have decoration, such as the terret from Letheringham which has punched dots in crescent shapes and a 'milled' edge (SHER: LRM013) (Martin *et al*. 1996: fig. 97F). This is paralleled by one from Kenninghall (NHER: 32862), of an 'unusual style with flat faces, a milled rim and dotted decoration' (Gurney 2000: 518).[7]

Hutcheson discusses miniature terrets alongside horse and chariot gear. She is sceptical of the votive interpretation and considers usage as fasteners for very fine straps more likely. She gives them a long date range of second century BCE to first century CE and a diameter of up to 20mm (2004: 28-30). Spratling's measurements are more generous than Hutcheson, allowing a diameter of 19-28mm. Although miniatures are sometimes found in pairs, he discounted their function as terrets, partly based on differences in use-wear. They may instead form part of other harness or cart fittings. A clue comes from Trevelgue, Cornwall, where a miniature terret and a linch-pin were concealed together in the wall of a structure demolished in the second century CE (1972: 50-54). One of the linch-pin heads from Colne Fen (see below) had an iron link attached. Miniature terrets have also been found in association with the heads of linch-pins in vehicle burials in East Yorkshire. There is

Figure 8.31. Miniature terret showing flat back, Oakley (PAS: SF-7BC364).

a strong possibility that such small terrets were attached by a strap to the linch-pin of vehicles as retaining rings, to stop them jumping out during transit (Hutcheson 2004: 29).

Miniature terrets are widely distributed, with fewer from Cambridgeshire and the west (Figure 8.28), which matches with harness generally. There are 41 examples from Norfolk, 21 from Suffolk, but only four from Cambridgeshire, reflecting the high proportions of horse harness from Norfolk. If they are indeed associated with transport, it may

---

[7] I have been unable to find an illustration of this to compare any more closely.

be that the marshy Fenland of Cambridgeshire did not lend itself to wheeled vehicles. No parish has a concentration of these artefacts, although there are two from Saham Toney, and Fring, not far from Snettisham, has three examples. Evidence for manufacturing comes from Ashwellthorpe in central Norfolk, in the form of a miscast or unfinished strap-mounted miniature terret (Rogerson PAS: NMS-6B7DF3).

An oddity from Marham in northwest Norfolk (PAS: NMS-44F9E6) (Figure 8.32) has three ovoid bezels arranged around the perimeter, rather like the full-sized platform-decorated terrets which seem to be a Norfolk speciality. No trace remains of what was held in the bezels, whether inlaid glass, enamel or gemstones. From Monk's Eleigh (SHER: MKE010), unfortunately unillustrated, is a bronze harness mount 'shaped rather like a miniature Westhall-type terret ring, with red and yellow enamelled decoration on a crescentic flange'. It is approximately 30mm high and dates from the first century CE (Martin *et al.* 1989: 63). This mount may be related to the enamelled button-and-loop fasteners (section 4.2), and demonstrates that miniature objects were being made which referenced other, full-size harness items.

An atypical object from Lound, in the extreme northeast of Suffolk, resembles a miniature terret, but has an attachment loop hidden behind a decorative 'button' and set at a 90-degree angle to the ring (PAS: NMS920). An unusual example from Stratford St Andrew (SHER: SSA002) is recorded as a small, or miniature, terret ring fragment, with triple pellet decoration. This is intriguing, given Davies's assertions about the symbolism of triple pellets on Icenian coins (2014: 27). The recorder noted that it was made from a high lead or tin copper alloy, reflecting other preferences for the colour or metal content of certain objects, particularly in Suffolk.

There are no confirmed leaden miniature terrets in my database, unlike other votive objects, particularly axes (section 6.7.2). This is a good argument against miniature terret rings being produced specifically for use as votives, although they may have served both purposes. Miniature objects are certainly present in special deposits (Haselgrove 2015: 34). A pair of miniature terrets was included in a coin hoard from Honley, West Yorkshire (Spratling 1972: 51-52). The linch-pin and mini terret at Trevelgue suggest a possible apotropaic concealment of objects linked in use. Dividing objects into ritual or practical categories may purely reflect modern considerations which have no bearing on how they were used and understood in the past. Multifunctional objects may have crossed conceptual distinctions during their lifetimes.

8.10. Harness Hoards and Production

Harness hoards appear to show the same impulse towards votive deposition as those of the torcs and jewellery previously discussed. They span the conquest and Boudican period, suggesting continuity of practice

Figure 8.32. Miniature terret with bezels, Marham (PAS: NMS-44F9E6).

beyond the rebellion. Evidence for manufacturing implies that the north of the area was a key production zone, in line with the overall deposition of harness fittings, with only the moulds from Waldringfield demonstrating the links with Suffolk (Figure 8.33). A look at several hoards reveals additional evidence for the mix of continuity and innovation in material culture which characterises the response to the occupation. The relationships between hoards, metalworking and burial are also explored further.

Horse gear follows a broadly eastern pattern from Kent to Yorkshire (Figure 8.1). The *civitas Icenorum* shows differential deposition to other parts of Britain, where horse harness tends to be found either in large hoards or associated with chariot burials. In addition to hoards, Norfolk has a greater number of individual finds and the distribution is more widespread (Hutcheson 2004: 18-19). This may reflect a higher proportion of horses and vehicles and therefore more casual losses, or greater metal-detector coverage and overall proportions of finds. Nevertheless, hoards have been found at several sites. In Norfolk, these include Ringstead (section 8.7), Santon and Saham Toney, which date to the first centuries BCE/CE. In Suffolk and Cambridgeshire, there are harness hoards from Westhall and Colne Fen respectively. These are well-known and significant finds, described briefly here with relevance to key research questions (for details of specific hoards see Clarke 1939; Davis 2014; MacGregor, M. 1976; Manning 1972; Smith 1909; Spratling 1972; for an overview see Garrow and Gosden 2012). A newly-reported hoard from Broadland (PAS: NMS-3E5C7E), including two lyre-shaped strap mounts, was dredged from a stream or boundary ditch and dates from *circa* 50 BCE-100 CE.

8.10.1. Westhall and Waldringfield

The Westhall hoard (found 1855) included six linch-pin terminals, two quadrilobe mounts and eight enamelled flat-ring terrets (BM: 1855,0519). The hoard was reportedly surrounded by charcoal and scorched earth. Davis also notes burning on the Polden Hills, Stanwick and Seven Sisters hoards (2014: 260). Both Westhall and Santon hoards included discs embossed with ambiguous quadrupeds, possibly horses, wolves or mythical beings

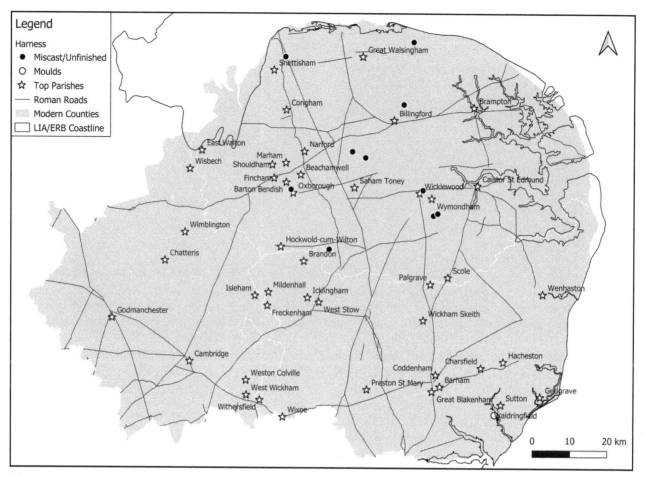

Figure 8.33. Distribution of harness moulds and miscasts.

akin to the Aylesford 'pantomime horses' (Clarke 1939: 65-69). As previously outlined, depictions of horses were rare, except on Iron Age coinage. Were these discs symbolic coins? Were they worn by horses in reference to some beast from folklore or religion? The Boudican narrative is used to pinpoint the dating, Clarke imagining its concealment during reprisals 'at the hands of the overzealous Roman troops' (*ibid.*: 68-69). Spratling attempted to debunk this notion, but still concluded that a mid-first century CE date was likely (1972: 307-9).

Enamelled flat-ring terrets from Weybread, Westhall and Rushmere are so similar that they are likely to have come from the same production centre. The distributions of such highly-distinctive, decorative artefacts in north Suffolk and Norfolk have been used to establish their Icenian manufacture (Gregory and Martin 1985: 35; Martin 1978: 137). However, evidence for production of Westhall-type terrets was subsequently found at Waldringfield, near Ipswich (Figure 8.33). Based on Iron Age coin distributions, this would be considered Trinovantian territory, bearing in mind these were Roman administrative categories, like modern counties, and are unlikely to refer to ethnic groupings.

Over 30 fragments of clay 'lost-wax' moulds for Westhall-style enamelled terrets and strap unions were found in a churchyard at Waldringfield (Rigby 2013: 27). Trial

trenches later unearthed several further fragments and both Roman and Iron Age ceramics. It is posited that the moulds had been placed in a pit, disturbed by later grave-digging. These may represent a workshop specialising in the manufacture of 'yoke furniture' i.e. sets of terrets and strap unions which fitted onto the yoke (Martin *et al.* 1986; Rigby 2013). Rippon views the Waldringfield moulds and Ipswich torcs as evidence for a territorial boundary in southeast Suffolk, suggesting that 'communities living in the Gipping valley regarded themselves as having an Icenian identity' (2018: 66). Alternatively, as these finds are both close to key inlets from the North Sea, the Rivers Deben and Orwell, they might be a sign of coastal trade links.

The Waldringfield fragments appear to have zoomorphic features encoded within them, as recognised on other LIA metalwork (Foster 2014). Birds' heads and eyes are part of the unique design, nevertheless within a specific aesthetic. This preference for zoomorphic decoration, which we have previously seen on the cosmetic grinders, seems also to be an important consideration on vehicles. Rigby suggests the complicated double-sided objects created within the moulds were items of conspicuous display, which embodied the metalworker's prowess as well as the acquisitive desire of their owner or commissioner (2013: 36). I would add a caveat about making assumptions about elite craft sponsorship; these items could be part of a gift exchange cycle, which alters the directional flow of personal display and prestige.

The individual moulds included two matched sets of five crescentic terrets and a pair of strap unions. Could this relate to the casting of specific designs meant for individual vehicles, persons or groups? One mould has been identified with the terret from Weybread. At Gussage All Saints, Dorset, a pit produced over 200 fragments of clay moulds estimated to be the equivalent for manufacture of around 50 sets of chariot fittings. Intentional or structured deposition is a common feature of disposal in this period: 'certain types of finds were regularly deposited together, in a certain order, and in certain places, while others were generally excluded' (Hill 1995a: 65, 95). Rigby determined an aspect of controlled deposition at Waldringfield, with 'contemporary sorting and recycling' resulting in only a small part of the manufacturing debris being deposited in the pit. This is reminiscent of the structured sorting of human and animal remains in pits and the deliberate nesting of torcs in hoards (2013: 26, 34).

8.10.2. Santon

The Santon hoard (found 1897) is a large mixed hoard which includes horse and chariot fittings as well as vessels, bronzeworking tools and scrap metal. Remarkably, there are no terret rings in this hoard, although linch-pins and nave bands from wheels suggest vehicles rather than riding horses. It is dated to *circa* 60 CE, again based on a Boudican explanation, and the inclusion of two Thistle (1-60 CE) and four sprung Colchester Derivative brooches (40-70 CE). All the brooches show signs of being worn or broken. A military connection cannot be ruled out, as the hoard also contains Roman legionary armour fittings and a Hod Hill brooch (40-70 CE). However, this brooch is unparalleled on the continent and may be an indigenous variant with no military association (Davis 2014; Hutcheson 2004; Spratling 1972, 1975).

The tools and scrap metal in the hoard suggest collection for recycling, reminiscent of the Snettisham Jeweller's Hoard (section 4.7.2). Perhaps the military objects were trophies from a battle or ambush, or had been brought to the smith for repurposing in a more peaceful climate. The presence of repaired, new and unfinished objects in the Santon and Ringstead hoards suggests they may be related to manufacturing (Garrow and Gosden 2012: 182-83). This calls to mind the mixture of ancient, repaired and unfinished torcs in the hoards at Ken Hill, Snettisham, at least one of which was centuries old and had been customised and curated before deposition (Joy 2016).

8.10.3. Saham Toney

The Saham Toney hoard, recorded in 1838, consists of five terret rings, a bridle-bit and a strap union (MacGregor, M. 1976: 26). It embodies the varied ornamental schemes which I have termed the 'similar but different' aesthetic. The terrets are of different sizes and display polychrome, geometric enamel decoration. Evidence for a nearby workshop is suggested by the matching platform-decorated terrets from Saham Toney and Carleton Rode (section 8.6.4). The Boudican narrative has been used to explain the design link between the enamelled strap union and one from the Middlebie hoard in Dumfriesshire. MacGregor suggested that the unrest in the Iceni territory led to the movement of craftspeople as refugees (*ibid.*: 179-80), much like Mackreth's diaspora of brooch-makers (2009: 147). It is unlikely that types of decoration were spread by mass movements of people, although, as we have seen, the imitation and adoption of 'outsider' objects was common. Indeed, this is one of several objects which connect Scotland and East Anglia over time, such as the Sedgeford/Netherurd torcs and the spiral armlet from Snailwell. Hunter has queried this diffusionist approach, considering that individuals, ideas and artefacts were mobile in more than one direction (1997: 109).

In the 1990s, metal-detecting and subsequent excavations at Quidney Farm, Saham Toney (NHER: 28294, 29429) uncovered a dispersed hoard of horse gear and a large quantity of ceramic metalworking debris. Crucibles and ceramic mould fragments, some of which may have been used to manufacture terrets were found, as well as evidence for iron-working. The report suggests this was a metal reprocessing hoard. This site shows overlapping LIA and Romano-British ceramic traditions, until at least the late first century CE (Bates *et al.* 2000).

Finds included five lipped terrets, a linch-pin, two bridle-bits, a matching roundel and plate brooch, an iron axehead and a pair of manacles. Thirteen mid-first century CE brooches and a miniature terret were also discovered in the same field. The terrets may represent a complete set from a single vehicle, although only two of the terrets are tightly matching in design. The largest terret is unparalleled. It has asymmetrical, projecting ribs similar to another fragment found at Saham Toney in 2002 (PAS: SF9412) (Figure 8.34). Another terret bridges the Iron Age lipped type and the Roman protected-loop terret, with geometric and swirling punched dot decoration on the 'skirt'. This shows the regional appetite for experimentation extends from brooches to horse gear (Bates *et al.* 2000).

Another 'creolised' object comes from a dispersed hoard discovered in 2011, approximately six miles from Saham Toney. It features a protected-loop terret with punched decoration on the skirt in the form of two back-to-back crescents, often found on coins and considered an Icenian device (Davies 2014: 27; Talbot 2015: 302) (Figure 8.35). The hoard also contained a lipped terret and a zoomorphic (bovid) tankard or bucket mount (PAS: NMS-E51D37). It is broadly dated 100 BCE-100 CE, but is most likely to be post-conquest, again showing a fusion between indigenous and external styles and preoccupations.

In conjunction with brooch production at nearby Old Buckenham (section 3.5.3), this is excellent evidence to support the theory that indigenous metalworkers

Figure 8.34. Unusual rotationally-lipped terret, Saham Toney (PAS: SF9412).

continued to produce small portable metal artefacts in the same workshops, while fusing both new and old techniques, materials and decorative styles. It also backs up Hutcheson's assertion that the Iceni were not wiped out after the revolt, but adapted to the conditions thrust upon them. These hybrid and unusual artefacts have the potential to show that the political clashes of the first century CE were not necessarily detrimental to the development of material culture and may in fact have prompted innovation.

8.10.4. Colne Fen

A hoard of five linch-pin heads was found at Colne Fen, Cambridgeshire, in an area of intensive Roman occupation. Three are the plain 'baluster' or vase-headed fittings known from the Santon and Westhall hoards. The other two linch-pins are highly decorative with enamelled heads, 'wholly in the Celtic tradition'. The dating is *circa* 1-40 CE. The two decorated heads were 'broken off short' from their pins, leading to the romantic notion that they were lost during a 'violent collision in fighting' (Tebbutt and Fox 1961: 236-38), no doubt drawn from the classical stereotype of Icenian chariot warfare. Alternatively, they may have been deliberately damaged before votive deposition.

One linch-pin has a swirling red pattern reminiscent of Westhall terrets. The second is an unusual example with recurving duck's head shaped terminals which are pierced for attachment, one of which still has an iron link looped through it. It has a projecting 'shelf' or cover with curvilinear enamelled decoration (MacGregor, M. 1976: 49-50; Tebbutt and Fox 1961: 235-38). Intriguingly, this echoes the design of the protected-loop terrets discussed above and supports the functional explanation of miniature terrets to retain the linch-pin (section 8.9). The crescentic head is enamelled with blue and red shapes, perhaps zoomorphic or birdlike, with 'eyes' as described in the Waldringfield terret moulds (Rigby 2013). The use of waterbirds' heads as terminals recalls the many examples found on cosmetic grinders (section 5.3.2) and other artefacts, such as the Crownthorpe cups.

All five pieces are different, leading again to the question as to whether these were scrap metal collected for recycling. The five terrets in other hoards reflects the number needed to join a team of horses to the vehicle, but is less explicable in relation to linch-pins, which must surely have secured two or four wheels to a vehicle. Was five an appropriate number for deposition? The 'patchwork' of mismatched

Figure 8.35. Hybrid protected-loop terret, Shipdham hoard (PAS: NMS-E51D37).

or different items grouped together in hoards and chariot burials (Chittock 2016: 181) is also paralleled by the terret moulds from Waldringfield.

8.10.5. Discussion

At Saham Toney and elsewhere mismatched sets are usually interpreted as replacements for worn or lost terrets (Garrow and Gosden 2012: 215-19). Is this part of the aesthetic of 'purposeful differentiation' (Spratling 2008: 197)? Or more prosaically, was 'close' good enough? Perhaps the uniqueness and individuality of harness items, like cosmetic grinders, was an important part of the design brief. Harness 'groupsets' can show considerable variability. Set-matched pairs of bridle-bits and cheekpieces were found in the Polden Hills hoard, which also has dissimilar terrets and horse brooches (Garrow and Gosden 2012: 188-89, 217-19). Davis's analysis of the metallurgy found paired bits were very similar (2014: 103-10). In the Yorkshire chariot burials, some harness sets may have been manufactured specifically for funerary rites, being virtually non-functional. Some were closely matched with deliberate pairing, whilst others never matched in the first place (Giles 2012: 196-97).

It is possible to see these finds in light of local workshops and product availability rather than 'tribal territories'. Local tastes and styles were influenced by, and influenced, the metalworkers' own aesthetics and methods. The debate over itinerant versus settled workshops can be revisited here (section 3.10). Westhall-type terrets have been found as much as 60 miles from Waldringfield, but the Carleton Rode terret was discovered only 13 miles from Saham Toney. The distributions of brooches and torcs show strong connections between southeast Suffolk and northwest Norfolk. Again, I would stress the need for thorough investigation into how decorative metalwork was produced and distributed.

Why were people burying horse harness in hoards? Were they offerings or metalworkers' caches? Do they relate to the Boudican revolt at all? Hutcheson challenges the Boudican ascription of Norfolk hoards, arguing for a much longer, more spread out chronology. Many key finds, including hoards, post-date the rebellion, in some cases by decades (2004: 34-35). This raises questions about the alleged devastation and the nature of the end of the Iron Age in the territory.

Webster proposed that workshops near military sites fed the Roman army's enthusiasm for attractive horse harness, local craftspeople quickly adapting to new markets, while retaining pre-conquest decorative styles (1993: 104). Comparison may be drawn again with the *civitas Batavorum*, on the Rhine *limes* in the Netherlands. This area has many similarities with the *civitas Icenorum*, including its low-lying wetland environment, which is particularly suitable for grazing horses (above other herbivores) all year round. Like the Icenian charioteers, Batavian horsemen also feature in the writings of Tacitus (*Hist*. IV). In the mid-Roman period, many rural sites show high proportions of horse skeletal material and widespread finds of harness. This is interpreted as part of a supply chain of riding ponies to the Roman cavalry and auxiliary units. Grain for fodder was also an important link in this chain (Vossen and Groot 2009: 85-100). If this parallel applies, significant harness finds around the presumed forts at Saham Toney (NHER: 4697, 8745) may be evidence of this sort of symbiosis. This may explain the many finds of openwork harness mounts with triskele decoration which are categorised as 'military' finds. At Swanton Morley (NHER: 17486), another early fort is deduced from air photography and metal-detector survey. As well as the bridles discussed earlier, a triskele mount and four terrets embody the aesthetic shift, with two crescentic Westhall-type terrets and a distinctive example with enamelled triangles (Davies 2009: 148-50; Hutcheson 2004: 29 and cat. #136-8).

By contrast, MacGregor considered the British harness system entirely alien to the Roman cavalry and noted that several hoards contain paired bits for draught horses (1976: 178-80). The association of British metalwork with forts is more likely to demonstrate discrepant responses to the occupation among indigenous people, than movements of the army around Britain making commissions from local workshops. The current evidence for production seems to follow the distribution of harness equipment more generally, with concentrations in central Norfolk. In the *civitas*, finds of harness are concentrated around the indigenous community and early forts at Saham Toney, and the settlement and temple complex at Wicklewood (Figure 8.4). Further excavation is sorely needed at these sites to gain a clearer picture.

Although the people of the Iceni polity did not favour chariot burials, or in fact burial at all, some of the components of harness hoards are very similar to funerary assemblages. Davis discusses the similarities and differences between hoards and LIA burials in the context of the Santon Hoard. Although she concludes that Santon probably did not accompany a burial, she draws parallels between the deposition of human remains and that of artefacts (2014: 213-15). As we have seen with the hoards at Snettisham (section 4.7), votive deposition is a long-lasting tradition in eastern Britain. I have suggested that hoards of jewellery might have represented proxy burials for significant members or groups within the community. The fragmentation of the chariot and horse equipment has parallels with the dispersal, mixing and partial integration of human and animal remains in some Iron Age deposits (Hill 1995a). There is a sense of selectivity at Waldringfield which echoes the small percentages of pyre remains in cremation burials (Pearce 1997: 177). Burning also seems to have featured in the deposition of some hoards, including Westhall.

The inclusion of tools, repaired and unfinished items, and scrap metal might be related to proxy burials of metalsmiths. Perhaps metalworkers were held in high esteem, with advanced cultural capital due to their important 'know-how' and magically-transformative abilities. Their role as significant people in the community, tinged by their dangerous or polluted work, maybe set them apart as liminal or taboo. This attitude to blacksmiths has been observed in anthropological studies, particularly in parts of Africa (Kusimba 1996; McNaughton 1993; Njoku 1991). After death, their belongings, products and tools were perhaps considered both sacred and contaminated, which needed to be safely contained and deposited.

8.11. Summary

What do vehicle and harness fittings tell us about group identity in the *civitas*? The practices of horse-breeding and training (and possibly also chariot warfare) span the conquest and revolt period. Perhaps this aspect of life in the 'Kingdom of the Horse' would have characterised the region more so than brooches. I have questioned the 'material elite' as an overly simple way of understanding social organisation in the LIA (section 2.3.3). There is little clear evidence of social hierarchy until the final Iron Age (Garrow and Gosden 2012: 33). Living assets, such as herds of horses, may have been communally owned and decorative harness may have reflected their importance within the community, rather than any single person's standing. The number or quality of horses and vehicles may have conferred status, which could be enhanced by their adornment with brightly-enamelled metalwork (Harlow 2018). Davis proposes that 'horses and related gear were maintained by parts of the community rather than by individual ownership', particularly those groups which resisted occupation in the first century CE (2014: 249).

Attitudes to representing horses in the iconography also changed. Horses held symbolic capital and may have been 'prestige' belongings. As Roman coins replaced Icenian issues, horses are not found on either the imported seal-boxes or indigenous cosmetic grinders, but became visible as pipeclay figurines and plate brooches often associated with burial and religious practices. The imagery of the 'Rider God' nevertheless suggests that horses remained a potent symbol, now tamed and dominated. Creighton views horses as 'significant in the conception of power and authority', possibly reflecting the shift from group to individual identities (2000: 104). For Davis, 'horse paraphernalia was for the symbolic show of rights, power, and land occupation as much as, if not more than for functionality. These items became essential in maintaining social systems, disputes and cooperation where necessary' (2014: 253).

Changes over time as well as hybridity can be seen through harness fittings. As in previous chapters, military and civilian, local and imported artefacts are not easily distinguished, especially where there is evidence for local manufacture. Decoration on harness reflects the broader shift in style from curvilinear towards geometric pattern in some personal ornament, like plate and Headstud brooches. Highly-coloured, symmetrical designs on horse gear and plate brooches became the new popular aesthetic after Roman colonisation (Garrow and Gosden 2012: 33). The shift in aesthetics is therefore applicable beyond objects worn on the person, reinforcing the idea that symbolism, colour and technical abilities displayed across categories of portable artefacts remained desirable to the people of the region.

Horse equipment represents a 'social currency recognisable within a diverse society, which was used, and then deposited in significant ways' (Davis 2014: 253). Hoards of horse and chariot fittings may demonstrate continuity of behaviour from earlier structured deposits of torcs and coins. I have suggested these might be proxy burials enacted as part of communal, ritual practices to commemorate important events or individuals. Sites which both pre- and post-date the rebellion have concentrations (Brampton, Caistor St Edmund, Saham Toney) and the use of terrets in the later first/second centuries CE shows continuity, although conspicuous decoration diminishes. This supports my argument against the destitution of the region in the Boudican aftermath. Manufacture, display and deposition of horse furnishings, particularly in central Norfolk and eastern Suffolk, imply that the equine 'economy' remained a significant aspect of identity before, during and after the client-kingdom.

Conclusions and Future Research

9.1. Introduction

This book has explored the formation of identities in the Iceni *civitas* through personal belongings. The final chapter considers how my research has addressed the key areas of enquiry and draws together some of the noteworthy trends which have been highlighted. It is divided into two sections: an assessment of the roles of belongings in the pre-conquest, client-kingdom and post-revolt periods, and a more thematic discussion of patterns observed during the study.

This project was ambitious in its research objectives and regional scope. I have created and interrogated a database of over 14,000 artefacts from three counties, with significant conclusions regarding Icenian identity, aesthetics and the historical narrative of the region. Nevertheless, there are ample opportunities for further investigations. Recommendations for setting the future research agenda are put forward at the end of each section.

9.2. Is there a distinctive material culture which can be identified with 'the Iceni'?

The principal research question raised complex issues which necessitated the deconstruction of the idea of 'the Iceni' as derived from Roman texts. Secondary considerations queried the idea of 'Doing Different' and the presentation of the Iceni as an 'Other'. I found a single unified social entity ('the Iceni') is not archaeologically visible across the study area, although there is intra-regional patterning.

The Iron Age people of East Anglia have been constructed as 'Iceni' through several mechanisms, starting with their naming in the classical literature. Naming is also essential in rooting this group firmly in space, constructing a 'tribal territory' around *Venta Icenorum*. The story is enhanced through the romantic notion of the indigenous underdogs rising up against their cruel and unjust oppressors, led by a strong female character. The conclusion in bloodshed and devastation birthed the idea of the stunted development of the *civitas* capital, the 'pacification' of the territory and the cultural backwardness of its people.

The Iceni have also been represented as 'Other', a foil against which the neophiles of the southeastern kingdoms, with their imports and 'chiefly burials' can stand out. They were rebellious, but not wild like the northern barbarians, beginning as friendly clients and only resorting to violence in extreme circumstances. Once the uprisings were quashed, the *civitas* settled into historical obscurity, perhaps divided up and settled by veterans and complicit

'elites'. In some cases, analysts have tried to make the material culture, particularly coins and brooches, fit with this narrative. Outside the *civitas*, the same archaeological evidence is interpreted differently, based on expectations of the Iceni to be resistant troublemakers or reactionary barbarians. Some of these attitudes also chime with the commonly-held stereotype of modern Norfolk as slow to change, lost in time, different and insular, summed up by the phrase 'Normal for Norfolk'.

This study has reassessed these discourses, using an archaeology-first approach which tests the material evidence against the written sources, taking a nuanced view of changes over time and space. My analysis of 'belonging and belongings' shows there is no archaeologically visible 'Iceni', as a bounded ethnic identity group, detectable through a consistent and shared material culture. This accords with other studies emphasising the complex relationships between artefacts and identity (Carr 2006; Crummy and Eckardt 2008; Gardner 2007; Hill 2007; Hutcheson 2004; Mattingly 2007, 2008; Revell 2016).

Nonetheless, my research has confirmed some distinctive material culture and practices which have traditionally been associated with Icenian identity. Certain artefact types show comparable deposition and recovery, suggesting patterns of indigenous settlement, perhaps also related to manufacturing centres. At the county level, Norfolk abounds with bridle-bits, linch-pins, miniature tools and weapons and vulvate mounts, but lacks Iron Age mirrors. Suffolk and Cambridgeshire, by contrast, have more miniature axes, phallic imagery, Baldock nail cleaners and pipeclay figurines. In central Norfolk, around Wicklewood and Wymondham, we find intense concentrations of Aesica, Rearhook and, to some extent, Headstud brooches. These are accompanied by hotspots of horse harness (Figure 8.4) and cosmetic grinders (Figure 5.5), but notably few seal-boxes (Figure 7.7).

In southeast Suffolk, with centres at Coddenham, Hacheston and Wenhaston, there are clusters of seal-boxes, cosmetic grinders and fasteners, plus almost all brooch types, although fewer Aesica and Langton Down variants than in Norfolk. Notably Coddenham and Wenhaston have strong signals for both Harlow and Rearhook Colchester Derivative brooches. Around the parishes in northwest Norfolk, many of the earlier brooch types are concentrated, along with seal-boxes and nail cleaners. Rippon has suggested that this subdivision into eastern and western parts persisted into the later Roman period, with the villa landscapes along the Fen-edge (2018: 164). Saham Toney, Caistor St Edmund and Brampton have high densities of harness fittings and fasteners. Hockwold has many plate brooches and cosmetic grinders, while Walsingham has numerous disc brooches and seal-boxes. Snettisham has its torcs, and in the Fens, Wimblington has a high rate of snake bracelets. How should we explain these patterns, when the idea of matching artefacts to ethno-cultural groups is no longer valid?

In his study of northeastern Gaul, Fernández-Götz (2014a) demonstrates how larger scale groups can incorporate and integrate diverse internal differences. He also critiques the disciplinary assumptions of hierarchically-structured, LIA warrior societies, in contrast to the much greater differentiation revealed by the archaeological evidence (*ibid.*: 35). In his view, the Treveran *civitas* was a loose aggregation or 'federation' of semi-autonomous *pagi*, a 'polycentric state' (*ibid.*: 155) which enabled multiple and overlapping identities to be expressed. There were perhaps six or seven *pagi* within the territory of the Treveri, each centred around an *oppidum* with a religious focus (*ibid.*: 156). The three major clusters of finds within the Icenian *civitas* may equally represent such a subdivision into *pagi*, as has been suggested for coinage. The focus on horse gear and other finds in central Norfolk perhaps backs up Allen's claims (1970) that Breckland was home to one such subgroup. Chadburn considered the numismatic evidence to show three Icenian *pagi*, centred on *oppida* at Thetford, Norwich and Stonea (2006: 477-83). By contrast, Talbot noted the three main mints were not static and may have been controlled by trade organisations rather than individual rulers (2017: 99-101).

Although coins and ornamental metalwork were occasionally produced at the same sites (e.g. Fison Way) and deposited together in hoards (e.g. Snettisham), personal artefacts display different geographical circulation zones to coins. Experimentation and hybridity in object manufacture are not mirrored in LIA coinage. Coins of this period show little wear, suggesting they were not everyday possessions carried on the person. Dies were issued and coins were minted by certain people or groups for specific uses. Later Icenian issues were tightly controlled and consistent in weight, metal content and design, with all reverses portraying the horse (Chadburn 2006; Leins 2012; Talbot 2015, 2017). This is very different from how we understand manufacture of most other artefacts, although a process of standardisation is often noted (for discussion see Pitts 2019). There was perhaps a democratisation of the production of decorative metalwork. The numismatic evidence does support the relatively late appearance of the *civitas* capital, which 'appears marginal to the main areas of coin-use' (Leins 2012: 185). The artefact assemblage confirms it was unlikely to have been built upon a pre-conquest *oppidum*, although it may have developed from a nearby ritual focus.

The complex distributions of brooches find parallels with LIA coin types, which appear geographically restricted, but have considerable crossover with neighbouring and far-flung issues. Colchester Derivative Rearhook brooches show strong patterning, which may be consistent with

Mackreth's view that this was the Icenian brooch type around the time of the conquest (2009, 2011). Likewise, Harlow brooches are widespread in the south of the area, as would be anticipated from a brooch considered characteristic 'of the Trinovantes' (Mackreth 2011: 50). I find this idea of mapping group identity directly onto brooches as 'badges of belonging' dissatisfying. It is unlikely that barely-visible differences in spring fixing were enough to distinguish one social grouping from another. However, the greater decoration on Rearhook brooches may have been more noticeable at a distance, and the textiles which they fastened may have identified people by clan or kin group. Certain craft traditions such as choices of spring fittings, decorative flourishes or enamel colourings could have been significant to different identity groups or passed down through generations of metalworkers.

Martin (1999: 88) proposed the eastern Fen-edge was in Iceni territory while the southwestern Fens were a contested zone between the Catuvellauni and Trinovantes. The 'ethnic identifier' concept is challenged by the popularity of the Harlow spring system in a broad swathe up the western side of the study area, perhaps following main routes. Harlow and Rearhook brooches are far from being mutually exclusive. The manufacturing evidence supports this assertion, with production of Harlow brooches in Norfolk and Rearhooks in Suffolk. A reassessment of the concepts of itinerant metalworkers and workshops in the light of the Boudican narrative has shown how archaeology can sometimes be blinkered. An unanswered question is why these types were occasionally made in one part of the region, but deposited in higher proportions in the other. Could this anomaly be related to the strong metalworking tradition in the north of the territory or is it solely down to loss and recovery?

Distributions of material culture demonstrate a multifaceted intra-regional picture. Some objects are closely tied with certain areas, most likely related to production centres and deposition foci. The Saham Toney area seems to have been important in the production of horse equipment and brooches. The evidence for coin minting is also characteristic of an *oppidum*. Was this the focal point of one of the Icenian *pagi*? Were these subgroups characterised by kinship, clan membership, trading arrangements or religious affiliation? Until the cropmark and surface survey evidence is tested by excavation, we cannot say for sure whether this site was an *oppidum* or equivalent political powerbase, but it certainly appears to have been a significant indigenous centre.

Hoards of torcs are an East Anglian phenomenon, with a probable religious focus in northwest Norfolk. Decorated horse harness also shows clear sub-regional distributions which are unlikely to result from recovery bias (chapter eight). The relationship between the Icenian territory and horses has long been established, with coinage and harness representing both a symbolic and practical preoccupation, arguably showing the regional importance of keeping wealth in livestock and portable objects. The people of the polity preferred displays of portable wealth and ornamented belongings over other status symbols. Torcs and harness may have also been essential in defining certain people in death, through hoards which I have suggested may have been substitutes for burial. Our understanding of the Iceni way of death is extremely limited, but the difference between northern East Anglia and neighbouring areas, such as Cambridgeshire and Essex, is marked. A survey like Hill's (1995a) on Wessex, bringing together disarticulated and fragmentary human remains would be revealing. Further research is needed to analyse the incidence and character of equine remains from sites across the region, to determine if breeding and training occurred.

9.3. Were personal belongings used to show resistance to Roman influence?

Iron Age modes of expressing status and identity persisted under Roman rule, through the manufacture, use and display of objects. The 'Do Different' narrative here presents two sides of the same story. Many objects and sites span the conquest, which reveals the division into LIA and Romano-British as a disciplinary fiction. Although some ways of articulating belonging and difference continued, there is an attendant increase in similarity with other parts of Britain and Europe. I found support for a shift from fragmentation and regional distinctiveness towards greater integration over time. However, it is important to establish that this observation is not 'Romanisation by any other name'. An explanation for this shift may be one of greater connectivity and cultural interchange, otherwise defined as 'globalisation' (e.g. Hodos ed. 2017; Pitts 2007; Pitts and Versluys eds. 2014; Versluys 2014; Woolf 2014).

How do the finds from the study area compare and contrast with their immediate neighbours, the wider region and other Roman provinces? As discussed above, there are complex and distinct intra-regional variations in belongings, which may suggest changing fashions or restrictions on certain objects or practices. The distribution of Westhall-type terrets shows a region-wide exchange network from a manufacturing point at Waldringfield (section 8.10.1). In some cases, items which may have been made in East Anglia have been found in Scotland (Middlebie) and *vice versa* (Snailwell). Long distance travel and communication must therefore be incorporated into our model of portable artefact manufacture and consumption. Martin (1999: 85) identified coinage and horse harness as Icenian cultural indicators in Suffolk, and a lack of early *amphorae*, imported Gallo-Belgic pottery and cremation cemeteries, seen as identifiers of the Trinovantes. Certainly, the widespread nature of harness and chariot fittings and the importance of hoarding, with the absence of individualised wealthy burials and enclosed settlements, are key features of the polity. I have argued that this may relate to a less-hierarchical social structure and the absence of an elite stratum focussed on displays of individual power. The communal aspects of hoards

and the potential for horse harness to represent a value system based on group ownership of livestock support these claims. Regionality and difference are defining features of the British Iron Age (Hill 1999: 186-88). In its individuality and distinctiveness, the region paradoxically achieves greater similarity with other LIA provinces.

A shift in geopolitical dynamics may be responsible for the increased links between East Anglia, Lincolnshire and the East Midlands in the mid-Roman period. This could be due to improved drainage of the Fens and the construction of transport infrastructure, including the Fen Causeway, Peddars Way and the putative ferry across the Wash (Margary 1967). The debate over an Imperial estate has highlighted the importance of the Fenland in the second century CE, with new settlements, farms and warehouses (Catling 2014). Like the *civitas Batavorum*, the wealth of this area was derived from grain and livestock, often explained in the context of military supply (Frere 1987: 268; Vossen and Groot 2009). Alternatively, this may signal expansion of the indigenous practice of horse-breeding into new areas, with many linch-pins and later terret rings on PAS from Norfolk and Lincolnshire. Other belongings reveal a distinctly religious connection between these areas: Hare brooches, Horse-and-rider brooches and figurines, snake jewellery and seal-boxes. This hints at a less economic, more spiritual, union between polities perhaps previously hindered by the perils of passage through the wetlands.

The people of eastern Britain were closely connected with their near neighbours on the mainland before the Roman invasion. My analysis of continental one-piece brooches (section 3.8) demonstrates that there were numerous early first century CE imports. There are also cultural, linguistic and material parallels with the Rhineland, home of the similarly rebellious Batavians, and a potential trade route across the North Sea between the Rhine Delta and the Great Estuary. Acquisition and appropriation of Gaulish material culture, along with items carried into Britain with the Roman army in the early post-conquest years, show that the Iceni were not resisting all imports or acting conservatively. During the contact period and occupation, 'intrusive' objects did flow into the region, accompanied by new people, ideas and practices. Some of these show geographically-restricted distributions, implying that they were treated as extraordinary in some way, such as the clustering of Wide-cuff bracelets in the parishes around West Wickham (Figure 4.19) and the numerous seal-boxes from Walsingham (Figure 7.7).

Was there a 'silent resistance' (Fernández-Götz 2014a: 236) of satire, subversion and defiance in the *civitas*? Certainly, adoption of object types remained highly selective. For example, while Norfolk and Suffolk display a similar taste for miniature votives to Lincolnshire and Gaul, local preferences were for model axes, tools and weapons at the expense of wheels (Gaul) or shields (Lincs.). At one level, the popularity of the cult of Mercury aligns East Anglia with other parts of Roman Britain and Gaul, but representations of the deity in pipeclay are extremely restricted compared to Venus, and pipeclay figurines as a medium show specific regional and social circulation in child burials from Cambridgeshire. Cambridgeshire shows greater connectivity with the southeastern polities focussed on *Verulamium* and *Camulodunum*. This multi-layering of identities as expressed through belongings demonstrates the nuanced results of exploring the data at a variety of scales.

Not only does the Icenian polity stand out against other Roman provinces and the 'classic' Wessex model, it exhibits key differences to neighbouring areas in modes of burial and deposition practice. These allegiances also changed over time, with a closer focus on connections with Lincolnshire and the Midlands developing in the second century CE. I have characterised this as a process of selectivity, rather than an outright rejection of all things Roman which perpetuates the dualistic view of 'Romans vs. Natives'. This is supported by Rippon, who observed that Icenian communities were discerning about which elements of 'being Roman' they wanted to adopt. He also notes the East Anglian people were 'lukewarm towards urban living' and expressed social standing in ways other than through grand architecture, such as the ownership of livestock (2018: 148). The communities of the Icenian *civitas* were not simply resisting Roman cultural forms and clinging blindly to their traditions. They were selectively acquiring and transforming material culture from Gaul, the Mediterranean and other parts of Britain in different parts of the region and at different times. As Pitts observes, 'resistance is too clumsy a term to explain the nuances of these local divergences' (2019: 176).

Much as cultural change has been shown to be multidimensional and discrepant, so what looks like continuity is more likely change that happens incrementally, through the small practices of everyday grooming behaviour, hybrid forms in personal adornment or the strategic adoption of literacy. People were experimenting with new forms and ideas as they presented themselves, modifying, adopting and adapting them to their own local aesthetics and tastes. In a region with a strong metalworking tradition and therefore highly skilled craftspeople, opportunities for experimentation took place at the forefront of some of these artefacts' evolutions, such as brooch production. Nail cleaners revealed regional patterning, with Norfolk having many more handles in the same plane as the loop, Suffolk more right-angle types and Baldock types found only in the south. Improved dating of other toiletry instruments, like tweezers and cosmetic spoons, would no doubt also be productive. Cataloguing and dating of *styli* would enhance analysis of the spread of literacy.

Continuity can also be seen in practices which persisted despite alterations in artefacts, perhaps relating to gender and religious activities. The ongoing importance of ritual deposition and the focus on horses is a good argument against depopulation of the region in the wake of the 'War of Independence'. Norfolk displays a preference for female over male imagery, including pipeclay figurines and vulvate mounts. Does this show women held a high position in Icenian society? Perhaps the story of Boudica is a distorted reflection of cultural norms and female leadership in the region.

9.4. What evidence is there for the post-rebellion famine, depopulation and reallocation of land?

Evidence is lacking for regional impoverishment and depopulation in the aftermath of the Boudican revolt. My research challenges the long-held hypothesis that the Iceni were heavily punished for their part in the anti-Roman rebellion. While an object-based approach cannot directly prove changes in populations, it corroborates the settlement continuity shown by the RRS Project (Smith *et al*. 2016: 214). 'Harried with fire and sword' (Tac. *Ann*. 14.38) is commonly repeated without any real recourse to archaeological evidence. Where are the burnt layers in Iron Age farmsteads? Where are the remains of families who starved to death in the 'ensuing famine' or who were massacred in retributive attacks by the Roman army? The general lack of Iron Age human remains and an identifiable burial tradition in the region make this problematic, although 'war cemeteries' and mass graves have been identified elsewhere (e.g. Redfern and Chamberlain 2011).

In comparison with other militarised zones, the fortresses, garrisons and other Roman military emplacements of the later first century CE are few and far between (Gambash 2012: 12). These include Saham Toney, Ashill, Horstead, Swanton Morley and Coddenham, although several of these sites are unexcavated and known only from aerial photography and surface finds. The stereotype of Iceni depopulation has also been used to make claims for centuriation and drainage schemes, with the 'unlucky remnants' of the rebels doomed to a life of forced labour (Bulst 1961: 506; Frere 2000: 350-55). Centuriation is unproven in Roman Britain and only usually applies around *coloniae*, of which there were none in the study area (Dilke 1971; Frere 2000: 351).

Analysis of Hod Hill and Aucissa brooches may indicate that the territory was not militarised during the first wave of occupation, which would be compatible with the client-kingdom, but saw more soldiers in the aftermath of the revolt. This could be used to argue both for and against the depopulation theory. Comparing the density maps of locally-produced Colchester one-piece brooches and Aucissa/Hod Hill types shows that both were being deposited in areas of indigenous settlement, rather than known forts or marching camps (Figure 3.35, Figure 3.48). Perhaps these 'pseudo-military' brooches were popular markers of status or fashion which caught on during this period and were adapted into local practices of production and display. The presence of *militaria*, including buckles, weaponry and armour, on civilian sites would benefit from further investigation, especially given the ambiguity over Hod Hill brooches. A comparative investigation of 'quasi-military' brooches from other *civitates* would make a useful future study.

My observations about the narrative of the Icenian 'Other' have shown that in neighbouring regions the same data can be interpreted differently. There are multiple opportunities for circularity in the dating of contexts and finds to the Boudican revolt. Archaeology has corroborated the destruction of Colchester and London described in classical sources; therefore, does it support the Icenian harrying at all? If the region were devastated, then repopulated with 'friendly' civilians and/or veterans, there would be no need to subdue the population with a heavy military presence. The genocide of the Rhenish Eburones is partly substantiated by pollen analysis which revealed decreased human exploitation of the landscape after the retributive destruction of their *civitas*, although complete depopulation was not indicated and certain forms of material culture, architecture and religious practice continued (Fernández-Götz 2014a: 235-36). A similar programme of analysis could be informative in East Anglia.

My data, spatial and chronological analyses do not demonstrate a major population shift in the Iceni polity, and most settlements appear to continue throughout the first century CE and onwards. Sites such as Hacheston and Saham Toney have pre-conquest, client-kingdom and post-revolt activity. Here, the brooch profiles (Figure 3.122, Figure 3.126) show early first century CE types, (Rosettes, Nauheim Derivatives, Langton Downs and Colchesters), mid-late first century CE brooches (the Colchester Derivatives and the Hod Hills) as well as the plate brooches, Polden Hills and Trumpets which stretch into the second century CE. The sheer quantity of material culture indicates that there was no widespread hiatus owing to a 'harrying' by occupying Roman forces. There are numerous brooches, other forms of personal ornament and horse harness which attest to this continuity. The 'hybrid' cremation burials from Norwich (section 5.6.1) also provide evidence against the cultural impoverishment hypothesis (Gurney 1998: 23-27).

There is occasional evidence for desertion of indigenous settlements. Sedgeford is one example of where there may have been population collapse and reuse of the landscape (SHARP 2014: 31-32). West Stow is another (West 1989: 109), although it is all too easy to ascribe abandonment to the Boudican rebellion. The brooch profiles show there was certainly activity in those parishes in the later first-third centuries CE, particularly the proportion of plate brooches from West Stow and Trumpets at Sedgeford (Figure 9.1, Figure 9.2). The abandonment at West Stow was not accompanied by great destruction. Similarly, the ritual site at Thetford was purposefully dismantled, perhaps with a relocation of the sacred focus (Hingley and Unwin 2005: 104-5), which I have suggested may have been at Hockwold-cum-Wilton. Likewise, the religious centre at Snettisham may have transferred to the shrine at Walsingham (Marsden 2014: 70). The construction of a road between Saham Toney and *Venta Icenorum*

via Crownthorpe (NHER: 52027) must also have been intended to ensure continued connection between these important sites.[1] A very recently announced discovery at Cressing, Essex has been interpreted as an Iron Age village destroyed in 'Boudiccan reprisals', although full results and dating evidence are yet to be published (Greef and Moan 2020: 12-13).

The boundary between the LIA and early Roman period is not especially clear in the small finds, nor the settlement or air photograph data, revealing it as a largely modern disciplinary construction. Neither does the material culture mirror the political changes so vividly described in classical literature. The real shifts seem to occur earlier (with the *fibula* event horizon) and later (the abandonment horizon).

9.5. The Object Abandonment Horizon

Hill's identification of the '*fibula* event horizon' (1995a: 66) drew attention to the appearance of significant numbers of brooches, as well as other small objects like grooming implements, in the century between Caesar's forays into southern Britain and the Claudian conquest. Gosden noted a consequent decline in the production of 'virtuoso' pieces often considered Iron Age 'art' (2005: 203). Pitts describes an 'object boom' of an 'ever-proliferating array of more ordinary objects' (2019: 38-39). Over the ensuing two centuries, certain object types flourished, but then fade from the archaeological record during the second century CE. This has been termed the '*fibula* abandonment horizon' (Cool and Baxter 2016a: 94-95). Mackreth also observed the dramatic decline in brooches around 200 CE, proposing that all later brooches were worn by military or official personnel, specifically men in powerful, or high-status, roles (2011: 236).

My study has shown that, like the event horizon, this extends well beyond brooches to many other small finds. It includes most bow brooches, fasteners, seal-boxes and signet rings, mirrors, pipeclay figurines, cosmetic grinders and possibly miniature votives. Other artefact categories abide, and sometimes proliferate, beyond the turn of the third century CE: finger-rings, bracelets, nail cleaners, and specific brooches such as Knee, Crossbow and Penannulars.

Explanations for this ebb and flow in the artefactual tide could include simple deposition, recovery and dating processes. Certain objects, such as linch-pins, change material from bronze and iron composites to all-ferrous versions, which would mean fewer survive in the ground. In other cases, the same practices may have continued with different material culture, like the reduction of votive miniatures at shrines in favour of deposition of large numbers of coins in the later Roman period (Bagnall Smith 1999). Pipeclay figurines crash at the same time as

---

[1] David Ratledge Travelling with the Romans http://www.twithr.co.uk/ norfolk/caistor-saham.htm

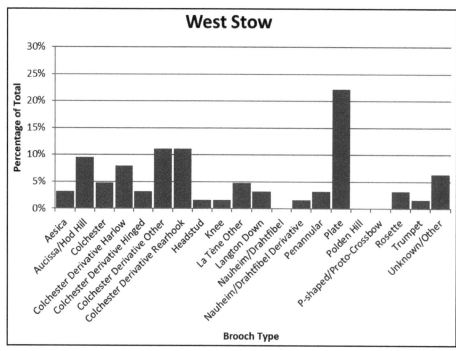

Figure 9.1. Percentages of brooches by type, West Stow (63 brooches).

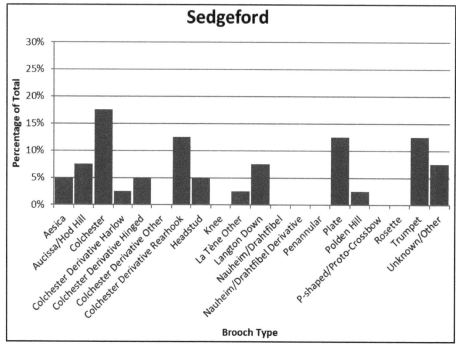

Figure 9.2. Percentages of brooches by type, Sedgeford (40 brooches).

the samian manufactories in Gaul. Toggles, fasteners and brooches could have been abandoned in preference for laces and thongs or sewn clothing. Changes in the display of gender roles, religious allegiance or social status may account for the restricted brooch types which persist beyond the abandonment horizon. Pitts suggests '*fibulae* had lost the power and allure that was part and parcel of social display in Late Iron Age Europe' (2019: 139).

It is worth noting that the abandonment begins earlier in Gaul than in the Icenian *civitas*, with a 'terminal decline' of *fibulae* in Gaulish cemeteries in the Flavian period

(Pitts 2019: 137-39). A sharp reduction in brooch deposition in Essex was also observed from *circa* 70 CE onwards (Wardle 2013: 203). This has been associated with the repression and military intervention due to the Boudican revolt (Perring and Pitts 2013: 246). This does not explain why the people of the Iceni heartland continued to produce and deposit brooches for longer than their southern neighbours. Neither is it a straightforward centre-periphery process of 'becoming Roman' (Pitts 2019: 139). Intra-regional variation also occurs, which may represent shifting allegiances within the *civitas*, and it is not simply items of Iron Age or indigenous origin which drop out of use. Further analysis and interpretation will be necessary to unravel the intricacies of these observations.

9.6. The Iceni Menagerie: Zoomorphics

Zoomorphic objects make up only a small proportion of the sample. Yet, broad trends in the various animals represented show how people's ideas of, and relationships to, the natural world may have changed. By cutting across individual artefact categories, it is possible to assess the prevalence of different species. Using this approach, what can be discerned about age or gender identities, indigenous or incoming attitudes, and regional or religious preferences?

Finds associated with Iron Age manufacture or usage (e.g. cosmetic sets, horse harness and drinking vessels) depict a limited selection of animals. These are mostly restricted to birds, particularly waterbirds, and bovids, perhaps associated with hunting or healing. The symbolism of 'wild' or powerful creatures like wolves and horses was appropriate on coins alone and, in the case of boars, helmets and shields. Despite Dio's evocative telling of Boudica's performance on the battlefield, hares are almost never represented on pre-conquest objects. Like horses, they begin to appear on Romano-British brooches and figurines (e.g. PAS: NARC-EA98E1, SWYOR-6EAEB1, KENT-9B0EB4).

Depictions of animals in the Iron Age were often highly stylised, such as the rather 'disjointed' horses and the crocodile-like wolf on East Anglian coinage, or the birds encoded within the Waldringfield terret moulds (section 8.10.1). By the conquest period, linch-pin terminals presented more mixed or hybrid messages, including dogs, waterbirds, horses' hooves and phallic imagery, probably apotropaic symbols for good fortune or protection during travel (Crummy 2011: 67). This aligns with cosmetic grinders which also display 'alien' phallic symbolism alongside the more 'British' bovids and birds.

Under Roman occupation, a novel range of animal imagery is represented on seal-boxes, figurines and plate brooches. While waterbirds continued to be popular, other species become recognisable, such as eagles and corvids on staff terminals (e.g. PAS: NMS-E9AF55, SF-D4D044), or chickens and owls on brooches. A wider assortment of mammals is represented, including *exotica* like lions, leopards and even an elephant from Crownthorpe temple (NWHCM: 1983.43.7). Conversely, the abstraction of animal forms continued to be a significant aesthetic. The carnelian intaglios from the Snettisham Jeweller's Hoard display a broad spectrum, from an ant to a dolphin, in a distinctive, schematic style. This reflects the need for multiple symbols to identify individuals, perhaps like medieval merchants' marks. Eagles were the most common animal motifs on both intaglios and seal-boxes, sometimes shown attacking a hare, a possible metaphor for imperial power over its provinces (Marshman 2015: 106, 117).

There is some evidence of gender preferences for zoomorphic personal adornment during the occupation. Cosmetic grinders are more often found in female graves (Jackson 2010: 50-62). Mackreth felt the evidence for gendered plate brooches, other than Châtelaines, was inconclusive (2011: 235), although those with cast attachment loops may have been worn with female attire. Associations of female gender with domesticated or prey animals simply replicate outdated structuralist distinctions which assume that women and children were rooted in the domestic sphere, while men focussed on warfare and economics. Zoomorphic pipeclay figurines are associated with burials of young children. Ivleva (2017: 86) suggests that zoomorphic plate brooches may have decorated children's clothing. Few contextual data are available to correlate brooch size with age group, although miniature plate brooches, including zoomorphics, are scarce. If diminutive bow brooches were used to fasten children's clothing, this may be indicative of an appropriate age for zoomorphic brooches, or that they reflect adult practices, such as religious adherence.

Clear regional preferences have been identified which vary over time as well as space. East Anglia has concentrations of animal symbolism, with more zoomorphic cosmetic grinders in Norfolk and Suffolk than elsewhere (Jackson 2010: 61). Birds are more common in central Norfolk and the northwest. Brooches depicting hares/rabbits and horses are especially common in the East and East Midlands. Marsden connects hare brooches with the worship of Venus, suggesting they may have replaced pipeclay figurines as votives when the industry collapsed (2014: 65). This adds further weight to the preference for female symbolism in northern East Anglia. A dozen hare brooches were found in Leicestershire, associated with the temple at Bosworth and a large quantity of Horse-and-rider brooches. Even these trends are subject to the intra-regional layering discussed above: Suffolk has a high proportion of brooches depicting horses without riders, while Norfolk has numerous Horse-and-rider brooches, but only horse figurines. Cambridgeshire has more of both types of figurines, but barely any equine brooches. This may purely reflect survival and deposition practices, or point to local interpretations of popular cults.

Zoomorphic brooches and figurines around temples signify devotional offerings of animals or their proxies to the gods (Marsden 2014: 54, 64). Plate brooches with animal symbolism are more common at sites with temples, such as Crownthorpe, Charsfield, Hockwold-cum-Wilton and Walsingham. It is intriguing that no zoomorphic seal-boxes have been recorded from Hockwold or Walsingham, while both have cosmetic mortars representing animals. This may reflect their mid-late Roman heyday or selective deposition of votives at specific shrines. A centre-looped mortar from Hindringham represents a fish or dolphin (NHER: 25007). Around *Venta Icenorum*, there are several brooches depicting fish, possibly denoting a shrine to Neptune, who is named on the Caistor *defixio*. There are also significant numbers of finds representing a likely Mercury cult at the *civitas* capital, including rings, figurines and seal-boxes depicting cockerels and sheep/goats.

Many zoomorphic object types discussed above were victims of the artefact 'abandonment horizon' in the third century CE. One of my observations is how poorly votive and miniature objects are dated and interpreted. Like many large-scale catalogues compiled during the mid-20th century, Green's volumes (1976, 1978) are overdue for an update. A revised catalogue of Romano-British religious small finds and a thorough review of their dates, roles and relationships is needed. Durham (2012) has gone some way by reassessing religious figurines. Roman magic and ritual have also been reconsidered by Parker and McKie (eds. 2018). Enamel colour schemes and the application of white metal trim (considered an indigenous invention by Mackreth) on plate brooches, seal-boxes and button-and-loop fasteners would make an interesting comparative study relating to manufacture and design.

9.7. How do metal-detector finds impact on the archaeological interpretation of the region?

Metal-detected surface finds have significant research potential when viewed across a wide area and in conjunction with stratified finds. The wealth of metal-detector data from East Anglia, particularly over the last few decades, has significantly changed our interpretation of the region's archaeology. Without it, we would be reliant on results from 'keyhole' excavations, which often focus on specific site types like towns and forts, or developer-led projects which are not based on specific research agendas. Despite certain, sometimes valid, question marks over ethics or recovery, my research shows that detector records are hugely beneficial, particularly when analysed *en masse*. The success of PAS shows there is a will to record and the number of research projects utilising PAS data is growing, with 772 thus far.[2] While the recovery of more artefacts from Norfolk and Suffolk than other parts of Britain may introduce an element of bias, it has been shown that finds are not purely concentrated in areas of high detector usage. The advantages of working with large datasets and distribution analysis allow for some of the inevitable inaccuracies to be evened out. Discussions with detectorists revealed a variable picture of recovery which depended on weather and soil conditions and the type of machine in use (Appendix B). Outreach to local detecting clubs and voluntary groups has already shared the results of my research with over 800 people, many of whom contributed to the original raw data by recording their finds with the HER or PAS.[3]

My study has also shown the value of an integrated approach which uses the PAS data to calibrate other sources, like HER records and grey literature. In some cases, this has helped to correct the perceived bias, such

as filling in Mackreth's 'black hole' in Suffolk (2011: 3), with the result that the figures for Trumpet brooches look much more consistent (section 3.11.4). Concentrations of surface finds can also flag up areas for future, more detailed, investigation. The many subtypes of brooches e.g. Trumpet, Headstud or Disc would profit from in-depth analysis, especially given Cool and Baxter's warnings about biases in the East Anglian dataset (2016a, 2016b). Raising awareness of possible morphological bias with detecting clubs and other participants is important. My research adds to the contributions made by recent PAS studies including Brindle (2014), Robbins (2012) and Statton (2016). The ongoing and sometimes dramatic increase in small finds from a variety of categories, even when compared to relatively recent studies (Figure 2.5), implies that more frequent reviews of material culture *corpora* must be made to ensure interpretation keeps pace with recovery and recording.

Duplication between PAS and HERs is also an issue which needs to be resolved. In future, an integrated online register and archive, along the lines of PAS or the Celtic Coin Index, would assist with searching and collating small finds from multiple sources. Streamlining of PAS descriptions and consistency in terminology is crucial for comprehensive searches. Best practice guidelines for the use of field-based GPS to fully geo-locate finds are to be encouraged. Romano-British mirror fragments are overlooked by detectorists and academics alike, leading to recording bias. Along with miniature lead axes and one-piece brooches, these often wind up in the scrap box. Training for other finders and recorders is recommended to reduce this bias and increase the geographical coverage.[4]

9.8. The Great Estuary

Plotting large-scale distributions of finds can also have unintended benefits. I observed that findspots rarely plot within the bounds of the 'Great Estuary' (Figure 9.3). There are two potential explanations: this may be evidence that in the Iron Age and Roman periods the Estuary was indeed roughly where projected. Alternatively, the distributions may be biased, partly because much of the relevant area is within the Norfolk Broads National Park or recorders deliberately do not plot finds there. The only finds which stray within the estuarine boundary are a few brooches from the Waveney Valley around Mettingham and Barsham. Other categories of finds largely respect the Estuary boundaries. An interesting cluster at Langley warrants further investigation. Peterson (2009) is one of the few who contested the idea of the Great Estuary. He argued that Roman period finds have been made in the area considered to have been submerged, and that the sandbar across the mouth of the Estuary at Great Yarmouth may have periodically been reoccupied. As in the Fenland, this

---

[2] https://finds.org.uk/research [Accessed: 22/11/2020].
[3] 'Closing the Loop' M4C post-doctoral project 2019.

[4] Since this research was carried out, I have delivered training on brooches to PAS staff, finders and volunteers, advised on brooch identification guidance and written a blog on Iron Age and Roman mirrors https://finds.org.uk/counties/blog/iron-age-and-roman-mirrors-from-east-anglia/

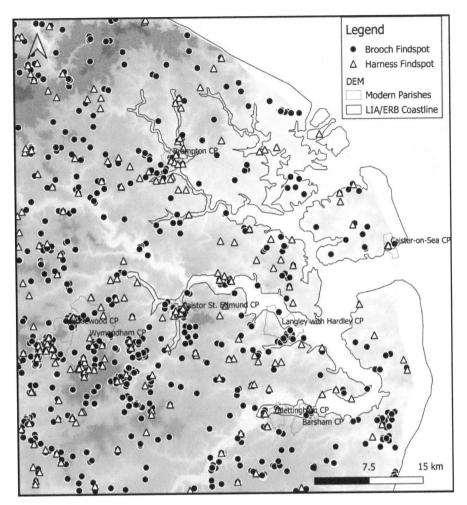

Figure 9.3. Brooch and harness finds around the Great Estuary.

coastal part could have become more habitable as water levels decreased throughout the Roman period.

Future research would be beneficial on the Great Estuary, plotting finds around contours, looking for evidence from dredgings, adding Lidar data to the NMP and most importantly testing on the ground. A targeted programme of research-led excavation in Norfolk directed at key sites known only from metal-detector, aerial photography and field survey, such as Saham Toney and Great Walsingham, is long overdue. The potential benefits are evident from the success of the Caistor Roman Project in reinterpreting the story of the *civitas* capital. Many of the research questions left open here, surrounding dating, military activity and ritual foci, could be answered by such excavations.

9.9. Summary

These results show the value of combining multiple datasets and the important contribution of responsible metal-detector use and recording. Looking for difference, oddities and hybrids has proved fruitful. This study has confirmed that interpretations based on classical narratives of the Icenian 'tribal territory', its militarisation and abandonment are questionable. This has wider implications for studies of other historically-attested peoples and regions. My study of portable artefacts demonstrates the complex and selective processes of resistance and connectedness, and shows that the people of the *civitas Icenorum* were highly innovative and engaged. In this way, I hope to have liberated discussions of the 'Iceni' from the constraints of cultural conservatism and the discourse of the Boudican revolt.

Bibliography

Classical Sources

Caesar (trans. H. Edwards). 1917. *Bellum Gallicum*. Loeb. DOI: 10.4159/DLCL.caesar-gallic_wars.1917.

Dio, Cassius (trans. E. Cary) 1925. *Historiae Romanae*, Books 61-70. Loeb. Cambridge, MA: Harvard University Press.

Martial (trans. D. Bailey). 1993. *Epigrams*. Loeb. DOI: 10.4159/DLCL.martial-epigrams.1993.

Ovid (trans. G. Showerman). 1914. *Amores*. Loeb. DOI: 10.4159/DLCL.ovid-amores.1914.

Pliny the Elder (trans. W. Jones). 1938. *Naturalis Historia*. Loeb. DOI: 10.4159/DLCL.pliny_elder-natural_ history.1938.

Propertius (trans G. Goold). 1990. *Elegies*. Loeb. DOI: 10.4159/DLCL.propertius-elegies.1990.

Strabo (trans. H. Jones). 1923. *Geographia*, Vol. 2, Books 3-5. Loeb. Cambridge, MA: Harvard University Press.

Tacitus (trans. M. Hutton, W. Peterson). 1914. *Agricola*. Loeb. Cambridge, MA: Harvard University Press. DOI: 10.4159/DLCL.tacitus-agricola.1914.

Tacitus (trans. M. Hutton). 1914. *Germania*. Loeb. Cambridge, MA: Harvard University Press. DOI: 10.4159/DLCL.tacitus-germania.1914.

Tacitus (trans. J. Jackson). 1937. *Annales*, Books 8-16. Loeb. Cambridge, MA: Harvard University Press.

Tacitus (trans. C. Moore). 1951. *Histories*. Loeb 249. London: Heinemann.

Online Sources

Allen, M., Blick, N., Brindle, T., Evans, T., Fulford, M., Holbrook, N., Richards, J. and Smith, A. 2016. *The Rural Settlement of Roman Britain*. York: ADS. https: //doi.org/10.5284/1030449

ADS: http: //archaeologydataservice.ac.uk

Cambridgeshire HER: http: //www.cambridgeshire.gov.uk/ info/20011/archives_archaeology_and_museums/318/ archaeology/5

Department for Communities and Local Government. 1990. *Planning Policy Guidance 16*. London: The Stationery Office. http: //webarchive.nationalarchives. gov.uk/20120919132719/http: //www.communities.gov. uk/documents/planningandbuilding/pdf/156777.pdf

Department for Communities and Local Government. 2010. *Planning Policy Statement 5*. London: The Stationery Office. http: //webarchive.nationalarchives. gov.uk/20120919132719/www.communities.gov.uk/ archived/publications/planningandbuilding/pps5

Durham, E. 2012. Depicting the Gods: Metal figurines in Roman Britain. *Internet Archaeology* 31. https: //doi. org/10.11141/ia.31.2.

FISH Thesaurus: http: //thesaurus.historicengland.org.uk/ thesaurus.asp?thes_no=144&thes_name=FISH%20 Archaeological%20Objects%20Thesaurus

Heritage Gateway: http: //www.heritagegateway.org.uk/ gateway/chr/default.aspx

Magic Map: www.magic.gov.uk/magicmap

MODES News. 2015. *Archaeology: Can you dig it?* http: //www.modes.org.uk/news/latest-posts/2015/02/25/ archaeology-can-you-dig-it/ [Accessed: 06/01/2017].

Norfolk Heritage Explorer: http: //www.heritage.norfolk. gov.uk

PAS: https: //finds.org.uk

Smith, A. 2013. *The Roman Rural Settlement Project*. http: //www.reading.ac.uk/web/files/archaeology/ Rural_settlement_Roman_Britain_AlexSmith.pdf [Accessed: 08/01/2014].

Suffolk Heritage Explorer: https: //heritage.suffolk.gov.uk

Treasure Act 1996: https: //www.legislation.gov.uk/ ukpga/1996/24/contents

Tyers, P. 2014. *Potsherd: Atlas of Roman pottery*. http: // potsherd.net/atlas/potsherd

UKDFD. 2007. *Lies, Damn Lies and the Hobby's Detractors*. https: //www.ukdfd.co.uk/pages/our-hobbys-detractors.html [Accessed: 28/07/2016].

Worrell, S. Autumn 2007. *Roman Brooch Timeline*. PAS Regional Newsletter North. www.finds.org.uk.

Modern Sources

Adams, S. 2013. *The First Brooches in Britain*. Unpublished PhD thesis: University of Leicester.

Albone, J., Massey, S. and Tremlett, S. 2007a. *The Archaeology of Norfolk's Broads Zone*. Gressenhall: Norfolk Landscape Archaeology.

Albone, J., Massey, S. and Tremlett, S. 2007b. *The Archaeology of Norfolk's Coastal Zone*. Gressenhall: Norfolk Landscape Archaeology.

Alföldi, A. 1949. The Bronze Mace from Willingham Fen, Cambridgeshire. *Journal of Roman Studies* 39(1-2): 19-22.

Aldhouse-Green, M. 2006. *Boudica Britannia*. Harlow: Pearson Education.

Allason-Jones, L. 1989. *Women in Roman Britain*. London: BM Press.

Allason-Jones, L. 2011. *Jet, Shale and other Allied Materials*. Roman Finds Group Datasheet 2. www.romanfinds.org.uk [Accessed: 09/11/2015].

Allen, D. 1970. The Coins of the Iceni. *Britannia* 1: 1-33.

Allison, P. 2008. Measuring Women's Influence on Roman Military Life. *Internet Archaeology* 24. https: //doi.org/10.11141/ia.24.5.

Andrews, C. n.d. *Roman Seal Boxes*. Roman Finds Group Datasheet 4. www.romanfinds.org.uk [Accessed: 09/11/2015].

Andrews, C. 2012. *Roman Seal-Boxes in Britain*. BAR British Series 567. Oxford: BAR Publishing.

Andrews, C. 2013. Are Roman Seal-boxes Evidence for Literacy? *Journal of Roman Archaeology* 26: 423-438.

Anon. 1951. Roman Britain in 1950. Britannia 41(1-2): 120-145.

Appadurai, A. (ed.) 1986. *The Social Life of Things*. Cambridge: Cambridge University Press.

Argent, G. 2010. Do the clothes make the horse? *World Archaeology* 42(2): 157-174.

Argent, G. 2016. Killing (Constructed) Horses, 19-32 in L. Broderick (ed.) *People with Animals*. Oxford: Oxbow.

Armour, N. 2007. *The ARES Site, Babraham Research Campus*. CAU Report 752. Cambridge: CAU.

Ashwin, T. and Bates, S. 2000. *Excavations on the Norwich Southern Bypass, 1989-91*. EAA 91. Gressenhall: NMS.

Ashwin T. and Tester, A. 2014. *A Roman Settlement in the Waveney Valley*. EAA 152. Gressenhall: NAU.

Atkins, R. 2011. *Bronze Age Beaker pits and a Late Iron Age into Roman Settlement on land off Stirling Way, Nr. Witchford, Ely*. OAE Report 1134. Cambridge: OAE.

Atkins, R. 2013. *Iron Age to Roman Settlement at Low Park Corner, Chippenham*. OAE Report 1275. Cambridge: OAE.

Atkins, R. and Connor, A. 2010. *Farmers and Ironsmiths*. EAA 134. Bar Hill: OAE.

Atkinson, D. 1931. Caistor Excavations, 1929. *Norfolk Archaeology* 24: 93-139.

Atkinson, D. 1932. Three Caistor Pottery Kilns. *Journal of Roman Studies* 22(1): 33-46.

Bagnall Smith, J. 1999. Votive Objects and Objects of Votive Significance from Great Walsingham. *Britannia* 30: 21-56.

Baharal, D. 1992. The Portraits of Julia Domna from the Years 193-211 A.D. and the Dynastic Propaganda of L. Septimius Severus. *Latomus* 51(1): 110-118.

Baldwin, A. and Joy, J. 2017. *A Celtic Feast: The Iron Age cauldrons from Chiseldon, Wiltshire*. Research Publication 203. London: BM Press.

Barnard, S. 1985. The *Matres* of Roman Britain. *Archaeological Journal* 142: 237-245.

Barrett, J. 1997. Romanization: A critical comment, 51-64 in D. Mattingly (ed.) *Dialogues in Roman Imperialism*. Journal of Roman Archaeology Supplementary Series 23. Portsmouth, R.I.: JRA.

Barth, F. (ed.) 1969. *Ethnic Groups and Boundaries*. Boston, MA: Little Brown and Co.

Bates, S., Ashwin, T., Davies, J., Gale, R., Lyons, A., Percival, S., Starley, D., Turner-Walker, C., Mortimer, C., and Davies, J.A. 2000. Excavations at Quidney Farm, Saham Toney, Norfolk 1995. *Britannia* 31: 201-237.

Bayley, J. 1989. Specialist Reports: Analyses of the brooches and crucibles, 179-181 in K. Blockley, *Prestatyn 1984-5*. BAR British Series 210. Oxford: Oxbow.

Bayley, J. 1995. *Crucibles and Moulds*. Historical Metallurgy Society: Archaeology Datasheet 1. http: //hist-met.org/images/pdf/hmsdatasheet01.pdf [Accessed: 17/01/2017].

Bayley, J. and Butcher, S. 2004. *Roman Brooches in Britain*. London: Society of Antiquaries.

Bayley, J., Gurney, D. and Mackreth, D. 2004. Two Roman Brooch Finds from Hockering and Felmingham. *Norfolk Archaeology* 44(3): 540-2.

Bayley, J., Mackreth, D. and Wallis, H. 2001. Evidence for Romano-British Brooch Production at Old Buckenham, Norfolk. *Britannia* 32: 93-118.

Beaudry, M., Cook, L. and Mrozowski, S. 1991. Artifacts and Active Voices, 150-191 in R. McGuire and R. Paynter (eds.) *The Archaeology of Inequality*. Oxford: Blackwell.

Bedikian, S. 2008. The Death of Mourning. *Omega* 57(1): 35-52.

de la Bédoyère, G. 2006. *Roman Britain*. London: Thames and Hudson.

Bell, C. 1992. *Ritual Theory, Ritual Practice*. Oxford: Oxford University Press.

Bendrey, R. 2010. The Horse, 10-16 in T. O'Connor and N. Sykes (eds.) *Extinctions and Invasions*. Oxford: Oxbow.

Bescoby, D., Bowden, W., Wallis, H., Green, F. and Fryer, V. (forthcoming) Late Holocene evolution of the Tas Valley in W. Bowden (ed.) *Venta Icenorum: Excavations and Surveys 2006-2014*. London: Society for the Promotion of Roman Studies.

Bird, J. 2011. Religious Life, 269-292 in L. Allason-Jones (ed.) *Artefacts in Roman Britain*. Cambridge: Cambridge University Press.

Blagg, T., Plouviez, J. and Tester, A. 2004. *Excavations at a large Romano-British settlement at Hacheston, Suffolk, 1973-74*. EAA 106. Ipswich: SCC.

Bliss, A. 2020. Re-appraising and Re-classifying: A new look at the corpus of miniature socketed axes from Britain. *Proc. Hampshire Field Club Archaeol. Soc.* 75(1): 1–27.

Blockley, K., Day, M. with Mackreth, D. Moulds, 183-192 in K. Blockley, *Prestatyn 1984-5*. BAR British Series 210. Oxford: Oxbow.

Booth, A. 2014. *Reassessing the Long Chronology of the Penannular Brooch in Britain*. Unpublished PhD thesis: University of Leicester.

Booth, P., Simmonds, A., Boyle, A., Clough, S., Cool, H. and Poore, D. 2010. *The Late Roman Cemetery at Lankhills, Winchester, Excavations 2000-2005*. Oxford Archaeology Monograph 10. Oxford: Oxford Archaeological Unit.

Booth, T. and Madgwick, R. 2016. New Evidence for Diverse Secondary Burial Practices in Iron Age Britain. *Journal of Archaeological Science* 67: 14-24.

Bourdieu, P. 1977. *Outline of a Theory of Practice*. Cambridge: Cambridge University Press.

Bourdieu, P. 2010. *Distinction*. London: Taylor and Francis. https: //ebookcentral.proquest.com/lib/nottingham/detail.action?docID=1433990 [First published 1979].

Bowden, W. 2011. Architectural Innovation in the Land of the Iceni. *Journal of Roman Archaeology* 24: 382–388.

Bowden, W. 2012. The Iceni Under Rome. *Current Archaeology* 270: 28-35.

Bowden, W. 2013a. The Urban Plan of *Venta Icenorum* and its relationship with the Boudican revolt. *Britannia* 44: 145-169.

Bowden, W. 2013b. Townscape and Identity at Caistor-by-Norwich, 47-62 in H. Eckardt, H. and S. Rippon (eds.) *Living and Working in the Roman World*. Journal of Roman Archaeology Supplementary Series 95. Portsmouth, R.I.: JRA.

Bowden, W. 2017. *Venta Icenorum*: 'Doing different' in the Land of the Iceni. *British Archaeology* 153: 20-25.

Bowden, W. (forthcoming) *Venta Icenorum: Excavations and Surveys 2006-2014*. London: Society for the Promotion of Roman Studies.

Bowden, W. and Bescoby, D. 2008. The Plan of *Venta Icenorum* (Caistor-by-Norwich). *Journal of Roman Archaeology* 21: 324-334.

Bowman, A. and Thomas, J. 1987. New Texts from *Vindolanda*. *Britannia* 18: 125-142.

Bowman, A. and Woolf, G. 1994. Literacy and Power in the Ancient World, 1-16 in A. Bowman and G. Woolf (eds.) *Literacy and Power in the Ancient World*. Cambridge: Cambridge University Press.

Božič, D. and Feugère, M. 2004. Les Instruments de l'Ecriture. *Gallia* 61: 21-41.

Bradley, R. 2000. *An Archaeology of Natural Places*. London: Routledge.

Bradley, R. 2003. A Life Less Ordinary. *Cambridge Archaeological Journal* 13(1): 5-23.

Bradley, R. 2005. *Ritual and Domestic Life in Prehistoric Europe*. London: Routledge.

Brailsford, J. 1968. A Hoard of Early Iron Age Gold Torcs from Ipswich. *PSIAH* 31(2): 158-9.

Braund, D. 1996. *Ruling Roman Britain*. London: Routledge.

Brindle, T. 2010. The Portable Antiquities Scheme and Roman Rural Settlement, 121-133 in S. Worrell, G. Egan, J. Naylor, K. Leahy and M. Lewis (eds.) *A Decade of Discovery*. BAR British Series 520. Oxford: BAR Publishing.

Brindle, T. 2014. *The Portable Antiquities Scheme and Roman Britain*. BM Research Publication 196. London: BM Press.

Brown, R. 1986. The Iron Age and Romano-British Settlement at Woodcock Hall, Saham Toney, Norfolk. *Britannia* 17: 1-58.

Brudenell, M. and Cooper, A. 2008. Post-Middenism. *Oxford Journal of Archaeology* 27(1): 15-36.

Bulst, C. 1961. *The Revolt of Queen Boudicca in A.D. 60*. Historia: Zeitschrift für Alte Geschichte, Bd. 10, H. 4: 496-509.

Burnham, B. and Wacher, J. 1990. *The 'Small Towns' of Roman Britain*. London: BT Batsford.

Butler, J. 2006. *Gender Trouble*. London: Routledge. [First published 1990].

Carr, G. 2001. 'Romanisation' and the Body, 112-124 in G. Davies, A. Gardner and K. Lockyear (eds.) *TRAC 2000: Proceedings of the Tenth Annual Theoretical Roman Archaeology Conference*. Oxford: Oxbow.

Carr, G. 2003. Creolisation, Pidginisation and the Interpretation of Unique Artefacts in Early Roman Britain, 113-125 in G. Carr, E. Swift and J. Weekes (eds.) *TRAC 2002: Proceedings of the 12th Annual Theoretical Roman Archaeology Conference*. Oxford: Oxbow.

Carr, G. 2005. Woad, Tattooing and Identity in Later Iron Age and Early Roman Britain. *Oxford Journal of Archaeology* 24(3): 273-292.

Carr, G. 2006. *Creolised Bodies and Hybrid Identities*. BAR British Series 418. Oxford: BAR Publishing.

Carr, G. and Knüsel, C. 1997. The Ritual Framework of Excarnation by Exposure as the Mortuary Practice of the Early and Middle Iron Ages of Central Southern Britain, 167-173 in A. Gwilt and C. Haselgrove (eds.) *Reconstructing Iron Age Societies*. Oxford: Oxbow Monograph 71.

Carroll, M. 2012. The Insignia of Women. *Archaeological Journal* 169(1): 281-311.

Catling, C. 2014. Excavating Earith. *Current Archaeology* 295: 28-35.

Chadburn, A. 2006. *Aspects of the Iron Age Coinage of Northern East Anglia with especial reference to hoards.* Unpublished PhD thesis: University of Nottingham [2 vols].

Champion, T. 2016. Britain before the Romans, 150-178 in M. Millett, L. Revell and A. Moore (eds.) *The Oxford Handbook of Roman Britain.* Oxford: Oxford University Press.

Chapman, E., Hunter, F., Booth, P., Wilson, P., Pearce, J. Worrell, S. and Tomlin, R. 2012. Roman Britain in 2011. *Britannia* 43: 272-354.

Chester-Kadwell, M. 2009. *Early Anglo-Saxon Communities in the Landscape of Norfolk.* BAR British Series 481. Oxford: BAR Publishing.

Childe, V. 1980. *Prehistoric communities of the British Isles.* New York: Arno Press. [First published 1940].

Clarke, R. 1939. The Iron Age in Norfolk and Suffolk. *Archaeological Journal* 96: 1-113.

Clarke, R. 1951. A Hoard of Metalwork of the Early Iron Age from Ringstead, Norfolk. *PPS* 17(2): 214-225.

Clarke, R. and Dolley, R. 1955. The Early Iron Age Treasure from Snettisham Norfolk. *PPS* 20(1): 27-86.

Clarke, S. 1995. Locational Models and the Study of Romano-British Small Towns, 81-91 in P. Rush (ed.) *Theoretical Roman Archaeology: Second Conference Proceedings.* Aldershot: Avebury.

Collingridge, V. 2005. *Boudica.* London: Ebury Press.

Collis, J. 2007. The Polities of Gaul, Britain and Ireland in the Late Iron Age, 523-528 in C. Haselgrove and T. Moore (eds.) *The Later Iron Age in Britain and Beyond.* Oxford: Oxbow.

Cool, H. 1983. *A Study of the Roman Personal Ornaments made of Metal, Excluding Brooches, from Southern Britain.* Unpublished PhD thesis: University of Wales.

Cool, H. 2000. The Significance of Snake Jewellery Hoards. *Britannia* 31: 29-40.

Cool, H. 2006. *Eating and Drinking in Roman Britain.* Cambridge: Cambridge University Press.

Cool, H. 2011. Funerary Contexts, 293-312 in L. Allason-Jones (ed.) *Artefacts in Roman Britain.* Cambridge: Cambridge University Press.

Cool, H. 2016. Clothing and Identity, 406-424 in M. Millett, L. Revell and A. Moore (eds.) *The Oxford Handbook of Roman Britain.* Oxford: Oxford University Press.

Cool, H. and Baxter, M. 2016a. Brooches and Britannia. *Britannia* 47: 71-98.

Cool, H. and Baxter, M. 2016b. Exploring Morphological Bias in Metal-detected Finds. *Antiquity* 90 354: 1643-1653.

Cooper, N. 1996. Searching for the Blank Generation, 85-98 in J. Webster and N. Cooper (eds.) *Roman Imperialism.* Leicester Archaeology Monographs 3. Leicester: University of Leicester School of Archaeological Studies.

Crawford, S. and Shepherd, G. (eds.) 2007. *Children, Childhood and Society.* BAR International Series 1696. Oxford: BAR Publishing.

Creighton, J. 1992. The Decline and Fall of the Icenian Monetary System, 83-92 in M. Mays (ed.) *Celtic Coinage.* BAR British Series 222. Oxford: BAR Publishing.

Creighton, J. 1994. A Time of Change. *Oxford Journal of Archaeology* 13(3): 325-334.

Creighton, J. 1995. Visions of Power. *Britannia* 26: 285-301.

Creighton, J. 2000. *Coins and Power in Late Iron Age Britain.* Cambridge: Cambridge University Press.

Creighton, J. 2006. *Britannia.* London: Routledge.

Crerar, B. 2006. Votive Leaf or Feather Plaques from Roman Britain, 71-89 in M. Henig (ed.) *Roman Art, Religion and Society.* BAR International Series 1577. Oxford: BAR Publishing.

Croom, A. 2004. Personal Ornament, 288-298 in M. Todd (ed.) *A Companion to Roman Britain.* Oxford: Blackwell.

Crumley, C. 1987. A Dialectical Critique of Hierarchy, 155-69 in T. Patterson and C. Gailey (eds.) *Power Relations and State Formation.* Washington, D.C.: American Anthropological Association.

Crummy, N. 1983. *The Roman Small Finds from Excavations in Colchester 1971-79.* Colchester Archaeological Reports No 2. Colchester Archaeological Trust. http://cat.essex.ac.uk/reports/CAR-report-0002.pdf

Crummy, N. 2002. Wax *Spatula* Handle from Yorkshire. Roman Finds Group Newsletter. *Lucerna* 23: 6-8.

Crummy, N. 2005. From Bracelets to Battle-Honours, 93-105 in N. Crummy (ed.) *Image, Craft and the Classical World.* Monographies Instrumentum 29. Montagnac: Mergoil.

Crummy, N. 2007a. Brooches and the Cult of Mercury. *Britannia* 38: 225-230.

Crummy, N. 2007b. Six Honest Serving Men, 59-66 in R. Hingley and S. Willis (eds.) *Roman Finds.* Oxford: Oxbow.

Crummy, N. 2011. Travel and Transport, 46-67 in L. Allason-Jones (ed.) *Artefacts in Roman Britain.* Cambridge: Cambridge University Press.

Crummy, N. 2012. Characterising the Small Finds Assemblage from Silchester's Insula IX (1997-2009), 105-125 in M. Fulford (ed.) *Silchester and the study of Romano-British Urbanism*. Journal of Roman Archaeology Supplementary Series 90. Portsmouth, R.I.: JRA.

Crummy, N. 2013. Attitudes to the Hare in Town and Country, 111-127 in H. Eckardt, H. and S. Rippon (eds.) *Living and Working in the Roman World*. Journal of Roman Archaeology Supplementary Series 95. Portsmouth, R.I.: JRA.

Crummy, N. 2016. Toilet Instruments: Symbols of dissent? *Oxford Journal of Archaeology* 35(3): 285–293.

Crummy, N. and Eckardt, H. 2003. Regional Identities and Technologies of the Self. *Archaeological Journal* 160: 44-69.

Crummy, N., Henig, M. and Ward, C. 2016. A Hoard of Military Awards, Jewellery and Coins from Colchester. *Britannia* 47: 1-28.

Crummy, P. and Wightman, A. with Crummy, N. 2015. The Fenwick Treasure. *Current Archaeology* 308: 22-29.

Curle, J. 1911. *A Roman Frontier Post and its People*. Armatura Press. Online edition 2004. http://www.curlesnewstead.co.uk [Accessed: 06/01/2017].

Darling, M. and Gurney, D. 1993. *Caister-on-Sea*. EAA 60. Gressenhall: NMS.

Dasen, V. 2014. Healing Images. *Oxford Journal of Archaeology* 33(2): 177-191.

Daubney, A. 2010. The Cult of Totatis, 109-120 in S. Worrell, G. Egan, J. Naylor, K. Leahy and M. Lewis (eds.) *A Decade of Discovery*. BAR British Series 520. Oxford: BAR Publishing.

Davies, J. 1996. Where Eagles Dare. *PPS* 62: 63-92.

Davies, J. 1999. Patterns, Power and Political Progress in Iron Age Norfolk, 14-43 in J. Davies and T. Williamson (eds.) *Land of the Iceni*. Norwich: Centre of East Anglian Studies.

Davies, J. 2009. *The Land of Boudica*. Oxford: Oxbow.

Davies, J. 2011a. Boars, Bulls and Norfolk's Celtic Menagerie, 59-68 in J. Davies (ed.) *The Iron Age in Northern East Anglia*. BAR British Series 549. Oxford: BAR Publishing.

Davies, J. 2011b. Closing Thoughts, 103-105 in J. Davies (ed.) *The Iron Age in Northern East Anglia*. BAR British Series 549. Oxford: BAR Publishing.

Davies, J. 2011c. Ten Years After, 1-2 in J. Davies (ed.) *The Iron Age in Northern East Anglia*. BAR British Series 549. Oxford: BAR Publishing.

Davies, J. 2014. The Boudica Code, 27-34 in S. Ashley and A. Marsden (eds.) *Landscapes and Artefacts*. Oxford: Archaeopress.

Davies, J. and Gregory, T. 1991. Coinage from a *Civitas*. *Britannia* 22: 65-101.

Davies, J. and Robinson, B. 2009. *Boudica*. Cromer: Poppyland Publishing.

Davies, J. and Williamson, T. 1999. Introduction: Studying the Iron Age, 7-13 in J. Davies and T. Williamson (eds.) *Land of the Iceni*. Norwich: Centre of East Anglian Studies.

Davis, M. 2014. *Technology at the Transition*. Unpublished PhD thesis: University of Cardiff.

Davis, M. and Gwilt, A. 2008. Material, Style and Identity in First Century AD Metalwork, 146-184 in D. Garrow, C. Gosden and J.D. Hill (eds.) *Rethinking Celtic Art*. Oxford: Oxbow.

Davy, J. 2016. *Miniaturisation: A study of a material culture practice among the indigenous peoples of the Pacific Northwest*. Unpublished PhD thesis: UCL.

Dawson, A. 2008. 'Minerva' Wax *Spatula* Handle from near Norwich. Roman Finds Group Newsletter. *Lucerna* 35: 2.

DeMarrais, E. 2016. Making Pacts and Cooperative Acts. *World Archaeology* 48(1): 1–13.

Derks, T. 1998. *Gods, Temples and Ritual Practices*. Amsterdam: Amsterdam University Press.

Derks, T. and Roymans, N. 2002. Seal-boxes and the Spread of Latin Literacy in the Rhine Delta, 87-134 in A. Cooley (ed.) *Becoming Roman, Writing Latin?* Journal of Roman Archaeology Supplementary Series 48. Portsmouth, R.I.: JRA.

Derks, T. and Roymans, N. 2009. Introduction, 10-21 in T. Derks and N. Roymans (eds.) *Ethnic Constructs in Antiquity*. Amsterdam: Amsterdam University Press. ProQuest Ebook Central. [Accessed: 29/05/2018]. https://ebookcentral.proquest.com/lib/nottingham/detail.action?docID=435488.

Deyts, S. 1983. *Les Bois Sculptés des Sources de la Seine*. Gallia Supplement 42. Paris: Centre National de la Recherche Scientifique.

Dilke, O. 1971. *The Roman Land Surveyors*. Newton Abbott: David and Charles.

Dobney, K. and Ervynck, A. 2007. To Fish or Not to Fish? 403-418 in C. Haselgrove and T. Moore (eds.) *The Later Iron Age in Britain and Beyond*. Oxford: Oxbow.

Dungworth, D. 1998. Mystifying Roman Nails, 148–159 in C. Forcey, J. Hawthorne and R. Witcher (eds.) *TRAC 97: Proceedings of the Seventh Annual Theoretical Roman Archaeology Conference, Nottingham*. Oxford: Oxbow.

Dungworth, D. 2016. Metals and Metalworking, 532-554 in M. Millett, L. Revell and A. Moore (eds.) *The Oxford Handbook of Roman Britain*. Oxford: Oxford University Press.

Eckardt, H. 1999. The Colchester 'Child's Grave'. *Britannia* 30: 57-90.

Eckardt, H. 2005. The Social Distribution of Roman Artefacts. *Journal of Roman Archaeology* 18: 139-160.

Eckardt, H. 2008. Technologies of the Body, 113-128 in D. Garrow, C. Gosden and J.D. Hill (eds.) *Rethinking Celtic Art*. Oxford: Oxbow.

Eckardt, H. 2013. Shoe brooches in Roman Britain, 217-234 in H. Eckardt and S. Rippon (eds.) *Living and Working in the Roman World*. Journal of Roman Archaeology Supplementary Series 95. Portsmouth, R.I.: JRA.

Eckardt, H. 2014. *Objects and Identities*. Oxford: Oxford University Press.

Eckardt, H. 2017. Age of Ink. *Current Archaeology* 328: 26-32.

Eckardt, H. 2018. *Writing and Power in the Roman World*. Cambridge: Cambridge University Press.

Eckardt, H. and Crummy, N. 2008. *Styling the Body in Late Iron Age and Roman Britain*. Montagnac: Monique Mergoil.

Effros, B. 2004. Dressing Conservatively, 165-184 in L. Brubaker and J. Smith (eds.) *Gender in the Early Medieval World*. Cambridge: Cambridge University Press.

Ehrenreich, R., Crumley, C. and Levy, J. (eds.) 1995. *Heterarchy and the Analysis of Complex Societies*. Ann Arbor: American Anthropological Association 6.

Emberling, G. 1997. Ethnicity in Complex Societies. *Journal of Archaeological Research* 5(4)4: 295-344.

Evans, C. 2003. Britons and Romans at Chatteris. *Britannia* 34: 175-264.

Fairclough, J. 2010. *Boudica to Raedwald*. Ipswich: Malthouse Press.

Farley, J. 2011. The Deposition of Miniature Weaponry in Iron Age Lincolnshire. *PALLAS* 86: 97-121.

Farley, J. 2012. *At the Edge of Empire*. Unpublished PhD thesis: University of Leicester.

Farley, J. 2015. The Celtic Riddle. *Current Archaeology* 307: 12-17.

Fernández-Götz, M. 2014a. *Identity and Power*. Amsterdam: Amsterdam University Press.

Fernández-Götz, M. 2014b. Reassessing the Oppida. *Oxford Journal of Archaeology* 33(4): 379–394.

Ferris, I. 2012. *Roman Britain through its Objects*. Stroud: Amberley.

Feugère, M. 1985. *Les fibules en Gaule Méridionale de la conquête à la fin du Ve s. ap. J.-C.* Revue archéologique de Narbonnaise, Supplement 12. Paris: Centre National de la Recherche Scientifique.

Fillery-Travis, R. 2012. Multidisciplinary Analysis of Roman Horse-and-rider Brooches from Bosworth, 135-162 in I. Schrüfer-Kolb (ed.) *More Than Just Numbers?* Journal of Roman Archaeology Supplementary Series 91. Portsmouth, R.I.: JRA.

Fincham, G. 2002. *Landscapes of Imperialism*. BAR British Series 338. Oxford: BAR Publishing.

Fittock, M. 2015. Broken Deities. *Britannia* 46: 111-34.

Fittock, M. 2016. *Pipeclay Figurines*. Roman Finds Group Datasheet 6. http: //www.romanfindsgroup.org. uk/public/files/datasheets/Pipeclay%20figurines%20 datasheet.pdf [Accessed: 04/07/2017]

Fitzpatrick, A. 1992. The Snettisham, Norfolk, Hoards of Iron Age Torques. *Antiquity* 66: 395-8.

Flitcroft, M. 2001. *Excavation of a Romano-British Settlement on the A149 Snettisham Bypass, 1989*. EAA 93. Gressenhall: NMS.

Foster, J. 1995. Metalworking in the British Iron Age, 49-60 in B. Raftery (ed.) *Sites and Sights of the Iron Age*. Oxbow Monograph 56. Oxford: Oxbow.

Foster, J. 2014. Hidden Faces and Animal Images on Late Iron Age and Early Roman Horse Harness, 56-67 in C. Gosden, S. Crawford and K. Ulmschneider (eds.) *Celtic Art in Europe*. Oxford: Oxbow.

Fowler, C. 2004. *The Archaeology of Personhood*. London: Routledge.

Fowler, E. 1960. The Origins and Development of the Penannular Brooch in Europe. *PPS* 26: 149-177.

Frere, S. 1971. The Forum and Baths at Caistor by Norwich. *Britannia* 2: 1-26.

Frere, S. 1972. The Caistor Intaglio. *Britannia* 3: 295-296

Frere, S. 1984. Roman Britain in 1983. *Britannia* 15: 265-332.

Frere, S. 1991. *Britannia*. London: Pimlico. [First published 1967].

Frere, S. 2000. A *Limitatio* of Icenian Territory? *Britannia* 31: 350-355.

Frere, S. 2005. The South Gate and Defences of *Venta Icenorum*. *Britannia* 36: 311-327.

Furger, A. and Riha, E. 2009. Definition und Verwendung der Siegelkapseln, 17-25 in A. Furger, M. Wartmann and E. Riha (eds.) *Die römischen Siegelkapseln aus Augusta Raurica*. http: //www.augustaraurica.ch/fileadmin/ user_upload/2_Arch%C3%A4ologie/7_Literatur%20 und%20Verlag/02_Forschungen_in_Augst/Fia44.pdf.

Gambash, G. 2012. To Rule a Ferocious Province. *Britannia* 43: 1-15.

Gardner, A. 2002. Social Identity and the Duality of Structure in Late Roman-Period Britain. *Journal of Social Archaeology* 2(3): 323-351.

Gardner, A. 2007. *An Archaeology of Identity*. Walnut Creek: Left Coast Press.

Gardner, A. 2013. Thinking about Roman Imperialism. *Britannia* 44: 1-25.

Garrow, D. and Gosden, C. 2012. *Technologies of Enchantment?* Oxford: Oxford University Press.

Geake, H. 2002. New Wax *Spatulae* from Suffolk. Roman Finds Group Newsletter *Lucerna* 24: 14-15.

Gell, A. 1998. *Art and Agency*. Oxford: Clarendon Press.

Gibbs, L. 1987. Identifying Gender Representation in the Archaeological Record, 79-89 in I. Hodder (ed.) *The Archaeology of Contextual Meanings*. Cambridge: Cambridge University Press.

Giddens, A. 1984. *The Constitution of Society*. Cambridge: Polity Press.

Giles, M. 2012. *A Forged Glamour*. Oxford: Windgather Press.

Gill, D. 2010. Forum: The Portable Antiquities Scheme and the Treasure Act. *Papers from the Institute of Archaeology* 20: 1-11.

Glare, P. (ed.) 2012. *Oxford Latin Dictionary*. Oxford: Oxford University Press.

Glob, P. [trans. R. Bruce-Mitford] 1971. *The Bog People*. London: Paladin.

Going, C., Green, M., Duhig, C. and Taylor, A. 1997. A Roman Child Burial with Animal Figurines and Pottery. *Britannia* 28: 386-393.

Gosden, C. 2005. What Do Objects Want? *Journal of Archaeological Method and Theory* 12(3): 193-211.

Gosden, C. and Hill, J.D. 2008. Introduction: re-integrating 'Celtic' art, 1-14 in D. Garrow, C. Gosden and J.D. Hill (eds.) *Rethinking Celtic Art*. Oxford: Oxbow.

Gosden, C. and Marshall, Y. 1999. The Cultural Biography of Objects. *World Archaeology* 31(2): 169-178.

Grahame, M. 1998. Redefining Romanization, 1-10 in C. Forcey, J. Hawthorne and R. Witcher (eds.) *TRAC 97: Proceedings of the Seventh Annual Theoretical Roman Archaeology Conference, Nottingham*. Oxford: Oxbow.

Greef, A. and Moan, P. November 2020. Tye Green, Cressing, Essex: An Iron Age village with evidence of Boudiccan reprisals? *In Touch* 54: 12-13. Oxford Archaeology Review 2019-2020.

Green, B. 1993. The Iron Age, 32 in P. Wade-Martins (ed.) *An Historical Atlas of Norfolk*. Norwich: NMS.

Green, H. 1977. *Godmanchester*. Cambridge: Oleander Press.

Green, M. 1976. *The Religions of Civilian Roman Britain*. BAR British Series 24. Oxford: BAR Publishing.

Green, M. 1978. *A Corpus of Small Cult-Objects from the Military Areas of Roman Britain*. BAR British Series 52. Oxford: BAR Publishing.

Green, M. 1981. Model Objects from Military Areas of Roman Britain. *Britannia* 12: 253-269.

Green, M. 1984. *The Wheel as a Cult-Symbol in the Romano-Celtic World*. Brussels: Latomus.

Green, M. 1998. God in Man's Image. *Britannia* 29: 17-30.

Gregory, T. 1980. Two Iron Age Linch-Pins from Norfolk. *Norfolk Archaeology* 37(3): 338-341.

Gregory, T. 1991a. *Excavations in Thetford 1980-1982, Fison Way*. EAA 53. Gressenhall: NMS.

Gregory, T. 1991b. Metal-detecting on a Scheduled Ancient Monument. *Norfolk Archaeology* 41(2): 186-196.

Gregory, T. and Gurney, D. 1986. *Excavations at Thornham, Warham, Wighton and Caistor St Edmund, Norfolk*. EAA 30. Gressenhall: NMS.

Gregory, T. and Martin, E. 1985. An Iron Age Terret from Rushmere. *PSIAH* 36(1): 34-5.

Gui, M. 2015. Button-and-loop Fasteners from *Porolissum* and the Rest of Dacia, 213-217 in A. Dobos, D. Petruţ, S. Berecki, L. Vass, S. Pánczél, Zs. Molnár-Kovács and P. Forisek (eds.) *Archaeologia Transylvanica*. Budapest: Opitz.

Gurney, D. 1986. *Settlement, Religion and Industry on the Fen-edge*. EAA 31. Gressenhall: NMS.

Gurney, D. 1993. The Roman Period, 34 in P. Wade-Martins (ed.) *An Historical Atlas of Norfolk*. Norwich: NMS.

Gurney, D. 1995. Small Towns and Villages of Roman Norfolk, 53-67 in A. Brown (ed.) *Roman Small Towns in Eastern England and Beyond*. Oxbow Monograph 52. Oxford: Oxbow.

Gurney, D. 1997. A Note on the Distribution of Metal-detecting in Norfolk. *Norfolk Archaeology* 42(4): 528-532.

Gurney, D. 1998. *Roman Burials in Norfolk*. EAA Occasional Paper 4. Gressenhall: NMS.

Gurney, D. 2000. Archaeological Finds in Norfolk. *Norfolk Archaeology* 43(3): 516-521.

Gurney, D. 2003. Archaeological Finds in Norfolk. *Norfolk Archaeology* 44(2): 356-368.

Halkon, P., Lyall, J., Deverell, J., Hunt, T. and Fernández-Götz, M. 2019. Arras 200. *Antiquity* 93 368, e11: 1–7.

Hanson, W. 1997. Forces of Change and Methods of Control, 67-80 in D. Mattingly (ed.) *Dialogues in Roman Imperialism*. Journal of Roman Archaeology Supplementary Series 23. Portsmouth, R.I.: JRA.

Harlow, M. 2004. Clothes Maketh the Man, 44-69 in L. Brubaker and J. Smith (eds.) *Gender in the Early Medieval World*. Cambridge: Cambridge University Press.

Harlow, N. 2016. Belonging and Belongings in the Land of the Iceni. NAHRG. *The Annual* 25: 43-60.

Harlow, N. 2017. Across the Great Divide, 75-82 in R. O'Sullivan, C. Marini and J. Binnberg (eds.) *Archaeological Approaches to Breaking Boundaries.* BAR International Series 2869. Oxford: BAR.

Harlow, N. 2018. Resistance is Useless! Culture, Status, and Power in the *Civitas Icenorum. Theoretical Roman Archaeology Journal* 1(1): 4. DOI: http://doi.org/10.16995/traj.350

Harlow, N. 2019. Roman Bone Gaming Counters from Caistor St Edmund. *Lucerna* 56: 7-13.

Harlow, N. (forthcoming) The Small Finds, in W. Bowden *et al. Venta Icenorum: Excavations and Surveys 2006-2014.* Britannia Monographs.

Haselgrove, C. 1985. Inference from Ploughsoil Artefact Samples, 7-29 in C. Haselgrove, M. Millett and I. Smith (eds.) *Archaeology from the Ploughsoil.* University of Sheffield: John R. Collis.

Haselgrove, C. 1992. Iron Age Coinage and Archaeology, 123-137 in M. Mays (ed.) *Celtic Coinage.* BAR British Series 222. Oxford: BAR Publishing.

Haselgrove, C. 1996. Roman Impact on Rural Settlement and Society in Southern Picardy, 127-187 in N. Roymans (ed.) *From the Sword to the Plough.* Amsterdam: Amsterdam University Press.

Haselgrove, C. 1997. Iron Age Brooch Deposition and Chronology, 51-72 in A. Gwilt and C. Haselgrove (eds.) *Reconstructing Iron Age Societies.* Oxbow Monograph 71. Oxford: Oxbow.

Haselgrove, C. 2002. The Romanization of Belgic Gaul, 45-71 in T. Blagg and M. Millett (eds.) *The Early Roman Empire in the West.* Oxford: Oxbow. [First published 1990].

Haselgrove, C. 2015. Hoarding and Other Forms of Metalwork Deposition in Iron Age Britain, 27-40 in J. Naylor and R. Bland (eds.) *Hoarding and the Deposition of Metalwork from the Bronze Age to the 20th Century.* BAR British Series 615. Oxford: BAR Publishing.

Haselgrove, C. and Moore, T. 2007. New Narratives of the Later Iron Age, 1-15 in C. Haselgrove and T. Moore (eds.) *The Later Iron Age in Britain and Beyond.* Oxford: Oxbow.

Hassall, M. and Tomlin, R. 1982. Roman Britain in 1981. *Britannia* 13: 396-422.

Hassall, M. and Tomlin, R. 1994. Roman Britain in 1993. *Britannia* 25: 293-314.

Hattatt, R. 1982. *Ancient and Romano-British Brooches.* Sherborne: Dorset Publishing.

Hattatt, R. 1985. *Iron Age and Roman Brooches.* Oxford: Oxbow.

Hattatt, R. 1987. *Brooches of Antiquity.* Oxford: Oxbow.

Hattatt, R. 1989. *Ancient Brooches and other Artefacts.* Oxford: Oxbow.

Hattatt, R. 2007. *A Visual Catalogue of Richard Hattatt's Ancient Brooches.* Oxford: Oxbow.

Haverfield, F. 1901. Romano-British Remains, 279-324 in Doubleday, H. (ed.) *The Victoria History of the Counties of England. A History of Norfolk Vol I.* London: Archibald Constable and Co. [1975 reprint by Dawson, Folkestone].

Hawkes, G. 1999. Beyond Romanization. *Papers from the Institute of Archaeology* 10: 89–95.

Hawkes, C. and Dunning, G. 1930. The Belgae of Gaul and Britain. *Archaeological Journal* 87(1): 150-335.

Heeren, S. and van der Feijst, L. 2017. *Prehistorische, Romeinse en middeleeuwse fibulae uit de Lage Landen.* Amersfoort: Eigen Beheer.

Henig, M. 1974. *A Corpus of Roman Engraved Gemstones from British Sites.* BAR British Series 8. Oxford: BAR [2 vols].

Henig, M. 1984. *Religion in Roman Britain.* London: B.T. Batsford.

Henig, M. 2002. *The Heirs of King Verica.* Stroud: Tempus.

Henig, M. 2006. *Engraved Gemstones.* Roman Finds Group Datasheet 1 http: //www.romanfindsgroup.org.uk/public/files/datasheets/Engraved%20gemstones%20(datasheet%201).pdf [Accessed: 09/11/2015].

Hill, J.D. 1995a. *Ritual and Rubbish in the Iron Age of Wessex.* BAR British Series 242. Oxford: BAR Publishing.

Hill, J.D. 1995b. The Pre-Roman Iron Age in Britain and Ireland. *Journal of World Prehistory* 9(1): 47-98.

Hill, J.D. 1997. The End of One Kind of Body and the Beginning of Another Kind of Body? 96-107 in A. Gwilt and C. Haselgrove (eds.) *Reconstructing Iron Age Societies.* Oxbow Monograph 71. Oxford: Oxbow.

Hill, J.D. 1999. Settlement, Landscape and Regionality, 185-207 in J. Davies and T. Williamson (eds.) *Land of the Iceni.* Norwich: Centre of East Anglian Studies.

Hill, J.D. 2001. Romanisation, Gender and Class, 12-18 in S. James and M. Millett (eds.) *Britons and Romans.* CBA Research Report 125. York: CBA.

Hill, J.D. 2007. The Dynamics of Social Change in Later Iron Age Eastern and South-eastern England, 16-40 in C. Haselgrove and T. Moore (eds.) *The Later Iron Age in Britain and Beyond.* Oxford: Oxbow.

Hill, J.D. 2011. How did British Middle and Late Pre-Roman Iron Age Societies Work (if they did?), 242-263 in T. Moore and X-L. Armada (eds.) *Atlantic Europe in the First Millennium BC.* Oxford: Oxford University Press.

Hill, J.D. and Hutcheson, N. 2004. Iron Age Horse Harness (2004 T301), 47 in *Treasure Annual Report 2004*. DCMS.

Hinchliffe, J. with Sparey-Green, C. 1985. *Excavations at Brancaster 1974 and 1977*. EAA 23. Gressenhall: NMS.

Hingley, R. 1996. The 'Legacy' of Rome, 35-48 in J. Webster and N. Cooper (eds.) *Roman Imperialism*. Leicester Archaeology Monographs 3. Leicester: University of Leicester School of Archaeological Studies.

Hingley, R. 1997. Resistance and Domination, 81-100 in D. Mattingly (ed.) *Dialogues in Roman Imperialism*. Journal of Roman Archaeology Supplementary Series 23. Portsmouth, R.I.: JRA.

Hingley, R. 2008. Not so Romanized? *World Archaeology* 40(3): 427-443.

Hingley, R. and Unwin, C. 2005. *Boudica: Iron Age Warrior Queen*. London: Hambledon and London.

Hodder, I. (ed.) 1991. The Meaning of Things. *One World Archaeology* 6. London: Harper Collins Academic.

Hodder, I. 2012. *Entangled*. Chichester: Wiley-Blackwell.

Hodder, I. and Hutson, S. 2003. *Reading the Past*. Cambridge: Cambridge University Press.

Hodos, T. 2017. Globalization. Some basics, 3-11 in T. Hodos (ed.) *The Routledge Handbook of Archaeology and Globalization*. London: Routledge.

Hodos, T. (ed.) 2017. *The Routledge Handbook of Archaeology and Globalization*. London: Routledge.

Holmes, B. 2012. *Gender: Antiquity and its legacy*. London: Tauris.

Horn, J. 2015. Tankards of the British Iron Age. *PPS* 81: 311-341.

Hukantaival, S. 2007. Hare's Feet Under a Hearth, 66-75 in V. Immonen, M. Lempiäinen and U. Rosendahl (eds.) *Hortus Novus*. Turku: Finnish Medieval Archaeology Society.

Hull, M. and Hawkes, C. 1987. *Corpus of Ancient Brooches in Britain*. BAR British Series 168. Oxford: BAR.

Hunter, F. 1997. Iron Age Hoarding in Scotland and Northern England, 108-133 in A. Gwilt and C. Haselgrove (eds.) *Reconstructing Iron Age Societies*. Oxbow Monograph 71. Oxford: Oxbow.

Hunter, F. 2007. Artefacts, Regions and Identities in the Northern British Iron Age, 286-296 in C. Haselgrove and T. Moore (eds.) *The Later Iron Age in Britain and Beyond*. Oxford: Oxbow.

Hunter, F. 2008. Celtic Art in Roman Britain, 129-145 in D. Garrow, C. Gosden, and J.D. Hill (eds.) *Rethinking Celtic Art*. Oxford: Oxbow.

Hutcheson, N. 2004. *Later Iron Age Norfolk*. BAR British Series 361. Oxford: BAR Publishing.

Hutcheson, N. 2007. An Archaeological Investigation of Later Iron Age Norfolk, 358-370 in C. Haselgrove and T. Moore (eds.) *The Later Iron Age in Britain and Beyond*. Oxford: Oxbow.

Hutcheson, N. 2011. Excavations at Snettisham, Norfolk, 2004, 41-48 in J. Davies (ed.) *The Iron Age in Northern East Anglia*. BAR British Series 549. Oxford: BAR Publishing.

Insoll, T. 2004. *Archaeology, Ritual, Religion*. London: Routledge.

Ivleva, T. 2016. Britons Abroad. *Current Archaeology* 311: 12-17.

Ivleva, T. 2017. Active Brooches, 69-93 in T. Martin and R. Weetch (eds.) *Dress and Society*. Oxford: Oxbow.

Jackson, R. 1985. Cosmetic Sets from Late Iron Age and Roman Britain. *Britannia* 16: 165-192.

Jackson, R. 1988. *Doctors and Diseases in the Roman Empire*. London: BM Publications.

Jackson, R. 1990. A new Collyrium Stamp from Cambridge and a Corrected Reading of the Stamp from Caistor-by-Norwich. *Britannia* 21: 275-283.

Jackson, R. 2010. *Cosmetic Sets of Late Iron Age and Roman Britain*. BM Research Publication 181. London: BM Press.

Jackson, R. 2011. Medicine and Hygiene, 243-268 in L. Allason-Jones (ed.) *Artefacts in Roman Britain*. Cambridge: Cambridge University Press.

Jackson, R. and Potter, T. 1996. *Excavations at Stonea, Cambridgeshire 1980-1985*. London: BM Press.

James, S. 2010. 'Romanization' and the Peoples of Britain, 187-209 in S. Keay and N. Terrenato (eds.) *Italy and the West*. Oxford: Oxbow. [First published 2001].

Jenkins, F. 1977. *Clay Statuettes of the Roman Western Provinces*. Unpublished PhD thesis: University of Kent.

Jenkins, F. 1983. Report on Venus Statuette from Brampton, in A. Knowles *Excavatores Brantunae*. CBA Group 6 Bulletin 28: 20-26.

Johns, C. 1995. Mounted Men and Sitting Ducks, 103-109 in B. Raftery (ed.) *Sites and Sights of the Iron Age*. Oxbow Monograph 56. Oxford: Oxbow.

Johns, C. 1996a. The Classification and Interpretation of Romano-British Treasures. *Britannia* 27: 1-16.

Johns, C. 1996b. *The Jewellery of Roman Britain*. London: UCL Press.

Johns, C. 1997. *The Snettisham Roman Jeweller's Hoard*. London: BM Press.

Johnson, C. 2002. Two Late Iron Age Warrior Burials Discovered in Kent. *Archaeology International* 6: 14–17.

Jones, B. and Mattingly, D. 1990. *An Atlas of Roman Britain*. Oxford: Blackwell.

Jones, S. 1997. *The Archaeology of Ethnicity*. London: Routledge.

Jordan, A. 2016. Her Mirror, His Sword. *Journal of Archaeological Method and Theory* 23: 870-899.

Joy, J. 2007. *Reflections on the Iron Age*. Unpublished PhD thesis: University of Southampton.

Joy, J. 2009. Reinvigorating Object Biography. *World Archaeology* 41(4): 540-556.

Joy, J. 2010. *Iron Age Mirrors*. BAR British Series 518. Oxford: BAR Publishing.

Joy, J. 2011. The Iron Age, 405-21 in T. Insoll (ed.) *The Oxford Handbook of the Archaeology of Ritual and Religion*. Oxford: Oxford University Press.

Joy, J. 2016. Hoards as Collections. *World Archaeology* 48(2): 239-253.

Joy, J. and Farley, J. (eds.) (forthcoming). *The Snettisham Treasure*. London: BM Press.

Jundi, S. and Hill, J.D. 1998. Brooches and Identities in First Century AD Britain, 125-137 in C. Forcey, J. Hawthorne and R. Witcher (eds.) *TRAC 97: Proceedings of the Seventh Annual Theoretical Roman Archaeology Conference, Nottingham*. Oxford: Oxbow.

Kiernan, P. 2009. *Miniature Votive Offerings in the North-west Provinces of the Roman Empire*. Mainz: Verlag Franz Philipp Rutzen.

Kimes, T., Haselgrove, C. and Hodder, I. 1982. A Method for the Identification of the Location of Regional Cultural Boundaries. *Journal of Anthropological Archaeology* 1: 113-131.

Knowles, A. 1977. The Roman Settlement at Brampton, Norfolk. *Britannia* 8: 209-221.

Knowles, A. 1981. *Excavatores Brantunae*. CBA Group 6 Bulletin 26: 12.

Knowles, A. 1983. *Excavatores Brantunae*. CBA Group 6 Bulletin 28: 20-26.

Krakowa, K. 2019. New Finds from the Pembrokeshire Chariot Burial. *Current Archaeology* 355.

Kurchin, B. 1995. Romans and Britons on the Northern Frontier, 124-131 in P. Rush (ed.) *Theoretical Roman Archaeology: Second Conference Proceedings*. Aldershot: Avebury.

Kusimba, C. 1996. *The Social Context of Iron Forging on the Kenya Coast*. Africa 66(3): 386-410.

L'Hour, M. 1987. Un Site Sous-Marin sur la Côte de l'Armorique. L'épave antique de Ploumanac'h. *Revue Archéologique de l'Ouest* 4: 113-131.

Lamb, A. 2018. The Curious Case of the Iceni and their Relationship with Rome, 106-127 in M. Janković and V. Mihajlović (eds.) *Reflections of Roman Imperialism*. Newcastle-upon-Tyne: Cambridge Scholars.

Laurence, R. 2001. Roman Narratives. *Archaeological Dialogues* 8.2: 90-101.

Laurence, R. 2012. *Roman Archaeology for Historians*. Taylor and Francis. https: //ebookcentral.proquest. com/lib/nottingham/detail.action?docID=981760. [Accessed 05/07/2017].

Leins, I. 2008. What can be Inferred from the Regional Stylistic Diversity of Iron Age Coinage? 100-112 in D. Garrow, C. Gosden and J.D. Hill (eds.) *Rethinking Celtic Art*. Oxford: Oxbow.

Leins, I. 2012. *Numismatic Data Reconsidered*. Unpublished PhD thesis: University of Newcastle.

Lethbridge, T. 1954. Burial of an Iron Age Warrior at Snailwell. *PCAS* 47: 25-37.

Levy, J. 1999. Gender, Power and Heterarchy in Middle-Level Societies, 62-78 in T. Sweeley (ed.) *Manifesting Power*. London: Routledge.

Lewis, A. 2015. *Iron Age and Roman-era Vehicle Terrets from Western and Central Britain*. Unpublished PhD thesis: University of Leicester.

Lewis, M. 1966. *Temples in Roman Britain*. Cambridge: Cambridge University Press.

Lewis, C. and Short, C. 1969. *A Latin Dictionary*. Oxford: Clarendon Press. [First published 1879].

Lloyd-Morgan, G. 1977. Mirrors in Roman Britain, 231-252 in J. Munby and M. Henig (eds.) *Roman Life and Art in Britain*. BAR 41.

Lyons, A. 2017. Roman Britain in 2016: East Anglia. *Britannia* 48: 384-391.

MacGregor, A. 1976. Finds from a Roman Sewer System and an Adjacent Building in Church Street. *The Archaeology of York* 17. York: CBA.

MacGregor, M. 1962. The Early Iron Age Metalwork Hoard from Stanwick. *PPS* 28: 17–57.

MacGregor, M. 1976. *Early Celtic Art in North Britain*. Leicester: Leicester University Press.

Machling, T. and Williamson, R. 2018. 'Up Close and Personal': The later Iron Age Torcs from Newark, Nottinghamshire and Netherurd, Peebleshire. *PPS* 84: 387-403.

Machling, T. and Williamson, R. 2020. *Thoughts on the Grotesque Torc and the Snettisham (Ken Hill) Hoards in the Light of New Research*. DOI: 10.5281/zenodo.4039630.

Mackintosh, M. 1995. *The Divine Rider in the Art of the Western Roman Empire*. BAR International Series 607. Oxford: BAR Publishing.

Mackreth, D. 2009. An Unusual Romano-British Brooch from Norfolk. *Britannia* 40: 137-149.

Mackreth, D. 2011. *Brooches in Late Iron Age and Roman Britain*. Oxford: Oxbow. [2 vols].

McKie, S. 2017. *The Social Significance of Curse Tablets in the North-Western Provinces of the Roman Empire*. Unpublished PhD Thesis: Open University.

McNaughton, P. 1993. *The Mande Blacksmiths: Knowledge, Power, and Art in West Africa*. Bloomington: Indiana University Press.

Malim, T. 2005. *Stonea and the Roman Fens*. Stroud: Tempus.

Manning, W. 1972. Ironwork Hoards in Iron Age and Roman Britain. *Britannia* 2: 224-250.

Margary, I. 1967. *Roman Roads in Britain*. London: John Baker.

Marsden, A. 2012. Piety from the Ploughsoil, 50-65 in T. Heslop, E. Mellings and M. Thøfner (eds.) *Art, Faith and Place in East Anglia*. Woodbridge: Boydell Press.

Marsden, A. 2014. Satyrs, Leopards, Riders and Ravens, 45-72 in S. Ashley and A. Marsden (eds.) *Landscapes and Artefacts*. Oxford: BAR Publishing.

Marshall, M. (In prep). *The Baldock Torc Tradition*.

Marshman, I. 2013. Return to sender? Letters, literacy, and Roman sealing practices. Review of Colin Andrews, Roman Seal-Boxes in Britain. *JRA* 26: 755-759.

Marshman, I. 2015. *Making Your Mark in Britannia*. Unpublished PhD thesis: University of Leicester.

Martin, E. 1978. A New Iron Age Terret from Weybread. *PSIAH* 34(2): 137-140.

Martin, E. 1988. *Burgh: The Iron Age and Roman enclosure*. EAA 40. Ipswich: SCC.

Martin, E. 1999. Suffolk in the Iron Age, 44-99 in J. Davies and T. Williamson (eds.) *Land of the Iceni*. Norwich: Centre of East Anglian Studies.

Martin, E., Feldman, H. and Plouviez, J. 1986. Archaeology in Suffolk 1985. *PSIAH* 36(2): 139-158.

Martin, E., Pendleton, C. and Plouviez, J. 1989. Archaeology in Suffolk 1988. *PSIAH* 37(1): 59-81.

Martin, E., Pendleton, C. and Plouviez, J. 1996. Archaeology in Suffolk 1995. *PSIAH* 38(4): 457-488.

Mattingly, D. 1997. Introduction: Dialogues of power and experience in the Roman Empire, 7-24 in D. Mattingly (ed.) *Dialogues in Roman Imperialism*. Journal of Roman Archaeology Supplementary Series 23. Portsmouth, R.I.: JRA.

Mattingly, D. 2007. *An Imperial Possession*. London: Penguin. [First published 2006].

Mattingly, D. 2008. The Unmaking of Iron Age Identities, 214-218 in D. Garrow, C. Gosden and J.D. Hill (eds.) *Rethinking Celtic Art*. Oxford: Oxbow.

Mattingly, D. 2011. *Imperialism, Power, and Identity*. Princeton: Princeton University Press.

Megaw, J. 1971. A Group of Later Iron Age Collars or Neck-Rings from Western Britain. *British Museum Quarterly* 35(1): 145-156. www.jstor.org/stable/4423078 [Accessed 23/06/20].

Merrifield, R. 1987. *The Archaeology of Ritual and Magic*. London: B.T. Batsford.

Millett, M. 1990. *The Romanization of Britain*. Cambridge: Cambridge University Press.

Millett, M. 2002. Romanization, 35-41 in T. Blagg and M. Millett (eds.) *The Early Roman Empire in the West*. Oxford: Oxbow. [First published 1990].

Millett, M. and Gowland, R. 2015. Infant and child burials rites in Roman Britain. *Britannia* 46: 171-189.

Moore, C. 1973. Two Examples of Late Celtic and Early Roman Metalwork from South Lincolnshire. *Britannia* 4: 153-159.

Moore, I., Plouviez, J. and West, S. 1988. *The Archaeology of Roman Suffolk*. Ipswich: SCC.

Moore, T. 2011. Detribalizing the Later Prehistoric Past. *Journal of Social Archaeology* 11(3): 334-360.

Moore, T. 2012. Beyond the *Oppida*. *Oxford Journal of Archaeology* 31(4): 391–417.

Moretti, D. 2015. Binding Spells and Curse Tablets through Time, 103-121 in N. Armitage (ed.) *The Materiality of Magic*. Havertown: Oxbow Books.

Morrison, W. 2013. A Fresh Eye on Familiar Objects. *Oxford Journal of Archaeology* 32(2): 221-230.

Mould, Q. 2011. Domestic Life, 153-179 in L. Allason-Jones (ed.) *Artefacts in Roman Britain*. Cambridge: Cambridge University Press.

Mudd, A. 2002. *Excavations at Melford Meadows, Brettenham, 1994*. EAA 99. Oxford: Oxford Archaeological Unit.

Myres, J. and Green, B. 1973. *The Anglo-Saxon Cemeteries of Caistor-By-Norwich and Markshall, Norfolk*. London: Thames and Hudson.

Nash Briggs, D. 2011. The Language of Inscriptions on Icenian Coinage, 83-102 in J. Davies (ed.) *The Iron Age in Northern East Anglia*. BAR British Series 549. Oxford: BAR Publishing.

Nash Briggs, D. 2012. Sacred Image and Regional Identity in Late-Prehistoric Norfolk, 30-49 in T. Heslop, E. Mellings and M. Thøfner (eds.) *Art, Faith and Place in East Anglia*. Woodbridge: Boydell Press.

Nash Briggs, D. 2017. Multilingual Coin Inscriptions and their Context in Pre-Roman East Anglia. *Philology* 3: 149-168.

Norfolk Archaeology. 1849. Appendix - Extracts from the Proceedings of the Committee. *Norfolk Archaeology* 4(1): 397-408.

Njoku, O. 1991. Magic, Religion and Iron Technology in Precolonial North-Western Igboland. *Journal of Religion in Africa* 21(3): 194-215.

Oosthuizen, S. 2016. Beyond Hierarchy. *World Archaeology* 48(3): 381-394.

Osborne, R. 2004. Hoards, Votives, Offerings. *World Archaeology* 36(1): 1-10.

Paites, B. 2016. The Manufacture and Symbolism of Radiating Designs on Brooches in Roman Britain. Roman Finds Group Newsletter. *Lucerna* 50: 14-21.

Palk, N. 1984. *Iron Age Bridle-Bits from Britain.* Occasional Paper 10. Edinburgh: University of Edinburgh Department of Archaeology.

Parker, A. 2020. His and Hers, 90-113 in T. Ivleva and R. Collins (eds.) *UnRoman Sex.* London: Routledge.

Parker, A. and McKie, S. (eds.) 2018. *Material Approaches to Roman Magic.* TRAC Themes in Roman Archaeology 2. Oxford: Oxbow.

Parker, B. 2006. Toward an Understanding of Borderland Processes. American *Antiquity* 71(1): 77-100.

Pearce, J. 1997. Death and Time, 174-180 in A. Gwilt and C. Haselgrove (eds.) *Reconstructing Iron Age Societies.* Oxbow Monograph 71. Oxford: Oxbow.

Pearce, J. 2017. The Upper Walbrook Valley Cemetery of Roman London, by C. Harward, N. Powers and S. Watson [review article]. *Archaeological Journal* 174(2): 489-490.

Perring, D. 2013. Town and Country in Roman Britain: Current Perspectives, 1-12 in D. Perring and M. Pitts (eds.) *Alien Cities.* Portslade: Spoilheap Publications.

Perring, D. and Pitts, M. 2013. Conclusions, 243-253 in D. Perring and M. Pitts (eds.) *Alien Cities.* Monograph 7. Portslade: Spoilheap Publications.

Perring, D. and Pitts, M. (eds.) 2013. *Alien Cities.* Monograph 7. Portslade: Spoilheap Publications.

Peterson, J. 2009. Towards a New History of Roman Broadland, 553-570 in M. de Dapper (ed.) *Ol' man river: Geo-Archaeological Aspects of Rivers and River Plains.* Ghent: Academia Press.

Pett, D. 2010. The Portable Antiquities Scheme's Database, 1-18 in S. Worrell, G. Egan, J. Naylor, K. Leahy and M. Lewis (eds.) *A Decade of Discovery.* BAR British Series 520. Oxford: BAR Publishing.

Pitts, M. 2007. The Emperor's New Clothes? *American Journal of Archaeology* 111(4): 693-713.

Pitts, M. 2010. Re-Thinking the Southern British *Oppida.* *European Journal of Archaeology* 13(1): 32–63.

Pitts, M. 2013. Comparative analysis, 231-242 in D. Perring and M. Pitts (eds.) *Alien Cities.* Monograph 7. Portslade: Spoilheap Publications.

Pitts, M. 2019. *The Roman Object Revolution.* Amsterdam: Amsterdam University Press.

Pitts, M. and Versluys, M. 2014. Globalisation and the Roman World, 3-31 in M. Pitts and M. Versluys (eds.) *Globalisation and the Roman World.* New York: Cambridge University Press.

Pitts, M. and Versluys, M. (eds.) 2014. *Globalisation and the Roman World.* New York: Cambridge University Press.

Plouviez, J. 2005. Whose Good Luck? 157-164 in N. Crummy (ed.) *Image, Craft and the Classical World.* Monographies Instrumentum 29. Montagnac: Mergoil.

Plouviez, J. 2008. Counting Brooches, 171-176 in J. Clark, J. Cotton, J. Hall, R. Sherris and H. Swain (eds.) *Londinium and Beyond.* CBA Research Report 156. York: CBA.

Plouviez, J. 2014. Some Roman Brooches from Scole and Elsewhere, 35-44 in S. Ashley and A. Marsden (eds.) *Landscapes and Artefacts.* Oxford: Archaeopress.

Potter, T. and Jackson, R. 1982. The Roman Site of Stonea, Cambridgeshire. *Antiquity* 56: 111-120.

Potter, T. and Robinson, B. 2000. New Roman and Prehistoric Aerial Discoveries at Grandford, Cambridgeshire. *Antiquity* 74: 31-2.

Pudney, C. 2010. Pinning Down Identity, 115-131 in D. Mladenovic and B. Russell (eds.) *TRAC 2010: Proceedings of the Twentieth Annual Theoretical Roman Archaeology Conference.* Oxford: Oxbow.

Pudney, C. 2018. Socio-semiotics and the Symbiosis of Humans, Horses, and Objects in Later Iron Age Britain. *Archaeological Journal* [online] 1-25.

Ralph, S. 2007. *Feasting and Social Complexity in Late Iron Age East Anglia.* BAR British Series 451. Oxford: BAR Publishing.

Rankov, N. 1982. Roman Britain in 1981. *Britannia* 13: 328-95.

Ranson, C. and Cooper, C. n.d. *Archaeological Test Pit Excavations in Chediston 2006, 2007, 2008, 2010 and 2011.* Report for Access Cambridge Archaeology. http://www.access.arch.cam.ac.uk/reports/published/ACA_Chediston_Report.pdf.

Rathbone, S. 2015. It's all gone Pear Shaped: Urbanism, Active Resistance and the Early Settlement Pattern of Ireland, 13-20 in *The Archaeology of Settlement.* Proceedings of the Spring 2014 IAI Conference 3.

Redfern, R. and Chamberlain, A. 2011. A Demographic Analysis of Maiden Castle Hillfort. *International Journal of Paleopathology* 1(1): 68-73.

Revell, L. 2013. Code Switching and Identity in the Western Provinces. *HEROM: Journal on Hellenistic and Roman Material Culture* 2: 123-141.

Revell, L. 2016. *Ways of Being Roman.* Oxford: Oxbow.

Ribeiro, A. 2016. Against Object Agency. *Archaeological Dialogues* 23(2): 229–235.

Richardson, J. 1984. *Roman Provincial Administration 227 BC-AD 117*. Bristol: Classical Press. [First published 1976].

Rigby, V. 2013. The Making of Iron-Age Horse Harness Mounts. *PSIA* 43(1): 24-37.

Rippon, S. 2018. *Kingdom,* Civitas, *and County*. Oxford: Oxford University Press.

Robb, J. 2010. Beyond Agency. *World Archaeology* 42(4): 493-520.

Robbins, K. 2012. *From Past to Present*. Unpublished PhD thesis: University of Southampton.

Robinson, P. 1995. Miniature Socketed Bronze Axes from Wiltshire. *Wiltshire Archaeological and Natural History Magazine* 88: 60-68.

Rodwell, W. 1975. Trinovantian Towns and their Setting, 85-101 in W. Rodwell and T. Rowley (eds.) *Small Towns of Roman Britain*. BAR British Series 15. Oxford: BAR.

Rogerson, A. 1977. Excavations at Scole, 1973, 97-224 in P. Wade-Martins (ed.) *Norfolk: Various papers*. EAA No 5. Gressenhall: NAU.

Rogerson, A. and Ashley, S. 2013. A Selection of Finds from Norfolk Recorded in 2013 and Earlier. *Norfolk Archaeology* 46(4): 554-68.

Ross, A. 1972. A Further Note on the Caistor St Edmund Intaglio. *Britannia* 3: 293-295.

Ross, C. 2011. *'Tribal Territories' from the Humber to the Tyne*. BAR British Series 540. Oxford: BAR Publishing.

Rosten, J. 2007. *Personal Adornment and the Expression of Identity in Roman Britain*. Unpublished PhD thesis: University of Leicester.

Rouvier-Jeanlin, M. 1972. *Les Figurines Gallo-Romaines en Terre Cuite au Musée des Antiquités Nationales*. Gallia Supplementary Series 24. Paris: Centre National de la Recherche Scientifique.

Roymans, N. 1996. The Sword or the Plough, 9-126 in N. Roymans (ed.) *From the Sword to the Plough*. Amsterdam: Amsterdam University Press.

Russell, L. 2004. Drinking from the Penholder. *Cambridge Archaeological Journal* 14(1): 64–67.

Rust, T. 2013. *Architecture, Economics, and Identity in Romano-British 'Small Towns'*. Unpublished PhD thesis: University of Leicester.

Salway, P. 1981. *The Oxford History of England: Roman Britain*. Oxford: Oxford University Press.

Sánchez Natalías, C. 2018. The Medium Matters, 9-16 in A. Parker and S. McKie (eds.) *Material Approaches to Roman Magic*. TRAC Themes in Roman Archaeology 2. Oxford: Oxbow.

Sauer, E. 2004. A Matter of Personal Preference? 114-133 in E. Sauer (ed.) *Archaeology and Ancient History*. London: Routledge.

van der Schriek, J. and van der Schriek, M. 2014. Metal Detecting: Friend or Foe of Conflict Archaeology? *Journal of Community Archaeology and Heritage* 1(3): 228-244.

Scott, E. 1995. Women and Gender Relations in the Roman Empire, 174-189 in P. Rush (ed.) *Theoretical Roman Archaeology: Second Conference Proceedings*. Aldershot: Avebury.

Scott, J. 1990. *Domination and the Arts of Resistance*. New Haven: Yale University Press.

Scott, W. 2017. *The Other Bosworth* Parts 1-6 (PAS blog posts 28/02/17-04/04/17). https: //finds.org.uk/ counties/leicestershire/blog/ [Accessed: 24/07/2017].

Sealey, P. 2015. The *Amphoras*, in M. Atkinson and S. Preston, Heybridge. *Internet Archaeology* 40. http: //dx.doi.org/10.11141/ia.40.1.sealey.

Sealey, P. 2016. Where Have All the People Gone? *Archaeological Journal* 173(1): 30-55.

SHARP (Sedgeford Historical and Archaeological Research Project). 2014. *Digging Sedgeford*. Cromer: Poppyland.

Slater, A. 2009. *Further Archaeological Investigation at the Waste Management Park, Waterbeach*. CAU Report 872. Cambridge: Cambridge Archaeological Unit.

Smith, A., Allen, M., Brindle, T. and Fulford, M. 2016. *The Rural Settlement of Roman Britain 1*. Britannia Monographs 29. London: Society from the Promotion of Roman Studies.

Smith, R. 1909. A Hoard of Metal Found at Santon Downham, Suffolk. *PCAS* 53: 146-163.

Snape, M. 1993. *Roman Brooches from North Britain*. BAR British Series 235. Oxford: BAR Publishing.

Sørensen, M. 1987. Material Order and Cultural Classification, 90-101 in I. Hodder (ed.) *The Archaeology of Contextual Meanings*. Cambridge: Cambridge University Press.

Spradley, K. 2001. Small Finds, 104–111 in G. Davies, A. Gardner and K. Lockyear (eds.) *TRAC 2000: Proceedings of the Tenth Annual Theoretical Roman Archaeology Conference*. Oxford: Oxbow.

Spratling, M. 1972. *Southern British Decorated Bronzes of the Late Pre-Roman Iron Age*. Unpublished PhD thesis: University of London Institute of Archaeology.

Spratling, M. 1975. Fragments of a *Lorica Segmentata* in the Hoard from Santon, Norfolk. *Britannia* 6: 206-7.

Spratling, M. 2008. On the Aesthetics of the Ancient Britons, 185-202 in D. Garrow, C. Gosden and J.D. Hill (eds.) *Rethinking Celtic Art*. Oxford: Oxbow.

Statton, M. 2016. *Dress, Adornment and Identity in Late Iron Age and Roman Britain*. Unpublished PhD thesis: UCL.

Stead, I. 1971. The Reconstruction of Iron Age Buckets from Aylesford and Baldock. *British Museum Quarterly* 35(1): 250-282.

Stead, I. 1991. The Snettisham Treasure. *Antiquity* 65: 447-65.

Stewart, P. 1995. Inventing Britain. *Britannia* 26: 1-10.

Stewart, S. 1993. *On Longing*. Durham: Duke University Press.

Sweely, T. (ed.) 1999. *Manifesting Power*. London: Routledge.

Swift, E. 1999. *Regionality in the Late Roman West*. Unpublished PhD thesis: UCL.

Swift, E. 2011. Personal Ornament, 194-218 in L. Allason-Jones (ed.) *Artefacts in Roman Britain*. Cambridge: Cambridge University Press.

Swift, E. 2017. *Roman Artefacts and Society*. Oxford: Oxford University Press.

Swift, E., Stoner, J. and Pudsey, A. (forthcoming*). A Social Archaeology of Roman and Late Antique Egypt*. Oxford: Oxford University Press.

Sykes, N. 2014. *Beastly Questions*. London: Bloomsbury.

Talbot, J. 2011. Icenian Coin Production, 69-82 in J. Davies (ed.) *The Iron Age in Northern East Anglia*. BAR British Series 549. Oxford: BAR Publishing.

Talbot, J. 2015. *What is Icenian Coinage?* Unpublished PhD thesis: University of Oxford, School of Archaeology.

Talbot, J. 2017. *Made for Trade: A New View of Icenian Coinage*. Oxford: Oxbow.

Talbot, J. and Leins, I. 2010. Before Boudicca. *British Numismatic Journal* 80: 1-23.

Taylor, A. 1993. A Roman Lead Coffin with Pipeclay Figurines from Arrington, Cambridgeshire. *Britannia* 24: 191-225.

Taylor, J. 2007. *An Atlas of Roman Rural Settlement in England*. CBA Research Report 151. York: CBA.

Taylor, J. 2013. Roman Urbanism. *Oxford Journal of Archaeology* 32(4): 413-432.

Tebbutt, C. and Fox, C. 1961. Celtic Linch-pin Heads from Colne Fen, Huntingdonshire. *Antiquaries Journal* 41: 235-8.

Tilley, C. 1990. Claude Lévi-Strauss: Structuralism and Beyond, 3-81 in C. Tilley (ed.) *Reading Material Culture*. Oxford: Blackwell.

Todd, M. 1970. The Small Towns of Roman Britain. *Britannia* 1: 114-130.

Todd, M. 1999. *Roman Britain*. Oxford: Blackwell. [Third edition].

Tomlin, R. and Hassall, M. 2006. Roman Britain in 2005. *Britannia* 37: 467-488.

Toynbee, J. 1973. *Animals in Roman Life and Art*. Baltimore: John Hopkins University Press.

Trett, R. 1983. Roman Bronze 'Grooved Pendants' from East Anglia. *Norfolk Archaeology* 38(3): 219-234.

Trigger, B. 2006. *A History of Archaeological Thought*. Cambridge: Cambridge University Press.

Trow, M. 2003. *Boudicca the Warrior Queen*. Stroud: Sutton.

Trow, S. 2002. By the Northern Shores of Ocean, 103-118 in T. Blagg and M. Millett (eds.) *The Early Roman Empire in the West*. Oxford: Oxbow. [First published 1990].

Trow, S., James, S. and Moore, T. 2009. *Becoming Roman, Being Gallic, Staying British*. Oxford: Oxbow.

Tullett, A. 2010. Community, 61-81 in M. Sterry, A. Tullett and N. Ray (eds.) *In Search of the Iron Age*. Leicester Archaeology Monograph 18. Leicester: University of Leicester School of Archaeology and Ancient History.

Turner, R. and Wymer, J. 1987. An Assemblage of Palaeolithic Hand-Axes from the Roman Religious Complex at Ivy Chimneys, Witham, Essex. *Antiquaries Journal* 67: 43-60.

Tylecote, R. 1969. Bronze Melting Remains and Artifacts from Caistor-by-Norwich. *Bulletin of Historical Metallurgy* 3: 46-7.

Ulmschneider, K. 2000. *Markets, Minsters, and Metal-Detectors*. BAR British Series 307. Oxford: BAR Publishing.

Van Driel-Murray, C. 1995. Gender in Question, 3-21 in P. Rush (ed.) *Theoretical Roman Archaeology: Second Conference Proceedings*. Aldershot: Avebury.

Versluys, M. 2014. Understanding Objects in Motion. *Archaeological Dialogues* 21(1): 1–20.

Vossen, I and Groot, M. 2009. Barley and Horses, 85-100 in M. Driessen, S. Heeren, J. Hendriks, F. Kemmers and R. Visser (eds.) *TRAC 2008: Proceedings of the Eighteenth Annual Theoretical Roman Archaeology Conference*. Oxford: Oxbow.

Wacher, J. 1976. *The Towns of Roman Britain*. London: Book Club Associates. [First published 1974].

Wallis, H. 2011. *Romano-British and Saxon Occupation at Billingford*. EAA 135. Gressenhall: NMS.

Walton, P. 2011. *Rethinking Roman Britain*. Unpublished PhD thesis: UCL.

Walton, P. 2012. *Rethinking Roman Britain*. Collection Moneta 137. Wetteren: Moneta.

Wardle, A. (with contributions by Trista Clifford and Dominic Perring) 2013. Registered finds, 189-230 in D. Perring and M. Pitts (eds.) *Alien Cities*. Monograph 7. Portslade: Spoilheap Publications.

Wason, P. 1994. *The Archaeology of Rank*. Cambridge: Cambridge University Press.

Watts, D. 2005. *Boudicca's Heirs*. London: Routledge.

Webb, T. 2011. *Personal Ornamentation as an Indicator of Cultural Diversity in the Roman North*. BAR British Series 547. Oxford: BAR Publishing.

Webster, G. 1993. *Boudica*. London: Routledge. [First published 1978].

Webster, J. 1997. Necessary Comparisons. *World Archaeology* 28(3): 324-338

Webster, J. 2001. Creolizing the Roman Provinces. *American Journal of Archaeology* 105(2): 209-225.

Webster, J. 2003. Art as Resistance and Negotiation, 24-51 in S. Scott and J. Webster (eds.) *Roman Imperialism and Provincial Art*. Cambridge: Cambridge University Press.

Webster, J. and Cooper, N. (eds.) 1996. *Roman Imperialism*. Leicester Archaeology Monographs 3. Leicester: University of Leicester School of Archaeological Studies.

Wells, P. 1999. *The Barbarians Speak*. Princeton: Princeton University Press.

Wells, P. 2001. *Beyond Celts, Germans and Scythians*. London: Duckworth.

West, S. 1989. *West Stow, Suffolk*. EAA 48. Bury St Edmunds: SCC.

Whimster, R. 1979. *Burial Practices in Iron Age Britain*. Unpublished PhD thesis: Durham University. http: // etheses.dur.ac.uk/7999/.

Whitmore, A. 2018. Phallic Magic, 17-31 in A. Parker and S. McKie (eds.) *Material Approaches to Roman Magic*. TRAC Themes in Roman Archaeology 2. Oxford: Oxbow.

Wild, J. 1970. Button-and-loop Fasteners in the Roman Provinces. *Britannia* 1: 137-155.

Williams, J. 2001. Coin Inscriptions and the Origins of Writing in Pre-Roman Britain. *British Numismatic Journal* 71: 1-17.

Williams, J. 2007. New Light on Latin in Pre-Conquest Britain. *Britannia* 38: 1-12.

Williamson, T. 1986. Parish Boundaries and Early Fields. *Journal of Historical Geography* 12(3): 241-248.

Wilson, D. 1971. Roman Britain in 1970. *Britannia* 2: 243-288.

Winkley, F. 2016. The Phenomenology of Metal Detecting. *Papers from the Institute of Archaeology* 25(2)13: 1–15.

Woolf, G. 1992. The Unity and Diversity of Romanisation [Review article]. *Journal of Roman Archaeology* 5: 349-352.

Woolf, G. 1994. Power and the Spread of Writing in the West, 84-98 in A. Bowman and G. Woolf (eds.) *Literacy and Power in the Ancient World*. Cambridge: Cambridge University Press.

Woolf, G. 1997. Beyond Romans and Natives. *World Archaeology* 28(3): 339-350.

Woolf, G. 2011a. Provincial Revolts in the Early Roman Empire, 27-44 in M. Popović (ed.) *The Jewish Revolt against Rome*. Leiden and Boston: Brill.

Woolf, G. 2011b. *Tales of the Barbarians*. Chichester: Wiley-Blackwell.

Woolf, G. 2014. Romanization 2.0 and its Alternatives. *Archaeological Dialogues* 21 (1): 45-50.

Worrell, S. 2007. Detecting the Later Iron Age, 371-388 in C. Haselgrove and T. Moore (eds.) *The Later Iron Age in Britain and Beyond*. Oxford: Oxbow.

Worrell, S. 2008. Roman Britain in 2007. *Britannia* 39: 337-367

Worrell, S. 2010. Roman Britain in 2009. *Britannia* 41: 409-439.

Worrell, S. and Pearce, J. 2015. Roman Britain in 2014. *Britannia* 46: 355-381.

Worrell, S., Egan, G., Naylor, J., Leahy, K. and Lewis, M. (eds.) 2010. *A Decade of Discovery*. BAR British Series 520. Oxford: BAR Publishing.

Worrell, S., Pearce, J., Moorhead, S. and Walton, P. 2011. Finds Reported under the Portable Antiquities Scheme. *Britannia* 42: 399-437.

Appendices

Database tables (Microsoft Excel) are provided at:

https://doi.org/10.30861/9781407357010.dataset1

Date ranges are drawn from the following sources: Appendix C (Bayley and Butcher 2004, Crummy 1983, Carr 2006, Hattatt 2007, Mackreth 2011, PAS database, Snape 1993 and Worrell Autumn 2007). Appendix D (Hutcheson 2004; PAS database).

Methodology and Data Collection

This appendix sets out the methodological approaches developed for this research and explains their appropriateness to my data. It also considers factors of collection and recording bias and the constraints imposed by working with a large body of surface finds.

The Icenian *civitas* represents an ideal arena to examine, through artefacts, the variety of provincial responses to Rome. By utilising surface finds in combination with stratified data, it is possible to explore the changing significance of different types of objects and materials, examining spatial and chronological variations in use and deposition. Intra-regional diversity and similarities can be investigated through mapping distributions and concentrations of finds in a GIS programme. Regardless of the challenges posed by decontextualised finds, they form a large proportion of archaeological data, and we must find appropriate ways to interpret them. Surface finds provide a resource with which to study different, yet complementary, research questions to the often 'keyhole' approach of modern excavation. Despite the trend towards contextual archaeology, I regard this as an opportunity to assess the value of low-context finds over a wide geographical distribution.

This section discusses the main sources of data: the county HERs, published excavations and the PAS database. It explains how my decision-making processes developed and some of the methodological issues and constraints which arose during creation of the database. Data collection was carried out 2014-2017, with a cut-off date for new entries of 30 April 2017. The PAS maps used for comparative UK-wide distributions in this publication were updated in April 2020.

Historic Environment Records

In the 1970s, HERs replaced county Sites and Monuments Records, often based on much older card index systems. By 2017, the Cambridgeshire HER had some 17,000 records from all sites and periods, Suffolk over 32,500 records and Norfolk more than 60,000 entries from 22,000 sites. These figures provide some sense of the proportion of finds from each county, which reflects their relative geographical extents and the frequency of metal-detecting.

Initial index searches were requested from the three county HERs using the recommended 'archaeological objects' termlists (FISH forum) and the date range 100 BCE-200 CE. I also requested a wider 'Iron Age-Roman' search for comparison. I subsequently visited each HER to consult the paper records, having drawn up a shortlist of sites to look at in more detail.

In Norfolk, sites are allocated an individual number, for example *Venta Icenorum* is NHER: 9786; the higher the number, generally, the more recently-created the entry. In Suffolk, sites are designated using a three-character parish code and three-digit site code. For instance, Coddenham is recorded as SHER: CDD017. The process of selecting records differed in Cambridgeshire. Each finds category (e.g. dress, written communication) was presented in a PDF document. These were searched in full within the shorter date range and the site codes extracted and then requested from the HER. Many records were only available online through the ADS due to the high proportion of 'grey literature' (see below).

One of the benefits of the scale of this research was to observe and compare the differences across three English counties. Variations occurred in recording styles and methods within and between counties. Data collection was carried out on the cusp of a digitisation programme in both Norfolk and Suffolk, which is now broadly complete. As my collection phase occurred before the full digital files were publicly available, there were some issues with the paper records which should no longer pose a problem to future researchers.

Working from the digital search results to the paper records threw up some inconsistencies. Some sites with dated artefacts failed to appear, or contained only references to lithics or ceramics, which could not be explained except in terms of human error or data entry limitations. Some objects returned by the digital search did not appear in the paper records. HER staff could not supply an explanation, but it may reflect the creation of 'digital only' records. The quality of accompanying images was highly variable in all three counties, from fine technical illustrations and high-resolution photos to faded black and white photocopies and blurry Polaroids.

In many HER records, small finds were categorised very broadly, 'RB *fibula*' being a case in point. This was more frequent in antiquarian records or imports from early card indexes. If there was no other description, image or dating evidence attached to the record, the object was excluded. If the record was a little more specific, such as 'Colchester type brooch', or the find was undated but recognisable, I recorded these and attempted a closer identification.

The Portable Antiquities Scheme

The PAS began in 1997 as a pilot scheme based in local authority museums and archaeological services, including Norfolk. In 1999, services including Suffolk joined the scheme and an online database was created. Since 2003, a network of Finds Liaison Officers (FLOs) has been employed to cover each English county and Wales. In 2020, the PAS database contains over 1.5 million records. To give a sense of relative proportions of finds of all periods, there are over 112,000 from Norfolk, 82,000 from Suffolk and 20,000 from Cambridgeshire.[1]

Public access to the database provides limited information, with restrictions on sensitive data such as finders' names and exact findspots. Researcher clearance allows greater access, more precise geo-referencing, and the ability to map data and export records. PAS searches were exported as .csv files for selected object types, based on my dating and functional criteria. It soon became apparent the narrow date range of -100 to +200 was restrictive, due to the lack of tight dating of many objects. Once the bulk of HER data collection was completed, additional PAS records were downloaded to make the two datasets comparable. A cut-off date (30 April 2017) was chosen and no PAS finds recorded thereafter were added.

During data cleaning, some clearly erroneous records were found, with imprecise data entry, misidentifications or mapping errors. Locational data were sometimes problematic, conceivably due to deliberate misinformation from the finder, but more usually from a mistyped grid reference. In a small number of cases, I replaced the PAS description with my own identification or dating of objects. I completed error reports and fed back mapping inconsistencies to assist with the precision of the database. Generally, however, the information was good, the locational data were precise, and most finds had high-quality zoomable photographs, which is one of the biggest advantages of PAS over HER records. One of my most striking observations from working with PAS finds is the increase in frequency across all categories and the continued rise in records of artefacts, in comparison to even recently published catalogues (Figure 2.5).

Variability in Recording

Individual finders use idiosyncratic recording methods, such as numbering systems for fields and finds. Archaeologists identifying and recording objects also have their own ways of describing and dating objects. Although computerised databases have ironed out some of these discrepancies, many remain. Earlier records are often the least well-identified and located. Recording also varies due to new catalogues and publications. For many years, the standard identification texts for British brooches were Hattatt's catalogues (1982, 1985, 1987, 1989, and 2007). However, these have been superseded by Mackreth's volumes (2011), and PAS/HER staff are generally expected to use Mackreth categories.[2] Unfortunately, Mackreth made little attempt to synchronise his brooch categorisation with Hattatt's, preferring to develop his own typo-chronology.

In my HER searches, patterns could be discerned. Some individual finders were particularly good at spotting non-metallic objects e.g. flints or bone; most concentrated on non-ferrous metalwork and discriminated accordingly. Geospatial information is another category in which personal ability, preference and technical know-how can affect results. I built up a mental picture of which detectorists regularly recorded 10-figure grid references and who never recorded specific locations. During interviews, eight of the nine respondents said they now use handheld GPS in the field, with only one preferring a map, ruler and pencil. It is important to remember that metal-detecting practice is changing over time, with improvements in technology, knowledge and recording. To analyse this, I included the finder's name and the date found (or recorded). This also assisted with identifying objects recorded pre-HER and flagging up PAS duplicates.

The potential overlap of HER and PAS finds posed a serious issue. Norfolk HER records were entered in digital-only format since 2012. All qualifying NHER finds should be entered on the PAS, although this is not necessarily the case in practice.[3] Reciprocally, PAS finds have been added to the NHER records. The PAS dataset, for Norfolk especially, has had fluctuations in entry levels, due to periodic uploads of bulk backlog entries (Andrews 2012: 57; Pett 2010: 3). This may well result in skewed interpretations of the records (Worrell 2008: 337, 2010: 410). In Suffolk, there was no determined effort to bring PAS records into the HER or *vice versa*, although there are certainly numerous PAS records within the HER.[4] In Cambridgeshire, there was no deliberate crossover between the two databases. Deduplication was undertaken to remove as much of this overlap as possible.

This highlights some of the difficulties found when working with multiple sources. A large synchronisation and data-cleaning period was necessary once the dataset was compiled. Consequently, my database only represents a sample of the total. The HER and PAS records are, of course, in themselves only a sample, defined by the chances of survival, discovery and reporting. The integration of HER and PAS finds, metal-detected and excavated materials, although sometimes laborious to achieve, is one of the strengths of my approach.

Locational Information

Norfolk and Suffolk HERs provided GIS shapefiles to be imported into mapping software for visualisation.[5] However, it quickly became apparent that it would be necessary to combine the two different datasets (HER and PAS) to fully express them in GIS. The Norfolk HER export

[1] https://finds.org.uk/database [Accessed 27/10/2020].
[2] Andrew Rogerson, former Senior Historic Environment Officer (Finds), NCC (pers. comm. 24/04/2015).
[3] A. Rogerson (pers. comm. 24/04/2015).
[4] Richard Hoggett, former Senior Archaeological Officer (HER), SCC, (pers. comm. 19/11/2014).
[5] In Cambridgeshire it is possible to create a map layer to overlay PAS finds onto the HER, although this was not offered as a research option. Gabrielle Day, former Assistant Archaeologist, CCC, (pers. comm. 15/01/2016).

included eastings and northings for each of the numbered sites, allowing a simple transfer to my database. These were generally centred on the field. Individual findspots with grid references were converted to coordinates for greater precision.

The Suffolk records were less straightforward, as there were often two or more entries with the same parish codes and different coordinates. Where possible, these were checked using MagicMap and where there were two points within the same area, a midpoint was selected. The Cambridgeshire GIS tables did not give locational data, instead providing a hyperlink to the Heritage Gateway, which showed the grid reference; these were individually compiled and converted to coordinates. Therefore, there will inevitably be small inconsistencies in the mapping, although hopefully within limited geographical areas, at the scale of the field or at most parish.

As the dataset was largely comprised of surface finds, I wanted to visualise concentration zones in GIS rather than signposting known sites or modern designations. The two sets of records were not necessarily compatible, so I decided to do this at the parish level. There were also discrepancies in the numbers of findspots by county (i.e. Cambridgeshire would have had very few in the top 5 per cent if combined with Norfolk and Suffolk). The top 5 per cent by county were used to create a shapefile of markers centred on the parish, which is included as a 'Top Parishes' layer on the maps.

Grey Literature and the Roman Rural Settlement Project

Since the 1990s, developers have been required to obtain archaeological information before starting work (DCLG 1990, 2010). Often, watching briefs and small-scale excavations are undertaken in advance or as construction work happens. These investigations are usually carried out by commercial archaeological contractors and are rarely published in full, leading to a large body of so-called 'grey literature'. These reports are held by the HERs and are usually deposited with ADS.

Few artefacts of relevance were found in these reports and the way they are indexed makes searching both time-consuming and unrewarding. For this reason, I chose to only look at grey literature for specific sites in Norfolk and Suffolk. In Cambridgeshire, the scale of recent development has meant that grey literature forms approximately half of the sources to be found in the HER.[6] Therefore, a slightly different approach was necessary and more grey literature was included in the sample.

The Roman Rural Settlement (RRS) Project was underway during my research period. As a response to the issues relating to grey literature, the RRS collated a large amount of information nationally from developments and produced a searchable online database and mapping tool. The project used East Anglia as one of its pilot studies.[7] RRS coverage of developer-funded literature is therefore complementary to my research as an alternative dataset.

Excavated Sites

Excavations across the East of England have added to our knowledge of the LIA and Roman periods. Selected artefact assemblages from excavated sites were incorporated to ground the research and broaden the dataset, in order to better understand patterns of deposition and recovery between surface and stratified finds. The EAA report series was of particular use, presenting a wealth of data in a consistent format. Local historical journals were also searched, including *Norfolk Archaeology*, the *Proceedings of the Suffolk Institute of Archaeology* and the *Proceedings of the Cambridge Antiquarian Society*.

Sites at Burgh, near Woodbridge (Martin 1988), Fison Way, Thetford (Atkins and Connor 2010; Gregory 1991a), Chatteris (Evans 2003) and Stonea (Wimblington) (Jackson and Potter 1996; Potter and Jackson 1982) span the conquest period. Excavations at Hacheston, near the River Deben, have contributed to the idea of a territorial boundary on the northern edge of the Trinovantian area (Blagg *et al.* 2004: 196). Settlements at Caistor-on-Sea (Darling and Gurney 1993), Billingford (Wallis 2011), Scole (Ashwin and Tester 2014), West Stow (West 1989) and Brampton (Knowles 1977) are also of interest. Sites at Brancaster (Hinchliffe 1985), Brettenham (Mudd 2002), Snettisham (Flitcroft 2001; Stead 1991) and Wighton (Gregory and Gurney 1986) provided additional excavation data.

The work of the Caistor Roman Project at the *civitas* capital and its hinterland, with which I have been closely involved for over a decade, has changed our understanding of the town's layout, dating and role as 'the marketplace of the Iceni' (Bowden 2012, 2013a, 2013b, 2017; Bowden and Bescoby 2008). The temples at Crownthorpe (Davies 2009: 137-39), Caistor St Edmund and Hockwold-cum-Wilton (Gurney 1986) were partly excavated in the 1950s and 1960s, while large assemblages of coins and other portable artefacts have been found at Walsingham (Davies and Gregory 1991: 69) and Saham Toney (Bates *et al.* 2000; Brown 1986), although to date there has been precious little excavation at these latter sites.

Many published site reports include a mixture of excavated and metal-detected finds, reminding us that these are not exclusive methodologies, but complementary tools for archaeological investigation, along with fieldwalking, geophysical and aerial surveying. Many HER records lack stratigraphy and context, due to surface or chance finds. Appendix B examines the practicalities and implications of using metal-detecting in research.

---

[6] G. Day (pers. comm. 15/01/2016).

[7] http://archaeologydataservice.ac.uk/archives/view/romangl/

Appendix B

Morphological Bias: A Response to Cool and Baxter

Interviews with Metal-Detectorists

One of my key arguments, upheld by my data and interpretation, is that metal-detecting is an important and useful resource for archaeological research. During this project, I encountered scepticism regarding the benefits of metal-detecting. I was often challenged about the veracity of records, findspots and issues surrounding looting of historic sites. This highlighted my own East Anglian bias, as an inheritor of the efforts of Tony Gregory and Barbara Green (NMS) and their successors, who developed positive relationships between archaeologists and detectorists in Norfolk over the past 30 years.

Cool and Baxter's research into morphological bias (2016a, 2016b) prompted me to enquire about detecting practices. Quantitative studies using questionnaires and interviews have previously been carried out with detectorists (Brindle 2014; Chester-Kadwell 2009; Robbins 2012; Winkley 2016). To explore these questions further, I recorded a short series of interviews with detectorists from Norfolk and Suffolk. These were intended more as oral histories than quantitative research, looking for opinion and personal experiences of retrieval practices, in the vein of the 'phenomenology of metal-detecting' (Winkley 2016). Verbatim quotes and summaries of the interviewees' responses are included where relevant.

Morphological Bias in Metal-Detector Finds

While other studies have explored recovery bias in terms of constraints on permissible metal-detecting (Brindle 2014; Robbins 2012), Cool and Baxter considered the impact of morphology upon artefact retrieval. They investigated this process using Mackreth's 2011 *corpus* of over 15,000 brooches, which covers published and unpublished excavations and both public and private collections. Mackreth was rather scathing of metal-detected material generally, although he assisted Norwich Castle Museum staff to record finds as the technology developed. He saluted the PAS, which was then still in its infancy, as a 'brave attempt'. Mackreth's data collection closed in 2004, meaning his *corpus* includes few, if any, PAS records (Cool and Baxter 2016a: 72, 2016b: 1643-644; Mackreth 2011: 4).

Cool and Baxter divided Mackreth's brooches into those collected prior to common metal-detector use, by survey, excavation or chance, which they term 'conventional' (meaning non-detected, but a somewhat loaded term, implying the opposite 'unconventional' for detected finds) and finds 'made most probably by metal-detectorists', namely those in private collections (2016a: 79-80).

They reserved Hattatt's collection as a special case as it drew on both sources. This methodology raises some questions about provenance. Many artefacts in museum collections are poorly provenanced antiquarian finds; many excavations use metal-detectors on site; and chance or surface finds made by eye are equally biased by artefact morphology, environmental conditions and visibility (see Robbins 2012: 41-43 on 'visual apparency' and 'detection probability').

East Anglia (Norfolk, Suffolk and Cambridgeshire) is the region with the highest proportion of metal-detector finds nationally. Here, 44 per cent of Mackreth's 2395 brooches derived from 'conventional' sources, 50 per cent from metal-detecting and 6 per cent from Hattatt's mixed collection. This compares, for example, to the southwest (2554 brooches) where conventional recovery stands at 92 per cent, metal-detector finds at just 4 per cent and Hattatt 3 per cent (Cool and Baxter 2016a: 81, table 2; 2016b: 1645). This stark contrast probably reflects the arable nature of the East Anglian landscape and strong relationships between detectorists and County Council archaeologists over several decades.

Cool and Baxter's analysis demonstrated that certain brooches were differentially recovered by metal-detecting, both in favour and against. Only one-third of the earliest types of bow brooches, Colchester one-pieces and Nauheim Derivatives, were retrieved by metal-detectorists. By contrast, Aesica brooches formed 14 per cent of conventional and 70 per cent of metal-detected finds. Penannular brooches also showed a dramatic difference, with only 11 per cent found by detector and 82 per cent by conventional means (2016a: 81, table 3). This appears to show that metal-detectorists are considerably less successful at recovering early one-piece brooches and penannulars, which have a 'wiry' or two-dimensional morphology. Larger examples like plate and Aesica brooches and decorative Headstud and Trumpet brooches were more commonly found. These brooch types are discussed in more detail in chapter three.

It is common practice for detectorists to discriminate against ferrous metals when detecting in fields with miscellaneous surface ironwork from agricultural activity and Victorian rubbish dumping.[1] This may explain the lower representation of simple one-piece brooches and penannulars which were regularly made in both iron and copper alloys. Booth suggests that some detectorists mistake penannular brooches for simple metal rings and

---

[1] A. Marsden (pers. comm. 09/12/2017).

discard them before recording (2014: 74).[2] Excavated ferrous finds are much more often retrieved, retained and are more likely to come from datable contexts than surface survey. The following responses were given by detectorists when asked in interviews whether they screened out certain metals:

Yes, unless we're on a dig of course, in which case then it's all metal. Screen out purely ferrous. You still have everything non-ferrous. Well, as I say, when it comes to official digs or something, it's all metal. Every nail, unfortunately, every nail.

We do discriminate [...] except for big bits of iron we do pick them up because you can't avoid it. Yeah you're right, the little tiny brooches, they're so...you get a really small signal so you're only going to get them shallow so you're not going to dig a big hole to find them.

[...] modern detectors, well the ones I use anyway, produce a different sound most of the time for ferrous but we do dig iron up sometimes, horseshoes, ploughshares, bits of cultivators, tractors in general.

If it's iron, it goes [makes noise] [...] you just walk on. But you have to be careful because next door to the iron could be a good object.

I try to discriminate as much iron out, or at least to be identified as iron because the modern detectors now you can assign a certain level of tone or a certain pitch to an iron signal, so you need to know that there's iron there to know that there's been habitation, but you don't necessarily want to dig it, I mean you can spend all day digging horseshoes and they're not very exciting I'm afraid.

There is also an element of anaerobic preservation in buried deposits compared to ploughsoil. Mackreth acknowledged this bias in his dataset, noting that ferrous finds were often rejected by pre-1960s excavators, museum curators and collectors, while others decayed beyond recognition in poor storage conditions (2011: 20). Degradation of metalwork in ploughsoil is also an increasing problem, due to the heavy usage of agri-chemicals on arable land:

The things which we are finding, especially the Roman coins, they're deteriorating due to fertiliser, they're in the topsoil and, maybe agriculture may change where they don't use so many fertilisers, but the damage has been done to a lot of those coins, they're really corroding. Fifty years' time, if there's any left, you may not even be able to identify them.

The survival in this sort of soil isn't good for ferrous items so most of the things we have retrieved have been

corroded beyond belief and, to be honest, most of them are fairly modern, probably 18th century or later.

Cool and Baxter's interpretation of Colchester Derivative brooches, of which there are high concentrations in East Anglia and which have played a key part in defining the Iceni in recent years (section 3.3), can also be called into question. According to their analysis, Colchester Derivative Rearhook brooches were represented by 32 per cent conventional and 63 per cent metal-detected finds. Colchester Derivative Harlow brooches, however, were 50 per cent conventional and 47 per cent detected. If morphology is the deciding factor in recovery bias, why should there be such a disparity between Harlow and Rearhook brooches, which are essentially similar in form and only differ in the mechanism which affixes the spring? This needs to be explained more fully before it can be accepted as a firm theory.

Lower recovery rates may be partly technological, as more two-dimensional artefacts are simply harder to detect and give weaker signals, 'no matter how skilled the detectorist is, how careful the recording is or how complete the item may be' (Cool and Baxter 2016b: 1647, 1651). Mackreth believed that brooches with brightly coloured enamelling, like Headstuds and Trumpets, show up well in the soil and so are more easily recovered (2011: 119). Certainly, some detectorists only search for the most complete, attractive, and therefore saleable finds, but there is a danger of reinforcing outdated 'treasure-hunter' stereotypes which vilifies many detectorists' longstanding experience and ability. Discussions with detectorists revealed that:

It's clear from our experience of retrieving finds that some things are going to give less of a signal and are easier to miss than others. It's not just the size and shape of an object, it's the chance aspect of how it lies in the soil [...] Randomness is an enormous part of that. The fact is that most of our machines don't go very deep, we're not digging anything below the plough depth, because we constantly search fields over and over again, eventually we find that most things will come to the surface within range of the machines, so that's smoothing out the bias that you might get in the statistics.

Yes certainly, thin wire brooches, the same as Roman hairpins, are far more difficult to detect. They give a very erratic signal whereas a large, reflective surface such as a plate brooch, will give you a very good signal no matter how it's lying in the soil. [Do you still dig up the erratic signals?] [laughs] You never lose that enthusiasm!

Obviously the smaller the find, the more difficult it is, or the less likely it is that you're actually going to detect it, and the classic one is a cut quarter penny for instance, which is really tiny, if it's horizontal you'll find it, down to probably five or six inches, if it's on edge with the pointed end upwards you won't get a signal from it, it's

---

[2] A. Marsden (pers. comm. 09/12/2017) also suggested that wiry one-piece brooches often go unrecognised and end up in the scrap bucket.

*too tiny. The bigger the item, obviously, the more likely
you are to find it.*

Research Implications

My research relies heavily on metal-detected artefacts and
Cool and Baxter highlight several potential biases. The
suggestion that the distribution and chronology of East
Anglian brooches is seriously undermined by the high
regional proportion of metal-detector finds merits closer
investigation. Some of my results are doubtless weighted
by recovery bias; this is an accepted and acknowledged part
of the process. The implications are twofold. Firstly, the
chronological signature of an assemblage may be distorted
by under-representation of certain types of brooches found
by metal-detector. The recovery of LIA and early Roman
brooches is biased in favour of conventional methods,
swinging towards metal-detector finds throughout the
second century CE (Cool and Baxter 2016a: 86, 2016b:
1648-650).

Secondly, Cool and Baxter insist that brooch data can only
really be understood in relation to other small finds. In
my analysis of cosmetic grinders (chapter five), I observe
that the smaller, more delicate 'pestles' are recovered
differently to the larger 'mortars'. This is also noted as
a possible cause for variations in finds of linch-pins and
the chronology of terret rings (chapter eight). While
Hutcheson uses PAS data to substantiate her claim that
the distribution of horse gear represents ancient practices
rather than modern recording bias (2004: 21-22), the
concentration of enamelled and highly-ornamented harness
fittings in Norfolk may confirm Cool and Baxter's theory.
The advantage of my research scope is that it incorporates
small finds from many different functional categories, of
all shapes and sizes, which have the potential to calibrate
the morphological bias against detected brooches and
other artefacts.

Appendix C

Brooch Date Ranges

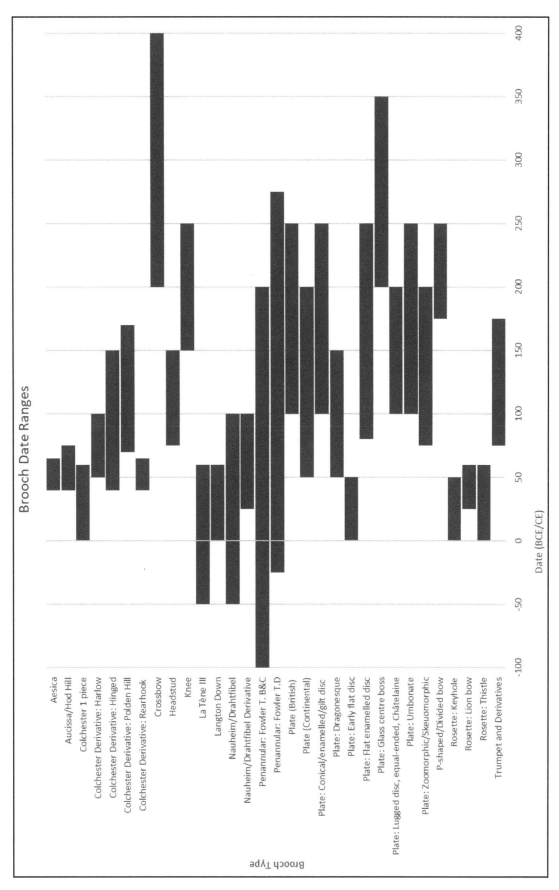

Appendix D

Harness Date Ranges

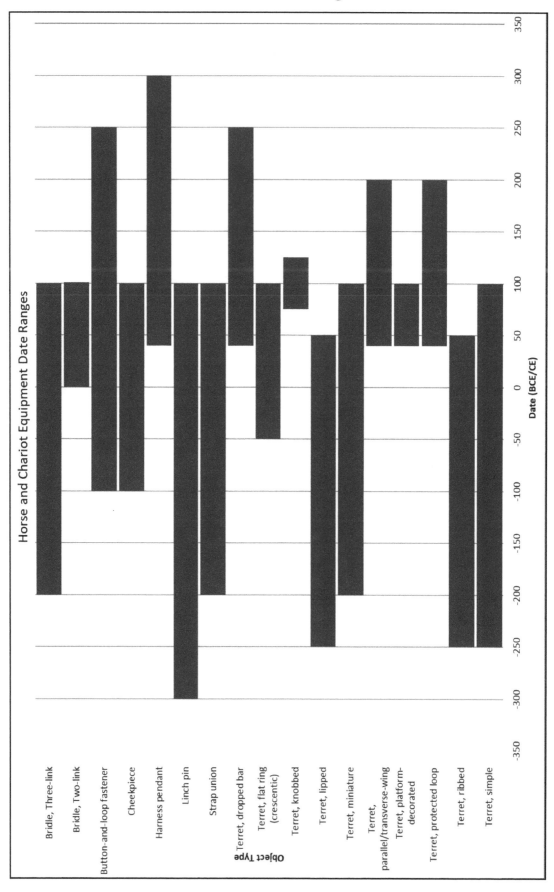

Index

Printed in the USA
CPSIA information can be obtained
at www.ICGtesting.com
CBHW061237071023
1266CB00019B/314